ABOUT THE AUTHOR

Born in 1958, Charles Grant studied modern history at Cambridge University. He then took a diploma in French politics at Grenoble University, where he learned to speak fluent French.

Returning to London, Grant joined *Euromoney*, the financial magazine. He moved to *The Economist* in 1986, where he wrote about the City. In 1987 he began a series of articles which exposed the County NatWest-Blue Arrow scandal. In 1988, together with David Goodhart, he wrote 'Making the City work', a pamphlet published by the Fabian Society, which proposed a programme of reform for Britain's financial markets.

In 1989 *The Economist* posted Grant to Brussels, to cover the European Community. During first-hand reporting of the negotiations which culminated in the Treaty of Maastricht, Grant got to know Jacques Delors as well as his friends and enemies. In 1992 Grant's writing on economic and monetary union won the Adelphi Foundation's Prix Stendhal. In 1993 he returned to *The Economist's* London office, to write about British affairs.

DELORS

Inside the House that Jacques Built

Charles Grant

NICHOLAS BREALEY
PUBLISHING
LONDON

First published in Great Britain by
Nicholas Brealey Publishing Limited in 1994
21 Bloomsbury Way
London WC1A 2TH

ISBN 1–85788–039–0

British Library Cataloguing in Publication Data
A Catalogue record for this book is available from the British Library.

Typeset by August Filmsetting, England

Printed in Finland by Werner Söderström Oy

CONTENTS

THE AGE OF DELORS AND THATCHER

For much of the twentieth century, the main fault line of Western Europe's political landscape has run between left and right, between those wanting more planning, state control and redistribution of wealth, and those wanting less. By the 1990s, however, the left had accepted much of the right's free-market philosophy. Only fine gradations separated their economic policies.

But as the left–right division diminished, a new fissure began to shape the political landscape. On one side stood the defenders of national sovereignty, such as Margaret Thatcher, who opposed the growing power of European institutions. On the other stood Jacques Delors, who argued that the European nations would decline unless they worked together to build common policies. This fault line bore little relation to the traditional left–right divide.

The debate on sovereignty had begun in the 1950s, when Jean Monnet inspired the movement for a federal Europe and General de Gaulle fought for a '*Europe des patries*'. Delors and Thatcher revived and developed the credos of Monnet and de Gaulle. But this argument only began to dominate Western Europe in the late 1980s when – partly because of Delors's impact on the European Commission – the European Community (EC) became a powerful and intrusive influence on national politics.

In the early 1980s the EC had been a dull, sleepy organisation that seldom achieved anything of note. Delors's presidency of the commission, which began in 1985, injected a new dynamism. He masterminded both the plan to create a single market by the end of 1992 and the Single European Act, which gave the EC the means to realise that ambition. Delors understood better than many Britons the paradox of the single market: the levelling of national barriers to the free flow of goods, services, capital and people would require a substantial transfer of sovereignty to European institutions. Delors then set new targets for the EC: economic and monetary union, and 'political union'.

I first met Delors in September 1990, when his influence was at its zenith, on a visit to Czechoslovakia. At Prague airport Jiri Dienstbier, the Czechoslovak foreign minister – a boilerman until the 'velvet revolution' of a year earlier – welcomed Delors as if he were a head of state. A band played the last movement of Beethoven's Ninth Symphony, the EC's unofficial anthem.

1

The European Community was gaining other trappings of statehood. As an eight-car motorcade whisked Delors towards the baroque splendours of Prague, a flag of 12 gold stars on a royal blue background fluttered all along the route. In January 1985 Delors had chosen that flag, which then belonged to the Council of Europe, for the commission. Later, without consulting any government, Delors and the administrations of the European Parliament and the Council of Ministers decided to make the flag a symbol of the EC. The 12 stars were unveiled as such in June 1986, at the Group of Seven's Tokyo summit – to the surprise of the European prime ministers who were present. Within a couple of years governments in Europe and beyond were using that flag to represent the Community.

The motorcade arrived at Prague Castle, where President Vaclav Havel and Alexander Dubcek, then speaker of the national assembly, would host a state banquet in honour of Delors. He delighted in the huge respect shown by Czechs and Slovaks for the EC, the commission and his office. 'Five years ago a commission president would never have received this treatment,' he said to me with pride.

Delors intrigued me not only because he had transformed the EC, and become the most successful European socialist of his generation, but because he himself had travelled such a distance. His grandfather had been a peasant in Corrèze, an impoverished region of central France, while Louis Delors, his father, worked as a messenger boy in the Banque de France. Born and brought up in a working-class district of Paris's east end, Delors had little formal education and never took a university degree.

A sense of mission, inspired by strong religious faith, drove Delors towards new horizons. His fierce intelligence, almost inhuman capacity for work and sharp sense of opportunism helped him on his way. Unusually for a politician, Delors combined a prodigious capacity to generate ideas with a pragmatic instinct for getting them implemented.

Delors is far from being the grey bureaucrat of some caricatures. He has played basketball for a French first-division team, written authoritatively on the music of Dizzy Gillespie and Dexter Gordon, and managed a cinema club which specialised in American films. Delors throws passion into whatever he does or says, which makes him an inspiring but awkward colleague. He brims with nervous energy and raw emotion, which he finds hard to control. For all his achievements, he often feels insecure.

Delors is riddled with contradictions which he cannot always reconcile. He is a socialist trade unionist who once worked for a Gaullist prime minister and describes himself as a closet Christian democrat. He is a practising Roman Catholic who takes moral stances and claims not to be ambitious; yet he is a crafty political tactician who enjoys power and has held the commission in an iron grip. He is a patriotic Frenchman with a vision of a unified Europe.

Delors may have pushed his federal agenda too far too fast, for many people neither understood the EC – which became the European Union in November 1993 – nor supported what he was trying to achieve. By increasing the might of 'Brussels', Delors contributed to the wave of anti-EC sentiment which swept through northern Europe in 1992 and 1993. Yet ever since the time of Monnet and de Gaulle, the rhythm of European integration has been two steps forward, one step back. While Delors led the dance some followed and some turned the other way, but none remained indifferent to his tune.

CHAPTER ONE

IN SEARCH OF AN IDEAL

IN FEBRUARY 1916 German forces attacked the French fortress of Verdun, on the River Meuse. By July of that year, when French armies had repulsed the Germans, more than half a million soldiers had been killed or wounded on the two sides. During the battle Louis Delors, a French private, suffered serious wounds and blacked out. His platoon retreated and left him for dead. Later, when Louis recovered consciousness, he saw a German officer moving from one wounded Frenchman to another, finishing each off with a pistol. Louis tried to flee but found that he could not move. The officer reached Louis but aimed poorly and hit him in the arm. Eventually French troops rescued the 21-year-old private, but the episode left him partially disabled and hateful of Germans. His war wounds would cause him pain for the rest of his life.

The movement for a federal Europe, which gathered strength after that other Franco-German conflagration of 1939–45, was born of the desire to ensure that battles such as Verdun could never happen again. Louis Delors's son would play a pre-eminent role in that movement.

Louis recuperated on the family farm at Le Lonzac, a village in Corrèze, a poor and hilly *département* of the Massif Central. Louis's father, Jean Delors, had 12 hectares and seven children. Peasant life did not appeal to Louis and, when his strength returned, he moved to Paris. He found a job with the Banque de France as a *garçon de recette* (messenger boy). Wearing a blue uniform and a pistol, he carried commercial bills around the city.

Louis married Jeanne Floc, whose family had come to Paris from Cantal, a *département* close to Corrèze. The Flocs ran a restaurant and a *bal-musette* (popular dance hall) in the 10th *arrondissement*. At the age of 19, Jeanne gave birth to Jacques Lucien Delors on 20 July 1925. He would be her only child.

The family lived in la Petite-Roquette, a popular *quartier* of the 11th *arrondissement*, in the east end of Paris. The *quartier* took its name from a nearby prison which had been a renowned home of brigands and rebels in past centuries. 'Sans-culottes' from the area had stormed the Bastille in 1789 and the neighbourhood raised a barricade at each of the nineteenth century's revolutions. La Petite-Roquette stretched from the Place de la Bastille in the west to the Père-Lachaise cemetery to the east. In May 1871, 1900 supporters of the Paris Commune were captured in the cemetery and then shot in the prison.

By the 1920s the *quartier* had become one of the respectable working class, with a sprinkling of lower-middle class families such as the Delors. However, the people resented anything posh or bourgeois. They felt they belonged to a community and they stopped to talk in the streets and markets. Some of that warmth survives in the 1990s, although the area has been smartened up and the prison demolished.

Jacques's father was stern, taciturn and mustachioed. Louis could not stand family arguments or political disputes, and liked to arrange compromises. He disliked extremes of left and right and supported the Radicals, a group of the political centre. During the week Louis worked conscientiously at the Banque de France, while on Sundays he became a ticket-collector at the Parc des Princes football stadium. Jacques inherited a penchant for work and a love of compromise from his father.

Martine, Jacques Delors's daughter, says her grandfather was 'quite selfish' because he was more interested in his work and friends than his family.[1] Delors denies his father neglected him. He says he was close to both parents, but admits his mother took more interest in his education.[2]

Unlike her husband, Jeanne had a strong Catholic faith. She nurtured Jacques's sense of religion – which he says he was born with – and accompanied him to church every Sunday. Intelligent, intuitive and cheerful, she could also be strong willed and temperamental. Jeanne took her son to cinemas, exhibitions, musicals and her mother's *bal-musette* – where, perched on a high stool, he watched the locals dance to accordion music. She read a lot, but her many interests did not extend to politics. She passed on a sense of curiosity and open-mindedness to her son.

Jeanne sent Jacques to a Catholic school at the age of six. He disliked it so much that she soon took him away. He went instead to the *école communale* in the Rue Saint-Maur, the same street as the Delors's apartment. He sang in the choir of Notre Dame du Perpetuel Secours, the local church. On Thursday and Sunday afternoons Jacques went to the *patronage*, a boys club run by the church curate. Having no brothers or sisters, Jacques threw himself into close friendships with boys at the *patronage*.

The *patronage* taught the catechism, arranged outings and – most important of all for Jacques – organised games of basketball on a pitch adjoining the church. Jacques's artfulness, strength and tactical skill compensated for his lack of height. He and his friends also played football against the walls of the prison. Jacques read *L'Auto*, a daily sports newspaper, assiduously. Having gained an encyclopedic knowledge of cycling, he took bets from his classmates on the Tour de France – and made money.

'Jacques used to hang around the streets with us, doing mischievous things like ringing doorbells, throwing bangers and annoying concierges,'

6

says Antoine Lejay, who was in the same school and *patronage* as Delors. Jacques even joined in the game of pissing in the shoes of the rival basketball team. 'But Jacques was less free than the rest of us to lark around – either because his father was strict or because he had to do homework.' Lejay says Jacques was 'one of us' but that the gang used to hesitate before calling on him. 'He wasn't a leader and he was more serious than the rest of us.' He was also better dressed than most of his friends.[3] Lejay's family, coloured immigrants from the West Indies, had a greengrocer's shop nearby.

Jacques became aware of politics in 1936, when Léon Blum's 'Popular Front' government presided over reforms such as paid holidays but also over strikes and demonstrations. He remembers people talking about the risk of a civil war. At a family party to celebrate Jacques's first communion, his uncle Henri (a member of the Communist Party) sang the 'Internationale'. In the same year the local priests tried to persuade Jacques to enter a seminary. He thought long and hard before deciding against the idea.

In June 1937 Jeanne Delors made her son sit the entrance exam for the Lycée Voltaire, the local secondary school. He succeeded and, at the age of 12, became the only pupil from his year at the *école communale* to enter a *lycée*. Delors's friends, such as Lejay, went to an *école professionelle* (technical school), which they would leave at 14. Lejay, who became a toolmaker and then spent his life with Catholic worker-education associations, remains a close friend.

'The day I went to the *lycée*, alone, leaving my friends behind, it was hell, it was not just,' says Delors, who was profoundly marked by the experience.[4] Delors felt angry about being privileged and the lack of opportunities available to most of his friends. 'This bad conscience has never left me since.'[5] The guilt made Delors political: from then on, he says, he wanted to combat social injustice.

At 13 Delors joined the junior wing of the Jeunesse Ouvrière Chrétienne (JOC), a nationwide movement of young Christian workers. He met his old friends at meetings of the JOC and at the *patronage*, where he still played basketball. Some of them thought it odd for a *lycée* boy to make an effort to keep up with them.

Delors spent summer holidays with Pépé Jean, his grandfather in Corrèze. He claims to have imbibed many of the values of his country cousins, such as hard work, frugality, the importance of saving against a bad year and the necessity of taking risks. Others would add stubbornness.

> *One bad season my grandfather took me to see the buckwheat: the harvest was terrible. But he didn't swear, he didn't inveigh against the*

7

*heavens or the government. He said, oh well, that's the way it is, we'll do
better next year. I kept that from him, pragmatism.*[6]

Pépé Jean told Jacques that nothing was ever won and nothing was ever
lost.

Delors claims his grandfather immunised him against communism by
explaining that people could not expect the state to improve their condition, and that they had to help themselves. Jacques used to attend mass at
the local church, alongside most of the village women. His father and
grandfather, like most of the men, would remain outside the church, chatting and drinking wine. The adult Delors has never lost a sentimental
attachment to rural life. When he became commission president, he would
oppose any policy which he considered damaging to small peasants.

In September 1939, at the outbreak of the second world war, Delors and
his mother went to stay with her family at Aurillac in Cantal. Delors went
to a new *lycée* and joined the *Jeunesse Etudiante Chrétienne* (JEC), the
Christian student movement. But after six months of the 'phoney war' he
persuaded his mother to return to Paris.

In June 1940, two days before German soldiers entered Paris, Delors,
his mother and grandmother Floc left in haste. Travelling by train, lorry
and foot, alongside fleeing soldiers, they scavenged for food and tried to
avoid bombs. Eventually they covered the 500 kilometres between Paris
and Aurillac.

The ignominious manner of France's collapse shocked the 14-year-old
Delors. 'The impression which fixed itself in my mind was that of a deca-
dent country,' Delors recalls. 'I said to myself the people who govern us are
very guilty.'[7]

On the journey Jacques wrote a draft constitution, which had something
in common with the one de Gaulle later designed for the Fifth Republic.
Delors downgraded the national assembly and strengthened the executive
authority, for the sake of efficiency.[8]

The Germans occupied the north and west of France but left the rest to
be run by Marshal Pétain's Vichy government. The Banque de France
transferred many of its staff, including Louis Delors, to the unoccupied
zone. Jacques and his mother followed Louis from one town to another
before the family settled at Clermont-Ferrand, close to Vichy.

The Vichy government's Ministry of Youth banned the JOC and the
JEC, sponsoring 'les Compagnons de France' as an alternative. Like most
adolescents of his generation, Jacques became an active member of this
scout-like movement. The *compagnons* propagandised for Pétain's
'national revolution' and helped farmers in the fields. Delors joined 'les

Joyeux Compagnons', a troop which toured the Massif Central in a gas-powered bus and performed both Molière and musicals. Delors had his first debates with communists and socialists in the *compagnons*. Until then his political views had been 'purely idealist, even sentimental. But they spoke of concrete economic and social realities.'[9]

When the Germans occupied southern France, in 1942, the *compagnons* folded. Like many of the French, the Delors had begun by being reserved towards the Vichy regime, rather than hostile. That soon changed. Henri Deschamps, who had led the *Joyeux Compagnons* and was two years older than Jacques, became his best friend at the Clermont-Ferrand *lycée*. Both Henri and his father carried messages for the Resistance. The Germans caught the pair and sent them to Auschwitz, where they died.

Delors listened to de Gaulle's broadcasts and thought him the only hope for France. He did not join the Resistance but he hovered on its fringes. 'I saw people who believed in nothing go on missions, who were ready to get killed, and some of them never came back. That shocked me: I learned there was no such thing as the superiority of Christians.'[10]

Despite spending the war at five different *lycées*, Delors excelled at his studies. His best subjects were mathematics, science and French, and his favourite authors Molière, Voltaire, Stendhal and Flaubert. When Delors passed a mathematical *baccalauréat* his teachers suggested that he pursue a degree in engineering. Instead, in October 1943, he joined the law faculty of Strasbourg university, which had decamped to Clermont-Ferrand. The following January German troops occupied the university and ended Delors's university career. Delors knew that if he got a job he risked being drafted by the Service du Travail Obligatoire for compulsory labour in Germany. So he went to Paris and remained incognito until the Allied troops arrived in August 1944.

CENTRAL BANKER

At the age of 19 Delors hesitated between finding work straight away, so that his parents would not have to support him, and pursuing a vocation. He thought of becoming a fashion designer, a film director or a sports journalist. Jeanne liked to indulge her son and approached a journalism school in Lille. She also enrolled him at the Institut des Hautes Etudes Cinématographiques.

But Louis insisted that Jacques join the Banque de France, where he had already got two of his brothers a job. 'As my father made himself ill over this, I wanted to make him happy.'[11] Delors took the entry examination and came 15th. Louis was angry that his son had not performed better, but the mark was good enough to get him a job.

Thus in October 1944, 45 years before the Delors Committee proposed a European central bank, Delors became a central banker. He says he was not upset to have to join the bank, for he was glad to earn his own living. His vocational ideas had been 'children's dreams, those from deprived backgrounds often dream.'[12]

When Delors started at the Banque de France he joined the Mouvement Républicaine Populaire (MRP), the Christian democrats, who supported de Gaulle's government. Delors soon became disillusioned with the right-wing stance of the party leadership and resigned in February 1946. 'I was scandalised by the gap I discovered between declarations of principle, on the one hand, and the concrete political practice, on the other.'[13]

Delors's first major assignment at the Banque de France was to take charge of 30 people who processed securities transactions. The team soon eliminated a six-month backlog. One of the keener members, Marie Lephaille, became the first woman in Delors's life. Small, dark and pretty, she had learned to speak Basque before French. They married in 1948 and rented a flat near the Gare de Lyon, in the east end of Paris. A strong Catholic, Marie buttressed her husband's faith, which had, according to Antoine Lejay, flagged during moments of his youth. Marie has the temperamental nature of many Basques and, like Delors's mother, is warm, instinctive and strong-willed. However, the wife and the mother have not always been the best of friends.

Delors had, in the autumn of 1944, enrolled in an evening class for a degree in literature. But he felt uncomfortable with the subject and, the following year, switched to a course in economics. In 1946, still unsure of his academic leanings, Delors changed again, to law. Delors's boss at the bank, a Monsieur Fruit, discovered about the evening classes. He realised that Delors's thirst for knowledge needed guidance.

Monsieur Fruit pointed Delors to the Centre d'Etudes Supérieures de Banque, France's most prestigious banking institute. Delors enrolled in the autumn of 1947 for a three-year diploma. After the first year's preparatory course, Delors came second in the exams. In the second year, which covered economics, Delors came top. In the third and final year, which dealt with banking, Delors finished fifth. Six years of evening classes were at an end.

'I still suffer from the lack of a full-time higher education,' Delors claimed in 1975. 'I never met great authors or had enough time to discuss things with professors and students. This set my career back at least 10 years.'[14] Delors exaggerates, for he bears a grudge against those who get to the top without having to work as hard as he did. He tends to dislike *énarques*, the graduates of France's elite Ecole Nationale d'Administration (ENA), who dominate the French establishment.

Delors's unconventional education may even have helped his career. Pierre Mendès-France, the outstanding politician of France's Fourth Republic (1944 to 1958), noted that 'Delors is a good workhorse – his asset is to be self-taught and therefore concrete.' One source of Delors's popularity in France is his preference for language which is simple and earthy rather than abstract and erudite.

Delors's impressive performance at the institute landed him a job, in 1950, in the 'cabinet' (private office) of the director-general of securities. In the same year the Banque de France offered him the chance of sitting the exams for its inspectorate. That job would have guaranteed a fast track to the bank's top échelon, but involved constant travel around France. Marie had just given birth to Martine and he had just joined the bank's branch of the Confédération Française des Travailleurs Chrétiens (CFTC), France's Christian trade union. He spent eight to ten hours a week playing sports, including basketball games for Jeanne d'Arc de Menilmontant, a first-division team based in Paris's east end. Delors thought he would not have enough time for the inspectorate, his family, the trade union and sport, so declined to take the exam.

In 1950 Delors and his wife set up a cinema club in the 20th *arrondissement*. Delors particularly liked American directors, such as Orson Welles, John Ford and William Wyler, and 'neo-realist' films with a political message, like Vittorio de Sica's *Bicycle Thief*. On a typical evening 30 or 40 people would turn up, most of them locals and some of them old friends from the *patronage*. They held a discussion after each film. On one evening some visitors argued vigorously for the films of Renoir, Hitchcock and Bergman, which were rather modern for Delors. He later discovered that François Truffaut and Claude Chabrol had been the visitors. The cinema club folded in 1953.

At the bank Delors put in long hours for his director-general, usually working on Saturdays. One of his biggest tasks was to prepare the securities department for computerisation. However neither the nature of the work nor the bank's culture inspired Delors. 'The bank was a very conformist place, the bosses wanted an easy life and didn't like change,' recalls Jean Leclere, who met Delors on a basketball pitch in 1945 and became his closest friend in the bank. 'Jacques's colleagues were utilitarian, concerned with money and getting on the world.'[15] Delors had a good reputation in the bank but was not happy there.

He was searching for ways of combating the injustice and backwardness of French society. By the mid-1950s he had committed himself to a trade union, a political party and a group of militant Christians. But none of these activities fully satisfied him.

EMMANUEL MOUNIER

Parisian intellectuals enjoyed a golden age in the years after the second world war. Jean-Paul Sartre, Albert Camus and Raymond Aron debated communism, existentialism and liberalism. The philosopher Emmanual Mounier, although less well known internationally, had as much influence as any of these writers on France. Mounier founded both 'personalism', a left-wing Catholic doctrine, and *Esprit*, a review, in the 1930s. He died in 1950, at the age of 45, at about the time Delors first read *Esprit*.

In the post-war years, many young, idealistic French men and women viewed left-wing or 'social' Catholicism as the most appealing cause on offer. The communists won a quarter of the vote but, because of their atheism, did not appeal to most Catholics. The socialists (known as the Section Française de l'Internationale Ouvrier, or SFIO), weaker and less inspiring than their British and German cousins, had an anti-clerical tradition. The Christian democratic MRP became discredited through its participation in ineffective right-wing coalitions.

No political party catered for the Catholic left, but more than a million people had some kind of link with it – through newspapers, reviews, clubs, the JOC, the JEC, the Jeunesse Agriculturel Chrétien or the CFTC. Mounier's ideas had a huge influence on left-wing Catholics, including the young Delors.

Delors became a 'personalist' in the 1950s and remains one. The personalist aims for a middle way between communism, which denies the individual, and liberalism, which denies the community. Unlike a social democrat, however, a personalist argues that man needs an internal, spiritual transformation no less than a new social order.

Delors offers this definition of personalism: 'I believe the individual is a person, and not only an individual, a person who cannot be reduced to other people, and that this person cannot live without participating in communities which bind him to people.'[16] Mounier himself wrote: 'Man masters himself through his relationship with other people and things, in work and in camaraderie, in friendship, in love, in action, in meeting, and not through standoffishness.'[17]

Mounier is hard for Anglo-Saxons to understand because the roots of his thought are mystical and because he resorts to Hegelian dialectics. Much of Mounier's writing is an angry polemic against totalitarianism and liberal capitalism. 'The classical notion of man has been broken up: people affirm the absolute of the individual, the race, the class, the nation.' The modern world had divided man into little pieces. 'Each broken fragment withers on its own: we search to rebuild him, to bring together his body and mind, meditation and works, thought and action.' Like Marx, Mounier stressed the unity of theory and practice. 'Man is only man when committed.'[18]

Mounier acknowledged that nineteenth-century liberalism had played a role in weakening absolute monarchies, but thought it redundant for the needs of the twentieth century. Liberalism was:

> *linked to individualism, its dominant trait is strongly egocentric, it saps the essence of our humanity, which is not only worrying about how to coexist within the mutual limitation of our fantasies, but also about collaboration, devotion, a common destiny and sacrifice for the common future.*

For the great majority of people, liberalism had brought nothing better than a declaratory or formal liberty. 'We must liberate liberty from liberals.'[19]

Mounier thought man's destiny to be the 'communication of consciences and universal comprehension.' He noted approvingly that the Christian tradition, before the Reformation, had been *communautaire* rather than individualist. He sought to revive 'Catholic' values of fraternity and internationalism (Mounier was not particularly interested in European union but favoured world government).[20]

Mounier thought communism contained an element of the kingdom of God and that the young Karl Marx, who wrote about human alienation, had been a personalist. 'Personalism tries to reconcile two contemporary alienations, of hyper-subjectivism and of hyper-materialism.' He wrote that capitalist structures prevented 'the liberation of man and they have to be destroyed for the sake of a socialist organisation of production and consumption.' He added, somewhat implausibly, that this change should be brought about democratically and by consensus. He favoured a decentralised, cooperative sort of socialism rather than the Soviet model. He attacked Christian democrats for their close ties to capitalist and bourgeois liberalism. 'The Christian world should break these fatal links.'[21]

Delors swallowed all of Mounierism, except for its communistic leanings. 'I've never been fascinated by communism and Marxism – I'm undoubtedly the only man on the French left who never has been. I believed one could improve society, but not change the society.'[22]

In 1975 Delors wrote that he owed his three principal criticisms of French society to Mounier. First, a political culture based on an over-mighty 'tentacular' state, and on social groups which preferred to insult each other rather than negotiate. Second, excessive individualism, reinforced by the struggle for social standing and consumer goods. And third, the inability of an essentially capitalist society to provide equal opportunities and to humanise the way people treated each other.[23]

Delors, who still rereads Mounier, says that personalism remains his principal analytical tool for understanding life and people. Like Mounier, Delors treats political issues as moral questions. Like Mounier, Delors mistrusts the world of politics and is torn between the desire to remain pure and analytical on the outside, and the wish to join the mêlée in an effort to implement his ideas. Unlike Mounier, however, Delors has usually joined the mêlée. Mounier found suffering a noble condition. 'Pain is embedded in the heart of our humanism, and we recognise our own kind to the extent that they refuse the temptation of happiness,' wrote Mounier.[24] Delors would not say anything so extreme, but sometimes takes a grim delight in bearing heavy burdens.

When Delors first fell for Mounier's ideas he discovered that *Esprit* ran a 'readers' group' for committed personalists. However Delors stayed away, fearing that he would be ill at ease among elite Parisian intellectuals. In 1952 he joined Vie Nouvelle, a personalist movement where he thought his deficient education would not matter.

Founded by André Cruiziat, who had been in the scouts and the Compagnons de France, Vie Nouvelle had 5000 to 6000 mainly middle-class members. The movement aimed to transform society through reflection, education and a commitment to action in three domains: spiritual life, personal life and political life. It consisted of neighbourhood fraternities, in which members invited each other to eat in their homes. They swapped experiences, debated contemporary issues and discussed how to become involved in parish life and social work. Marie Delors became as active as her husband. The Delors took their children to Vie Nouvelle holiday camps.

Members paid a proportion of their salaries into the collective coffers, which financed good works. Vie Nouvelle shared Mounier's contempt for the MRP. Unlike that party, Vie Nouvelle campaigned for Algerian independence, a new liturgy and modern forms of birth control. The movement did not evangelise. 'It was secular: we distinguished between politics and faith but we kept the humanism of Christianity,' says Delors.[25] In 1955 Cruiziat appointed Delors as Vie Nouvelle's political education officer.

Delors found Vie Nouvelle's ambience of free debate congenial. All through his career, he has felt more at home in movements and clubs than in political parties. He finds them more tolerant and fraternal and less prone to personal rivalries. He considers them an ideal place for testing his raw ideas against the arguments of others. Nevertheless, political animals such as Delors are seldom able to avoid parties for long. Vie Nouvelle drew Delors ever closer to the world of party politics, as did his trade union.

BROTHER JACQUES

The Confédération Française des Travailleurs Chrétiens (CFTC) had close links with the Catholic Church and the MRP. The union preferred moderation and caution to militant action on behalf of its members. A reform movement, based around the review *Reconstruction*, aimed to make the CFTC more secular and radical. *Reconstruction* opposed French colonialism, demanded better rights for workers and championed 'democratic planning', which meant involving the trade unions in the national planning process. Paul Vignaux, a professor of medieval history, and Albert Detraz, a labourer, led the movement, which sought to bridge the gap between workers and intellectuals. Many of the union's younger members, including Delors, supported the reformers.

Vignaux and Detraz heard about a young man at the Banque de France who had the ability to explain complicated problems in simple terms. In 1953 they asked Delors to become *Reconstruction*'s economic expert and he jumped at the opportunity. He wrote articles, under the pseudonym Roger Jacques, and lectured groups of workers in the evening.

Delors discovered he enjoyed teaching. Thirty years later, François Mitterrand said to him: 'You have the clarity of Giscard and, what is more, people believe you. How do you manage that?' Delors replied: 'If I am clear, it's because I've had little education. As I'm not clever, before understanding something I have to make a huge effort.'

In 1957, at the CFTC's annual conference, the reformers won a share of power and appointed Delors to head the research department. The Banque de France released him on Tuesdays to work for the union. Delors had to write reports on subjects ranging from the Common Market to the Algerian war. He says:

> I had to explain to these Christian trade unionists what the unions were doing in the rest of the world. That's how I got my passion for Sweden and Britain, which I studied closely. I followed the debates between the New Statesman *and the* New Left Review. *From then on I was no longer* franco-français *[narrow-mindedly French].*[26]

In 1961 Delors wrote most of a CFTC report on incomes policy, which became known as the Bonety Report, after one of the union's leaders. If public enterprises were to be competitive, said the report, the Ministry of Finance should stop laying down their employees' wages and conditions. Instead, state enterprises should negotiate freely with trade unions. Both sides should agree on a contract which specified that pay increases would reflect the level of inflation and the overall performance of the economy.

In the same year Roger Jacques (Delors's pseudonym) wrote an article for *Esprit*, 'A trade union approach to the Commissariat au Plan' (France's planning commission). He proposed an annual meeting of the government, the employers and the unions. This would fix a minimum wage and an average level of pay rise, leaving some freedom to managers and unions to negotiate specific pay deals. The unions would accept binding agreements in return for being fully associated with the planning process.

The Bonety Report and the *Esprit* article sketched out many of the ideas later known as *politique contractuelle*. There is no English translation of this concept, although 'social contract' and 'corporatism' have some of the same meaning. The essence of *politique contractuelle* was that the two sides of industry should negotiate regularly over pay and conditions. In Britain and the then West Germany such behaviour was normal. In France, where the trade union movement was weaker, neither the government nor employers had the habit of negotiating with them. Delors would later become the father of France's *politique contractuelle*. Later still he would use the presidency of the European Commission to promote similar ideas at a European level.

Delors believed that negotiation, rather than state intervention or class struggle, would improve the lot of workers. Jean Leclere recalls a conversation with Delors one morning in 1953, when they walked to the Banque de France because of a metro strike. 'He told me all conflicts could be prevented or solved by negotiation, by mutual understanding of each point of view, and by taking the trouble to find a compromise that satisfied each side.'[27] Delors's almost mystical faith in the powers of negotiation has never abandoned him.

Delors's work for the CFTC brought him into contact with the great and the good of the French left. Michel Debatisse, who led the Centre Nationale des Jeunes Agriculteurs, a farmers' union, and José Bidegain, the president of Jeunes Patrons, a left-of-centre employers' lobby, shared Delors' Christian faith and befriended him. Delors also met Edmond Maire, who was to lead the trade union in the 1970s and 1980s. '*Reconstruction* found it useful to have Delors's support, for he, unlike many who backed it, was known for his faith' says Maire. 'He was more interested in making the union efficient than in the factional disputes.'[28] *Reconstruction* won control of the union in 1961, when Eugène Descamps became general secretary. The union's more radical stance attracted growing numbers of members.

Delors's job at the Banque de France, plus the trade union, politics, Vie Nouvelle and sport made heavy demands on his time. Marie had given birth to a son, Jean-Paul, in 1953. 'I consecrated the necessary time for my children, but it was tough on my wife,' he admits.[29] In 1960 Delors gave up sport so he could spend more time with his family. Martine, his daughter, remembers her father being 'busy but not absent. We'd see him a couple of evenings a week and then on Sunday he'd take me to an art exhibition or my brother to a sporting event such as cycling.'[30]

Delors turned down the chance to work full-time for his trade union. But in 1959 he became the CFTC representative on the Conseil Economique et Sociale, a consultative body which brought together French employers and trade unions. In 1961 the Commissariat au Plan (generally known as Le Plan) asked the Conseil Economique et Sociale to report on how the fruits of economic growth should be shared out. The Commissariat au Plan was looking for ideas to put into its plan for the years 1962 to 1965.

Delors wrote the report and emphasised the importance of collective rather than personal consumption. He suggested defining the standard of living not only by salary, but also by the provision of services, such as roads, health, education and culture, by social benefits and by the amount of free time. Pierre Massé, the commissaire-general of the Plan, was impressed. The new plan, which reflected Delors's report, proposed a slower growth of private consumption. General de Gaulle asked for Delors's report to be distributed to each ministry.

Massé asked Delors to set up a social affairs department at the Commissariat au Plan. Louis Delors firmly opposed such a move, for his son was on the way to becoming a director-general of the Banque de France. The Plan would also pay less than the bank. 'He didn't understand that I don't focus uniquely on the material,' says Delors. 'He found that I was too idealistic, too much of a believer and rather naïve.'[31]

At that time the Plan was one of France's most influential and prestigious institutions. Founded by Jean Monnet in 1945, with the task of directing scarce resources to where they were most needed, the Plan had taken the credit for France's economic boom in the 1950s. Delors had long championed 'democratic planning' and saw a chance of putting it into practice. He took the job, prompting Louis to vent his rage on Marie, who had refused to persuade Jacques not to move. Louis died in 1964, aged 69.

In January 1962 Delors began the job which would, for the first time, give him influence over public life. The Commissariat au Plan obliged

Delors to resign from the CFTC – which in 1964 would signal its independence from the Catholic Church by becoming the Confédération Française et Démocratique du Travail (CFDT).

When Delors started at the Plan he bought a flat on the top floor of 19 Boulevard de Bercy, in the 12th *arrondissement*. This poor *quartier*, bisected by large and sombre railway bridges, lies between the 11th *arrondissement*, where Delors grew up, and the Seine. The Delors kept this small and sparsely furnished flat for 30 years, because they liked the area's friendliness and sense of community. The Delors often ate in the Bar Restaurant de la Gare, the bistro opposite their flat, where the clientele was and is mainly blue-collar.

Martine and Jean-Paul went to the local state schools. Delors regularly took his family to the cinema but did not allow a television in the house until the 1964 Tokyo Olympics. He encouraged his children to read a lot and pushed them hard at school. Martine says she was not often allowed to go out with friends, but that her younger brother had an easier time.

Marie Delors became one of the neighbourhood's best known characters. She taught children the catechism and gave immigrants lessons in how to read and write. She visited the elderly and the sick, and always found time to chat in the shops. Sometimes, on a Sunday morning, Jacques Delors would lead a group of children down the Rue Proudhon (named after France's leading socialist-anarchist) to Notre Dame de Bercy, the austere local church.

Local people say the couple were popular because they did not take on airs and graces, even when Delors became famous. Delors made a political virtue of staying in the *quartier*. 'I've never changed my lifestyle, for I knew that if I did I would never understand the rest of society,' he said on French radio in 1975. He admitted that his *haut fonctionnaire* career had tended to make him indifferent to what was going on in the rest of France. That made it 'a very important point to stay in osmosis with these [popular] milieux.'[32] Delors stuck to his principles and, in the early 1980s, was the only socialist minister who lived in a predominantly working-class area.

CHAPTER TWO

MENDÈS-FRANCE AND THE SECOND LEFT

THE FOURTH REPUBLIC spanned the years between de Gaulle's resignation in 1946 and his return in 1958. All its governments were coalitions, and most of them were ineffectual and short-lived. Pierre Mendès-France's government, formed in June 1954 after France's military defeat by the Vietnamese at Dien Bien Phu, proved an exception. This Jewish radical set a deadline for pulling France out of Indochina and, by acting decisively, kept to it. He also began to disengage France from Tunisia and Morocco. He explained his policies in a series of radio broadcasts, which made him popular. A solitary, principled figure, he showed little interest in party politics or wheeler-dealing – which is one reason why, after his coalition collapsed in February 1955, he never regained the prime ministership.

In the early and mid-1950s Delors, like many of his generation, found Mendès-France an inspirational figure. 'Without Mendès I might have continued as a trade unionist. He is responsible for my passage to politics,' says Delors, who today has the collected works of Mendès-France displayed prominently behind his desk. Delors found his blunt language, his concern to inform public opinion and his accent on economic modernisation appealing.[1] Mendès-France sought a middle way between economic intervention and free markets, and favoured a strong currency.

In 1953 Delors joined Jeune République, a small Mendèsist party. Unlike the socialist SFIO, Jeune République was strongly anti-colonial and committed to France becoming a neutral country. For the 1956 general election the party joined the 'Front Républicain', whose leaders included Guy Mollet of the SFIO, François Mitterrand, who led a small party of war veterans, Jacques Chaban-Delmas, a moderate Gaullist, and Mendès-France. Delors printed leaflets and stuck up posters for the Front Républicain, which won the election. However Jeune République picked up only one parliamentary seat.

Mollet formed a left-of-centre government but disgusted many who had voted for the Front Républicain by prosecuting the Algerian war with renewed vigour. A 'Second Left' began to emerge, rejecting both the Stalinism of the communists and the unprincipled, managerial and colonialist politics of the SFIO, the Christian democratic MRP and the Radical

Party. Magazines such as *L'Observateur* and *Témoignage Chrétien* spoke for this side of the left. In 1957 several Second Left groups, including Jeune République, merged into the Union de la Gauche Socialiste. Delors sat on the new party's central committee.

In May 1958 the French army in Algiers mutinied. The rebels were fed up with weak governments and demanded the return of General de Gaulle. Faced with the prospect of a military coup, the National Assembly voted to abolish the Fourth Republic and asked de Gaulle to form a provisional government. The general drafted a new constitution, which would give the president a pre-eminent role in foreign and defence policy. The president would choose a prime minister, whose job would be to manage domestic policy. The National Assembly would be weaker than the parliaments of most other democracies.

In September 1958 de Gaulle put this constitution to the people in a referendum. Delors met Mendès-France for the first time during the campaign. Mendès-France opposed the new constitution because he doubted de Gaulle's commitment to democracy. He said of de Gaulle's government: 'This regime, born in the street, will perish in the street.' However Delors, like 78 per cent of those who voted, supported what became the Fifth Republic. 'I had been traumatised by the feebleness of the Fourth Republic, and I thought de Gaulle was the only person who could get France out of Algeria.'[2]

In 1962, when de Gaulle held a referendum on the introduction of direct presidential elections, Mendès-France, Mitterrand and most of the left campaigned against the general. Delors was among the 62 per cent who voted in favour of the reform, which further weakened parliament. He thought direct presidential elections would increase the visibility of the political process, and encourage the public to take an interest.[3]

Delors and Mendès-France also disagreed on the Common Market. In the last days of the Fourth Republic, Mendès-France had voted against the Treaty of Rome because he feared it would lead to German domination. Yet despite their differences, Delors saw Mendès-France as a role model. He recognised several of Mendès-France's traits – disdain for the scrum of party politics, pragmatism, sincerity and a gift for pedagogy – in himself.

The advent of the Fifth Republic shattered the traditional parties of the centre and the non-communist left. The socialists, radicals and Christian democrats had proved unwilling or unable to prevent de Gaulle's return to power. The general's restoration of firm government and his retreat from Algeria made him extremely popular. In the referendum of April 1962, 91 per cent of the French approved Algerian independence. The left appeared to have no chance of winning an election.

The clubs, magazines and small parties of the Second Left thrived on the disenchantment with established political forces. Some of the activists of these groups were militant Catholics, while others backed the *Reconstruction* wing of the CFTC union. The Second Left defined itself by a vigorous opposition to colonialism, a preference for devolved rather than statist forms of socialism and a belief that class struggle was not the only struggle with mattered. It branded the other left 'Jacobin' and out of date.

The traditional left viewed those involved in the Second Left as middle-class trendies who ignored the needs of the working class. It preferred the communist-led Confédération Générale du Travail (CGT) to the CFTC/CFDT, and it wanted state control of the commanding heights of the economy. The traditional left was readier to consider an alliance with the Parti Communiste Français (PCF) in order to gain power. The cultural divide between these two lefts would mark French politics for the next 30 years. François Mitterrand, who came to personify the traditional left, seldom trusted those with a Second Left pedigree.

The Club Jean Moulin, one of the most influential clubs of the Second Left, had a membership of *résistants*, *hauts fonctionnaires* and academics. Delors frequented the club and met several of the senior civil servants who would later help his career, including François Bloch-Lainé (director-general of the Caisse des Dépôts, a French credit agency), Simon Nora (who worked for the European Coal and Steel Community) and Jean-Yves Haberer (who would later be director of the Treasury when Delors became finance minister). These *hauts fonctionnaires*, aware of their ignorance on trade union matters but eager to learn, cultivated the intriguingly different Delors. But he felt uncomfortable among so many *énarques* and intellectuals and decided not to join the club.

If Pierre Mendès-France was the intellectual godfather of the Second Left, Jacques Delors and Michel Rocard became its leading lights and chief ideologues. Rocard, five years younger than Delors, had quit the SFIO in September 1958 and helped to form the Parti Socialiste Autonome. That party fused with the Union de la Gauche Socialiste in 1960, to create the Parti Socialiste Unifié (PSU). Rocard hoped the idealistic and 'genuinely' socialist PSU would, in time, replace the discredited SFIO. Delors joined the PSU but not its central committee. He left after a few months because the factional intrigues annoyed him.[4]

For the next 30 years Delors and Rocard would rival each other for power and influence on the French left. There is some mutual affection, and they respect each other's intelligence. They have nearly always agreed on the same social-democratic, pro-European, anti-statist policies. Yet they have never formed an alliance and have seldom helped each other. One reason is that their policies are too close: they appeal to similar political constituencies, and neither will accept the other's leadership.

A second reason is that their personalities clash. Rocard is a bourgeois Protestant whose father won the Nobel prize for physics. For Jacques Moreau, a leader of the CFDT and one of the many friends the two men share, 'Rocard has inherited a spirit of free inquiry from the Protestant tradition, while Delors is a man of certainty.'[5] After passing through the elite Ecole Nationale d'Administration, Rocard became an even more elite *Inspecteur des Finances*. Rocard likes to sail and ski, while Delors's sports are cycling, basketball and football. And while Rocard has a fun-loving streak and has been married three times, the sobre Delors has been content with one wife.

Rocard has always believed that in order to win power it is necessary to control a political party. Delors has taken a more unusual approach. Being ill at ease with political infighting but a prolific creative thinker, Delors has sought to impose himself through the power of ideas. So while Rocard turned the PSU into a vehicle for his ambitions, Delors poured his energies into Citoyen 60, a review and a club of the same name, which he founded in 1959.

CITIZEN JACQUES

Delors's declared intention, in creating Citoyen 60, was to aid the political, economic and social education of Vie Nouvelle members. Delors hoped the review and the club would inspire them to play an active role as citizens, working in youth groups, family associations, social centres and their neighbourhoods. However, Citoyen 60 soon appealed to a wider audience than Vie Nouvelle.

Most other Second Left clubs, such as the Jean Moulin, had no more than a few hundred members and were based in Paris. Delors's club had branches in 30 towns, with trade unionists, teachers and middle-ranking civil servants among its members. He says the club attracted 2000 members in addition to 5000 from Vie Nouvelle who automatically belonged. The review had 3000 to 4000 subscribers and sold 5000 copies of some issues.

Citoyen 60 made an explicit attempt to apply Mounierist principles to politics. Some years later Delors wrote:

> Our concern was to bridge the gap between, on the one hand, politics and
> the science of the state, which are the preserve of an elite and, on the
> other, the attempt at the base to transform society, led by cultural, social

and trade union activists. For Citoyen 60, political action was insepar-
able from the daily action of men and women in their various milieux,
the quartier, the town or the job.[6]

The first issue of the review *Citoyen 60* carried a masthead which reap-
peared in every issue:

The idea which inspires those responsible for this magazine is to be AT
THE SERVICE OF MAN, OF ALL MAN AND OF ALL MEN.
Its guiding principle is the desire to promote the communal side of
humanity, inspired by Christian personalism. But we believe our pos-
ition is universal enough to interest people who do not follow a religious
faith.[7]

The review did not carry articles on religion as such. However, Delors
notes that 'unlike many socialists, and above all Marxists, we said man
wasn't simply a product of economic and social systems, but that each
person was a unique being – of course conditioned by his economic situation, birth and culture.'[8] In 1963 the reference to personalism disappeared
from the masthead. Instead, 'its guiding principle is a desire to promote
humanity, inspired by democratic socialism.'[9] By then Delors was hoping
that *Citoyen 60* would help to revive the whole of the French left, rather
than just its Christian wing.

Citoyen 60 became influential for two reasons: the Second Left was fresh,
amorphous and looking for guidance; and the review, which appeared
every two months, was worth reading. The articles were written in clear
and simple French, with a rigorous and pedagogic tone – not unlike *The*
Economist. Delors, who edited the magazine under the pseudonym Roger
Jacques, wrote many of the articles. Cruiziat and other friends from Vie
Nouvelle provided the rest.

Citoyen 60 had an international flavour. The first issue carried articles on
German politics and the Algerian economy. In the second issue Delors
wrote 'Le Petit Guide du Marché Commun', which summarised the
Treaty of Rome in two pages. The fourth number featured a debate on the
future of socialism between Mendès-France, Britain's Nye Bevan and
Italy's Pietro Nenni.

Delors's editorials strongly favoured European integration. That of
December 1961 – exactly 30 years before the Maastricht treaty was agreed
– complained of the

profound scepticism towards all supranationality which afflicts the
Gaullists and part of the Jacobin left. We all feel there is something

about classical nationalism which is out of date and ill fitting, while the
world increasingly needs large-scale organisations, and while the prob-
lems of humanity require solutions at the planetary level.[10]

The appeal of the European adventure, he wrote, would pull France
forwards and allow it to 'bandage the wounds of decolonisation, to overcome its terrible divisions and its rancour, to regain a minimum degree of
unity and consensus, without which it risks, once more, tearing itself apart
and sinking into feebleness.' Delors called for Europe to move beyond a
common market, which was compatible with de Gaulle's *'Europe des*
patries', towards a 'common political project'.[11] A year later *Citoyen 60* ran
an article praising the European Commission's plans for monetary union.

An editorial of September 1963 attacked de Gaulle's European policy.

> *His will to establish French hegemony over Europe is the surest obstacle*
> *to the construction of this Europe. His aggression towards American*
> *capitalism is more spectacular than efficient, for stamping on political*
> *Europe will brake the implementation of a common economic policy*
> *which, alone, can allow us to regulate American investment in all the*
> *European countries.[12]*

Citoyen 60 took a strong line on decolonisation. It called for the decentra-
lisation of the French state and for regional government. It rejected protectionism and demanded a stable currency in order to achieve low inflation.
Citoyen 60 championed a new system of industrial relations in which the
trade unions would play a greater role. These ideas had much in common
with those of Mendès-France and CFTC.

Thirty years on, Delors claims that Citoyen 60 created a reservoir of
ideas 'on which governments of left and right drew for the next 20 years'.[13]
He has a point. Delors's own work in the early 1970s transformed French
industrial relations, while in the early 1980s President Mitterrand gave
more power to regional government. However some of the review's other
themes, such as 'democratic planning', slipped out of fashion.

Père Henri Madelin, a Jesuit priest and an *eminence grise* of the French
left, says the influence of Citoyen 60 cannot be underestimated.

> *Through Citoyen 60 Delors became a seducer of men, promoting ideas of*
> *sharing, justice, openness and participation among leaders of liberal*
> *opinion. He took Roman Catholics, turned them into left-wingers and,*
> *later on, many of them forgot their Catholicism.[14]*

The success of Citoyen 60 created jealousies. The MRP detested a club
which drew young Christians from its own ranks. In some parts of France

bishops tried to prevent meetings of Citoyen 60. Relations with the PSU were strained. 'Rocard was upset we'd left the PSU,' says Delors. 'They wanted to replace capitalism, we thought there were several capitalisms and that one could live with some of them.'[15] In July 1963 Rocard dined with Delors at the Belvedere restaurant, near the Banque de France. Rocard implored Delors to bring the membership of Citoyen 60 into the PSU. When Delors said no Rocard replied: 'I will break you, you will be wiped out.'[16]

Every time that someone tried to unify the non-Communist left they courted Citoyen 60, the largest club and the one which spoke, more or less, for left-wing Christians. Gaston Defferre, an SFIO leader, made overtures at the 'Assizes de la démocratie', a gathering of socialist groups in Vichy in April 1964. Defferre wanted to represent a 'third force', bringing together everyone between de Gaulle and the Parti Communiste Français, in the presidential election of December 1965. Delors thought Defferre's scheme unrealistic and would have nothing to do with it. Defferre's candidacy collapsed in September 1965, when the Christian democrats withdrew their support.

Mitterrand, who emerged as the left's new candidate, believed he could not win the election without support from the communists. Delors shared this analysis and joined Mitterrand's campaign team. He swung Citoyen 60 behind the Fédération de la Gauche Démocratique et Sociale, Mitterrand's umbrella organisation. Mitterrand gained the backing of the Communists and achieved an impressive 46 per cent in losing to de Gaulle.

A few days after the election Georges Pompidou, the prime minister, telephoned Pierre Massé at the Plan. 'Is Delors a civil servant or an adviser of the opposition?' he asked. Delors got the message and resigned from Citoyen 60.

At the same time Mitterrand established a six-man shadow cabinet on the British model. He offered Delors a place as the Christians' representative, adding that a parliamentary seat could be arranged. But Delors still viewed the political world with trepidation. He thought Mitterrand's offer incompatible with his job at the Plan. Delors's refusal maddened Mitterrand, but in any case the shadow cabinet fell apart a few months later.

At many points in his career, Delors has faced a choice: to hold power, but accept limits on what he may say; or to renounce power, but gain the right to speak freely. Delors has usually chosen power rather than political purity. To Delorists, this is proof of his desire to serve humanity through practical action. To anti-Delorists, he is a master opportunist.

HAUT FONCTIONNAIRE

The job of the Commissariat au Plan, since Monnet's day, had been to set out the choices confronting the French economy, and to provide research on the pros and cons of each. The Plan also hosted a series of committees where the 'social partners' – employers and trade unions – could debate each industry's problems. These tasks stimulated Delors, who describes his seven and a half years at the Plan as 'the most beautiful period of my life: one could reflect and act at the same time. I had the time to promote ideas.'[17]

Pierre Massé, an economist and engineer who had run Electricité de France before the Plan, became Delors's friend and mentor. He wanted Delors to increase the involvement of the social partners in the planning process. Massé believed the market could not be trusted to take account of the long term or to provide collective goods. 'The Plan imposed itself as a support, correction or substitute for the market,' wrote Delors after he had left the institution. He came to share Massé's belief that 'the government of men is a profoundly haphazard business', and that the Plan was therefore needed to 'embody the will of a society to master its future.'[18]

In March 1963 France suffered a bitter and prolonged miners' strike. Prompted by Delors, Massé suggested to Georges Pompidou, de Gaulle's prime minister, that he appoint mediators. Pompidou agreed, choosing Massé, Bloch-Lainé and Pierre Masselin, another senior civil servant. The three wise men made Delors their secretary and left much of the negotiating to him.

This role brought out two Delorist qualities: an attention to detail which enabled him to master the intricacies of how miners' pay scales compared with those of other workers; and a flair for finding a compromise that everyone could accept. He invited the union leaders to his home for boeuf bourguignon and, by listening to their concerns, won their confidence. The wise men's report concluded that miners' salaries had slipped by 8 per cent, compared with comparable private sector workers. The government and the unions accepted the report and the strike ended.

The miners presented Delors with a lamp which he still proudly displays in his office. De Gaulle summoned Delors to discuss the report – at the same time that Roger Jacques was attacking his foreign policy in *Citoyen 60*. 'I wasn't a Gaullist but he was a man for whom I had a great deal of admiration and respect,' says Delors. 'He had an amorous rapport with France of a very special kind.'[19]

The experience of the miners' strike reinforced Delors's belief in incomes policy, both as a weapon against inflation and as an instrument of social justice. He visited Britain's National Incomes Commission to see how another country managed wage restraint. In October 1963 Delors invited employers and unions to a conference on incomes. Afterwards he wrote a report which proposed a centralised prices and incomes policy for France. Every year the Plan would consult the social partners before setting pay increases for the various categories of worker. In addition, each company would distribute a profit-share to its workforce. An 'economic magistracy' would punish those who broke the new system's rules.

The trade unions rejected the report, fearing incomes policy would curb pay rises. The Patronat, the employers' lobby, criticised the report for enhancing the role of unions. The government thought the report would give the Plan too much power, so Delors's ideas gathered dust.

Delors took this failure, his first in public life, as a personal blow. But he soon recovered his zest for work, chairing committees, writing articles and delivering speeches on subjects as varied as adult training, welfare benefits and equality of opportunity in education. 'Because so few civil servants interested themselves in these questions, I was considered a social innovator,' he says.[20] From one side, François Mitterrand would seek Delors's help with policy proposals; from the other, ministers such as Jacques Chirac, the youthful secretary of state for employment, would ask his advice on new legislation.

Delors's work at the Plan made him aware, for the first time, that he had the potential to make an impact on France. 'For a young man of 37 who hadn't been to a grande école – where the Plan's other top officials had been – the ambience was formidable,' says Delors. 'When they saw this trade unionist arrive they gave him a funny look – he was like the ugly duckling.'[21]

Delors had to put up with educational snobbery from some of the senior officials. At one point his name was mentioned as a potential deputy head of the Plan. The prevalent view, however, was that someone so uneducated could not be a serious candidate. Such attitudes provoked Delors to bristle with self-importance. He trod on many territorial toes while building the social affairs department. Jean Ripert, the deputy head of the Plan, complained that Delors behaved as if he was deputy head.

The Plan allowed senior staff such as Delors the freedom to pursue their own interests. It lacked the formal hierarchy of a government ministry, and encouraged a free exchange of ideas. Delors found the Plan's sense of mission congenial. Many years later, he rediscovered similar qualities at the European Commission. That was not entirely coincidental, for when Jean Monnet had founded the High Authority (which became the commission) he modelled it on the Plan. Both bodies had to take a long-term perspective and to warn of the future. Both searched for consensus among parties with divergent interests – the Plan among the social partners, and the commission among the member-states.

Delors's team at the Commissariat au Plan found him a demanding taskmaster. 'The pressure was constant: since he was always stressed, we were,' recalls Marie-Thérèse Join-Lambert, one of his assistants. She notes the contrast with Michel Rocard, in whose cabinet she worked when he was prime minister. No workaholic, Rocard would let his staff get on with their jobs and sometimes tolerated fun and games. Delors, by contrast, 'saturated the work with his emotions. He was very involved, wanting to do everything himself.' Delors mixed friendship with work, and she recalls laborious Sundays spent at his flat.[22]

France's economic growth slowed in the mid-1960s. 'The government was becoming distant, the people were becoming indifferent and discontent, rather like today [September 1992]', recalls Delors.[23] His speeches in 1967 carried two themes: that economic growth had not reduced inequalities, and that the spread of consumer goods had not defused social tensions. He told anyone who would listen that France was heading for a social explosion – although he had no idea how it would come about. He took his worries to Edouard Balladur, one of Pompidou's advisers. As a result the prime minister asked the Plan to report on the social consequences of industrial modernisation.

Delors wrote the report with François-Xavier Ortoli, who had replaced Massé as commissaire-general (and who would later become president of the European Commission). Pompidou reacted favourably and, in August 1967, invited the social partners to a round-table discussion of several issues raised in the report. These included higher unemployment pay; a requirement for employers to give notice before making collective dismissals; and the creation of committees of employers and trade unions to look at restructuring in each industrial sector. The talks began in February 1968; for the first time in 20 years, the Patronat and the communist CGT had seats around the same table. This small step towards *politique contractuelle* delighted Delors.

Les événements of May 1968 intervened before the talks had got very far. For a month, the combination of student riots and a general strike threatened to topple the Fifth Republic. Martine, an economics student of 18, joined the protests, while Jean-Paul, a schoolboy of 15, slept out on the barricades of the Latin quarter. Any disciple of Mounier was bound to have some sympathy for students who rejected the consumer society and the centralised state. Yet Delors kept a low profile; demonstrations were not his style of politics and he abhorred the violence.

He complained that if the Gaullists had implemented the reforms he had championed – on industrial relations, on a fairer division of incomes and on the education system – the explosion need not have happened. Delors thought the protestors would lose. He advised Mendès-France, who tried to stage a political comeback, not to speak at a rally of students and workers on 27 May. Mendès-France took no notice and, at the rally, offered to lead a provisional government.

By 30 May Pompidou had restored order. De Gaulle broadcast to the nation, announcing a general election and attacking Mendès-France with venom. That provoked Delors and some of his colleagues at the Plan to issue a statement. They said that de Gaulle had not understood the crisis and that the protestors had their sympathy.

This statement came far too late to impress anyone on the left, but it earned a punishment from the right. Delors was on the point of becoming director of a new research institute for urban problems. Pompidou refused to sign the decrees which would have established the institute. On 30 June he won a thumping majority for the right in the general election.

A senior civil service post, that of secretary-general for professional training, became vacant in October 1968. Delors had the best qualifications but had to continue his punishment by spending six months as 'acting' rather than full secretary-general. Delors found the time and energy to combine this new job with his post at the Plan.

In April 1969 de Gaulle resigned after losing a referendum on constitutional reform. Pompidou, whose popularity had grown as the general's had waned, easily won the presidential election of June. The left suffered a catastrophic reverse. The communist candidate won 21.5 per cent of the votes, but the SFIO's Defferre (who ran with Mendès-France as his prime minister-designate) achieved 5 per cent and the PSU's Rocard only 3.5 per cent.

Although he had trounced the left, Pompidou feared a return of social strife. He thought that France's staid political system needed fresh ideas. So he chose the debonair Jacques Chaban-Delmas, a Gaullist committed to social reform, as his prime minister. Chaban-Delmas had been mayor of Bordeaux since 1947 and was president of the National Assembly. Although a hero of the Resistance, a rugby international, a charismatic speaker and a tremendous hit with women, Chaban-Delmas lacked intellectual depth and devotion to detail. He needed solid and industrious advisers.

Bloch-Lainé suggested two names to Chaban-Delmas: Nora, who had worked in Mendès-France's 1954 'cabinet', and Delors. Both were men of the left rather than Gaullists, yet Chaban-Delmas sent Bloch-Lainé to offer Nora the job of *directeur de cabinet* and Delors the post of adviser on social affairs. Delors asked for 24 hours to think about it. Marie and Martine advised him to take the chance. So did Eugène Descamps, the secretary-general of the CFDT, although he warned Delors that the left would hate him. Delors wrote a memorandum on the reforms he considered necessary, which Chaban-Delmas approved. 'We agreed that, with society unstable, the time was ripe to get two or three social reforms passed,' says Delors, who was 43 when he accepted the offer.[24]

Delors had believed that being a trade unionist or a *haut fonctionnaire* could bring about change. 'After the shock of the presidential election I thought the only way to realise my ideas was to work with the system,' he says. 'I knew I wouldn't stay long, and that I would therefore have to pay one day, and I paid.'[25] Before paying, however, Delors would enjoy his first taste of political power.

CHAPTER THREE

CHOOSING SIDES

Delors has often had doubts about where he stands in the French political spectrum. He spent the 1960s moving away from the left: in 1961 he quit the far-left PSU, in 1962 he resigned from the CFTC trade union, in 1965 he abandoned *Citoyen 60* and in May 1968 he lay low. Then he spent three years working for a Gaullist prime minister.

After that experience he remained unsure of where his loyalties lay. He said in 1975:

> *The political world simplifies everything, but I'll always be on the right of the left or on the left of the right, rejected by both. I am le mal aimé. My route is uncomfortable and doubtless unrealistic, but one also needs people like me.*[1]

Ultimately, Delors's desire to be a serious politician – or as he would put it, to be useful – forced him to make choices. In the 1960s the weakness of the French left had encouraged him to drift away from it. In the 1970s its revival would draw him back – just in time to hold office in the socialist governments of the 1980s.

France had only one radical, reforming government between the fall of Mendès-France in 1955 and the election of Mitterrand in 1981: that of Chaban-Delmas. The broadly-based ministerial team included not only Gaullists but also 'independent republicans', such as Valéry Giscard d'Estaing, the finance minister, and Christian democrats.

On 16 September 1969, Chaban-Delmas unveiled his government's programme to the National Assembly. He described France as 'a blocked society' and 'a country of castes'. He complained of archaic social structures; of a fragile, under-industrialised economy; and of a 'tentacular' state which suffocated local government. Chaban-Delmas spoke of social reforms which would, he hoped, build a '*Nouvelle Société*'. The flavour of the speech harked back to Mendès-France, and the ideas came from Nora, his *directeur de cabinet*, and Delors.

The prime minister's programme implied that Gaullism should open itself to the left. However, many Gaullists feared this strategy would lose the support of right-wing electors without gaining new votes from socialists. They also resented the presidential style of Chaban-Delmas's speech. The prime minister appeared to have forgotten that in the Fifth Republic his role was to execute presidential policies rather than determine strategy.

Pompidou shared none of Chaban-Delmas's radicalism. While the prime minister talked of making the French freer and happier, the president stressed the creation of wealth and social order. Yet Pompidou was content to let the government introduce a series of reforms, in the hope that it would prevent a repeat of May 1968. Chaban-Delmas freed television stations from government control, gave greater autonomy to state enterprises and reduced the length of military service. He raised family allowances and the minimum wage.

Chaban-Delmas gave Delors a free hand to try out his ideas of *politique contractuelle*. Delors explains:

> *In France senior civil servants and politicians thought everything*
> *should be done by law or decree. Against that I pushed the contract,*
> *between the economic partners, with or without the state according to*
> *circumstances, on salaries, working conditions and employment policy.*
> *It's better to change society by contract than by decree.*

Delors's *politique contractuelle* had two strands: an implicit incomes policy, which some trade unionists disliked, and negotiations on matters other than incomes, which most of them liked 'since they had the right to speak, which was a real revolution in France.'[2]

In November 1969 a strike at Electricité de France (EDF) gave Delors a chance to try out his ideas. He persuaded EDF and the unions (bar the communist CGT) to sign a *Contrat de Progrès*. Each year the unions and the management would negotiate on salaries and much else, while the government would not get involved. The *Contrat de Progrès* guaranteed a minimum pay rise every year, but the size of the increase would depend on the state of the French economy and on EDF's performance. Neither side could renounce the contract without three months' warning. The unions at Gaz de France signed a similar *Contrat de Progrès*.

No sooner were these contracts signed than Chaban-Delmas told a conference of business people that the result would be no strikes for two years. Delors was furious, for such triumphalism would make the negotiation of further contracts harder. He accused the prime minister of humiliating the union leaders and slammed the door on him. Despite their suspicions, however, union leaders did sign about 60 *Contrats de Progrès*, in public industries such as railways, coal, atomic power and Parisian transport. Most of these contracts covered not only pay but also working hours, training provisions and employment guarantees. In February 1971 even the CGT added its signature to the contracts for the gas and electricity industries. A law of July 1971 laid down negotiating procedures for management and unions in private sector companies.

Delors frequently invited trade union leaders to the Matignon palace, where the prime minister and his staff work in gilded rococo splendour. Never before – or since – had a French government courted trade unions with such ardour. The French economy's strong growth in the early 1970s helped Delors to convince them that his policies were worthwhile.

However during these years the unions were shifting to the left. At the CFDT's annual conference in 1970, delegates complained of Delors's 'scandalous' work for a reactionary government. Edmond Maire, who became the union's general secretary in April 1971, recalls:

> The majority of the CFDT wanted a radical transformation of society, rather than [Delors's] pragmatic approach. The first Contrats de Progrès would, in certain circumstances, restrain pay, so we only accepted a few of that sort.[3]

Later contracts left out pay restraint.

Although the *politique contractuelle* proved less far-reaching than Delors had hoped, it transformed industrial relations in France. He is prouder of this than anything else he achieved before he became president of the European Commission. 'After everything I did, everyone was for *politique contractuelle*,' says Delors. 'Before, the right was against it because of union power, and the left because it thought only politics could change society.'[4] Delors's policies helped to bring about social peace. In each of 1970, 1971 and 1972, the number of days lost through strikes was less than in the preceding year. By the end of 1970, 70 per cent of French people thought Chaban-Delmas a good prime minister.

Delors had a second success with *formation permanent*, adult training. In July 1970 he asked the trade unions and employers' organisations to negotiate, without the government, a national convention on training. Delors annoyed both sides by trying to influence the talks. However the social partners agreed on a convention, which Delors and Chaban-Delmas turned into a law – known as the *Loi Delors*. Twenty years later, the Treaty of Maastricht included a provision for conventions among the social partners to become European law.

The *Loi Delors* required all companies to give employees the right to training throughout their careers. Employers and the government would finance the scheme. The law also created the institutions to carry out the training. In 1973 200,000 workers followed training courses based on the law.

Chaban-Delmas trusted Delors and gave him a long leash. In theory Delors was an official rather than a politician. In practice he became the only luminary of the French left to wield power at a national level in the 1960s or 1970s. Delors adored his master because 'he's not a killer, he's a charming man, open, friendly, warm, spontaneous, faithful, energetic and not pretentious.'[5] Chaban-Delmas returned the affection.

The right wing of the Gaullist party thought Delors's influence on Chaban-Delmas unhealthy. Gaullists opposed to 'Chabanism' included the shadowy figure of Pierre Juillet, Pompidou's closest counsellor; Marie-France Garaud, a striking and determined Amazon who advised the president; Jacques Chirac, budget minister; and Charles Pasqua, a Corsican deputy. However other Gaullists, including Edouard Balladur, Pompidou's adviser on social affairs, supported Delors's initiatives.

Delors's cabinet colleagues noted that he always concentrated on the immediate task and that he never relaxed. 'Unlike most civil servants, Delors had strong convictions and a sense of mission,' says Nora. 'The upside was that he motivated people. The downside was that he could be convinced he was right against everyone else.'[6] Other colleagues found Delors's impulsiveness and fits of pique trying. When he did not get what he wanted he sometimes threatened to quit. In July 1970, prompted by Delors, Chaban-Delmas tried to remove the ceiling on the national insurance contributions of those on high salaries. Pompidou and Giscard d'Estaing blocked the scheme. Delors said he would resign, but did not.

Delors's regular briefings to journalists helped to get Chaban-Delmas a good press. 'He was more political than the rest of us,' says Yves Cannac, another member of the cabinet. 'He promoted himself, thanks to his court of journalists, and willingly appeared as a deputy prime minister.'[7] In 1970 Delors made the cover of *L'Express*, a weekly magazine, as '*l'Inconnu du Matignon*' (the unknown man of the Matignon). The magazine coined the term '*social-delorisme*' to define the government's policy.

Thiérry de Beaucé, another member of the cabinet, says:

> To begin with Nora was the real force in the cabinet – he had the brilliance and experience, the énarque education and the establishment contacts. Yet Delors became a more powerful force behind Chaban-Delmas than most of the ministers.

Was Delors then a megalomaniac?

No, more of a paranoid, he liked to see himself as a victim of personal attacks by the right – but in truth the right did plot against us.[8]

In June 1971 François Mitterrand took control of the Parti Socialiste (as the SFIO had become in 1969) and began to reinvigorate it. Chaban-Delmas's hope of winning over some socialists to a centre block in French politics began to appear unrealistic. In July Nora quit to become president of Hachette. Delors took over as *directeur de cabinet*, adding the economy to his other responsibilities. By that time the cabal of right-wingers around Pompidou had convinced the president that the prime minister was leading Gaullism into a dead end.

Garaud says:

> *The problem between Chaban and Pompidou was less about policy and more about Chaban's 'Fourth Republic' style of government. In the Fifth Republic, the inevitable conflicts between president and prime minister are sorted out in private. Chaban used the National Assembly and the press [in his arguments against Pompidou].*[9]

Pompidou began to limit the prime minister's freedom of manoeuvre. A succession of scandals tarnished Chaban-Delmas's reputation and made Pompidou's task easier. The most serious scandal concerned the prime minister's tax form, which someone in the ministry of finance leaked to the *Canard Enchaîné*, a satirical weekly. The form revealed that Chaban-Delmas had not paid any tax for four years, although he had not broken the law. Some suspected Giscard d'Estaing of mischief. The finance minister, like the prime minister, had his eyes on the presidency. At that time, however, neither of them expected an election sooner than 1976.

Chaban-Delmas always had Delors at his side, so the right considered, correctly, that he was more than a counsellor. '*Enlevez Delors, il n'y a plus rien*' (take away Delors and there's nothing left), said Garaud at a Gaullist convention. She and her friends persuaded Pompidou that he must change prime minister if the Gaullists were to win the 1973 legislative elections. 'Chaban was riddled with scandals like a dog with fleas,' says Garaud.[10] In fact Chaban's opinion poll ratings, although slipping, remained at a respectable 40 per cent. In a referendum of April 1972, 67 per cent of the French voted for the government's policy of allowing Britain to join the European Economic Community.

In June the Parti Socialiste and the PCF agreed on a *Programme Commun de Gouvernement*, containing radical socialist policies. Chabanism had failed to prevent a revival of the left which, for the first time under the Fifth

Republic, appeared to have a chance of winning power. In July Pompidou sacked Chaban-Delmas, installing the conservative and colourless Pierre Messmer in the Matignon. French politics was becoming sharply polarised between left and right. Those with centrist inclinations, such as Delors, would have to make choices.

THE PRODIGAL SON

After leaving the prime minister's office, Delors waited more than two years before joining the Parti Socialiste. Delors says that he and Chaban-Delmas always knew their 'moral contract' would be a short one and that when it ended he would rejoin the left. He says he did not join the Socialists immediately because he was busy with a new job and a new club, and because it would have been indecent to turn his back on Chaban-Delmas so soon. 'That's the Don Quixote side to me.'[11]

At the time, however, Delors's commitment to the left did not seem so obvious. Chaban-Delmas says that in October 1972 Delors both offered to work for him and said he was thinking of joining the Socialists.[12] In the event Delors did not join that party until November 1974, after Chaban-Delmas's bid for the presidency had failed.

During his three years in the Matignon, Delors had remained secretary-general for adult training, attending to that post at weekends. From July 1972 he worked full time at the job, which involved implementing the *Loi Delors*. Some Gaullists spread unfounded stories that he used the position to channel public funds to far-left organisations. In January 1973 Giscard d'Estaing, still the finance minister, appointed Delors to the prestigious general council of the Banque de France. But in August, fed up with the way the Messmer government was treating him, Delors resigned.

'People offered me jobs in banks, companies and universities,' says Delors. 'For ethical reasons I chose the university.'[13] He adds that, having never taken a degree, the thought of being an academic flattered him. He became a professor at the Paris Dauphine university, where he had an office on the same corridor as Jacques Attali. Delors taught comparative political economy, with the focus on Western Europe. He also created a research centre for employment.

At first the students gave this 'right-wing collaborator' a hard time. Later, after word spread that his lectures were unorthodox and fascinating, he became a popular figure. Delors also taught at the ENA, where, during his years with the Plan, he had given courses on industrial relations. In the mid-1970s Delors's ENA students included Pascal Lamy, who later became his chief aide in Brussels, Joachim Bitterlich, who became Helmut Kohl's chief foreign policy adviser, and his own daughter.

Martine finished sixth in her final exams at ENA, in 1975. Unusually for an *énarque* with such high marks, she chose the 'soft option' of going to work in the ministry of labour. She had inherited her father's interests, brains and ambition, but her combative and forceful character owed more to her mother.

Unlike Martine, Jean-Paul had some of his father's mental fragility. The liveliest and most cheerful member of the family, he was also creative, intuitive and sensitive. Jean-Paul's politics were more idealistic than his sister's and, as an active member of the PSU, he disapproved of his father's sojourn with Chaban-Delmas. Jean-Paul rebelled against parental authority more often than Martine. At the age of 18 Delors dissuaded him, with great difficulty, from living in a commune.

Antoine Lejay recalls visiting the Boulevard de Bercy flat in the early 1970s. 'There was always a lively discussion, all four of them arguing with conviction. They shouted at each other but were a very close family.' Marie joined in the arguments but made an effort to keep the peace.[14] After a degree in economics, Jean-Paul began a career in journalism at *La Nouvelle Economiste*, a weekly magazine. Then he moved to Ajaccio, where he reported on Corsica for *Libération*. He fell in love with the island and wrote a book about it.

In 1973 many left-wingers rallied to the Parti Socialiste. Delors, however, set up a new club, Echange et Projets, which sought to bring together left and right in reasoned debate. The club's purpose, said its review, was to 'imagine, and then create a more fulfilling, just and democratic society.' While Citoyen 60 had aimed to educate Christian activists throughout France, Echange et Projets targeted the Parisian elite. Founder members included civil servants such François Bloch-Lainé, Jean-Yves Haberer and Jean-Baptiste de Foucault (later commissaire-general at the Plan); entrepreneurs such as José Bidegain, Antoine Riboud (of BSN) and François Dalle (of Orient); and diverse writers, lawyers and trade unionists. There were socialists, Christian democrats and Gaullists – many of them Catholics.

Only those who received invitations and then underwent a rigorous vetting could join. Those holding political mandates were barred. The club took the equivalent 10 per cent of each member's tax bill, to pay for premises and publications. Not surprisingly, membership stuck at 200. Delors, the president, spent two days a week on the club.

Pierre Mialet, a mathematician, inventor and sometime president of Camping Gaz, recalls:

> *Echange et Projets was very different from the other clubs, where you just talked. It was hard work, with committees, reports and presentations,*

though there was also camaraderie. Delors had a kind of mysterious radiance: it was hard to classify where he came from or where he was going.[15]

The monthly general assembly had to approve everything the club published. Echange et Projets' review, a more turgid read than *Citoyen 60*, appeared every three months. It ran articles on subjects such as international relations, the EEC, employment, the condition of women, local democracy and *autogestion* (self-management) for workers. The club also organised seminars, including a tempestuous event in 1975 which brought together ecologists and proponents of nuclear power.

Delors's preface to *La Révolution du Temps Choisi*, an Echange et Projets book on the politics of time, showed he had not forgotten Mounier. Delors attacked the modern world for depriving people of the ability to control their time. Time had been 'Taylorised', subordinated to industrial organisation. Instead, Delors argued, people should manage the hours in which they chose to work. He called for job-sharing to reduce unemployment, better leave for childcare, and time off for training and political activity. Older people should be allowed to phase out their careers gradually.[16]

Delors demanded an end to the conflict between the alienation of work and the fulfilment of leisure. He suggested that the growth of the service economy and 'post-Taylorist' production techniques provided the answer. Production was shifting towards smaller, geographically dispersed units, and more sorts of work could be done at home.[17] (In 1988 *Marxism Today*, a British review, presented almost identical ideas as the theory of 'post-Fordism'.) When Delors became a minister he remembered some of these ideas and pushed through a law allowing civil servants to work part time.

Echange et Projets proved influential when the left won power. About 50 members of the club joined ministerial 'cabinets' in the Mauroy government of 1981. Jean Auroux, the minister of labour, had Delors's daughter Martine and Gills Bellier, both members of the club, in his cabinet. Together they produced the *Lois Auroux* of 1982, the Mauroy government's most significant set of social reforms. These laws required each company's management and unions to negotiate, annually, on pay, hours and conditions; gave rights to part-time and temporary workers; and established, in every company, a health and safety committee. The *Lois Auroux* drew heavily on a 1976 report for Echange et Projets by Martine and Bellier.

When Pompidou died in April 1974, Chaban-Delmas became the Gaullist candidate for the presidency. The competition in the first round of the election included Giscard d'Estaing and Mitterrand. Chaban-Delmas says Delors was 'not a stranger' to his campaign.[18] If Chaban-Delmas had won, would Delors have become a minister, or perhaps prime minister? 'No, no, that wasn't my political family,' says Delors. 'I didn't campaign for him in 1974. I went round to his place two or three times, through friendship.' Delors also refused to help Mitterrand. 'It was all very delicate.'[19]

Delors says one reason he did not campaign was that he knew Chaban-Delmas would lose. After Chirac and a group of right-wing Gaullists declared their support for Giscard d'Estaing, Chaban-Delmas's campaign faltered. On 5 May Mitterrand, who represented the Union of the Left, an alliance of the socialists, the PCF and the small left-radical party, won 43.3 per cent of the vote. Giscard d'Estaing won 32.9 per cent and Chaban-Delmas 14.6 per cent. In the second round Giscard squeaked home with 50.6 per cent, against Mitterrand's 49.3 per cent.

Mitterrand's narrow defeat settled the argument over which strategy the left should adopt in order to win power. The Mitterrandist route, via an alliance with the communists, appeared viable. Alternatives, such as Rocard's PSU – fizzling out amidst its own internal divisions – or an alliance with the centre, did not.

In October 1974 Mitterrand organised the 'Assizes du Socialisme', a conference designed to broaden the base of the Parti Socialiste. Before the assizes Mitterrand sent his faithful aide Pierre Bérégovoy to Delors's home. Bérégovoy announced that Mitterrand wanted Delors to join the party and that a place would be found on the committee organising the assizes. Later on, however, the Rocardians objected that a 'right-winger' without a band of supporters did not deserve a seat on the committee, so the offer was withdrawn.

The assizes proved a triumph for Mitterrand. Many of those who had been active on the Second Left – in the CFDT or in groups such as Vie Nouvelle – joined his party. Rocard brought in part of the PSU, in return for a seat on the executive. 'I put myself in the back row' Delors recalls. 'Mitterrand signalled that Delors should come to the front, so that he could be seen by the cameras, but I refused.'[20]

The following month Delors bit the bullet and applied to his local branch of the Parti Socialiste, in the 12th *arrondissement*. At a branch meeting in the Tambour restaurant he – rather than any meat – underwent a grilling. 'Are you not ashamed to have collaborated with the Gaullists?' asked one member. Delors said he was not, citing trade union leaders who had praised his *politique contractuelle*. Was it true that Giscard had offered him a ministry? No, but Jean-Jacques Servant-Schreiber, one of Giscard's ministers, had asked him to be his *directeur de cabinet*. Would he use the branch as a springboard to becoming a deputy? Delors promised he would not be a candidate in that district or any other. 'We would have much preferred a plumber to join today!' shouted a member of CERES (a faction of national-ist Marxists led by Jean-Pierre Chevènement). Delors pledged that he would accept the *Programme Commun*. After two hours of questions, 70 per cent of the members voted to accept Delors. The ordeal left scars.

The following week Delors wrote about his decision to join the party in the *Nouvel Observateur*, a weekly magazine. 'Some people try and make the *Programme Commun* into a kind of monument under which you absolutely must pass, curving your spine, before you have the right to speak in the name of the left,' he wrote. The programme was 'the most important political gesture of the past few years', but nothing more.[21] Such words raised the hackles of many party members.

Rocard says:

> *I advised Jacques to enter quietly and to wait a year before doing anything. But he was impatient enough to announce he was joining with press releases and communiqués, and so provoked the odious treatment he received.*[22]

Delors says there were no press releases or communiqués and that Rocard's memory is 'completely mistaken'.[23]

In February 1975 Delors published *Changer*, the most interesting of his half-dozen books. Written in the form of an interview, the book described Delors's involvement in trade unions, clubs and political parties in the 1950s and 1960s. Delors wanted to show the younger generation of socialists, who linked him with Gaullism, that he had authentic left-wing credentials. He wrote that France needed nationalised industries and banks to safeguard its independence; to take on tasks in the national interest where the private sector was too weak; and to strengthen the state against private economic forces. Yet Delors praised the market as:

> *a good instrument for dealing with large quantities of information, assuring consumers a certain amount of choice, sending out signals which facilitate entrepreneurial and investment decisions, and stimulating economic activity.*[24]

Delors saw positive elements in Eastern Europe, pointing to 'a less unequal society than our Western societies, and a development of collective consumption, which is one of the foundations of a more balanced lifestyle.' Those countries' dissidents went unmentioned, but he advised the West to learn from China's model of modernisation, which had 'avoided excessive industrialisation.' As for America, it had messed up the global economic system, tried to weaken European unity and forced Europe to make economic concessions in return for the maintenance of its nuclear umbrella. 'American imperialism is a fact,' and the best remedy for that, wrote Delors, was a united Europe.[25]

FOR FRANÇOIS, AGAINST MICHEL

Delors busied himself with Echange et Projets and his teaching, but kept a low profile in the Parti Socialiste.

I was waiting to be called to the end of the table, to be close to the seigneur. That's a general rule with me, I never vaunt myself. That's my pride. There is a lot of similarity between pride and humility.[26]

The call came in 1976. 'You can't stay like that, the period of purgatory is over,' said Mitterrand, who gave Delors a place on his committee of experts. Delors also took over the party's international economics department.

Most French politicians have a local power base, as mayors or deputies. But Delors, despite prompting from Mitterrand, showed little enthusiasm for getting elected. While he enjoyed speaking to politicians, business people, trade unionists or civil servants, he felt ill at ease with the general public. Furthermore, Delors could not seek election without immersing himself in socialist faction-fighting, which he disdained.

In 1976 Mitterrand sent Delors to the Parisian suburb of Créteil, where the Parti Socialiste was riven with conflict. Mitterrand wanted Delors to sort out the local party, lead it into the 1977 municipal elections and become the mayor. However the CERES tendency gave Delors such a rough time that he pulled out of Créteil. Before the 1978 legislative election, Delors turned down the chance of standing in the constituency of Roanne, near St Etienne.

Then Mitterrand offered him a seat in Corrèze, his ancestral home. Delors almost accepted but his mother, who had moved to Corrèze, persuaded him not to stand. She feared the jibes of peasants and traders, many of whom supported Jacques Chirac, who had made Corrèze his political base. She had never wanted her son to be a politician. Delors declined the offer, prompting Mitterrand to wonder if he was a serious politician. Delors admits that his electoral shyness is 'a weakness, a fault, but I could only do it by causing pain for my family.'[27]

Meanwhile Rocard, who lacked Delors's fastidiousness, had begun to make his mark on the party. At the socialists' congress in Nantes, in 1978, Rocard unveiled his own policy platform. His theme was *autogestion*, which meant direct democracy in the workplace and the devolution of power to regions and local authorities. He attacked the Jacobin traditions of nationalism, protectionism and the centralised state. Delors agreed with this implicit criticism of Mitterrand's ideology – while noting ruefully that Rocard's programme drew heavily on his own ideas.

The socialists expected to win the general election of March 1978 – and might have done so, if the communists had not broken the Union of the Left and heaped abuse on their erstwhile allies. Delors helped to run the socialists' campaign at the party headquarters. On the evening of the right's victory, Rocard went on television and made a thinly veiled attack on Mitterrand. He said the socialists had gone astray, that they should have waged a better campaign and that they should be more responsible.

Delors reacted indignantly to Rocard's intervention.

> *I felt sick, he had spat in the soup, I was absolutely scandalised by that. I always thought that François Mitterrand was the only man who could bring the left back to power. That he should contest his leadership, I understood, but on the evening of the defeat!*[28]

The next morning Delors went to see Mitterrand to assure him of his support. Mitterrand took Delors to the Palais Bourbon, the home of the National Assembly. For an hour they walked around the lobbies, attracting puzzled looks. Delors is proud of this moment of fealty.

On 20 June a group of Mitterrand loyalists published the 'Manifesto of 30', a vicious attack on Rocard's policies. Describing a 'rupture with capitalism' as necessary, the manifesto warned that revisionism was a 'mortal danger' for the Parti Socialiste. 'We have to reaffirm the need to take over the commanding heights of the economy and the pre-eminence of the Plan over the market.' At the end of the manifesto came the predictable signatures of Mitterrand loyalists such as Lionel Jospin, Louis Mermaz, Charles Hernu and Paul Quilès – and, to many people's surprise, that of Jacques Delors.

Delors says he signed because he was mad at Rocard's behaviour on the night of the election defeat. 'I don't regret having signed it.'[29] Although Delors does not say so himself, that signature helped to expiate the years with Chaban-Delmas and to show the Mitterandists he was one of them.

'Signing the manifesto was a great injustice,' says Rocard. 'He later told me he had done it for the "*droit d'exister au politique*" [the right to exist in politics], which in a sense was true, for he was alone.' Rocard notes that while he fought his corner in the Parti Socialiste

> *Jacques was not at my side, which was hard to explain in terms of his intellectual coherence. He and I were always on the same wavelength, but*

he affected to preserve his liberty and shunned factions. Frankly, the
situation wasn't such that I was going to beg him to support me : he had no
battalions. He is a producer of ideas – one is never very sure if he is really
in politics.[30]

So Delors threw in his lot with Mitterrand, although he preferred Rocard's policies. Rocard continued to attack the party leader. 'We have to condemn a certain political style and a certain archaism,' he said on television in September 1978, adding that socialists should speak more truthfully and respect facts. Rocard prepared to bid for the leadership at the party congress due in Metz in April 1979. Pierre Mauroy, Mayor of Lille and leader of a faction of moderate socialists, backed Rocard. Delors met Rocard in Brussels and tried to persuade him not to challenge Mitterrand. 'I said to him, you'll lose. He said "no, I'm going to win." It was his habitual optimism.'[31]

Delors's judgement proved correct. In Metz Mitterrand's motion won more votes than that of Rocard, but only with the support of Chevènement's CERES tendency. The Rocardians claimed that Delors had betrayed 20 years of his political life by signing Mitterrand's motion. Yet Delors would not tolerate personal abuse of Rocard. Laurent Fabius, Mitterrand's young protégé – and, as a bourgeois *énarque*, the sort of socialist Delors does not warm to – delivered a vitriolic attack on Rocard. 'They tell us there is nothing between the market and rationing,' said Fabius, pointing to Rocard. 'But yes, there is socialism!' The delegates cheered but Delors stormed out of the chamber shouting 'this is shameful!'

Delors says he likes Rocard personally, 'but less his entourage, they're killers.'[32] He sometimes complains of Rocard being unpredictable and lightweight. 'Rocard has ideas, but doesn't deepen them.'[33] Delors sometimes seems jealous; he has built a career on dogged work and the solid production of ideas, while Rocard has often got by with sheer brilliance and charisma.

Mitterrand rewarded Chevènement for his support by asking him to write the *Projet Socialiste*, the party programme. Strongly anti-American, Chevènement's offering included phrases like 'the disembowelling of the French economy on the altar of multinational capitalism.' In 1980 the Parti Socialiste – with a more middle-class membership than any other socialist party in Western Europe – adopted this semi-Marxist programme. Delors voted against it.

The first-ever direct elections to the European Parliament were held in June 1979. France's system of proportional representation requires each party to present a national list of candidates. The higher a candidate's position on the list, the better his or her chances of election. Delors hoped that his European expertise would ensure a high ranking on the socialist list. However, Mitterrand refused to intervene in his favour and the party bureaucrats gave priority to loyalists. Ranked 21st, Delors's chances seemed slim. In the event the first 22 socialists qualified and Delors – for the first and probably the last time in his life – was elected to a parliament.

At that time the European Parliament had few powers, and its role was mainly consultative. But Delors enjoyed the work, which took him to Strasbourg for plenary sessions and to Brussels for committee meetings. Delors became chairman of the economic and monetary affairs committee, one of the most influential in the parliament. His committee's report on the European Monetary System (EMS), which had started in January 1979, welcomed the venture. The committee covered the free circulation of people, goods, services and capital, so Delors soon learned that there was no such thing as a single market.

Delors had a strained relationship with the socialist group of Euro-MPs. A majority of them opposed any step towards monetary union and delayed his report on the EMS. Simone Veil, a French centrist who was then the parliament's president, recalls Delors's temper fraying. 'He thought the parliament should do more technical and economic work, instead of wasting time on foreign-policy motions that achieved nothing,' says Veil. 'He didn't like all the ideological confrontation.'[34]

Together with some of the parliament's brighter socialists, Delors formed the 'Amigo group', named after the Brussels hotel where they met. Members included Piet Dankert, a Dutchman who later became the parliament's president, Carlo Ripa di Meana, an Italian who later became a European commissioner, and Jacques Moreau, a French trade unionist who later became president of the European Community's Economic and Social Committee. The Amigo group prided itself on being open to new ideas and free from the banal thinking of many socialist Euro-MPs. But in May 1981, before either Delors or the Amigo group had made much impact, France's presidential election whisked him away.

Ever since Delors had joined the socialists, Mitterrand's treatment of him had alternated between encouragement and indifference. Mitterrand attached a huge importance to longstanding personal loyalty. Having shunned him in the 1960s and early 1970s, Delors was never accepted – as were courtiers such as Edith Cresson, Laurent Fabius and Jacques Attali – as 'family'. Mitterrand was suspicious of a man whose 'Second Left' ideas resembled those of Rocard.

Yet in February 1981 Mitterrand started to use Delors as a close economic adviser. Delors accompanied the party leader on his travels and coached him before interviews. As the election approached, Mitterrand – whose ignorance of all things economic is legendary – realised that Delors's experience of government would be useful if the socialists won. He knew that Delors would help to reassure those in France and abroad who feared that a socialist victory would lead to economic disaster. The more Mitterrand used Delors, the less he had need of Rocard. Alone of the socialists, Delors could put Rocard in the shade, where Mitterrand wanted him.

CHAPTER FOUR

THE APOSTLE OF RIGOUR

FRENCH MEN and women above a certain age will never forget the night of 10 May 1981. Mitterrand's defeat of Giscard d'Estaing, with a vote of 51.8 per cent, gave France its first socialist government since 1956. A wave of joy swept supporters of the left on to the streets. Strangers embraced and the revelling continued for days. Many French socialists remained in a dreamworld for months. Having accomplished the seemingly impossible task of winning power, they assumed that implementing socialism would be relatively easy. The socialists had been out of power for so long that only a few of them, such as Delors, expected to meet the kind of problems which had beset left-wing governments elsewhere in Europe.

Mitterrand appointed the bluff and genial Pierre Mauroy as prime minister. Mauroy had broken with Rocard after the congress of Metz and devoted himself to Mitterrand. The president asked Delors what job he wanted. Delors said that he would rather be secretary-general of the Elysée – the major domo – than a minister. Delors's experience with Chaban-Delmas had taught him that real power lay in the Elysée. However Mitterrand did not want Delors that close and offered him the Ministry of Finance.

Delors's three years in that ministry won him fame and popularity in France, and a considerable international reputation. Yet they were among the most miserable years of his life, personally and politically. Jean-Paul had been suffering from leukaemia since September 1978. He had moved from Corsica to Toulouse, where he set up a weekly newspaper. When Jean-Paul's health deteriorated he returned to Paris, where his family and Jacqueline Housseaux, his partner, cared for him. He continued working, writing about Corsica for *Libération*.

Delors had the unenviable job of running the French economy when the ruling party was committed to a statist, hard-left brand of socialism. France had failed to adjust to the oil shock of 1979: in 1980 it had experienced inflation of 13.7 per cent and growth of only 1 per cent. By 1981 France's trading partners were in recession. Few of Mauroy's ministers cared about inflation, the currency or the balance of payments. Mitterrand's belief in the primacy of politics over economics encouraged his party to imagine that dreams could be realised and that *volonté politique* (political willpower) could surmount any problem.

Delors had little authority in the Mauroy government, ranking 16th in the official hierarchy. In theory Laurent Fabius, the budget minister, reported to Delors. In practice Fabius had the president's ear and did what he wanted. Many Mitterrandists, the communists, who held four ministries, and Chevènement, the research minister, attacked Delors's policies as 'right-wing' and 'pro-banker'.

Delors had no faction of rank-and-file supporters who would campaign for his policies. Rocard, who had the peripheral job of minister for the Plan, shared Delors's cautious instincts on economic policy. But Rocard thought he should have been minister of finance and the two men kept to themselves. Delors saw a lot of Mendès-France, who gave him moral support in his battles against the hard left. But Mendès-France was nearing the end of his life and, shunned by Mitterrand, had little influence. 'I quickly understood that I had less power here than I did when I was in the Matignon,' Delors said after a year in office.[1]

In June 1981, in an effort to create jobs, the government boosted public spending by FFr30 billion (about 1 per cent of GDP), mainly in the form of higher welfare benefits. Most economic forecasts predicted the world economy would pick up before the end of the year. If the forecasts had been right, France's reflation might not have proved disastrous. In the event global growth did not revive until the end of 1982. The reflation sucked in imports, stoked inflation and encouraged speculation against the franc. In 1981 the budget deficit doubled to FFr75 billion (£7 billion).

'On board this locomotive, I was the one demanding that we put less coal in the engine,' says Delors, who failed to persuade his colleagues to reflate more modestly.[2]

> As the left hadn't been in power for so long, we had to satisfy a part of its dream, without compromising the economic situation ... The speculators were against us. One can't say I was against everything the government did, but I tried to limit the damage.[3]

In July Mitterrand told his government that he wanted the state to buy 100 per cent of the share capital of 36 banks, two *banques d'affaires* (Paribas and Indosuez) and five industrial groups (Saint-Gobain, Thomson, CGE, Rhône-Poulenc and Péchiney). Delors thought some banks and companies so under-capitalised that they would benefit from nationalisation. But he argued for buying only 51 per cent of the five industrial groups, the two *banques d'affaires*, and five, rather than 36 banks.

When the Conseil de Ministres (the equivalent of the British cabinet) debated nationalisation, only Claude Cheysson, the foreign minister, and

Robert Badinter, the minister of justice, supported Delors. Rocard irked Delors by saying nothing, although he would offer support in later meetings. Mauroy, keen to keep the communist ministers content, backed Mitterrand. Delors accused his colleagues of pandering to the coming socialist congress and, saying he would resign, walked out. He went to see Chaban-Delmas, who persuaded him that he would be more useful in the government.

In September Fabius prepared the 1982 budget without consulting Delors. Fabius made the unrealistic assumption that the economy would grow by 3.3 per cent in 1982 and proposed a budget deficit of FFr95 billion. When Delors returned from the annual meeting of the International Monetary Fund (IMF) he tried and failed to get the budget changed. He particularly objected to Fabius's idea of a wealth tax. Delors's refusal to sign the budget had no effect. Jean Peyrelevade, a member of Mauroy's cabinet, says Delors was in tears in the prime minister's office.[4]

On 4 October speculation against the franc forced Delors to accept a 3 per cent devaluation, combined with a D-mark revaluation of 5.5 per cent. Delors knew the realignment would not restore the trade balance without a matching austerity package. He proposed spending cuts but Mauroy and most of the ministers took no notice. When Delors threatened to resign, Mitterrand agreed to some of his demands and froze FFr15 billion of spending. But it was not enough to restore the confidence of financial markets. Delors's threats annoyed the president, who complained that he was '*un professionel de l'état d'âme*' (a professional soul-barer). Most ministers were by now fed up with Delors's predictions of doom and gloom.

Delors hit back on 29 November during an interview with RTL radio. 'We have to make a pause in the announcement of reforms, but we must also carry out, carefully, those which have been decided.' He said public opinion had not had time to understand the reforms and the government should explain them. 'In Sweden, when people said they wanted to make a reform, they began by thinking about it for five years, then they put it into place and then they made it work.' The Swedes had thus achieved many reforms, while the French suffered from 'the Mediterranean style, which means that we talk three kilometres away from the reality.'[5]

Mitterrand and his ministers found this talk scandalous, for the word 'pause' had a historical resonance. Léon Blum had called for a pause in 1937, shortly before the collapse of his Popular Front government. Mauroy rebuked Delors in public by promising that the reforms would continue. In February 1982, against Delors's advice, the government cut the working week to 39 hours, without reducing pay. It lowered the retirement age to 60 and introduced a fifth week of paid holiday.

Delors ran the Ministry of Finance very differently from his predecessors. He invited trade union leaders as well as employers to lunch. Edmond Maire of the CFDT says:

> *More than any other minister of finance I knew, and more than any other socialist minister, he always listened. If we brought Rocard a problem, he would try and understand what it meant, and then fit it into his intellectual framework before he sought a solution. Delors was more pragmatic and would, spurred on by his convictions, try and deal with a problem straight away.*[6]

Delors did the unions a favour by promoting a law on *fonds salariaux* (wage-earner funds), based on the Swedish model. The law required each company to set aside a slice of profits for an investment fund, to be run by management and trade unions. The French right scrapped these funds when it returned to power.

Delors's voracious appetite for memoranda and papers perturbed officials. Before taking any decision he required long debates on the pros and cons of each option. The *fonctionnaires* had to stay later in the office and some complained of Delors's indecisiveness. He circumvented the ministry's hierarchy by working with junior officials who were directly responsible for particular subjects.

The strains of the job, and of Jean-Paul's illness, often made Delors's temper snap. On one occasion, during a speech to the National Assembly, he accused his critics of being 'fascistic thugs'. On another, when the inflation figures turned out worse than expected, Delors shouted at his cabinet that it was their fault. Philippe Lagayette, the *directeur de cabinet*, helped to smooth out such awkward moments. Delors had become a close friend of this relaxed, consensual *énarque* in Echange et Projets.

Elizabeth Guigou, who would later work for Mitterrand, joined Delors's cabinet in February 1982. She remembers a 'convivial' atmosphere and says Delors was 'a very human boss'. He told her his daughter had a similar position in the Ministry of Labour and that if she had problems she should ask for help. 'It was gratifying for we civil servants that he went into the depths of a problem.' She describes Delors as 'an engineer who knows how to make things work between people, and how to unblock one problem by finding the right way of linking it to another.'[7]

Jean-Paul died in February 1982, at the age of 29. The next day Delors was at his desk in the ministry. He has told friends he could not have coped without his faith in God, yet work became a way of escaping the tragedy. Henceforth, Delors's devotion to his job became manic. Marie had no solace but her faith.

Martine proved a pillar of strength for the family. She had married Xavier Aubry, an accountant, and given birth to Clementine in 1978. A high-flying official in the Ministry of Labour, she had her father's perfectionism and capacity for work.

THE BATTLE FOR THE FRANC

In the spring of 1982 the foreign exchange markets stepped up their speculation against the franc. The budget deficit appeared likely to breach FFr150 billion in that year. Delors struggled to convince his colleagues that the French economy could not become competitive without a further devaluation, more austerity and a lighter burden on industry. In April he cut employers' national insurance contributions by 10 per cent.

Mauroy's chaotic management of the Matignon exasperated Delors. The prime minister often agreed with several viewpoints at the same time, and tended to change his mind. Some ministers took little notice of what the prime minister said. Jacques Attali, Mitterrand's special counsellor, noted in his diary that Delors thought Mauroy should be sacked. In May Mauroy decided to finance loss-making state industries with forced credits from the newly nationalised banks. Delors told Mauroy he could not remain in a government which practised such lax policies. Mauroy said it would not happen again and applied his bonhomie to persuading Delors not to resign.

By June Delors had convinced Mauroy and some of Mitterrand's advisers of the need for a U-turn. On 12 June, at a meeting of EEC finance ministers, Delors negotiated a 5.75 per cent devaluation of the franc and a 4.25 per cent revaluation of the D-mark. Mitterrand approved spending cuts which aimed to hold the year's budget deficit to FFr108 billion. There would be a four-month wage and price freeze. Delors believed that Margaret Thatcher's remedy for inflation – monetarism without incomes policy – would cause more pain than his own more eclectic approach.

'The time of austerity has arrived,' Delors told the press. But Mitterrand warned Delors and Mauroy that if the austerity package did not work he would take the franc out of the EMS. Few ministers were prepared to speak out in favour of Delors's *politique de rigueur*. Edith Cresson, the minister of agriculture, recalls Delors explaining to her why the devaluation was necessary. 'He had doubts, he was always torn apart by his own questions. He wondered if he was doing his job well.'[8]

In the autumn of 1982 France had to borrow about $10 billion for its depleted foreign-currency reserves. In October 1982 Michel Jobert, the trade minister, took the desperate – and infamous – step of routing all imports of video equipment through one office in Poitiers. Yet the trade deficit continued to swell, totalling FFr90 billion over the whole year. In November, when the pay freeze ended, Delors persuaded the trade unions to negotiate the de-indexation of public-sector wages. From then on inflation headed down rather than up.

Two rival camps struggled for the mind of Mitterrand. The outcome would determine the future not only of the French economy but also of the EMS. In the daytime Delors and Mauroy told the president that France needed the external discipline of the EMS. They demanded a further dose of austerity in order to put right the balance of payments. Presidential advisers such as Jean-Louis Bianco, the secretary-general of the Elysée, and Attali agreed. In public Edmond Maire called for more rigour.

Another group – called 'les visiteurs du soir' by Mauroy and Delors – used to visit Mitterrand late in the evening. Fabius, Pierre Bérégovoy, who had just become minister of labour, and Jean Riboud, a businessman friend of the president, proposed leaving the EMS. They argued that floating the franc would allow interest rates to fall from their then level of 15–18 per cent. They wanted import controls and massive borrowing to pay for industrial modernisation. Chevènement and the PCF backed these policies, which Delors branded 'Albanian'.

In the middle of these arguments, Delors made public a government decision to lower the interest rate on state savings accounts. Some ministers feared this would harm the socialists in the forthcoming municipal elections and, behind Delors's back, overturned the decision. Delors confronted Mitterrand and said he would have to resign. Mitterrand admitted Delors had been treated shabbily, but begged him to stay, which he did. Mitterrand also asked him to fight in the municipal elections. Delors stood as socialist candidate for the mayordom of Clichy, a suburb of Paris. Many of the local socialists were CERES members who made Delors unwelcome.

In January 1983 Delors and Mauroy realised that a third devaluation was inevitable and began work on a matching austerity plan. They warned Mitterrand that leaving the EMS would damage the EEC and, since the international markets would lend no more, throw France into the arms of the IMF. Bianco says that Mitterrand had decided to stay in the EMS as early as December 1982.[9] However Attali and other presidential advisers claim that he was genuinely undecided until mid-March 1983, and that for much of this period he inclined towards leaving the EMS. In any case Mitterrand, who delights in ambiguity, continued to ask both camps to feed him with papers and arguments.

The 10 days which began on 13 March, with the second round of the municipal elections, were among the strangest in modern French political history. The unpopular socialists lost many towns, although Delors, who had campaigned hard, won Clichy by 439 votes. Mitterrand thought it time to change his prime minister. Bianco says Mitterrand thought about Bérégovoy, Rocard and Delors, as well as keeping on Mauroy.[10]

The franc had sunk to the bottom of its band in the Exchange Rate Mechanism (ERM), which sets parities among the currencies of the EMS. With French inflation six points higher than German inflation, the currency markets knew the franc could only lose value. Mitterrand asked Fabius, Bérégovoy and Riboud to supply him with an economic plan to accompany leaving the EMS. On 14 March Mitterrand told Mauroy he had decided to leave the EMS, and asked him to head a new government. When Mauroy refused, Mitterrand made the same proposition to Delors, who gave the same answer.

On 15 March Delors had a long *tête-à-tête* with Mitterrand. In his best professorial style, he explained that protectionism always led to decline, as French history showed, and that all the best economists were against it. He said that lifting controls was usually beneficial, and that Britain had been most prosperous in the mid-nineteenth century, when it had followed the precepts of Adam Smith. He predicted that leaving the EMS would lead to a devaluation of 20–30 per cent, setting off a huge rise in the price of imports – and in the cost of servicing FFr400 billion of foreign debt. Foreign currency reserves had shrunk to FFr30 billion – half their level of May 1981 – which meant the Banque de France could defend a floating currency for only a couple of weeks. Thus floating would mean higher, not lower interest rates.

Mitterrand did not trust Delors's figures and sent Fabius to check them with Michel Camdessus, the director of the Treasury. A pale-looking Fabius returned to say the figures were correct and that France had no choice but to stay in the EMS. Neither he nor Bérégovoy nor Riboud had ever provided the economic plan which Mitterrand had asked for. Mitterrand said later: 'During this period I saw many people. In the end Delors had the best-crafted arguments. So the Delors plan won.'[11]

On 16 March Mitterrand and Delors agreed on a strategy for a forthcoming meeting of EEC finance ministers. They would try to make the Germans believe they wanted to leave the system. Germany might then accept a large revaluation of the D-mark and a small devaluation of the franc, for the sake of keeping France in the EMS. Mitterrand and Delors knew that if they avoided a simple franc devaluation, they would be able to claim that Germany's policies had caused most of the problem.

In Brussels on Saturday 19 March, Delors showed that although he had failed to become a film director, he knew how to act. Gerhard Stoltenberg, the German minister, refused French demands for a D-mark revaluation. 'Before such arrogant and incomprehending people [as the Germans], what on earth can I do?' Delors asked the ministers. 'There's no reason for France to stand in the corner just because the other countries are under an oxygen tent.' He told the ministers to go ahead and make their realignment without France and, at 1 am, the session ended without agreement.[12] Delors now says he called the Germans 'arrogant' because 'it's the personal shocks which count, in a negotiation you're either the weakest or the strongest.' He had wanted to 'give France the impression she had won something, so that she would believe in Europe.'[13]

Mitterrand, annoyed that nothing had been decided, telephoned Delors in the night and told him to come home. On Sunday morning Delors briefed the Brussels press: 'This meeting has to be finished before midday, for important things will happen in Paris today and I have to be there.'[14] Delors then went into another session with the finance ministers. His dramatisation of the recall to Paris convinced some of them that he would be sacked, and others that he would become prime minister. Stoltenberg started to feel guilty for having caused the French so many problems.

Arriving at the Elysée that afternoon, Delors found that the president had interpreted his words to the press as a bid for the prime ministership. An angry Mitterrand told Delors that it was too early to reshuffle the government and that he should hurry back to Brussels and clinch a deal. Delors duly returned. Helmut Kohl, the German Chancellor, rang Stoltenberg and told him to give in to the French as long as they promised an austerity package. So on Monday morning, 21 March, EEC ministers agreed on 2.5 per cent franc devaluation and a 5.5 per cent D-mark revaluation.

That afternoon Mitterrand arrived in Brussels for a regular EEC summit. Attali explained to Mitterrand that Delors had won a 'formidable' victory for France. 'All that for two points of difference?' said an unimpressed Mitterrand. He then spent a couple of hours with his finance minister, talking about the future. Without saying so directly, Mitterrand made it clear that he envisaged Delors in the Matignon. Delors pointed out that a big problem for the next government would be that he, Bérégovoy and Fabius did not agree on economic policy. He suggested that the four of them should discuss their differences over lunch. Mitterrand agreed and fixed the lunch for Tuesday.

On Monday night, back in his Paris flat, Delors discussed with Lagayette and Pascal Lamy (his deputy head of cabinet) what he should say to Mitterrand. They knew the president wanted Fabius in the Ministry of Finance, to prevent a prime minister Delors from veering too far to the right. Delors thought such an arrangement would render him an ineffective prime minister, given that he and Fabius loathed each other. By 3 am the coterie had agreed that if Mitterrand offered the Matignon, Delors should ask for guarantees.

At the lunch Mitterrand, Bianco, Bérégovoy, Fabius and Delors discussed everything except the choice of prime minister. None of them ate much and at the end of the meal Delors remarked that they did not agree on economic policy. Mitterrand said he would see them in his study, one at a time, starting with Delors.

Mitterrand offered the prime ministership. 'Given that Fabius and I do not agree, I'd be reassured if I had charge of the Treasury, though not the whole Ministry of Finance,' said Delors, meaning that he wanted to control the Banque de France and monetary policy. 'I told him that would not be astonishing since the situation with Raymond Barre [who held both jobs under Giscard d'Estaing] had been the same.' Mitterrand said nothing, but showed his anger by twisting a handerchief in his hand. 'He was humiliated, rather wounded,' recalls Delors, who went back to his office.[15] Attali says that when he called him to say Mauroy would remain prime minister, Delors became hysterical.

One year later Mitterrand explained to Delors, a propos of this incident, that he had not wanted to share power: 'You would have been the grand vizier, and I would have been the *roi fainéant* [lazy king].'[16] Ten years later, Delors says he does not regret setting the condition which cost him the job. Delors argues that he and Mauroy together were more likely to persuade the socialists of the need for rigour than he alone. 'From the point of view of my career, it would have been much better to follow Mauroy. But I don't care a damn about my career, I was just trying to be as useful as possible.'[17]

Delors had lost the job but won the policy. France would stay in the EMS. In Mauroy's new government Delors became minister for finance, economics and budget, ranking first in protocol. Fabius became minister of industry and Bérégovoy remained minister of labour. Delors and Mauroy's new austerity package was the toughest yet, deflating demand by FFr65 billion, or 2 per cent of GDP. The burden fell on the government, through spending cuts, and on consumers, through a 1 per cent levy on all incomes, rather than on companies. By the summer Delors's policies seemed to be working. The balance of trade improved. Ministers who had opposed austerity started to praise it.

Shortly after the traumas of March 1983, Delors let Mitterrand know that he would be interested in the presidency of the European Commission. He thought of it as second best to the unattainable job of prime minister. The Luxembourger Gaston Thorn was due to complete his term as president in December 1984.

Delors's interest in Europe had ripened slowly throughout his career. His own war-time experience, and that of his father, made him predisposed to any idea which sought to eliminate war between European nations. In the 1950s he picked up the ideal of a federal Europe from his left-wing Catholic friends. He began to learn about other European countries when he ran the CFTC research bureau and his work at Dauphine University taught him about the interdependence of European economies.

Two years in the European Parliament stimulated Delors's curiosity, but it took the crisis of March 1983 to convince him that France could not solve its problems without the EEC. Delors told *Euromoney* in October 1983: 'I've always believed in the European ideal, but today it's no longer a simple question of idealism, it's a matter of necessity.' He said Europe had to speak with a single voice in order to tackle

> *the vagaries of the dollar, the refusal of the Japanese to accept the worldwide responsibilities which go with their economic power [and] the fate of third-world countries being choked by a combination of high interest rates and the decline in world trade. Our only choice is between a united Europe and decline.*[18]

Delors impressed his fellow EEC finance ministers. 'Both he and I had to sustain tough policies against much of public opinion,' says Geoffrey Howe, Britain's Chancellor of the Exchequer from 1979 to 1983. 'I learned that Delors was a man of insight, tenacity, determination, courage and emotion.' Howe believes that he and Delors had a significant effect on each other's policies. 'Delors absorbed my ideas on fiscal and monetary stability, while he convinced me of the virtues of currency stability.' Howe recalls that in June 1982, at the Versailles summit of the Group of Five (as it then was) industrialised countries, Delors managed to insert a reference to the goal of stable exchange rates in the conclusions.[19] Howe had no serious problems with Thatcher until Delors convinced him of the benefits of ERM membership.

THE PROPHET VINDICATED

Delors and Mitterrand had a difficult and complicated relationship. Ever since joining the Parti Socialiste, in 1974, Delors had viewed Mitterrand as a political role model. 'He fascinates me, he's the only one,' says Delors. 'He taught me everything in politics.'[20] Mitterrand appreciated Delors's unswerving loyalty and his ability to explain complicated problems. He once remarked that of all the socialist ministers, Delors performed most effectively on television. Delors's Tintin-like enthusiasm amused Mitterrand.

Yet Delors's resignation threats – Attali says there were seven or eight, Delors says only three of them were serious – infuriated the president. Mitterrand noted waspishly that Delors never had the guts actually to resign. Lagayette says Delors had to issue these threats since, lacking a power base within the party, he had few other means of influencing policy.[21]

'Delors smells of the sacristy', Mitterrand once said. He tended to dislike Catholic politicians, whose 'conscience' could make them intransigent and ill-suited to the wheeler-dealing of party politics. Cresson, who is close to both Delors and Mitterrand, says:

> Mitterrand likes cunning, crafty, very political men, like Roland Dumas [his second foreign minister]. Delors felt Mitterrand did not recognise him enough. He thought Mitterrand had shown more favour to those who had done less for his cause.[22]

Delors became extremely nervous before his weekly meetings with the president. An unkind word would leave the finance minister distraught. He found it hard to cope with Mitterrand's habitual postponing of important decisions, and his fostering of rivalries among courtiers. Their different personalities and interests bred a state of mutual incomprehension. Delors is direct, Mitterrand sibylline. Delors reads books about economics and social problems while Mitterrand prefers literature and history.

During Delors's final year as a minister, ending in July 1984, his relationship with the president deteriorated. Mitterrand often opposed Delors's policy initiatives, and vice versa. The Elysée interfered more often in the daily running of the finance ministry. It did not consult Delors on appointments to the newly nationalised banks. An exhausted Mauroy became less supportive of Delors's policies; knowing that his prime ministerial days were numbered, he wanted to retire with the image of an authentic socialist. Delors's whining and sulking irritated the other ministers, yet he had become – through the vindication of his policies and the force of his personality – more influential than any of them.

In June 1983 Delors prepared the following year's budget. The government's promise that the budget deficit would not surpass 3 per cent of GDP was starting to look untenable (the deficit would reach 3.5 per cent in 1984, compared with 1.9 per cent in 1980). Delors therefore proposed doubling the special levy on income to 2 per cent, extending it to all benefits and calling it the *contribution sociale*. Bérégovoy said that a new tax would be unpopular and spiked the proposal. Delors failed to get all the spending cuts he wanted – and maddened Mitterrand by suggesting that grand projects such as the Opéra-Bastille be shelved. Attali had to persuade Delors not to resign. The budget turned out just stringent enough to convince the foreign-exchange markets that *la rigueur* remained the rule.

In February 1984 France's lorry drivers went on strike and blocked many main roads. With Mauroy absent in Austria, Delors moved into the Matignon and, aided by Charles Fiterman, the communist minister of transport, managed the crisis. He went on television and praised the lorry drivers for doing such a difficult and useful job. The following day the lorry drivers returned to work. Delors felt proud of his role in ending the strike, but had a surprise at the next meeting of the Conseil de Ministres. 'No one spoke of it, no one said a word to me, as if we'd lived through 10 days of calm!' he recalls. 'That really hurt.'[23]

The Mitterrandists believed Delors had tried to profit from a strike which, in their opinion, Fiterman had solved. Delors claims that the ministers behaved strangely because they had, since March 1983, resented his being proved right on economic policy.[24] Despite these strained relations, Delors still won arguments in the Conseil de Ministres. In April 1984, when Fabius demanded extra subsidies to prop up bankrupt steel-makers, Delors succeeded in blocking them.

In the June 1984 European elections, the socialists won 21 per cent of the vote, their lowest score since 1973. Delors went on television to say there had been too many laws and that the government had not put enough emphasis on liberty. He advised the president to become less involved in the everyday business of government and to unite the French behind a national consensus. Delors no longer worried about the consequences of tweaking the president's whiskers. He knew his chances of becoming prime minister were minimal.

Mauroy resigned on 16 July. Mitterrand summoned Delors and told him he was not sufficiently left-wing or popular with the party to become prime minister. 'I told him I could not stay in the government because I considered that the Elysée got too involved in the business of ministers, and that the smooth-running of government suffered,' says Delors.[25] Later in the day Mitterrand appointed the 39-year-old Fabius prime minister.

Delors's meeting with Mitterrand had left him no wiser on his chances of going to Brussels. Horse-trading among governments would decide the presidency of the European Commission, and it was the Germans' turn. In Paris on 28 May Mitterrand had told Kohl that if the Germans did not have a candidate, he would suggest Cheysson – his clever, choleric and unpredictable foreign minister – or Delors. On 25 June, at the EEC's Fontaine-bleau summit, Delors had an inkling that he might be in the running. Delors recalls:

> *I'd come to welcome Kohl when he got out of the helicopter. He took me*
> *aside and said [in German, of which Delors got the gist] that he'd agree*
> *to a French president as long as his initials were JD and not CC.*[26]

Delors's tenure of the finance ministry had impressed Kohl.

At the summit there was no formal discussion of commission presidency. Nevertheless Attali's *Verbatim* recounts a conversation over break-fast between Kohl and Mitterrand. Kohl said he would not insist on a German president, and hinted that, because of Cheysson's friendship with Hans-Dietrich Genscher, his own foreign minister whom he mistrusted, he would prefer Delors to Cheysson.[27]

On the margins of the summit Thatcher told Mitterrand that she could accept Delors but not Cheysson. Howe had told her Delors would be a good president. She records in her memoirs:

> *At that time all I knew was that M. Delors was extremely intelligent*
> *and energetic and had, as French finance minister, been credited with*
> *reining back the initial left-wing socialist policies of President Mit-*
> *terrand's government and with putting French finances on a sounder*
> *footing.*[28]

On 18 July the EEC governments named Delors to the presidency of the European Commission. He says that if he had not got the job he would have gone back to university teaching and become an active Mayor of Clichy.[29] Delors's new responsibilities obliged him to vacate that post.

Delors felt justly proud of his record as finance minister. The austerity packages had done their job. During his last 12 months as a minister, booming exports more than compensated for falling domestic demand, and industrial output rose by 2.5 per cent. Manufacturing investment increased by 10 per cent over the same period, helping France to avoid a recession. But as Table 1 shows, unemployment refused to respond to Delors's imprecations.

The socialists' nationalisations did not turn out to be the disaster many had feared. Delors's banking law of June 1983 gave the managers of state-owned banks considerable autonomy. Among the publicly-owned indus-trial groups, Péchiney, Rhône-Poulenc and Saint-Gobain performed better, by many criteria, than they had under the private ownership which had starved them of capital.

Table 1 French economic performance 1980–1984

Year	Inflation %	Trade deficit (billion francs)	Growth %	Unemployment %
1980	13.7	60	1.1	6.3
1981	14.0	59	0.3	7.3
1982	9.7	99	1.6	8.1
1983	9.3	43	0.7	8.3
1984	6.7	26	1.4	9.7

Delors had persuaded the Parti Socialiste that reflation in one country, import controls and quitting the EMS were not viable policies. He taught the left that private-sector companies and entrepreneurs had to be nurtured. 'Jacques is one of those who played a fundamental role in reinserting a vision of the market economy in French social democracy,' judges Rocard. 'The intellectual thrust of that battle depended on both of us.'[30]

The hard facts of France's economic predicament helped Delors to win the argument. So did his skilful use of television interviews, press briefings and dinners with newspaper editors. Like Mendès-France before him, Delors emphasised the need for public opinion to understand government policy. Delors won for himself, in France and abroad, the image of an honest realist pitted against socialist dinosaurs. Few people blamed him for France's dire economic straights. In May 1981 an opinion poll gave Delors an approval rating of 44 per cent. He left office with a respectable rating of 47 per cent, despite what had happened to the French economy in between.

Delors wanted all the French, however poor, to take part in a collective effort to restore the economy's health. Thus the wages freeze and the 1 per cent special levy on incomes applied to everyone. In April 1983 Delors introduced the *carnet de change*, a little book limiting holiday-makers' access to foreign currency. He knew the economic impact would be minimal, but hoped the *carnet* would bring home the gravity of the crisis and show that everyone had to do their bit. Some of Delors's collaborators claim that such policies reveal the application of Christian personalism to politics.[31]

Before March 1983, France had a high-inflation economy. Since then it has had lower inflation than most of its trading partners. France's socialist experiment – both the mistakes of the first two years, and the remedies – made an impact on the rest of Europe. By the mid-1980s Britain's Labour Party had abandoned policies of socialism in one country, partly because it had seen them fail in France.

After 1984 French governments of left and right continued Delors's *franc fort* policy. Not until 1992, when the strains of German unification undermined the ERM, did any mainstream politicians question that policy's wisdom. Even after the near collapse of the ERM, in August 1993, Edouard Balladur's government maintained the old parity with the D-mark. Balladur knew a floating franc would damage not only 10 years of anti-inflationary credibility, but also the prospects of economic and monetary union (EMU). One consequence of Delors's victory in March 1983 had been that EMU became a possibility. Without a stable and successful ERM, which included the French franc, Europe's politicians would not have put monetary union on their agenda.

CHAPTER FIVE

RELAUNCHING EUROPE

JACQUES DELORS could not have arrived at the European Commission at a more propitious moment than January 1985. Although the European Economic Community was becalmed and listless, there were hints of a fair wind. Anyone becoming president in January 1985 would have faced exciting opportunities. Yet it is doubtful that many would have seized the opportunities with such skill as Delors.

The commission, like the Community it served, had experienced 35 years of chequered history. The Community's origins had been political: France and Germany wanted never again to fight a war. The means they chose were economic: a common market for coal and steel, the raw materials of war. In 1950 Robert Schuman, France's foreign minister, Konrad Adenauer, Germany's chancellor, and Jean Monnet, commissaire-general of France's Plan, dreamed up the European Coal and Steel Community (ECSC). Humiliated by allied control of their coal and steel industry, the Germans jumped at the chance of becoming equal partners with the French in a new international organisation. The French, worried by a possible resurgence of German nationalism, wanted to see those German industries managed by a supranational body.

The ECSC started work in 1952, with Italy, Belgium, Holland and Luxembourg joining in. Its institutions remain, broadly, those of today's European Union: a High Authority (which became the European Commission), a civil service with a monopoly of the right to propose laws; an assembly to debate legislation; a Court of Justice to adjudicate in disputes; and, representing national governments, a Council of Ministers which votes on laws and takes the major executive decisions.

The High Authority's first president, Jean Monnet, shared the hope of Schuman and Adenauer that gradually, over decades, European governments would cede powers to federal institutions. He thought it best to begin with limited, economic goals, and that in the long run the supranational bodies would spread their authority – through a process he called 'engrenage' (spill over) – into ever-widening areas.

The ECSC proved a success but a parallel plan for a European Defence Community collapsed in 1954: France's parliament, worried by the prospect of German rearmament, refused to ratify the treaty. From then on the federalists focused on economics. In the mid-1950s the six members of the

61

ECSC experienced strong economic growth, cheap oil, fixed exchange rates, stable monetary policies and trade surpluses – all of which encouraged them to think of deepening their ties. The Six also worried that their economies would fall behind America's unless they had the benefit of a common market. In 1955 they held a conference at Messina to consider how they could build one.

A British diplomat called Bretherton, who attended the conference as an observer, made the following contribution:

> *The future treaty which you are discussing has no chance of being agreed; if it was agreed, it would have no chance of being ratified; and if it was ratified, it would have no chance of being applied. And if it was applied, it would be totally unacceptable to Britain. You speak of agriculture, which we don't like, of power over customs, which we take exception to, and of institutions, which frighten us. Monsieur le président, messieurs, au revoir et bonne chance.*[1]

Bretherton then walked out.

Hoping to prove Bretherton wrong, the Messina conference set up a committee under the chairmanship of Paul-Henri Spaak, the Belgian foreign minister. The work of the Spaak Committee led to the Treaty of Rome, signed in March 1957, which established the European Economic Community (EEC). Another treaty signed at the same time set up Euratom, an atomic energy community. 'These institutions appeared to be economic and technical, but their purpose was political,' wrote Monnet at the time.[2]

The Treaty of Rome laid down a timetable for the abolition of internal tariffs and for the creation of a customs union by 1970. It also called for the building of a Common Agricultural Policy (CAP). The essential bargain behind the EEC was that German industry would be able to boost its exports while French agriculture would gain new markets and subsidies from the CAP.

All ran smoothly until General de Gaulle began to fear the growing power of the Brussels-based commission, whose president, Walter Hallstein, was an able and arrogant German. In 1960 de Gaulle launched a scheme for European Union, named the 'Fouchet plan' after the diplomat who drafted it. 'Inter-governmental' bodies would manage joint policies on economics, culture, defence and foreign affairs. The role of the EEC and its commission would diminish.

During the negotiations on the Fouchet plan, de Gaulle declared his aim in a note sent to Adenauer:

the supranational organisms of the Six, which tend inevitably and abusively to become irresponsible superstates, will be reformed, subordinated to governments and used for the normal tasks of the council and technical business.

In 1962 the Benelux countries vetoed the scheme, because they wanted a strong commission to protect them against the larger countries. Thirty years later, during the negotiation of the Treaty of Maastricht, Delors and other federalists accused France of seeking to revive the Fouchet plan.

In 1965 Hallstein enraged de Gaulle by proposing that the EEC should have its own budgetary resources and that the commission and the assembly should have more say over how the budget was spent. De Gaulle responded by refusing to accept the Treaty of Rome's provision that from January 1966 the Council of Ministers should take certain decisions by majority vote. The other five, still angry with de Gaulle for vetoing Britain's application in 1963, backed Hallstein. For six months France left an empty chair in the Council of Ministers.

The 'Luxembourg Compromise' of January 1966 allowed France to end its boycott. France declared that when vital interests were at stake, it would not accept majority voting. From then on all governments used this principle to justify vetoes on even the smallest matters. For the next 20 years the Council of Ministers passed laws either very slowly or not at all.

De Gaulle appeared to have halted the ebb of power from governments to supranational institutions, and from 1966 to 1984 the EEC had a dull and unspectacular image. Nevertheless, many of the foundations for later progress were laid during those years. In 1967 the ECSC, Euratom and the EEC merged their bureaucracies. In 1969 members began to coordinate foreign policy through a process known as 'European Political Cooperation'. The EEC gained its own financial resources in 1970.

The Paris summit of 1972 committed the EEC to monetary union – although the 'snake', a system which linked its currencies, soon fell apart. Britain, Denmark and Ireland joined in 1973. The leaders' occasional summits turned into regular and formal events, known as 'European Councils', in 1975. There was plenty of 'spill over'. The EEC moved beyond trade and farm policy into environmental and labour law. It established R&D programmes and 'structural funds' to aid poorer regions.

In 1979 Helmut Schmidt, the German chancellor, Valéry Giscard d'Estaing, the French president, and Roy Jenkins, the commission president, established the European Monetary System. The EMS's 'exchange rate mechanism' (ERM) tied currencies together through setting upper and lower limits on their values, subject to periodic realignments. Britain stayed out of the ERM. In the same year Euro-MPs – Delors among them – were directly elected for the first time. Greece joined the EEC in 1981.

Despite these small steps forward, the late 1970s and early 1980s were a particularly dark age in the Community's history. The oil shock of 1979 threw Europe into recession. At that year's Dublin summit Margaret Thatcher, enraged that Britain paid much more into the EEC budget than it got out, declared: 'I want my money back'. The others, struggling to contain swelling budget deficits, were in no mood to oblige. The argument over Britain's budget contribution paralysed the Community for five years. Gaston Thorn, the Luxembourger who became president of the commission in 1981, proved ineffectual, and morale in that institution sank low.

Meanwhile business people fretted about 'Eurosclerosis', the idea that Europe's economy could not compete with those of Asia or America because of inadequate R&D, poor training and inflexible labour markets. They complained that the Treaty of Rome's promise of a common market had never been fulfilled. Governments had removed internal tariffs but erected hidden barriers – often in the form of technical standards – which prevented trade. For instance Lancing Bagnall, a British firm, could not sell fork-lift trucks in France because the rules there required a particular layout of pedals in the cab. In 1983 the 'Kangaroo group' of Euro-MPs – whose name reflected their belief in hopping across frontiers – campaigned for a timetable for the abolition of hidden barriers to trade.

In June of that year the Stuttgart summit agreed to a 'Solemn Declaration on European Union', which called for the deepening of existing policies, the development of new ones and the strengthening of 'European Political Cooperation'. The Stuttgart Declaration was long on pious principles and short on practical proposals. But it called for the treaty's provisions on majority voting to be applied. Britain, France, Ireland and Denmark added a rider that they remained attached to the Luxembourg Compromise.

In February 1984 the European Parliament voted for a draft treaty on European Union that had been inspired by Altiero Spinelli, an Italian member. This proposed that majority voting should become the rule in the Council of Ministers and that legislation should be settled by 'codecision', meaning that the council and the parliament would have an equal say. President Mitterrand declared that the Spinelli draft merited examination and that the existing treaties needed revision. He wanted the Fontainebleau summit of June 1984 – which would conclude France's six-month stint as EEC president – to relaunch the Community rather than merely focus, as had previous summits, on Britain's budget payments.

At Fontainebleau the heads of government agreed to control farm spending (by inventing milk quotas), to increase the structural funds and to unblock the talks on Spain's and Portugal's membership applications. With the help of Jacques Delors, his finance minister, Mitterrand settled the budget question: Britain would receive a rebate of two-thirds of the difference between the share of its VAT revenues that it paid to the budget and what it got back in EEC spending. The summit concluded by setting up a committee to look into how the workings of the EEC and European Political Cooperation could be improved.

The committee, chaired by James Dooge, a former Irish foreign minister, consisted of one representative from each government. The Dooge Report, published in March 1985, proposed a broadening of the EEC's objectives to include a 'homogenous internal economic space', a technological community and a 'European social space'. It wanted a stronger common external policy to include the discussion of security matters. It proposed majority voting in the Council of Ministers and 'codecision' for the European Parliament, although the British, Danish and Greek delegates dissented from those points. The Dooge Report suggested that an inter-governmental conference should draw up a Treaty of European Union, to be based on itself, on the existing treaties and on the Stuttgart Declaration, and to be inspired by the Spinelli draft.

DELORS'S GREATEST HIT

Delors inherited a bureaucracy quite unlike any national administration. In most democratic states the role of the civil service is purely administrative, while elected governments take political initiatives and major decisions. The commission administers the European Union's policies, such as regional aid, and enforces its laws and treaties, if necessary by taking governments to the European Court of Justice. But it also negotiates with other countries on behalf of the Union, for instance on trade agreements or membership applications. And it has a monopoly of the right to propose European laws.

The commission is thus a political civil service with its own agenda. That agenda always has been, and probably always will be, broadly federalist, since the commission would benefit from a more unified Europe. The institution's power lies with the commissioners, who numbered 14 at the time of Delors's arrival. Each of the large countries appoints two commissioners, and the smaller countries one (the number rose to 17 when Spain and Portugal joined the EEC, in January 1986).

When Delors began his first term as commission president, which ran from January 1985 to December 1988, he found that some of his most influential colleagues held economic philosophies far removed from his own. Lord Arthur Cockfield, a former British trade secretary and a Thatcherite, became commissioner for the single market. Peter Sutherland, who had been Irish attorney general, brought charm, pugnacity and a faith in market forces to the post of competition commissioner. Willy de Clercq, a Belgian who had the trade portfolio, and Lorenzo Natali, an Italian who managed the negotiations with Spain and Portugal – and who, having already served for eight years, played the role of wise uncle – were less fervently liberal. However, none of the commission's heavyweights was a socialist.

Delors had spent the autumn of 1984 searching for a 'Big Idea' to relaunch the EEC. He considered institutional reform, monetary union, closer cooperation on defence and an economic revival based on the completion of the internal market. He toured each of the capitals to discuss these ideas. Only the internal market won the support of all ten governments.

That autumn, in Brussels, Delors had met a group of officials and industrialists brought together by Max Kohnstamm, who had been Monnet's chief assistant. After Monnet's death in 1979, Kohnstamm had become one of the guardians of the sacred flame of federalism. The Kohnstamm group advised Delors to make the internal market his priority and to lay down a timetable of eight years (the life of two commissions) for its achievement. The idea of a timetable came from the Treaty of Rome, which had set a 12-year schedule for the creation of a customs union. The group warned Delors that an internal market would require greater use of majority voting in the Council of Ministers. At the same time Wisse Dekker, the chairman of Philips, made several speeches calling for the EEC to remove its internal barriers by 1990.

Delors picked a Big Idea whose time was ripe. Margaret Thatcher was at the height of her powers and eager for the EEC to take on a practical and liberal objective. West Germany's coalition of Christian Democrats and Free Democrats was committed to the principle, if not the practice, of freer markets. France's socialists had veered towards pro-business policies and financial deregulation. Right-of-centre coalitions held power in Holland, Belgium, Italy and Denmark. Privatisation, tax cuts and competition were in the air. Most important of all, the EEC's annual growth rate was picking up. Having averaged 1.6 per cent in the three years 1982 to 1984, it rose to 2.6 per cent from 1985 to 1987 and 3.6 per cent from 1988 to 1990. The Community has always thrived during periods of strong growth and stagnated in recessions.

On 14 January 1985, Delors declared to the European Parliament that the commission intended to suppress the EEC's internal frontiers by the end of 1992. He drew attention to the institutional paralysis and blamed it on decision-making procedures which required unanimity. He said it would help if, within the framework of the existing treaties, governments agreed not to use the Luxembourg Compromise. But that would not be enough: a new treaty was needed.

Delors did not enthuse about the single market because he was a born deregulator. He thought it would arrest Europe's economic decline, relative to America and the Asian economies. Delors revealed a concern for Europe's rank in the world which echoed de Gaulle talking of France. Europe's future would be hopeless, he told the parliament, unless it learned

> to speak with a single voice and to act together . . . But are we Europeans capable of it? Whether it concerns currency instability, prohibitive rates of interest, hidden protectionism, a decline in aid to the poorest countries, no, Europe has not known how to lead the way and influence.

Delors's speech set out exactly what he planned to do over the four-year life of his commission. A 'European social space' would be a priority.

> What would become of us if we didn't have a minimum harmonisation of social rules? What do we already see? Some member-states, some companies who try to steal an advantage over their competitors, at the cost of what we have to call a social retreat.

Monetary union would not be feasible in the next four years. However 'a substantial strengthening of monetary cooperation and a controlled extension of the ecu's role is possible, [and then] we could discover the so-desired paths to economic and monetary union.'[3]

Delors's plan for a single market could not be implemented unless three conditions were fulfilled. Business people had to understand the objective and mobilise in its support. The commission had to come up with a coherent and practical set of proposals. And governments had to pass them into law.

The slogan '1992' captured the imagination not only of business people and bankers but also of a wider public. Lord Cockfield claims to have thought up the idea of a deadline for the end of 1992. Pascal Lamy, Delors's then *chef de cabinet*, claims the slogan came out of a meeting between Delors, himself, Gunter Burghardt (the deputy *chef de cabinet*) and François Lamoureux (Delors's institutional expert) – after they had rejected 1990, 1995 and 2000. Both Delors and Cockfield say they chose 1992 as it would allow the span of two commissions for the fulfilment of the goal.

Delors had few expectations of the 68-year-old Cockfield. Neither had been elected to a national parliament, but they had little else in common. Michel Petite, who has worked in the 'cabinets' (private offices) of both, says their minds could not have been more different.

> *Cockfield is a cool Cartesian, whose logic is so deadly that he can push systematically to extremes. You need that kind of mind to work through the consequences of abolishing frontiers. Delors is less consistent than Cockfield but more intuitive and flexible. Delors is more political and has more of a vision of the future.*[4]

Yet the odd couple of a French socialist from humble origins and a British Conservative aristocrat got on well and made a powerful combination. 'Much of the success of the 1992 programme depended on our relationship,' says Cockfield. 'Delors left me to get on with it. I fathered it, launched it and drove it to the point of success.'[5] Although never one to underestimate his achievements, Cockfield's assessment of his own role is fair.

Cockfield unveiled *Completing the Internal Market*, a white paper containing 297 proposals and a timetable for their implementation, just before the Milan summit of June 1985. The first chapter covered the removal of physical barriers at borders between EEC countries. Customs formalities would be scrapped. Controls on plants, animals and foodstuffs would be carried out at the point of dispatch rather than at frontiers. Member-states would no longer apply restrictive quotas on imports from third countries.

The second chapter dealt with the elimination of technical barriers to the trade of goods and services. 'Mutual recognition' would mean that a member-state could not exclude another's goods on the grounds that they did not comply with national standards. Any product conforming to one member-state's standards could be sold anywhere in the Community, so long as it satisfied minimum levels of health and safety set by EEC directives.

The white paper promised to strengthen the rules which required public bodies to put major contracts out to tender, and to extend those rules into the transport, energy, water and telecommunications sectors. Laws on the mutual recognition of diplomas and professional qualifications would promote the free movement of people. There was a vague promise to liberalise capital movements.

One of the white paper's most original features was the application of mutual recognition to service industries. For banking, stock broking, insurance, life assurance and unit trusts, a 'single passport' would allow a firm authorised in one member-state to establish itself in another and to sell services across frontiers. Airline routes and airfares would undergo partial liberalisation. Road-haulage firms would gain the right to operate in any member-state. Television companies would be able to broadcast anywhere in the EEC so long as they complied with common rules on decency, advertising and European content. A Community trademark would protect intellectual property.

The third and final chapter covered fiscal barriers. If frontier controls disappeared while large differences of VAT rates and excise duties remained, shoppers would distort trade by thronging into low-tax countries. Cockfield therefore proposed some harmonisation of VAT rates and excise duties. Under the EEC's system of VAT collection, goods exported from one member-state to another were zero-rated in the country of origin, controlled at the frontier and liable for VAT in the country of destination. Cockfield wanted to abolish frontier controls by collecting VAT in the country of origin; intra-Community commerce would be treated like trade inside a member-state. This system would shift VAT revenue from countries which imported a great deal to the big exporters. Cockfield therefore proposed a 'clearing house' to rebalance revenues so that no country lost out.

All the white paper's major proposals had become law by the end of 1993, except for the new VAT system. Governments mistrusted the idea of a clearing house and designed an interim system which came into force in January 1993. This collects VAT in the country of destination but, by requiring companies to inform tax authorities of their trade with other member-states, has allowed frontier controls to be scrapped. Governments have promised to introduce the full Cockfield system in 1997.

The commission wanted the member-states to abolish passport controls between each other but, having no legal competence on the matter, said nothing in the white paper. Britain, Ireland and Denmark decided to keep passport controls, while the other nine – signatories of the Treaty of Schengen, named after a village in Luxembourg – planned to end theirs.

Cockfield and his staff wrote most of the white paper, although Delors added to the sections on company law and VAT harmonisation. The president's more important contribution was to sell the 1992 programme with energy and enthusiasm. He spoke at many employers' conferences, and regularly met the European Round Table, a group of industrialists then led by Volvo's Pehr Gyllenhammar. Delors cultivated, among others, Jacques

Solvay of Solvay, Jean-Louis Beffa of Saint-Gobain and Karl-Heinz Kaske of Siemens, all of whom backed the commission's plans.

Delors's support for the white paper led him to swallow larger doses of deregulation, for instance on insurance, than he felt comfortable with. Thatcher, by contrast, liked financial services liberalisation more than anything else in the document. She fretted that the chapters on frontier controls and indirect tax would erode national sovereignty. She was soon complaining that Cockfield had 'gone native'. 'Cockfield fell out of love with Thatcher and in love with Delors,' recalls Charles Powell, her diplomatic adviser.[6]

Thatcher viewed the single market as an end in itself. Delors and Cockfield saw it as a means to an end, as the white paper's conclusion made clear: 'Just as the Customs Union had to precede Economic Integration, so Economic Integration has to precede European Unity.' In 1993 Delors admitted on French radio, with some hyperbole, that 'if this job was about making a single market I wouldn't have come here in 1985. We're not here just to make a single market – that doesn't interest me – but to make a political union.'[7]

The single market might not have interested Delors, but he had spotted the strategic significance of a project which would gather support from nearly all shades of the political spectrum. Delors foresaw that the impact would be political as well as economic. Once the Community had such an ambitious goal on its agenda, the pressure for constitutional reform would grow. Better than many British politicians, Delors had understood that if the European nations wanted an efficient market, with fair competition and without national protection, they would have to transfer a sizeable dose of sovereignty to the Community.

THE MOUSE THAT ROARED

Spain and Portugal had been trying to join the Community since the late 1970s. The negotiations over their accession provided the new commission president with his first big challenge, and brought out the best and the worst in him. In February 1985, at the end of a session of talks, Delors confronted a group of Spanish television journalists. He attacked the Spaniards for their pretensions and a lack of vision. '*C'est au pied du mur qu'on rencontre les maçons*,' he declared with contempt. That French proverb – literally, one finds stonemasons at the base of a wall – meant 'we'll see if they remain so tough when the crunch comes.' However, many Spanish television viewers thought Delors had insulted them by saying they were no better than building-site workers. 'It looked like he had had a glass too many,' remembers a Spanish diplomat. 'But whether he had or not, the burst of temper was a controlled attempt to soften our negotiating position.'

The Spaniards soon forgave Delors, for he displayed his uncanny ability to root out compromises where others had failed to find them. In March Delors proposed a package including 'Integrated Mediterranean Programmes' (regional aid for the olive belt), rebates on budget payments and some creative accountancy with fish quotas, which settled the differences between the Iberians and the Ten.

The publication of the Dooge Report in the same month set off an inter-governmental battle over the Community's future. Italy hoped to conclude its stint as EEC president, at June's Milan summit, by convoking a conference to revise the Treaty of Rome. Only the Benelux countries backed Italy. Geoffrey Howe, Britain's foreign secretary, led a counter-offensive to improve decision making without changing the treaty. He suggested governments should make 'gentlemen's agreements' to abstain, rather than wield the Luxembourg Compromise, if they opposed an internal-market law. He also proposed a new treaty for European Political Cooperation (EPC), to codify existing practice and add some of the Dooge Report's recommendations. When the foreign ministers met at Stresa in Italy, in early June, a majority backed Howe.

The day before the Milan summit, France and Germany unveiled a draft treaty for European Union which proposed a heavyweight 'secretary-general' to guide the union's foreign policy. The plan maddened Delors since its 'inter-governmental' approach was bound to weaken the commission. 'I read it and I went to see Mitterrand, furious, and told him: "it's the Fouchet plan". Saying that is an insult. So he withdrew it.[8]' Most governments rejected the draft for the same reasons as Delors.

When Bettino Craxi, Italy's prime minister, opened the summit on 28 June, Britain's plan for gentlemen's agreements dominated the debate and seemed likely to win. Thatcher said bluntly that since any treaty revision had to be unanimous, and Britain was opposed, there could not be one. Her stridency contributed to an ebbing of support for the British proposals. She frequently said 'we and the Irish think', which upset Garret Fitzgerald, the Irish prime minister. Howe recalls:

> Her tone appealed to Andreas Papandreou [the Greek prime minister], and the Danes liked it too. We became part of a bloody-minded minority instead of working for a solution with our partners. So we provoked Craxi.[9]

Delors argued that if the EEC was serious about implementing the white paper on the internal market, there would have to be treaty changes. Even if governments agreed not to use the Luxembourg Compromise, most of the white paper's proposals would, under the Treaty of Rome, require unanimity. He pointed out that a law allowing architects to work anywhere in the EEC had taken 15 years to get through the Council of Ministers, and that a proposal for vetting mergers had been stuck there since 1973. He proposed the immediate amendment of three articles in the Treaty of Rome, so that the council would decide all single-market laws by majority vote, and so that the European Parliament would gain powers of amendment. Delors suggested tacking these amendments to the treaty of accession for Spain and Portugal, which had been signed on 12 June but still had to be ratified.

Delors's intervention helped to swing the meeting against the British line of no treaty change. Summing up at the end of the first day, Craxi backed Delors's plan and asked the foreign ministers to prepare a proposal to amend the treaty the following day. However Britain, Greece and Denmark made it clear they would veto treaty amendments. So during the night Giulio Andreotti, Italy's wily foreign minister, aided by Delors's officials, prepared an alternative proposal which, unlike a treaty amendment, would not require unanimity.

Craxi opened the summit's second day with an unprecedented step. Having been briefed by Andreotti, Craxi called for a vote on the holding of an inter-governmental conference (IGC). Article 236 of the Rome Treaty says the Council of Ministers may decide to hold an IGC by a simple majority vote. A flabbergasted Thatcher objected that the European Council always worked by consensus. Poul Schluter, the Danish prime minister, complained of rape and Papandreou of a *coup d'état*. But seven, including Kohl and Mitterrand, voted for the IGC.

Luxembourg took on the presidency of the EEC in July and, together with the Council of Ministers' secretariat, managed the inter-governmental conference. Starting in September, the IGC consisted of a series of meetings of the foreign ministers and their officials. Spain and Portugal attended as observers. Their imminent arrival in the EEC reinforced the case for more majority voting: 12 would find it harder than 10 to reach unanimity.

The commission had no formal role in the IGC, but Delors attended the meetings of foreign ministers and Emile Noël, the commission's secretary-general, took part at the level of officials. Delors, Noël and Lamoureux drafted the commission's contributions without consulting the other commissioners.

In the first weeks of the conference a clutch of commission proposals helped to define the agenda and dissuaded many governments from putting forward ideas of their own. Delors's first contribution, a draft treaty chapter on the internal market, pleased the British by stressing the importance of completing the 1992 programme. The British, who had begun by objecting to the idea of a treaty revision, started to think something good might come of the IGC.

Delors put forward draft chapters on the environment, research and 'cohesion' (regional aid for poorer members) – areas where the EEC had become active but on which the Treaty of Rome said nothing – and on the European Parliament. He argued that when ministers decided laws by majority vote, the European Parliament should have a greater say since national parliaments could not control the outcome. So he suggested a 'cooperation procedure' which would allow the parliament to impose an amendment on the Council of Ministers, so long as the commission accepted it and the council was not unanimously opposed.

Delors held back his draft chapter on economic and monetary union (EMU) until the end of November. This codified the practice of the EMS and contained a provision that would allow governments to agree unanimously on the creation of an autonomous 'European Monetary Fund' – an embryo central bank. This was too much for the Germans, British and Dutch, who wanted no mention of EMU in the treaty.

The foreign ministers maddened Delors by inserting a long list of exceptions to his proposals on the internal market and by replacing the goal of a 'space without frontiers' with the more mundane 'common market'. When the foreign ministers met on 25 and 26 November, Delors complained that the text had 'more holes than Gruyère' and threatened to boycott the rest of the conference. Delors went to see Kohl and Mitterrand, with spectacular results. At the next ministerial meeting a Franco-German initiative led to the restoration of the Delorist version of the internal market chapter.

The Luxembourg summit of 2 and 3 December concluded the IGC. Delors helped Kohl and Mitterrand to reach an informal bargain: Germany – abandoning Britain – would accept a modest mention of EMU, while France would accept the principle of free capital movements. Thus the new treaty's preamble recalls the 1972 commitment to the 'progressive realisation of economic and monetary union'. A chapter entitled 'Cooperation in Economic and Monetary Policy (Economic and Monetary Union)', containing a mere 110 words, said that any changes to Europe's monetary institutions would require an IGC.

The chapter on EMU and much else in the new treaty infuriated Thatcher, who very nearly applied a veto. Just before midnight on the second and final day the Foreign Office convinced her that wrecking the summit would not help British interests. The 10 heads of government approved two distinct documents: a revision of the Treaty of Rome, covering the EEC, and a new, inter-governmental treaty on EPC.

After the summit Thatcher said at her press conference that the treaty's words on EMU did not mean anything and that if they did she would not have agreed to them. For Delors, however, that diminutive chapter was a signpost for the future. 'It's like the story of Tom Thumb lost in the forest, who left white stones so he could be found. I put in white stones so we would find monetary union again.'[10]

Despite the mention of EMU, the new treaty fell far short of Delors's federalist hopes. The morning after the summit, at a meeting of foreign ministers, Delors harangued them for failing to rise to the challenge of doing something for Europe, and for having given birth to a 'monstrosity'. He tried to reopen the text on the arcane subject of 'comitology', which he – but no one else – considered of the utmost importance. Delors wanted the treaty to specify that the commission rather than national officials should control the committees which managed the single market. The ministers ignored him.

However, when the ministers met again on 19 December to tidy up the text, Delors convinced them that if the inter-governmental text on EPC remained separate from the rest of the new treaty, it could weaken the Community's institutional principles. So they framed both with a preamble which repeated the federalist rhetoric of the Stuttgart Declaration and stressed the common role of EPC and the Community in constructing a union. The ministers also accepted Delors's idea of calling the whole bundle *L'Acte Unique* – the Single European Act or Single Act – to stress the coherence of its two parts.

The Single Act could not come into force until ratified by all 12 members. Ten of them held parliamentary votes. In a referendum of February 1986, 56 per cent of the Danes approved the Single Act. A challenge to Ireland's High Court led to a referendum in May 1987, with a positive vote of 70 per cent. The Single European Act came into force on 1 July 1987.

The new treaty attracted little attention beyond Eurocratic circles. Thatcher called it a 'modest decision'. *The Economist* said it was 'a smiling mouse', meaning that it was well intentioned but too diminutive to make much difference. Few politicians or commentators expected the treaty to alter the nature of the European Economic Community – which had become an out-of-date name since the new treaty referred to the 'European Community' (EC).

But the mouse carried sharp teeth. The chapter on the single market committed the EC to remove all internal barriers by the end of 1992. The Council of Ministers would take decisions on the single market by 'qualified majority vote', although unanimity would remain the rule where the free movement of people, employee rights or taxation were concerned. Under the council's complex system of weighted voting, a qualified majority meant that two large countries and one small one could veto a law. Laws on the health and safety of workers would henceforth be settled by qualified majority. The new chapters on the environment, cohesion, R&D and the parliament – which won the 'cooperation procedure' – were more or less as Delors had proposed.

The treaty on European Political Cooperation (EPC) committed the 12 to 'endeavour jointly to formulate and implement a European foreign policy,' and to consult each other and to consider each other's interests before acting. They would cooperate on the political and economic aspects of security. The commission would be 'fully associated' with EPC, which would establish a Brussels secretariat.

Mouse or monster, the Single European Act satisfied governments with markedly different views on the EC's long-term objectives. The poorer, southern members expected – correctly, as it turned out – that the articles on regional policy would translate into concrete commitments of money. The pragmatic British and Danes thought the act was mainly about implementing the 1992 programme. The more idealistic six founder members stressed the sections on EMU and the European Parliament and viewed the treaty as a stepping-stone to a more federal Europe. Despite his petulance after the Luxembourg summit, Delors agreed. 'I knew that if this treaty was accepted, it was an important moment and that historians would one day recognise the value of this mouse.'[11]

He now speaks of the Single European Act with the warmth of a father who has watched his child grow into a star. He says he decided to

> make a treaty in the style of that of the Coal and Steel Community, without fat, on the point. [The Single Act] was precise – which is not at all the case with the Maastricht treaty. We said clearly what we should and should not do.[12]

The Single Act is, as he says, written with a clarity and precision wholly absent from the much longer Rome and Maastricht treaties. But Delors's estimate that he and his officials wrote 85 per cent of the Single Act is an exaggeration. Other participants in the IGC think 60 to 70 per cent a fairer figure.

Only when the Single Act came into force did Europe's politicians start to appreciate how much it shifted power from national governments to Community institutions – and to the commission more than to the parliament. The commission gained fresh 'competences' – areas where it could propose laws – from the new treaty chapters. More importantly, the spread of majority voting allowed many more of the commission's proposals to become law. When unanimity had been the rule, few people bothered about the commission's schemes, for they seldom passed the Council of Ministers.

THE CZAR OF BRUSSELS

The successes of the 1992 programme and of the Single European Act were inextricably linked. There would not have been a Single Act without Cockfield's white paper. Equally, many of the proposals in the white paper could not have been implemented without the new voting rules of the Single Act.

Delors viewed the single market and the Single Act as two parts of what he termed a 'triptych' of reforms. He thought the 'Delors package' of budgetary measures, agreed in February 1988, no less important than the other two achievements of his first commission. Under Delors's presidency the Community moved closer to a federal system of government in two respects. Member-states transferred powers to EC institutions, through constitutional changes and new laws. They also transferred money from their own budgets to that of the Community.

The Community's most intractable arguments have always concerned money. Nothing consumed more time, energy and good will than the annual budgetary haggle between the member-states, the commission and the European Parliament. The Common Agricultural Policy (CAP) took about two-thirds of the budget. It supported farmers by promising to buy their food, at artificially high prices, even when there was no demand for it. This incentive to overproduction led to mountains of cereals, beef and butter being stored. The CAP subsidised the export of these surpluses which, when dumped on third-world markets, sometimes damaged the livelihood of local farmers.

At the London summit, on 5 and 6 December 1986, Delors delivered a detailed exposition on the state of the EC's finances, concluding that it would be bust within a year. Thatcher asked him to work on a plan that would tackle a range of problems, including the swelling cost of farm surpluses, the demands of poorer members for larger structural funds and the overall size of the budget.

Until then Delors and Thatcher had got on quite well. She could hardly complain about Delors's emphasis on the single market. They fell out for the first time at their joint press conference at the end of the London summit. Thatcher fielded all the questions and appeared oblivious to the presence of Delors, who fumed silently.

When a journalist asked if the summit had ignored the issues of finance, agriculture and regional aid, an official reminded Thatcher that Delors was beside her. She said Delors had been asked to tackle those subjects during a tour of the member-states, and asked him to comment.

Delors's attention had wandered. 'No, no, I am obliged to such a discretion,' he said, looking rather a fool.

She persisted: 'Would you very kindly confirm that what I said was absolutely strictly accurate and that you are looking forward to this, and rising to the challenge it represents, and that you will hope to solve it during your coming two years of presidency of the commission?'

'I hope.'

'I had no idea you were such a strong silent man.'[13]

Delors felt snubbed and patronised, and thought she had tried to humiliate him, which was probably not the case. On 9 December they both went to the European Parliament in Strasbourg to report on the summit. Thatcher spoke first and was barracked. Delors's speech, cheered by the Euro-MPs, berated the lack of progress on a coordinated EC growth strategy, on new R&D programmes and on Erasmus, a programme of student exchanges – all of which Thatcher had blocked.

A flustered Thatcher took the floor to respond. 'I wish he had said some of these things in London. I invited him to do so while he was sitting at the press conference with me. He was singularly quiet.' Afterwards Thatcher sat next to Cockfield during a lunch in Strasbourg's Orangerie. She fulminated against Delors in language which brought blushes to the lord's cheeks.

In February 1987 Delors unveiled what became known as the 'Delors package' to the European Parliament. He called on the EC to fix each major category of spending (the CAP, administration, R&D and so on) for five years in advance. The annual budget would merely fill in the details and the Community would be spared its yearly financial wrangle. Delors proposed doubling the structural funds over five years and allowing Britain to keep its budget rebate. He suggested curbing farm surpluses with 'stabilisers', a device which would cut prices automatically if production exceeded a pre-set quantity.

Delors entitled his package *Réussir l'Acte Unique* (making a success of the Single Act) to emphasise that the new treaty required a budgetary counterpart. He thought the Single Act's chapters on research and regional aid would prove meaningless unless financial flesh was grafted onto their legal bones.

Delors knew the Community's poorer members worried about being hurt by the 1992 programme. He hoped that bigger structural funds would

win them round by softening the single market's hard edges. More generally, he thought greater transfers from richer members to poorer ones
would promote a family spirit within the EC.

Delors's proposals stood no chance of implementation unless Germany
agreed to pick up the largest share of the bill. He approached the Germans
with both carrots and sticks. He told the *Financial Times*:

> *We can't make Germany move from a sense of guilt which is 40 years
> old, I'm trying to convince them Europe must be their design and not a
> chance project. They need it to express their will to play a role in the
> world.*[14]

Yet on French television he complained of Germany's waning interest in
European integration.

> *We say to you [the Germans], if you see Europe as a way of increasing
> your trade surplus with other countries, because you are good fellows we
> understand that. But if you don't understand that you also have to take
> part in the construction of Europe, don't be surprised if one day this
> Europe bursts apart and you lose your surpluses and you have more
> unemployed.*[15]

The Copenhagen summit of December 1987 was supposed to settle the
Delors package but ended in rancorous discord. Germany, which took on
the EC presidency in January 1988, called an emergency summit in an
attempt to break the deadlock.

On 27 January the commissioners discussed the summit, which would
take place in Brussels the following week. After a break for lunch Delors
brought a large glass of Fernet Branca – a dark and spicy *digestivo* – to the
commission table. His mood was no less dark and spicy. He thought the
prospects of an agreement on his package were bleak. He also suspected
that some commissioners had criticised his budget proposals to their
governments, behind his back.

Delors told his colleagues that if the Brussels summit did not pass the
budget package, he would resign and they should too. When none of them
offered to do so, he accused the commissioners of cowardice and disloyalty.
He said if anyone engaged in dirty tricks after the summit he would resign
and name in public those who had broken ranks. If there was a shipwreck,
he said, they were all in it, and he would denounce any survivors. If they
wanted someone else to represent them at the summit, so be it.

Unfortunately for Delors, the two commissioners who might have calmed him down, Natali and Cockfield, were absent. When Frans Andriessen, the Dutch farm commissioner, suggested they discuss the structural funds, Delors launched a personal attack on Grigoris Varfis, the amiable but ineffectual Greek who ran the funds. He accused Varfis of incompetence and treachery, saying he and his directorate-general were '*une honte*' (shameful) and '*une scandale*'.

Stanley Clinton-Davies, the British environment commissioner, was unwise enough to ask Delors if they could discuss car exhaust emissions. Delors attacked him for trivialising the debate and for proposing intrusive rules which upset the member-states. Manuel Marin, who ran the social fund, asked Delors to explain what he meant. The president told the Spaniard that he had had enough of 'jungle warfare' in the commission and of 'your little games'. During this performance, which lasted two hours, Delors four times told his colleagues they should be ready to resign with him. Eventually Delors stormed out, followed by Lamy.

For several days Delors spoke to none of the commissioners. Claude Cheysson, the commissioner for development, suggested to colleagues that Delors should skip the Brussels summit, take a long holiday and spend it in a hospital. A mischievous Italian Euro-MP tabled a question about alcohol consumption during commission meetings.

In the event Delors never had to put his colleagues' loyalty to the test. At the Brussels summit the southern countries demanded more structural money, and Thatcher more controls on farm spending than Kohl, in the chair, was offering. Kohl, Delors and their officials sought to break the impasse by crafting a new compromise. Kohl agreed to a doubling of the structural funds over six years, although Germany would foot the lion's share of the increase. The EC budget would gain a new source of finance, on top of the customs dues, levies on farm imports and VAT revenues it already received: a contribution based on the size of members' GDPs, which would benefit the poorer states. The overall ceiling on EC spending would rise from 1.05 per cent of Community GDP in 1988 to 1.2 per cent in 1992 (which turned out to be 70 billion ecus, in 1992 prices, or £51.5 billion).

Thatcher rejected the Kohl-Delors compromise, finding the structural funds too large and the agricultural stabilisers too weak. At midnight on the second day, the summit was on the brink of breakdown. Delors asked for the session to be suspended and, together with Geoffrey Howe, David Hannay, Britain's EC ambassador, and David Williamson, the commission's new secretary-general, worked on Thatcher. At 3 am she ceded, attracted by the package's 'agricultural guideline', which would limit the growth of farm spending to 74 per cent of the total budgetary growth.

Delors had been on peak negotiating form, scurrying from one delegation to another and showing himself sensitive to the priorities of each. Everyone – except perhaps Thatcher – felt they got a good bargain. In a week Delors had moved from the depths of depression and the brink of disaster to triumph and acclaim. For the first time the world's media feted Delors as star. Budgetary arguments had been swept aside for five years.

Meanwhile the 1992 programme was turning from a great idea into a practical reality. Even before the ratification of the Single Act, the Council of Ministers had begun to pass more laws because of an understanding that the Luxembourg Compromise would not be used (the new treaty had ignored, rather than abolished or codified, that weapon). After the new voting rules came into force, the council passed single-market laws rapidly. Actual votes were rare, for a minister who saw that he or she was going to lose an argument would often back down and seek a compromise. Cockfield tended to dominate meetings of single-market ministers, where his clear explanations of the most abstruse technicalities proved telling. He hurried everyone along with regular reports on how many proposals the commission had tabled and how many the council had passed.

Delors worked hard to rally support for the 1992 programme. In August 1986 he told Democracy 2000, a forum of French socialists:

> I've always thought, notably in France, that there was not enough market and that the state was, for historical reasons, omnipresent and too often suffocating or dominating. Most of the French have not yet learned this mentality of openness to the world, without which we cannot build a competitive economy and prosper ... The market will teach us better than any speech to think, act and produce according to the diverse needs and tastes of the world's consumers.[16]

In March 1988 the commission unveiled a study on the economic impact of 1992, written by a team working for Paolo Cecchini, an Italian economist. The Cecchini Report estimated that the disappearance of frontier controls would boost Community GDP by 0.2 to 0.3 per cent; that the removal of technical barriers would add 2.0 to 2.4 per cent; and that economies of scale and greater competition would contribute 2.1 to 3.7 per cent. That added up to a one-off gain of 4.25 to 6.5 per cent of GDP, or 119–175 billion ecus. The report predicted a short-term rise in unemployment but a long-term gain of about 5 million jobs. The Cecchini Report received widespread publicity and, whatever the merits of its forecasting, helped convince business people to take 1992 seriously.

In the late 1980s business people faced an incessant series of conferences, books, articles and reports, all offering advice on how to restructure in advance of 1992. Government advertising campaigns urged them to think European. Many companies increased investment or resorted to cross-border takeovers in preparation for the new market. Industrial investment, having been flat in the three years 1982–84, grew by an annual average of 3.5 per cent from 1985–87 and by 7.5 per cent from 1988–90.

In the first half of 1988 the EC's German presidency pushed through a series of single-market laws, including a unanimous agreement to end controls on capital movements by 1 July 1990 (Spain, Portugal, Ireland and Greece were allowed longer). By the end of the year the Council of Ministers had passed more than half the white paper's proposals. This success transformed the world's image of the commission and of the Community. The countries of the European Free Trade Association worried about being left out of the market and thought about joining the EC. Americans took note of the man who symbolised both: in February 1989 Delors made the cover of *Newsweek* as 'The Czar of Brussels: Building the Euro-empire of 1992'.

PARIS AND THE POPE

The successes of the Delors package and the single market turned the commission president into one of the brightest stars of the French political firmament. Newspapers lauded his achievements and speculated on his return to Paris. Throughout his years in Brussels, Delors remained on the Parti Socialiste's governing council, and he never took his eye off developments in France.

After the right-wing parties won the legislative elections of March 1986, France experienced 'cohabitation', with Jacques Chirac in the Matignon and Mitterrand in the Elysée. Delors hoped that if that pair fell out, he might head a coalition government of socialists and centrists. In September 1986 Delors said that if Mitterrand wanted to present him as his successor, he would be ready. But 'morally' he could not do anything against Rocard, his potential socialist rival, for they agreed on 90 per cent of policy.[17]

A year later, during a television interview, Delors shocked many socialists by saying that he would serve as prime minister if Raymond Barre, a man of the centre-right, became president – if, in doing so, he could rally 65 to 70 per cent of the French. Despite such open ambition, Delors said three times in the same interview that he had not caught the virus of politics. When asked if he had fits of rage, Delors turned the question into an explanation of how he differed from other politicians.

> *Yes, some calculated, some not. But what do you want? In this political life, where everything is covered in felt and there's a code, nothing ever gets done if you don't bawl at people!*

He had only been active in politics for eight years, so he had not 'got the virus and I don't want to adapt my behaviour to it, even if [behaving nicely] is considered wise and tolerant.'[18]

This television programme revealed three of the reasons for Delors's growing popularity in France. First, he is a master of the extended, hour-long interview. His frankness and passion engage the viewer. He is worth listening to because he is certain to say something he should not. The format allows him the time to vaunt his wit, and to explain complex issues – such as the workings of the CAP – in his clearest schoolmasterly style.

Second, Delors's repeated claim that he is different from other politicians proved a winner. In the late 1980s and early 1990s the French grew increasingly disenchanted with their scandal-ridden political elite. Many of them began to like this non-politician who remained distant from the squalid struggles of Parisian party politics.

Third, the reference to Raymond Barre highlighted Delors's concern to appeal to the centre and centre-right of French politics. He wanted to show he was not a sectarian left-winger and that he sought to bring together all reasonable French people. Delors's preaching of consensus struck a chord with many French electors. Since the late 1980s opinion polls have shown Rocard's support to be solidly based on voters who define themselves as left of centre; Delors has relatively more supporters among electors who are right-wing, centrist or practising Catholic.

By the end of 1987, Mitterrand had not said whether he would run for a second term. Many Mitterrandists worried that if he stood down, their enemy Rocard would grab the socialist nomination. Pierre Joxe and Louis Mermaz, two of Mitterrand's most faithful lieutenants, paid Delors a secret visit to implore him to stand if Mitterrand did not.

In the event Mitterrand decided to fight his fourth presidential election and, in May 1988, trounced Chirac. Once again Delors had hopes of the prime ministership, only to see Rocard preferred. However during Rocard's three years in the Matignon he was overtaken by Delors in the opinion polls.

Meanwhile in Brussels, the commission's growing authority had attracted a stream of visiting statesmen and dignitaries. When Pope John Paul II paid a visit, in May 1985, he and Delors did not get on. The Pope told Delors that the EC was incapable of helping Eastern Europe, and that European unity had to be based on Christianity rather than economics. The Pope then chatted to Natali, the Italian Christian Democrat. According to some reports, the Pope made disparaging remarks about the left-wing Catholic bodies, such as the Jeunesse Ouvrière Chrétien and the CFTC, which had helped to shape Delors. When he heard about these comments Delors became upset.

Subsequently Cardinal Lustiger, the archbishop of Paris, has tried to arrange further meetings between Delors and the Pope. At the time of writing the cardinal had not succeeded. On one occasion, when Lustiger assured Delors that John Paul II liked him and wanted to meet him again, Delors asked why the pontiff could not issue an invitation himself.

Delors becomes embarrassed when asked about his *malentendu* with the Pope:

> *He says I misunderstood him ... perhaps the Church considers that the project I promote is too materialist – which is absolutely stupefying! One hears things but we've never had an in-depth conversation.*[19]

THE EUROPEAN MODEL OF SOCIETY

From his first month at the commission, Delors wanted to balance the plan for a single market with an effort to improve the lot of workers. In January 1985 he invited Unice, the confederation of European employers' organisations, CEP, its public sector equivalent, and Etuc, the European trade union confederation, to a 'social dialogue'. 'Delors called us in and said let's stop the ideological polemics' recalls Zygmunt Tyszkiewicz, general secretary of Unice. 'He said he would cease throwing directives at us if we and the unions talked to each other. So for four years there were no more directives.'[20]

These meetings of the 'social partners' – employers and trade unions – led to joint opinions on matters such as safety in the workplace and training. But the unions, the European Parliament and Delors soon became frustrated with the results. They wanted the dialogue to deepen into the negotiation of binding agreements on subjects such as worker participation and working conditions. Unice wanted to avoid such negotiations.

In 1988 Delors began to worry that the 1992 programme was turning the Community into a mere cornucopia for capitalists. He listened to the unions' worries about 'social dumping' – the idea that investment would flow to countries with the lightest labour regulations – and to their pleas for EC directives to prevent it. 'I was worried that the trade unions might not continue to support the [1992] project politically,' he says.[21]

So in May 1988, at an Etuc conference in Stockholm, Delors revealed a new strategy. He promised that a series of EC labour laws, to be inspired by a 'Social Charter', would lay down minimum standards. A 'European Company Statute' would allow firms to incorporate under EC law – giving them tax advantages if they did so – but oblige them to set up procedures for worker consultation. He also promised that workers would have access to training throughout their career.[22]

Delors's new line ensured the unions' loyalty to the commission but soured his relations with industrialists. In November 1988 Tyszkiewicz publicly criticised the commission for spending too much time on social policy and not enough on the market. Later that month, when Unice celebrated its 30th birthday, Tyszkiewicz took the heads of its national associations to meet the commission president. Delors launched a blistering attack on Tyszkiewicz, admonishing him for (supposedly) having damaged the commission by attacking its president. Delors then turned on the Unice chiefs, telling them their opposition to the 'social dimension' was undermining the construction of Europe. If they did not realise that Europe had to be more than a free-trade zone, he said, there would be problems. 'If you want a class war, you'll get one.'

In the same month Delors asked the Community's Economic and Social Committee – a consultative body of employers, trade unions and professional associations – to draft a Social Charter. Delors disliked the result, for it covered the rights to a clean environment, health and education, as well as consumers' and childrens' rights. He wanted a charter focused on workers' rights.

In June 1989 the commission presented its own Social Charter to governments. Ministers spent the next six months watering it down, in the hope that Thatcher would sign the document at the Strasbourg summit of December 1989. Thus references to a minimum wage and to a maximum level of working hours were cut. But in Strasbourg only 11 heads of government signed the Social Charter.

The charter had no legal force and contained no proposals for legislation. It consisted of 30 vague and worthy aspirations, such as 'all employment shall be fairly remunerated' and 'every individual must be able to have access to public placement services free of charge'. There were many references to subsidiarity, the idea that the EC should act only when strictly necessary. Hence 'information, consultation and participation for workers must be developed along appropriate lines, taking account of the practices in force in the various member-states'.

Yet Thatcher hated the charter. She regarded the taming of Britain's trade unions as one of her greatest triumphs and saw the Social Charter as a symbol of the corporatist values she despised. She even branded it (in June 1989) as 'Marxist interventionism'. Thatcher liked the commission's 'social action programme', published in November 1989, no better. Based on the principles of the Social Charter, this white paper contained 47 proposals, 27 of them for binding directives.

Delors came under heavy pressure from the European Parliament – where the socialists had become the largest group after the June 1989 elections – not to compromise on social policy. In 1990 the parliament held up several single-market directives and demanded a speedier implementation of the social action programme. The commission responded by bringing forward the publication of several draft directives on labour law.

Unlike the commission, the Council of Ministers took little note of the parliament's huffing and puffing. Ministers treated social directives less urgently than single-market laws. The confrontational and uncompromising stance of Vasso Papandreou, the Greek social affairs commissioner from 1989 to 1992, sometimes added to the delays. Some directives failed to pass because they required the unanimous approval of ministers. Thus Britain blocked a directive that would require any company with 1000 or more employees in two or more EC countries to set up a consultative workers' council, and another which would give part-time and temporary staff the same rights as full-time workers.

Other directives survived the mangling and wrangling of the Council of Ministers and, in 1992 and 1993, reached the statute book. One gave mothers the right to 13 weeks of maternity leave, with pay of no less than health benefit in their own country. A second set a maximum working week of 48 hours (with exemptions) and a minimum of four weeks annual paid holiday. A third regulated the hours that children could work. Britain opposed these laws, all of which were passed on a qualified majority vote.

When the commission tables a draft law it must cite the treaty article which justifies the proposal. The article will specify the appropriate voting procedure. To avoid a British veto the commission tabled several directives – including those on maternity leave, working hours and child labour – as health and safety measures, and therefore subject to qualified majority. The British government called this cheating, on the grounds that these measures were not primarily about health and safety. The commission resorted to the same ruse on several environmental laws, proposing them as 'single-market' measures that would be decided by qualified majority.

Nothing did more to turn Britain's Conservative Party against the commission's plans for a social dimension than its cavalier approach to the legal base of its proposals.

Delors's campaign for a social dimension won him little thanks. Trade unions and the European Parliament complained that he should have done more. Yet in 1993, during the debate on Europe's faltering competitiveness, employers' lobbies and the British government claimed that EC labour laws had destroyed jobs.

Delors's staff admitted that some commission proposals had been more detailed than necessary. The commission's future proposals, they said, would set objectives and leave governments to decide how to meet them. But they maintained that very few of the action programme's 47 measures would raise the cost of labour. For instance, the burden on companies of the proposal for workers' councils would be no more than 10 ecus a year per worker. As for the law on working time, Delors's staff pointed out that the commission had proposed merely to limit the hours of nightwork; government amendments had added the 48-hour and four-week rules.

Such justifications do not impress Unice's Tyszkiewicz.

> *Delors's proposals on social law have been a brake on the single market programme. He got the balance wrong because he is too emotionally attached to his CFDT roots. The decline of the trade unions upset Delors and he wanted to help them through the EC.*

Tyszkiewicz says that whether a particular directive increases costs is not the point, for the overall impression of more regulation deters investment – especially from American companies which may be allergic to a phrase like 'worker consultation'.[23]

Such comments only confirm Delors in his belief that the 'European model of society', as he calls it, is at risk. Delors has used two justifications for the EC's involvement in social legislation. Some directives – such as those on minimum standards of health and safety – are needed to prevent social dumping. The point of others – for instance rules limiting child labour – is to express common European values.

Delors's enthusiasm for the social dimension comes from a deep-rooted desire to protect certain traits of European society.

> *European society is different from the Japanese model to the extent that society doesn't exert this psychological or sociological pressure on the individual; there is a bit more space to blossom. But at the same time society is more present than it is in the United States. The Europeans*

have always had a kind of balance between the individual and society.
That goes back to the base of their civilisation, to Christianity, to
Roman law, to the Greek civitas, *and in the recent period, to the influ-*
ence of social democracy.[24]

Some of Delors's definitions equate the European model with the ideal of
Christian personalism: 'The individual must be able to fulfil himself, to be
a real citizen, to be an active man in his work, but he also has obligations
towards society.'[25]

Speaking in Bordeaux in March 1991, Delors praised the Social Charter
for defending a model of society which gave space to the market yet allowed
the state, public bodies, local government and the social partners to act. He
moved beyond conventional definitions of social democracy by declaring
the pattern of rural settlement to be an essential feature of the European
model.

> *The specific way in which the European land, and not only France, is*
> *peopled, spread out over the whole territory in a diversified pattern*
> *which contrasts with the massive urban conglomerations that one sees in*
> *other countries, next to totally empty zones; the desire of many Euro-*
> *peans to be rooted in the land, and the search, often so difficult today, for*
> *a feeling of belonging to a settlement that is close to its own history;*
> *that's why I believe we can speak of the rural world as a mainstay of our*
> *civilisation.*[26]

Does the European model apply to Britain?

> *Yes, in Britain's foundations but not in Thatcherism. The English*
> *remain attached to many grass-roots collective organisations. Their*
> *tradition is the same even if they still dream of being at the heart of three*
> *circles – America, the Commonwealth and Europe.*

Thatcher's love of the individual and disdain for society place her, Delors
believes, in a tradition of American radicalism.[27]

JACQUES AND MAGGIE

Jacques Delors and Margaret Thatcher had more in common than either
would care to admit. They stood out as rare ideologues in an age of grey and
managerial politicians. They cared deeply about principles but were
inclined to be authoritarian and made the mistake of identifying them-

selves with what they believed in. The achievements of both lay in their first five or six years of power; by the end of their reigns they had lost much of their authority.

Not until 1988 did they fall out irreparably. In that year Delors shifted the EC's agenda from the single market to the social dimension and to economic and monetary union (EMU). After the success of the Delors package, in February 1988, his self-confidence soared. In June, at the Hanover summit, Thatcher seconded Delors's appointment for a second four-year term (she knew she could not prevent the reappointment, since all the others wanted Delors). The same summit created the Delors Committee on EMU. Delors's moods, whether high or low, are seldom moderate, and in the summer of 1988 he floated on cloud nine.

On 6 July 1988, in an elated state, Delors addressed the parliament in Strasbourg. He noted that in the last six months the EC had taken more decisions than it had between 1974 and 1984, but sounded a note of caution. Only the British and German parliaments were aware that law-making was shifting to the EC, and that there needed to be more dialogue between the European and the national parliaments. 'In 10 years, 80 per cent of economic legislation, perhaps even tax and social, will come from the EC.' He said the Community had so many decisions to take that, for the sake of efficiency, it would need the beginnings of a European government by 1995. He asked everyone to reflect on the best formula for achieving it.[28]

Delors's critics immediately picked on the '80 per cent' phrase as proof of his megalomaniac tendencies. 'His over-the-top comments are absurd because they frighten people,' Thatcher told BBC Radio's Jimmy Young in July 1988. 'He would never say such extreme things to me.'[29] Two months later Delors explained that his job was to provoke a debate on where the EC was heading. In Strasbourg he had tried to make national parliaments take more interest and to 'set out clearly what was at stake in a way that doesn't disguise history's progress, so that there isn't one day an explosion or a sort of exasperation.'[30] The explosion came in 1992.

On 7 September Delors visited the annual conference of the Trades Union Congress (TUC) in Bournemouth. The TUC had, traditionally, been hostile to the Community. Yet when Norman Willis and the other union leaders held a dinner in Delors's honour, they sang 'Frère Jacques' – and moved him to tears. The following day, when Delors addressed the congress, he sought to quell the unions' hostility to the 1992 programme. He said the Hanover summit had agreed that the single market would benefit all individuals and that it would not harm social welfare. As in Stockholm he spoke of a minimum level of workers' rights, of the European

Company Statute and of a right to training.[31] The delegates gave Delors a standing ovation and passed a resolution in favour of the single market.

Delors's Bournemouth speech enraged Thatcher, perhaps because he had delivered it in Britain. Delors says Thatcher should not have taken offence because he had spoken to the Confederation of British Industry in 1985. 'She cannot find a single passage in which I interfered in Britain's domestic politics. My goal was to change the stance of the trade unions. I succeeded.'[32]

Britain's labour movement shook off its old antipathy to Europe in 1988. Thatcher brought about some of this change: if she hated the EC so much, there had to be something good about it. Delors's trumpeting of the social dimension and his Bournemouth speech achieved the rest. Under Delors's influence, the unions began to see Brussels as a counterweight to the Conservative power of Westminster.

Thatcher had had enough. She attempted to squash Delors and his ideas in a speech to the College of Europe in Bruges, on 22 September.

> *It is ironic that just when those countries such as the Soviet Union which have tried to run everything from the centre, are learning that success depends on dispersing power and decisions away from the centre, there are some in the Community who seem to move in the opposite direction. We have not successfully rolled back the frontiers of the state in Britain only to see them reimposed at a European level with a European super-state exercising a new dominance from Brussels.*

Thatcher's words inspired Conservative Europhobes to found the Bruges Group. The speech's virulence wounded Delors, who lay low for several months.

'From 1984 to 1987 British diplomacy in Europe was very successful: we got the EC to focus on enlargement and the single market,' says Charles Powell, Thatcher's diplomatic adviser. 'We thought Delors responsible for spoiling this period.' He says Thatcher wanted the commission to become a mere civil service for carrying out the Council of Ministers' wishes.[33]

Another of her advisers remembers how Delors's pontificating on foreign policy – such as his insistence on the need to preserve the Soviet Union at the October 1990 Rome summit – infuriated Thatcher. She thought the commission president not competent (neither in the sense of legally entitled, nor in the sense of knowledgeable) to speak on such matters. The adviser notes that since Thatcher had an instinctive dislike of both Frenchmen and commissioners, Delors did not stand much of a chance.

Geoffrey Howe shared Thatcher's ideal of free markets and Delors's ideal of Europe, and felt frustrated that his efforts to bring them together came to nothing.

> *He never understood the history of British governments' struggles against trade unions. Delors wasn't well advised on the impact of his policies on other countries, and had a lack of cultural sensitivity. So did Thatcher, who didn't understand other cultures and classes in her own country, let alone foreign ones.*

Howe reckons Delors made more of an effort with Thatcher than she did with the commission president, for he saw it as part of his job.[34]

A senior British diplomat who spent a lot of time with both reckons that personalities rather than ideology caused the biggest problems between them.

> *Delors made the mistake of being visibly frightened of her. Because she's a bully she kicks harder if she sees someone is scared. He'd never say boo to her in the room, then he'd go out and criticise her. But he found her fascinating and hated her much less than she hated him.*

For all that, Delors had more respect for Thatcher than he has for Major. 'I never wasted my time when I talked with her; she was always well informed on economic and monetary matters.' He says their relationship did not deteriorate until her last year, after she had removed Howe from the Foreign Office in July 1989. 'She began to regret having signed the Single Act, and to see that there was a "spill over" effect. She hardened and, having a sort of fixation against me, used excessive language.'[35]

Thatcher's contempt for Delors ensured that her supporters would vilify him as the Beast of Brussels. For the British right, Delors became the symbol of everything bad about the EC. The combination of a federalist commission president and a Eurosceptic prime minister, in the late 1980s, placed huge strains on Britain's relationship with the Community. The polemics between Brussels and Downing St fuelled Britain's European debate and worsened the Conservative Party's divisions – which, ultimately, contributed to Thatcher's fall.

CHAPTER SIX

THE HOUSE THAT JACQUES BUILT

THE EUROPEAN COMMISSION inherited by Jacques Delors had drifted, rudderless, for many years. The commission had few successes to its credit and scant respect from the rest of the world. Individual commissioners and officials ran parts of the organisation as semi-independent fiefs. Discipline was slack, working hours were short and morale was low.

Delors turned the commission upside down. He gave it a sense of purpose and taught it to respond to his will. Power and ideas started to flow top-down instead of bottom-up. The commission's achievements, such as the 1992 programme, won international acclaim, and its officials put a swagger in their stride.

However, Delors brought about this revolution by concentrating power in the presidency. His methods were often unorthodox, sometimes dubious and occasionally improper. By the end of his reign, Delors's personal system of command and control had begun to damage the commission's internal organisation, sap the enthusiasm of its officials and contribute to the tarnishing of its image.

The commission's civil servants tend to be very different from those who work for national bureaucracies (by 1993 the commission had 17,000 full-time and 1000 temporary staff). Many of them applied to work for the commission because they find the ideal of European unity inspirational. Most commission officials speak several languages fluently (all documents have to be translated into the nine official languages, but French, English and German are the three 'working languages').

Many of them have spouses or lovers of a different nationality, or both at the same time. Commission officials escape the prying gaze of friends, relations and neighbours when they come to Brussels – which may explain why the institution is something of a *baisodrome* (French slang for a place containing much dalliance). According to some surveys, nearly half of commission officials are divorced.

The money helps commission staff to enjoy their jobs. In 1993 the 4000 administrative officials (whose grades range from 'A8' at the bottom to 'A1' at the top) earned between 1.6 million and 6.2 million Belgian Francs (£32,000 and £124,000). A middle-ranking 'A4' official, aged between 45 and 50, earned BFr3.6 million (£72,000). On top of their salary they receive allowances for living away from home and for having children. Instead of Belgian tax they pay a European Union tax, but for lower- and middle-ranking officials this is often no more than the allowances (The EC became the European Union in November 1993).

People who work for the commission look rich. The men almost never wear grey suits, preferring colourful jackets and ties. Many of the women wear expensive suits, often Italian, with make-up and jewellery. A lot of the most senior officials work hard, spending 50 or 55 hours a week at their desks; many others put in well under 40. They all believe in the sanctity of a civilised lunch: nobody will pick up a phone between 1 pm and 3 pm.

Most administrators find the cultural mix and the nature of the work stimulating. The Union and its various policies are continually in a state of flux. Officials have a chance to study problems and propose solutions which may, one day, end up as European laws. Britons who have worked for both the commission and the home civil service note that the former puts a much greater premium on creativity, while the latter stresses regular procedures and the need to write everything down on paper. The commission brims with ideas but never hums with the smoothness and efficiency of the best parts of the British or French civil services. Staff come from diverse backgrounds so there is no single administrative culture which encourages them to work harmoniously. Officials tend to pursue their own personal or political objectives and the results can be chaotic.

Any president of the commission faces the problem that he – there has yet to be a she – has few formal powers. The 'college' of 17 commissioners holds executive authority. The president is *primus inter pares*, with one vote, like the other commissioners. He cannot determine policy unless at least eight other commissioners are ready to vote in his favour.

The president does decide, after consulting the governments, which commissioner does which job. He also represents the commission to the rest of the world, having a seat at G7 summits and at European Union meetings of heads of government and of foreign ministers. But he cannot sack a commissioner, although a government can (the European Parliament has always had but never used the power to sack the whole college).

The commissioners are not, like ministers in a government, bound by a common affiliation to a party or coalition. Britain, for instance, sends one commissioner from the governing party and one from the opposition. Commissioners have little incentive to bury their differences for the common good or to respect the president.

Each commissioner is responsible for one or two of the 23 'directorates-general', the commission's equivalent of ministries. Thus DG1 deals with foreign trade, DG2 economic and monetary affairs, DG3 industry, DG4 competition policy, and so on. The top official in each is the director-general.

Yet the directors-general are not, in practice, the most powerful officials. Each commissioner has a 'cabinet' (private office), consisting of a *chef de cabinet* and five other officials (the president, exceptionally, has a cabinet of 12). These advisers cajole the directorates-general into carrying out the commissioner's wishes. They also sift the ideas that come up from the directorates-general and keep an eye on the work of other commissioners. Most cabinet officials are recruited from the directorates-general, but some come from the national civil services. Most share their commissioner's nationality, although Delors introduced a rule that one in each cabinet must be from a different country.

The *chefs de cabinet* generally have more clout than the directors-general. They deputise for their commissioner in his or her absence. The weekly meeting of *chefs de cabinet*, every Monday, goes through the business that the commissioners are due to consider at their own weekly meeting, on Wednesday. The *chefs de cabinet* initial many decisions which the commissioners will later rubber-stamp, and they leave only the more contentious matters to be discussed in commission (the word commission, confusingly, can mean either meetings of the college of 17 commissioners or the entire bureaucracy).

Even ordinary members of cabinets may wield more influence than directors-general. Each cabinet sends a member to 'special *chefs*', meetings which consider proposals prior to the *chefs de cabinet*; there is a telecoms special *chefs*, a financial services special *chefs*, and so on. Directors-general are not invited to 'special *chefs*' or to meetings of *chefs de cabinet*.

Several of the commission's most important departments – with a thousand officials between them – report directly to the president. The legal service advises the commission on the conformity of its proposals to the Union's treaties and laws. The spokesmen's service provides each commissioner with a press officer, holds a daily press briefing and publishes 50–100 press releases a week. The Cellule de Prospective is an in-house think tank. The secretariat-general coordinates the work of the directorates-general. The secretary-general, the commission's top official, chairs a weekly meeting of the directors-general.

Some of the commission's worst features have survived the Delors decade. Ability is only one factor that influences promotion. Directors-general decide junior appointments and the full commission rules on senior ones. But decisions on jobs are seldom made without months of struggle between rival networks of influence.

The European Union

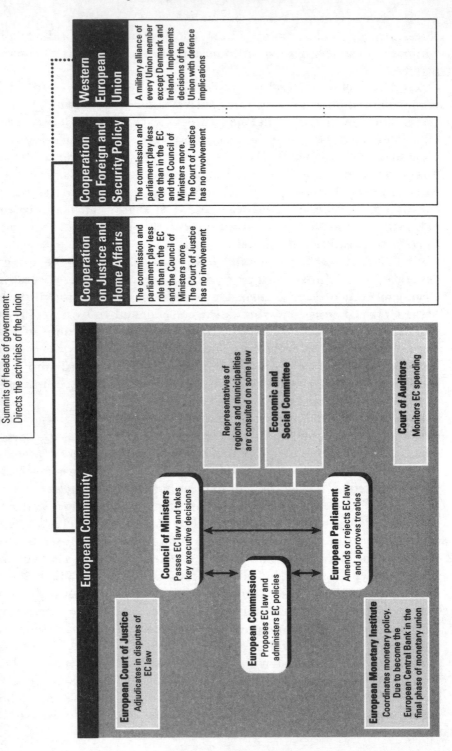

European Council

Summits of heads of government. Directs the activities of the Union

Western European Union

A military alliance of every Union member except Denmark and Ireland. Implements decisions of the Union with defence implications

Cooperation on Foreign and Security Policy

The commission and parliament play less role than in the EC and the Council of Ministers more. The Court of Justice has no involvement

Cooperation on Justice and Home Affairs

The commission and parliament play less role than in the EC and the Council of Ministers more. The Court of Justice has no involvement

European Community

Representatives of regions and municipalities are consulted on some law

Economic and Social Committee

Court of Auditors
Monitors EC spending

Council of Ministers
Passes EC law and takes key executive decisions

European Parliament
Amends or rejects EC law and approves treaties

European Commission
Proposes EC law and administers EC policies

European Court of Justice
Adjudicates in disputes of EC law

European Monetary Institute
Coordinates monetary policy. Due to become the European Central Bank in the final phase of monetary union

Political parties have a say over promotions. Many Italians, especially, owe their jobs to support from what were the Italian Christian Democrat and Socialist parties. Networks of loyalty to particular commissioners overlap with national lobbies. Governments work through 'their' commissioners and cabinets to push favoured officials into slots they judge to be important. Crude bargaining among the governments has ensured that some of the most important jobs are not open to competition: the director-general of financial services is always a Briton; that of agriculture, a Frenchman; that of competition policy, a German; that of regional policy, a Spaniard; and that of economic and monetary affairs, an Italian.

Governments insist that the appointment of directors-general should reflect an informal system of national quotas. If a slot becomes free and the Portuguese, say, are owed one, candidates from other countries will not be considered. If the Portuguese have no suitable internal candidate, they will 'parachute' a Lisbon official into the director-generalship. Such *parachutage* upsets staff who see their career prospects blocked. This political picking of directors-general means that their quality is variable (the quality of cabinet officials is no less variable).

In the lower ranks there are no national quotas. But in recent years governments, commissioners and their cabinets have interfered in promotions down to the level of A3. In March 1993 the European Court of Justice annulled the appointment of several Spaniards and Italians in the fisheries directorate, on the grounds that nationality had been the determining factor. Whatever the long-term impact of that ruling, officials who wish to rise fast will need to be skilled at lobbying and at ingratiating themselves with networks.

The directors-general run their departments as independent baronies. Each directorate has its own priorities – DG5 proposed a law to ban cigarette advertising at the same time that DG6 raised subsidies to tobacco farmers – and takes little notice of the others. If Mr Smith in DG7 wants to write to his opposite number Mr Dupont in DG8, his letter must pass up to the director-general of DG7, across to the director-general of DG8 and down the other side. The secretariat-general tries to impose coherence on the whole, and occasionally succeeds.

Many commission units are understaffed, particularly those dealing with new areas of activity such as Eastern Europe. Other units, such as those that administer the Common Agricultural Policy (CAP), are less busy. Yet personnel policy remains inflexible: directors-general with more than enough staff resist the secretariat-general's efforts to make them deliver posts to overstretched colleagues. All these and other problems remain, yet Delors and his team transformed the way the commission worked.

JACQUES DELORS

DELORS'S EXOCET

Delors owes much of his success in Brussels to Pascal Lamy, his *chef de cabinet* from January 1985 to May 1994, who planned and implemented the presidential regime. Lamy's intellect, energy, efficiency and forcefulness invariably impress those who meet him. Lamy chose and trained the president's cabinet as an elite squad of commandos, dedicated to enforcing the president's will. A political scientist who studied Delors's cabinet noted that their task was 'to make the commission function more like a real government and less like a college, while simultaneously preserving the collegiate forms and ethos.'[1]

Delors's cabinet monitors and guides the work of the other commissioners, their cabinets and the directorates-general. One member will follow the environment, a second energy, a third social policy, and so on. Delors' cabinet also helps the secretariat-general with its task of coordination, feeds the president with ideas and information, and liaises with EC governments.

Lamy exercised more power than most of the commissioners, and he terrified many officials. Tall and lean, with a crew cut and a square jaw, he has the appearance and the manner of a French paratrooper (although he spent his national service in the navy). His military brusqueness allows little time for small talk. He speaks concisely, precisely and slowly, in a deep, gruff voice.

Lamy's working method was simple. Each day he cleared his desk before going home. This meant he worked very fast, kept meetings short, and refused lunch invitations. Lamy's incessant glancing at his wristwatch reminded his visitor to hurry up. A man of speed, Lamy ran several times a week in the Forêt de Soigne and several times a year in marathons.

Large photos of the family château – in the department of Eure, Normandy – covered his office wall. Hailing from this prosperous area, where he was born in 1947, Lamy has a different *Weltanschauung* from Delors. Lamy does not get sentimental about French peasants. He is more enthusiastic about free trade and GATT, and tempered some of Delors's hostility to the Japanese. Childhood holidays with British families have given him an impressive command of English.

Lamy gets on easily with the British and the Americans in a way Delors does not. Lamy's close friendship with Robert Zoellick – chief aide to James Baker, President Bush's secretary of state – proved useful for Delors. So did Lamy's close relationships with Joachim Bitterlich, Kohl's adviser on Europe, and Elizabeth Guigou, who played that role for Mitterrand and later become France's minister for Europe. Lamy oversaw

Delors's links with other governments and acted as his 'sherpa' before G7 summits. Although Lamy and Delors did not always share the same views, they never came close to falling out. 'We discuss, we don't argue,' said Lamy. 'Once he knows what I think, it's he who takes the decisions.'[2]

In 1975 Lamy graduated second in his year at the Ecole Nationale d'Administration – where he had befriended Martine Delors. He then became an *Inspecteur des Finances* and an active member of Delors's club Echange and Projets. In 1981 Delors gave him a job in his cabinet, soon making him deputy *chef*. In 1983 Pierre Mauroy, the prime minister, poached Lamy as his deputy *chef*, with responsibility for the government's austerity package.

Delors rehired Lamy on his appointment to the commission. Lamy spent the autumn of 1984 in a small commission office, gathering information on how the bureaucracy worked. He designed the *système Delors* to suit the strengths and weaknesses of both the commission and its president.

> *From my experience of working with Delors, I knew what he liked and didn't like doing, and what he could and could not do. It was like designing a custom-built racing car for a driver who has particular skills. If you want to make good use of Delors's resources, you should leave strategy, communication and negotiation to him, and let the system take care of the rest.*[3]

Lamy's role was to run the administration, which has never interested Delors, and to be ruthless when necessary, for, as Lamy says, 'Delors dislikes blood'.[4] Delors sometimes sent Lamy to argue with a commissioner rather than do it himself.

Lamy also had to push the president to take decisions. Delors is inclined to prevaricate. In the first three months of 1993, Leon Brittan, the commissioner for external relations (economic) and Hans van den Broek, the commissioner for external relations (political) argued over who would do what. Their often public dispute made the commission appear ridiculous. Delors kept his distance for too long before knocking heads together. Significantly, Lamy was absent for much of that period, campaigning in France's parliamentary elections (he stood as a Socialist in Eure, but won fewer votes than the National Front).

Lamy was often a delight to work for. He gave cabinet members the freedom to manage their portfolios as they saw fit. He supported them in their battles within the commission. Wherever in the world he was, he would respond to a colleague's note in minutes.

Yet he could also be a brutish taskmaster. He expected everyone else to work as hard as he did – which was an average of 12 or 13 hours a day, six days a week. He would call a cabinet member at home at the weekend, and without bothering to use such a superfluous word as 'hello', ask why he or she was not in the office. Joly Dixon, who covered EMU in the Delors cabinet from 1987 to 1992, says: 'When I first met Lamy, what struck me as odd was that he assumed anyone can do anything instantly. Then I discovered that there were a whole lot who could – *énarques*.'[5]

Lamy shared Delors's obsession with frugality. The cabinet did not hold birthday or leaving parties. Members did not turn up at diplomatic soirées. In September 1993 Lamy confessed that in all his time in Brussels he had held only two parties and attended five.[6] On a rare occasion when the author persuaded Lamy to leave his office for lunch, he would eat only rice and lentils in the staff canteen.

Leon Brittan meets his cabinet daily, as a group. The Delors team is more hierarchical. Apart from a weekly lunch which Delors occasionally attends, cabinet members do not see each other together. Nor do they see the president unless he happens to be working on their subject. The *chef de cabinet* alone has an overview of the cabinet's work.

The point of this hierarchy is to save the president time. Most modern politicians are, essentially, managers, whose work revolves around meetings and briefings from staff. Delors likes to spend time by himself, reading, thinking and writing. But the hierarchy harms team spirit. Cabinet members have seldom had a please or thank you from Delors or Lamy. Only the strongest personalities flourish in such a high-pressure environment; several have dropped out after a year.

Delors and Lamy worked symbiotically. Lamy's cool and sober temperament balanced Delors's changeable emotions. Lamy's down-to-earth realism restrained Delors' flights of fancy. Jérôme Vignon, head of the Cellule de Prospective, says that Lamy's role was to listen to Delors's 20 ideas and tell him which was the one which would work.

Delors says simply of Lamy, 'I wouldn't have made it without him.' Delors offers this list of Lamy's virtues:

> *an impeccable working method, a very good headhunter, a great ability to learn and the temperament of a leader. He's one of the few top administrators who doesn't base their power and influence on knowing things they hide from others. As soon as he knows or does something, he writes a note to the cabinet. That's the key to the good functioning of a team.*

Delors praises Lamy for decentralising work to members of the cabinet, noting that he himself has a tendency to want to do everything.[7]

Explaining his need for Lamy, Delors says:

> *I trust people and my ideas, I don't see blows coming, I don't analyse things realistically. If one was nasty one would say I was a bit naïve. Lamy is from my daughter's generation, these people are much more realistic than me.[8]*

Lamy helped Delors to guard his moral image. When something nasty happened in the commission, people assumed Lamy and not Delors was responsible.

Lamy set the style – aggressive, dedicated and frugal – for the Delors cabinet, which, in turn, transmitted these values to many other parts of the commission. Having been bashed by Lamy – and sometimes Delors – members of the cabinet bashed those in other cabinets and in the directorates-general. The justification was simple: there was no other way to get things done, given the president's relatively weak formal powers.

One member of Delors's cabinet chairs every meeting of the 'special *chefs*'. He or she will have read all the relevant files the night before, unlike many others at the meeting. The Delors representative may tell an awkward official that his attitude is 'harmful to the construction of Europe' – a euphemism for saying the president will get annoyed if you do not back down. Thus the Delors line often prevails.

Some of the weaker commissioners, such as Vasso Papandreou, responsible for social affairs from 1989 to 1992, had to put up with Delors's cabinet virtually running parts of their portfolio. One cabinet member recounts that a commissioner

> *was doing stupid things. So we had to 'rape' him and work directly with the directorate-general to achieve our ends . . . The president advised me not to do it, but because of the job I had to interpret that to mean I should do it but make sure there was not too much noise.[9]*

François Lamoureux, Delors's deputy *chef de cabinet* from 1989 to 1991, played a key role in the imposition of presidential discipline. Known as 'the ayatollah' for his fervent federalism, Lamoureux is a fearsome debater. His ruthless logic and caustic criticism often traumatised those who crossed him.

Lamy was unashamed of the regime he and Delors created: 'As Delors likes ideas a bit more than power, if the system is to work well I have to focus a bit more on power than ideas.'[10] Lamy's apparent obsession with power has led some to speculate that he believes in nothing. Yet that speculation is, in a sense, a tribute to Lamy. 'He is a superb civil servant because he gets things done for his master without pursuing his own agenda,' said Peter Sutherland, who dubbed Lamy 'Delors's Exocet'. He added, with some uncertainty: 'I would not say he does not have a heart.'[11]

Lamy says he is a socialist and a Catholic, but that his faith is less strong than Delors's. He says he reads Mounier, though less than Delors. He says he has a strong sense of guilt, but that it is less extreme than Delors's. Did it bother him that cabinet members complained they seldom saw their children? 'Yes . . . probably we've made the job too much of a priority – because it's so absorbing, because we believe that we can achieve something – compared with family needs. It's not a system I'm very happy about.'[12]

Delors can appear more human than Lamy, and may even ask after his staff's children. One weekend he rang a member of the cabinet at home and told him to come into the office to finish some work. 'But my wife is away, so I have to look after the children,' was the reply. 'Bring them,' said the president. While the official worked, Delors crawled around on his office floor with the children.

But even in a good mood Delors finds fault in almost every document he receives, particularly in the details. In May 1991 Delors delivered a speech to the Senegalese parliament, but afterwards felt it had been a poor one. So he harangued the cabinet member who had written the speech and kicked his own briefcase hard. But usually Delors fumes rather than shouts when he is angry. He will say very little and then make a barbed comment like: 'I'm not blaming you, but if only we had put in a bit more effort.' He feels guilty when he is not working and has a gift for making his staff feel the same.

'The British and German cabinets in the commission are more convivial,' says one member of Delors's cabinet. 'Even if I've finished work I feel I ought to stay in the office.' Cabinet members are desperate to impress the president. Underneath their sober, determined exteriors, they suffer hot jealousies. Each member counts the number of presidential smiles, comments or calls he receives, compared with his colleagues.

Delors is at his most unreasonable before a big event such as a summit or a television interview, when, in front of others, even Lamy was liable to be branded as incompetent. Delors admits to having 'a very fragile nervous system'. He says that when he overworks he has no warning mechanism, and that he does not see exhaustion looming. 'And then I pay, with moments of depression. Then I mustn't take decisions for half a day.'[13]

Delors is not a man to say sorry. Yet the most bludgeoned cabinet members remain loyal, for they share a militant ethos. They want to work harder than other officials, to be better prepared, to think further ahead and to do whatever is necessary to enforce the president's will. They are committed, body and soul, to a unique figure and his goal of European union.

The commission became a more spritely and powerful machine with Delors in the driving seat. Thus by the end of 1988 the commission had published 90 per cent of the draft laws it had promised in the 1992 programme. As the EC's fortunes revived in the late 1980s, officials began to work harder. They were delighted to have a star at their head, whose views were respected beyond Europe. The Delors regime – at least until 1992 – nurtured their idealism and creativity. Many of those bullied and bruised by the Delors cabinet nevertheless granted it a sullen respect. They knew the EC could not have achieved so much without Delors and Lamy converting the unwieldy, unfocused and unhurried bureaucracy into one capable, if pushed, of acting with speed and efficiency.

RAISON D'ÉTAT

Delors's system of command and control depends on more than his cabinet. Ever since January 1985 Delors and Lamy have placed their own men in key posts, creating a network of supporters. The point of the Delors network, like the cabinet, is to gather information and to carry out the president's wishes.

In 1987 Delors installed Jean-Louis Dewost, a Frenchman, as head of the legal service – displacing a German. From then on political considerations were more likely to colour that service's advice. If Delors disagreed with another commissioner's proposal, an opinion from the legal service would, on occasion, help him to win the argument. When Leon Brittan was competition commissioner, the legal service sometimes parried his efforts to make French companies repay state aid.

Until 1990 the commission's chief spokesman and the president's spokesman were different people. In that year Bruno Dethomas, a former *Le Monde* journalist and Delors's spokesman, took on the additional role of chief spokesman. Henceforth Delors's interests in media management equalled those of the commission. When Leon Brittan's spokesman put out press releases on illegal subsidies to French companies, they were sometimes rewritten lest too tough a tone embarrass Delors in France. In March 1993, when the commission reached an agreement with the Japanese on that year's level of car imports, the spokesmen's service stressed that the number of imports would fall. Another spin – less pleasing to French sensibilities – could have been that Japan's share of the EC car market would rise.

Most of the 650 journalists accredited to the commission treat its president with a great deal of respect. The French press almost never criticise Delors. Those that do offend are liable to be punished. In June 1993 the Brussels correspondent of *Libération* wrote an innocuous preview of the Copenhagen summit. The article ended by saying that Delors's initiative on job creation 'could well be a huge flop'. Tame stuff, but the piece followed another which had compared the president to the emperor with no clothes. Shortly afterwards Delors dined with Serge July, the editor of *Libération*, and criticised the correspondent at length. Lamy then forbade members of the cabinet to talk to the man from *Libération*.

In 1989 Delors appointed Jérôme Vignon to head the Cellule de Prospective, the commission think tank. Vignon is strongly committed to the social teaching of the Catholic church and is, among those close to Delors, the least enamoured of free markets. The Cellule has provided Delors with papers on issues ranging from energy taxes, to the future of the welfare state, to the theological antecedents of the principle of subsidiarity.

The boundaries between Delors's cabinet and the Cellule are blurred, as are those between the cabinet and the secretariat-general. When Delors arrived in Brussels the secretary-general was Emile Noël, a wily Frenchman who had had the job since 1958. Inclined to secrecy, Noël would sort out a problem between two commissioners by mediating behind the scenes. Although not a methodical manager, Noël supplied the institution with some of the political vision which the commissioners often lacked. Noël's retirement in September 1987 left no serious counterweight to Lamy's power over the administration.

Noël's British replacement, David Williamson, could not have been more different. Williamson is an efficient, self-effacing and conscientious administrator, with an impish sense of humour. He has tried, with partial success, to impose a more open and regular style of management. But true to the traditions of the British civil service whence he came, Williamson is not a politician *manqué* who is eager to push a personal strategy.

Ironically, the British Williamson has become more enmeshed in the Delors network than the French Noël ever was. Delors has total confidence in Williamson's loyalty. Every day he sees the secretary-general two or three times (more than anyone else except his *chef de cabinet*) and sends him a dozen notes or queries. Williamson has not stood up to Delors or Lamy, but, as one director-general puts it, 'how can any official stand up to them except by resigning?'

Those close to Leon Brittan are particularly critical of Williamson for having allowed Lamy to rewrite the minutes of commission meetings. The written record matters, for it may be referred to at a later date – when people have forgotten what was said and decided – to justify an action or an argument. An official of the secretariat-general takes the minutes of the commission, of the *chefs de cabinet* and of the 'special *chefs*'. The secretariat-general sends drafts of all these minutes to the president's cabinet, who may make changes. For instance, if two *chefs de cabinet* spoke for a presidential proposal, and five spoke against, the presidential cabinet might alter the minutes to read that a majority spoke in favour. Or, after an evenly balanced argument, opinions which conflicted with the president's could receive less space. The changes are usually distortions rather than inventions.

The Delors cabinet returns the minutes to the secretariat-general, which sends them on to other cabinets. If the Brittan cabinet, say, did not like the minutes, they could ask Williamson to alter them. Williamson would then have talked to Lamy. If the outcome did not satisfy Brittan, he could have raised the matter at the next commission meeting. But Brittan would not have been sure of winning his point, for many commissioners think twice before opposing Delors. Brittan may therefore have preferred a compromise whereby Lamy agreed to some changes but not to others.

Sometimes substantial issues are at stake. The competition directorate vetted state aid in poorer regions by one set of criteria; the regional directorate used another set to decide each region's eligibility for EC funds. In December 1991 Delors sought to harmonise the two sorts of criteria, while Brittan fought to keep the competition directorate's own rules. Brittan believed he had won the argument, but the commission's minutes said he had lost. Williamson refused to change the minutes and the dispute dragged on for months. Eventually the Brittan cabinet offered concessions on another subject in order to obtain partial satisfaction.

Lamy denies stories of the minutes being rewritten. 'It's not by fabricating the minutes that one holds on to power. The minutes of the commission are always approved by the college.'[14] But he has told colleagues that in an efficient system of government the minutes have to be 'managed'.

Delors's network extends beyond the commission. On 28 October 1987, in the aftermath of the biggest stockmarket crash since 1929, Delors addressed the European Parliament:

> *If the Americans are unable to obtain an assurance of increased growth*
> *in Europe, will they not seek to apply pressure by means of the falling*

dollar? . . . Let there be no illusions, the Americans are prepared to let it drop as far as DM1.60.[15]

Delors's words caused the dollar to dip two pfennigs to DM1.73. Several finance ministers rebuked him for speaking out of turn. Lamy appeared in the Brussels press room to say Delors had been misquoted. Then he sent one of Delors's cabinet to the Brussels office of the European Parliament. The envoy hunted down a Monsieur Parfait, the Frenchman who edited reports of parliamentary proceedings, and bullied him into deleting the offending words. The report of 28 October was printed and on the point of distribution – when Lord Henry Plumb, the parliament's British president, discovered Lamy's ruse. He ordered the report's destruction and told Parfait to start again with the true text.

Any official who is French, socialist and competent, with a useful area of expertise, is almost certain to be invited into the Delors network. Anyone with a couple of those qualities would be seriously considered, as long as one of them is competence. Membership varies according to the subject under discussion. 'Often, one doesn't understand why someone argues a particular line – then later on you realise the Delors cabinet had phoned their friends in advance,' says one of Brittan's team.

The 'Delors mafia', as its enemies call it, has strengthened during Delors's second and third commissions. Riccardo Perissich, an able Italian and a Delors loyalist, became director-general for the single market in 1990. Jean-Louis Cadieux, a friend of Lamy's, became deputy director-general for Eastern Europe in the same year. In 1993 Gunter Burghardt, Delors's deputy *chef de cabinet* in his first commission, became head of the new directorate-general for foreign policy.

Delors had less need of a network during his first term as president, when the initial successes bound the commissioners together. Delors could count on senior figures such as Lorenzo Natali, Lord Cockfield and Willy de Clercq to be loyal, and his authority was seldom challenged. In his second term Delors found it harder to make his views prevail. Commissioners who came on board in 1989, when the ship was sailing forwards with a fair wind – such as Leon Brittan, the competition commissioner – felt no special obligation to support the president. Delors missed Natali, who had acted as a peacemaker, and found himself outvoted more often.

For instance in April 1991, during a commission debate on the farm budget, Delors proposed raising the statutory ceiling on farm spending by 1.3 billion ecus (£900 m). He argued it would cost that much to integrate former East Germany into the Common Agricultural Policy. Ray

MacSharry, the farm commissioner, opposed Delors and won the vote. When Delors said he would not defend the result in public, MacSharry asked if he was refusing to accept a collegiate decision. Delors snapped back that he would not take moral lessons from MacSharry. Delors later retaliated by ordering Lamy to break off communications between his cabinet and the Irishman's team. Luckily for Joly Dixon, whose wife worked with MacSharry, the order was soon forgotten.

Delors and his cabinet became increasingly dependent on the network, especially when important tasks had to be carried out rapidly. In July 1989, when the Paris G7 summit asked the commission to coordinate the West's aid to Eastern Europe, Delors mobilised the network rather than the directors-general. The secretariat-general and the president's cabinet wrote most of the budgetary plans which Delors launched in 1987 and 1992. The network drafted the commission's contributions to the inter-governmental conferences of 1986 and 1991. The commissioners did not even see the draft treaty on EMU – published in their name in December 1991 – before they read about it in the newspapers. Delors did not consult other commissioners before making a presentation on European competitiveness to the Copenhagen summit of June 1993.

The Delors cabinet justifies all this centralisation in the name of efficiency. If every commissioner could propose amendments to presidential initiatives, the results would be watered down and meaningless, says one member. 'You can't delegate much while there is no constitutional means of exerting authority.'

Any commissioner who wishes to make a proposal at a commission meeting must – according to the rules – notify the president's cabinet 10 days in advance. This allowed Lamy effective control of the agenda. If he disliked a proposal he would badger the commissioner's cabinet to withdraw it. Only the strongest of commissioners, such as Brittan, generally resisted such pressure.

In France's administrative tradition, geographical and organisational centralisation is regarded as a virtue. *Hauts fonctionnaires* have fewer qualms about the ends justifying the means than they do in some countries. The tradition values strategic thinking.

But Delors and Lamy have done much more than import the French tradition to Brussels. They have transformed a horizontal power structure into a vertical one, resembling a steep pyramid. The secretariat-general, the president's cabinet and Delors form the apex. Brittan is one of the few commissioners to have established a foothold on the upper slopes of the pyramid. The weaker commissioners languish at the bottom, excluded from the decisions which matter.

The commission's physical move at the end of 1991 symbolised its meta-morphosis under Delors. The commission had to leave the Berlaymont – a 1960s block of concrete and glass, famed for its ugliness – because of the health risks of asbestos. Delors had shared the 13th floor of the Berlaymont with other commissioners. But when they moved to the Breydel, a more modern building close by, Delors kept the 12th floor for himself, his cab-inet and the secretary-general. The other commissioners had to make do with floors nine, ten and eleven.

Most of the commissioners, naturally, resent the concentration of power in Delors' hands. Some of them blame him for the frosty ambience – particularly marked during his second and third commissions – among the 17. Some commissioners find it hard to get an appointment to see Delors. Unlike previous presidents, he has not sought to rule through an 'inner cabinet' of the most able commissioners. The president rarely seeks a chat with a commissioner, in order to win his or her support or to tackle a looming problem. If, during a meeting of the college, a commissioner lost an important vote, Delors would not put a hand on his or her shoulder and say, 'let's have a drink'.

However, many of the president's colleagues have been remarkably unsociable. During Delors's second term Frans Andriessen, the external relations commissioner, engaged in turf disputes with half a dozen of his colleagues. Solitary and awkward people such as Manuel Marin (the senior Spaniard), Vasso Papandreou (the Greek commissioner) and Ray MacSharry (the Irish commissioner) were not the sort to go off together for a weekend's hiking in the Ardennes.

Delors accepts the criticism that he is not a team player. 'I don't find enough time in my timetable to see each commissioner. I could organise myself differently and say: "I'll spend 40 per cent of my time seeing com-missioners." ' But he does not plan to do so:

> *If I do that, I don't do other things. And then if I was more collegial, if I surveyed everything, they'd say I was too authoritarian. I surveyed everything from 1985 to 1987 because I had the time. Now I have to receive the prime minister of Croatia, the president of Mali, the head of a big company, and so on.*

Talking to commissioners is clearly not his priority. 'Collegiality doesn't bring ideas. I struggle to gain time to advance ideas, because I think the world advances by ideas.'[16]

Delors complains, with justice, that the EC's governments have seldom sent him their best and brightest. The only stars of the first commission were Cockfield and Sutherland. In the second, only Brittan could match Delors intellectually. Andriessen did not have sufficient imagination, negotiating skills or charisma to make a success of his huge external relations portfolio. The considerable talents of Martin Bangemann, a German who had charge of industry in the second and third commissions, were undermined by a lack of application (in 1993 Bangemann often spent no more than a couple of days a week in Brussels). Two heavyweights of the third commission, Brittan and Van den Broek, spent much of their time scrapping.

Many of Delors's fellow commissioners have been inconsequential politicians who made no mark on their portfolios and have already been forgotten. The appointment of such people gave Delors an excuse for augmenting his own power.

THE GREEN MAN OF BRUSSELS

Delors's intense and tempestuous relationship with Carlo Ripa di Meana – a charming, humorous and flamboyant socialist – revealed how hard he found it to get on with other commissioners. Delors became friends with the Italian in 1979, when both were elected to the European Parliament. In 1985 Ripa became commissioner for cultural and institutional affairs. Although Ripa did not like reading the details of his dossiers, he proved to be one of the few commissioners who stood up to Delors. He urged the president to be more socialist and more federalist.

In 1989 Delors gave Ripa the environmental portfolio, but soon regretted it. Ripa put EC environmental policy on the map by publicising the failure of most governments to follow the rules. When Spain endangered bird habitats by destroying wetlands he took them to the European Court. He prosecuted Britain for breaching EC directives on the purity of drinking water and bathing water.

Public opinion in most member-states welcomed Ripa's efforts to give the Community a green tinge. But the governments being prosecuted were not amused. 'I caused Delors more trouble – especially with Major, Gonzalez and Kohl – than any other commissioner,' Ripa says with pride.[17]

In October 1991 Ripa wrote to Malcolm Rifkind, then Britain's transport minister, asking for work to halt on seven construction projects, pending legal proceedings. Britain had failed to carry out 'environmental impact assessments', as required by EC rules, before authorising projects such as the M3 extension over Twyford Down near Winchester, and a dual carriageway through Oxleas Wood in London. Ripa leaked this letter to the press. An infuriated Major sent a stinging letter to Delors, saying that such interference was 'exactly how the commission should not behave' and that it jeopardised the success of the imminent Maastricht summit.

Relations between Ripa and Delors sank lower in 1992, when Delors tried to apply subsidiarity – the principle that the EC should act only when strictly necessary – to environmental policy. Delors thought Ripa an over-zealous regulator. 'Whenever we discussed subsidiarity in the commission, I saw Delors glaring at me,' he recalls. Delors squashed Ripa's plans for an EC environmental inspectorate. A regulation which would have required industrial firms to carry out environmental audits ended up merely asking governments to set up voluntary audit schemes. 'Lamy torpedoed many of my legislative proposals, filibustering so they did not come to commission,' complains Ripa.

Ripa makes two criticisms of Delors.

> *He aims his politics too much at governments and businessmen. When he was attacked as a scapegoat I told him to use environmental policy as a way of rallying the public behind him. But he didn't want to provoke the governments, it's his* haut fonctionnaire *training. He's out of touch with popular gut-feelings and sympathies.*

Ripa's second complaint is that 'Delors is not very tolerant. He's rather monarchical, and likes yes men more than no men.' As for his entourage,

> *I pay homage to their intense work and knowledge of dossiers. But they were inhuman, people of sheer rationality rather than emotion. So they were not good advisers for Delors. He needs warming up for he is inclined to dry logic.*[18]

The United Nations-sponsored 'Earth Summit', held in Rio de Janeiro in June 1992, damaged Ripa's friendship with Delors irreparably. Ripa was preparing a commission directive for a CO_2 tax, as a means of reducing greenhouse gas emissions.

Ripa claims that Lamy hid from him what Delors and the other EC leaders had agreed in advance of the summit: that the convention on global warming would say little of substance, so that President Bush could sign it. 'When I learned about this diplomacy I realised that Rio would be a display of empty words and hypocrisy', says Ripa, who made a public announce-ment that he would not go. 'The real betrayal was when Lamy persuaded Delors to go instead of me, making me look silly.' In fact Ripa's refusal to go looked silly enough on its own. But he was upset, and when, at the end of June, Giulio Amato offered him the job of environment minister in his new government, Ripa quit the commission.[19]

Ripa had his revenge. His green eyes twinkle with delight when he recalls what befell Delors on 14 June in Rio. The Brazilians' chaotic organisation led to the hour of Delors's speech being shifted several times. Just when they had given Delors a slot at the end of the day, Mitterrand walked into the conference chamber saying 'Where's Delors? I'm going.' Delors had arranged to fly home in Mitterrand's Concorde, and the French president would not wait. Delors took a car to the airport, clutching his undelivered speech. However the driver got lost, so Delors arrived long after Mitterrand. Furious at having to wait, the French president assumed Delors had stayed to give the speech.

Is Delors green? 'He makes an effort, but it's not his vocation,' says Ripa. The Italian notes that Delors supports the philosophy of a balanced ecosystem and the principle of a CO_2 tax. 'But his Roman Catholic background is anthropomorphic so he is not very concerned with animals and plants.'

Ripa says that, although he believes Delors does not like him, he still likes Delors, for 'his honest, stern and courageous commitment to Europe. He has not used his position to promote French interests.'[20] Others disagree.

THE FRENCH CONNECTION

All commissioners, on taking office, swear an oath in the European Court of Justice to serve only European interests. All commissioners break this oath to a greater or lesser degree. A certain amount of responsiveness to national sensibilities is desirable. The institution would probably come up with more unpopular ideas than it does if commissioners did not tell each other which issues were sensitive in their own countries. For instance if officials were preparing a law on the treatment of young bulls, the Spanish commissioners might argue that bullfighting was an intrinsic part of Spain's heritage and should therefore be exempt.

Yet if commissioners were to become mere government agents, the institution could no longer justify its existence. The commission is supposed to be an unbiased ringmaster which considers general rather than particular interests. Governments have their representatives in the Council of Ministers.

The Spanish commissioners are often the most blatantly nationalistic. In November 1992 the commission discussed a proposal of Brittan's that

Spain should not be allowed to build a steel mill in the Basque country because of European overcapacity. Abel Matutes, one of the Spanish commissioners, said he would resign if the proposal went through. The other, Manuel Marin, said he had been on the phone to Felipe Gonzalez and that he had no room for manoeuvre (article 157 of the Treaty of Rome requires commissioners to 'neither seek nor take instructions from any government').

Several commissioners share Cockfield's judgement that 'Delors was better than average' at disregarding his own country's interests. Cockfield remembers the difficulties Delors had in 1987 when he supported Williamson for the secretary-generalship against the French, who wanted to keep the post for themselves.[21] However while Delors may be less nationalistic than many of his colleagues, he has more clout, which has benefited France.

In November 1986 Peter Sutherland, then competition commissioner, tried to make Boussac, a textile firm, repay FFr600 million of aid to the French government. After a heated argument in commission Delors accused Sutherland of trying to destabilise him. He then threatened to resign if his colleagues made Boussac repay the aid. The worried commissioners postponed a decision for six months, pending an outside inquiry into the matter. In the end the commission decided against Boussac but required only FFr340 million to be repaid.

Subsequently Delors has usually had the sense to keep his hands clean. A pattern has emerged whereby his cabinet will argue a forceful French line at meetings of *chefs* or 'special *chefs*', while Delors will remain studiously neutral in commission. Thus when Sutherland and his successor as competition commissioner, Brittan, sought to make Peugeot, Renault and Thomson repay state aid, they had to fight Delors's cabinet rather than Delors himself. But there were occasions – such as Brittan's battles against subsidies to Bull and Péchiney – when Delors stepped in.

In 1991 Brittan proposed a 'communication' which would require state-owned companies to file annual reports to the commission on their relations with shareholders. This would enable the commission to check whether capital injections from governments were disguised state aid. France viewed the proposal as a political onslaught on the public sector. Delors's cabinet opposed the communication but he abstained when the commissioners voted, which allowed it to pass. In 1993 the European Court struck down the measure on the grounds that the commission had exceeded its powers.

Utilities such as Gaz de France and Electricité de France have always found a sympathetic ear in Delors's cabinet. The president never championed the commission's plans to liberalise the gas and electricity markets, which by 1992 had stalled in the Council of Ministers. For much of 1992 Delors's cabinet annoyed Brittan by keeping a white paper on telecommunications deregulation – opposed by France Telecom – off the agenda.

Sutherland reckons that Delors's unleashing of his cabinet in defence of monopolies or subsidies reflects a pro-public service and interventionist ideology, rather than French bias.[22] For instance when Sutherland tried to make Fiat repay state aid, Delors defended the Italian firm. However under Delors's presidency ideology and national bias were hard to untangle, for many of the most controversial state aid cases concerned French firms.

The French sometimes complained that Delors did not give them more support. In 1991 a consortium of France's Aerospatiale and Italy's Alenia tried to buy de Havilland, a Canadian aircraft maker. Brittan, responsible for vetting mergers, said the deal would create a monopoly for some types of small passenger aircraft and should therefore be vetoed. Brittan won the argument in an October commission meeting by one vote – and probably would have lost if Delors had spoken against him. The president said nothing and abstained. French ministers attacked Delors in public and newspapers portrayed him as a creature of Anglo-Saxon liberalism.

Delors had understood the commission's authority was at stake, and that it could not be seen to bow to the wishes of one powerful country. He also saw that Brittan's credibility as competition commissioner was at risk. Delors has often supported senior colleagues in their own fields, even when – as with de Havilland – he disagreed with them on the substance of an argument.

Delors's pragmatism sometimes gets the better of his French or socialist viewpoint. The commission and Japan argued for many years over the level of Japanese car exports to the EC. The deal finally struck in 1991 allows quotas for Japanese cars to rise until 1999, after which there will – in theory – be no controls. Delors thought the European car industry needed stronger protection than the agreement provided. But he saw he could not win the argument against the liberal trio of Andriessen, Bangemann and Brittan, and stood by the deal they negotiated.

If a commissioner argues the same line as a national government, he may not be following instructions. The commissioner and the government may simply share a similar view of the world. This explains much of Delors's behaviour in November 1992, when he tried to block an agreement in the GATT trade talks (see Chapter 8).

'Like many of his compatriots, Delors believes that what is good for France is good for Europe,' says Sir David Hannay, Britain's EC ambassador from 1985 to 1990. Unlike the British, the French have an idea of

Europe and feel self-confident about it, 'so it comes naturally to them, rather than being vainly self-serving, to say that Europe should be as France would wish it to be.'[23]

UNTAMED MONSTER

As Delors's presidency entered its third and final term, in January 1993, commission officials began to speculate that his style of government was doing more harm than good. 'By relying excessively on informal channels, the formal channels have become atrophied and the morale of the senior officials has suffered,' was one view. Such words might be expected from a director-general who had suffered from cronyism. But they came from a long-serving member of the Delors cabinet. He thinks the commission's poor morale in 1992 and 1993 can only partly be blamed on the external shocks – economic recession, the Yugoslav war and Denmark's *Nej* to Maastricht – which damaged the EC. He believes the institution would have better weathered the crisis if the Delors network had not undermined its structures and stability.

A member of the Brittan cabinet says any good president would need a network. 'He cannot rely solely on his fellow commissioners or on directors-general, for some of them will be incompetent, or display national prejudice, or simply not be on the same wavelength.' He says that if Delors is going to brainstorm with the best people he has to use unorthodox channels. But he regrets that Delors has 'established a largely *franco-français* network, thus departing from a truly European spirit.'

Many commission officials believe the power of the cabinets and the networks has increased, is increasing and ought to be diminished. When Delors arrived in Brussels he promised the directors-general he would restore their authority. Yet he has done nothing to restrain the cabinets' power, and in 1989 even increased the size of each from five to six officials.

Today's directors-general are often preparers of files for their commissioners rather than true advisers. The ablest believe they are an under-used resource. Delors seldom consults a director-general on a major initiative unless he is in the network. Delors's speech to the directors-general in February 1991 did nothing for their morale. 'If I could hire and fire, I'd go after at least five or six of you,' he said. 'I know which ones among you don't take me seriously. Here you're all bosses, it's hard to shake you up, but I'll get you none the less.' He even singled out the heads of DGIII and DGIV – two of the ablest directors-general – for criticism. They had provoked Delors's rage by blocking a paper on aid for electronics firms. The outburst had its desired effect: the electronics paper soon passed.[24]

Delors has dabbled with reform at various times during his presidency. In 1991 Carlo Trojan, the Dutch deputy secretary-general, drew up a report on the commission's inadequacies. Its hint that the cabinets had too many staff annoyed enough commissioners to ensure that the report gathered dust. In the summer of 1993 Delors held a series of meetings with the directors-general to discuss the workings of the commission. As a result they won the right to discuss policy initiatives as a group, and a little more power to reorganise their departments.

The president's meagre formal powers undoubtedly make reform of the commission a daunting task. Decisions which national prime ministers would take on their own must, in Brussels, pass the college of 17 commissioners. Yet if Delors had made reform a priority, he could surely have cajoled the commissioners to support him. Other more interesting subjects have always grabbed the president's attention.

Neither Delors nor Lamy nor Williamson has tried to tackle the fundamentals of what is wrong with the commission – whose running costs in 1993 totalled 2.3 billion ecus (£1.8 billion). For instance the number of directorates could be reduced, to prevent duplication of resources. Some of the departments which administer existing policies rather than plan new ones could become autonomous agencies. If the influence of cabinets on promotions was reduced, ability would count for more; an independent appointments body could ensure a fair balance among the nationalities.

Most commissioners have no idea how odious their institution can appear to outsiders – consultants, lobbyists, researchers, business people, recipients of regional aid or anyone searching for information – who have to deal with it. During 1991 and 1992 the senior partner of a leading Brussels law firm sent 25 letters to commissioners and directors-general, on various problems, and had five replies.

The commission is much better at drafting laws and proposing programmes than managing the results. 'Phare' and 'Tacis', which are, respectively, the EC's aid programmes for Eastern Europe and the former Soviet Union, show how much the commission still needs to learn about management. The commission's administration of these programmes – together worth 5 billion ecus (£3.6 billion) in the four years 1990–93 – has been shambolic.

Procedures for project approval are so slow that, by April 1993, only 70 per cent of Tacis's funds for 1991 had been spent. The commission has annoyed the Russians and the East Europeans by refusing to consult them over which consultants should be chosen to run projects. Those hired often receive contracts from the commission 6–12 months after starting work. They are typically paid 3–12 months late. The management of these programmes is so overcentralised that project managers have to refer the minutest of decisions to Brussels – where overworked officials may take months to reply. Phare and Tacis have undoubtedly done some good. But many of the East Europeans and Russians experiencing these programmes complain that the commission's slowness, inefficiency, arrogance and unhelpfulness remind them of their old regimes.[25]

Lamy concedes that the Delors system has concentrated too much on taking short-cuts to get things done.

> *Probably we should have changed the structure of the institution, but we thought it wasn't a priority. The problem is that officials spend too much time managing tasks and not enough time on the tasks themselves. The circuits are too complicated, there's too much paper. The bureaucratic noise of the house is too loud compared with what it produces.*[26]

Lamy has only praise for Williamson but others in the Delors entourage blame the Briton for not trying harder to reform the commission. One says:

> *The cabinet has tried to concentrate on strategy, leaving the management of the house to the secretariat-general. Williamson is a very good transmission channel but, as a typical British civil servant, he hasn't had the strategic vision that would have enabled him to shake up the system.*

Williamson's defenders reply that neither he nor anyone else could have undertaken major reforms without Delors's express support.

The centralisation of the Delors system should be kept in perspective. Brittan says:

> *Compared to the British cabinet, the commission is infinitely less centralised. More information is made available to commissioners than is to British ministers. Delors sometimes loses votes and he doesn't always use his influence to the full: he will often ask the commissioner responsible to introduce a debate, and not speak himself until the end. But he should talk more to colleagues, rather than rely on his cabinet. Their behaviour is not improper, but it can be unattractive and counter-productive.*[27]

Officials outside the network sometimes feel gratitude towards it. One of the ablest directors-general – who has never had a *tête-à-tête* with Delors or Lamy – has had to contend with a weak commissioner and an obstructive cabinet. On several occasions, when the director-general has sought help from a member of the president's cabinet, the obstacle has been removed.

Delors has listened to criticism of his governance:

> *The pyramidal structure became too strong. It's true that Lamy held the system in an iron grip, to change it. But this authoritarianism was necessary for a while, since nothing worked.*

He says that in December 1992, just before the start of his third commission, he asked his cabinet to loosen its grip for two reasons. First, his own authority, inside and outside the commission, had been grievously damaged by the GATT rows of November 1992. Second, 'I wanted to let the new commissioners bloom, to see how it worked out.'[28]

The style of Delors's cabinet had already mellowed, following the departure of Lamoureux in July 1991. His replacement as deputy *chef de cabinet*, Jean-Pierre Jouyet, was a gentler soul. Delors says:

> *After the pyramidal phase there is a phase of relaxing the constraints, to try and get more collegial behaviour. That implies that my collaborators don't reign by terror, that they're a bit more open and that they refer to me before hitting hard.*

By the summer of 1993 Delors was grumbling that the softening had slowed the commission's capacity to take decisions.[29] But the relaxation continued when, in May 1994, Lamy left the commission to take on the number two job at Crédit Lyonnais. Jouyet became *chef de cabinet*.

However much Delors's mind has focused on loftier matters, he has known about the methods used by Lamy and his band and must take responsibility. It is ironic that Delors's public image in many countries is that of an arch-bureaucrat. For Delors is a natural dreamer, thinker, strategist and negotiator, who prefers to leave bureaucracy – and dirty work – to others.

CHAPTER SEVEN

THE PUSH FOR A FEDERAL EUROPE

In the spring of 1986 Tommaso Padoa-Schioppa, a senior Bank of Italy official, visited Delors with a warning. The two men had become friends in 1979 when Padoa-Schioppa had been director-general for economic and monetary affairs in the European Commission, and Delors had been chairman of the European Parliament's economic and monetary committee. Padoa-Schioppa is a leading authority on the economics of EMU. He told Delors that the 1992 programme's provision for the abolition of exchange controls, although desirable *per se*, could weaken the Exchange Rate Mechanism (ERM) of the European Monetary System (EMS) and hence threaten the single market.

The controls had dampened speculation against the ERM's parities. Since the crisis of March 1983, France, Italy, Denmark, Ireland and the Benelux countries had achieved fairly stable exchange rates and a level of inflation that was getting closer to that of West Germany. They had had to subordinate their domestic economic policies to the external discipline of an ERM that was dominated by one member. When the Bundesbank changed its interest rates, the others usually had to follow.

Delors asked Padoa-Schioppa to write a report on the implications of the 1992 programme for the future of the EC. The Padoa-Schioppa Report appeared in April 1987, warning that

> the complete liberalisation of capital movements is inconsistent with the present combination of exchange-rate stability and the considerable national autonomy in the conduct of monetary policy.

The report hinted that it was time to consider EMU: 'Capital mobility and exchange rate fixity together leave no room for independent monetary policies.' Padoa-Schioppa recommended that

> monetary policy coordination and the mechanisms of the EMS will have to be significantly strengthened if freedom of capital movements and exchange rate discipline are to survive and coexist.[1]

This report influenced the 'Basel-Nyborg agreements', signed by finance ministers and central bank governors in September 1987. These sought to strengthen the ERM by improving the rules for central bank cooperation in support of weak currencies.

After the stockmarket crash of 19 October, Delors declared that the storms set off by the dollar's gyrations risked destabilising the EMS. 'The next step can only be the creation of a European central bank ... and the promotion of the ecu as an international reserve currency.' He said the EMS had worked as a D-mark zone for long enough.

> Now the system must become symmetrical: the cost of adjustment must be shared among all the member countries. If the ecu today shared the role of a reserve currency with the dollar and the yen, we would have been able to avoid so many financial, even stockmarket crises.[2]

The project of Economic and Monetary Union had virtually disappeared from the European agenda in the mid-1970s. Early in 1988 it again became intellectually fashionable to talk of EMU. The argument for a single European currency was that people and companies would no longer face the bother and cost of having to change money or take out insurance against currency risk. By making prices more transparent and by freeing companies from the worry of exchange-rate losses, a single currency would promote trade within the EC. It would also encourage investment, for firms would find it easier to calculate their costs several years ahead.

A monetary union that was managed by an independent central bank, as most models assumed, would spread the benefits of low inflation to all its members. A virtuous circle of lower interest rates, higher investment and higher employment would result. The discipline of EMU would prevent governments from making an inflationary dash for growth, either by cutting interest rates or by devaluing.

Those against EMU argued that governments should keep control of interest rates and the exchange rate, so that they could react to the shocks and strains that hit different economies at different times. They feared an independent European central bank would run a deflationary monetary policy, biased against growth. They also thought it undemocratic for politicians to lose control of interest rates.

Opponents of EMU highlighted the differences between the EC and genuine federations. An American state survives an economic depression without devaluing because federal spending cushions the hardship, and because many workers are prepared to move elsewhere. The EC's budget, at about 1 per cent of Community GDP, is too small to make much difference to a recession-hit area, while European labour is less mobile.

The big political argument for EMU was that it would push Europe towards a federal system of government. The big political argument against EMU was that it would push Europe towards a federal system of government.

The debate on the pros and cons of EMU was not a new one. Nevertheless in 1988 a group of West European leaders decided that it was the right moment for the Community to move towards EMU. They did so for four reasons. First, the single-market programme was proving a success. The Community's new-found self-confidence made the pursuit of more ambitious goals seem feasible. Many argued that the absence of a single currency discouraged trade among EC members and thus prevented the market from being truly single.

Second, the agreement on the 'Delors package' in February 1988 gave EC leaders – including Delors – the time to consider fresh objectives. That package doubled the EC's structural funds, making them macroeconomically significant for the poorer members. By 1993 Ireland would depend on those funds for 3 per cent of its GDP. The poorer members would have been reluctant to consider the potentially painful project of EMU without the boost to regional aid.

Third, the stockmarket crash of October 1987 had failed to darken Western Europe's mood of economic optimism. In 1986 oil prices had dropped from $30 to $15 a barrel, giving an extra kick to a worldwide economic boom. Economic confidence reduced fear of the unknown and fear of EMU.

Fourth, many of those running Europe's governments – Kohl, Mitterrand, Gonzalez, Ruud Lubbers of Holland, Wilfried Martens of Belgium, Jacques Santer of Luxembourg and Poul Schluter of Denmark – had been in power since early in the decade. They knew and trusted each other, and Delors. Enthusiastic Europeans, they wanted to make their mark on history.

The Basel-Nyborg agreements provoked a wide-ranging discussion on the future of the ERM. In January 1988 Edouard Balladur, France's finance minister, sent EC governments a memorandum. This argued that too much of the burden of supporting a weak currency fell on the central bank directly concerned, and that a European central bank would resolve the problem. A paper from Giulio Amato, Italy's finance minister, attacked the ERM for imposing deflation on all its members except West Germany. Amato wrote that he would prefer an agreed loss of autonomy, via a European central bank, to an ERM in which West Germany imposed a loss of autonomy on its partners.

West Germany had no obvious interest in abandoning the D-mark, its chief symbol of post-war economic success. Yet Hans-Dietrich Genscher, its foreign minister, believed that West Germany could not run the ERM for ever. His memorandum to governments of February 1988 concluded: 'The creation of a single European monetary zone, with a European central bank, constitutes the economically indispensable centrepiece of a European internal market'. In March Helmut Schmidt and Valéry Giscard d'Estaing unveiled a joint plan for EMU.

Paying another visit to Delors in March 1988, Padoa-Schioppa argued that the EC's draft directive on free capital movements made EMU urgent. He recalls that Delors had doubts over the timing of a push for EMU: 'With the Delors package just through, he was reluctant to open a new front against Thatcher. He thought EMU an imprudent *fuite-en-avant* [precipitate rush].'[3] The Italian changed the Frenchman's mind. Delors says:

> *When I saw the movement accelerating, I said to myself, we need –*
> *following the method which has always worked so well – a committee*
> *which would provide the intellectual and technical framework for subse-*
> *quent political decisions.*[4]

The Spaak Committee had preceded the Treaty of Rome and the Dooge Committee the Single European Act.

Helmut Kohl, whose government held the EC presidency in the first half of 1988, was sceptical about monetary union. Genscher asked him to put the subject on the agenda of the summit that would be held in Hanover in June. However Kohl mistrusted Genscher and it was Delors, during a series of private meetings, who played the key role in converting the chancellor to EMU. On 13 June EC finance ministers agreed to abolish exchange controls, a decision which helped to convince the German government that EMU was feasible.

Genscher proposed a group of five wise men to carry out the preparatory work. Delors preferred a committee of central bank governors. He had attended the governors' monthly meetings since 1985 and knew many of them to be EMU-sceptics. But he thought their technical expertise and economic orthodoxy would add weight to whatever they could agree on. Delors recalls:

> *Kohl invited me round on a Sunday, before the European Council of*
> *Hanover. I persuaded him to go for a committee [of governors], and –*
> *what audacity! – to give me its chair, which was not necessarily what the*
> *governors would want.*[5]

Karl Otto Pöhl, president of the Bundesbank from 1980 to 1991, complains of Delors and Kohl deceiving him over the creation of the Delors

Committee. He recalls attending a meeting of a German cabinet committee shortly before the Hanover summit. He says Kohl told him the government line in Hanover would be either to follow Genscher's idea, and let the wise men write a report which could be forgotten; or to ask the central bank governors to make limited technical proposals on how to improve monetary coordination, as a step towards EMU. 'Then I dined with Delors in Brussels, and told him about these ideas, and I thought we were all agreed on one of these low-key ways forward,' says Pöhl.[6]

On the first evening of the summit, 27 June, Kohl hosted a dinner in Schloss Hernhausen. The commission president introduced a discussion on EMU, which ended with Kohl proposing that Delors should chair a committee. Neither Thatcher, caught off guard, nor anyone else opposed the proposal outright. Kohl asked Delors to prepare some formal conclusions for the following day.

Most of Delors's text got through, although Thatcher cut out references to a single currency and a central bank.

> *The European Council recalls that, in adopting the Single Act, the member states confirmed the objective of the progressive realisation of economic and monetary union. They therefore decided to examine at the European Council meeting in Madrid in June 1989 the means of achieving this union. To that end they decided to entrust to a committee the task of studying and proposing concrete steps leading towards this union. The committee will be chaired by Jacques Delors.*

The committee would consist of the 12 central bank governors, acting in a personal capacity, supplemented by Frans Andriessen, a commissioner, Miguel Boyer, a Spanish banker and former finance minister, Alexandre Lamfalussy, the Belgian general manager of the Bank for International Settlements (BIS) and Niels Thygesen, a Danish economist. Delors had suggested these extra names to counterbalance the scepticism of some governors.

Thatcher declared at her press conference that there was no prospect of EMU in her lifetime. According to Charles Powell, her diplomatic adviser, she swallowed the conclusions because

> *we thought the Delors Committee was a good way of sidelining the idea. We expected the governors to be sceptical and to keep the wide-eyed commission officials out. They disappointed. Kohl told us it was just a committee. We underestimated the other side.*[7]

On hearing about the Delors Committee, Pöhl raged that his government had, he thought, reneged on an agreed policy.

> *My first instincts were, I won't sit on this heterogeneous committee. Why is Delors in the chair? He's not an expert, the Rome treaty gives the commission no competence in monetary policy – I was against two commission guys on the committee.*

Pöhl's Bundesbank colleagues persuaded him that he should take part in order to make sure the committee produced nothing ridiculous, and to avoid insulting the governments of Europe.

Pöhl says he thought about resigning from the Bundesbank, but did not because he had just been reappointed. Pöhl now judges it

> *a mistake to take part in the Delors Committee, I couldn't defend German interests. If I had boycotted it I could not have stopped the process, but I could have slowed it down. I would have been freer to criticise the Delors Report.[8]*

Delors and Pöhl, who feuded throughout the negotiations on EMU, were not cut out to be friends. Pöhl is a cosmopolitan *bon vivant* who turns up at meetings with his golf clubs or his skis. He sports a tan 12 months a year. Nobody has ever suspected Delors of being tanned. Pöhl does not share Delors's enthusiasm for details and dossiers, but often gets his way through sheer brilliance and force of personality.

Pöhl says:

> *Like a lot of French bureaucrats Delors does not understand market mechanisms, he believes in administration. Like Kohl and Mitterrand, he believes in a moral drive for European integration, derived from World War Two. But this view is based on circumstances which are out of date.*

Pöhl wants a looser, liberal, decentralised European Union, but he never teamed up with Thatcher because he disliked her nationalism and believed that sovereignty was limited in a modern economy.[9]

THE DELORS COMMITTEE

The Delors Committee met eight times between September 1988 and April 1989, at the Basel offices of the BIS. The committee's technical brief

– to examine what EMU should look like and how the Community should get there – ignored the question of whether EMU was desirable. This enabled the committee to work fast and helped sceptics such as Pöhl and Robin Leigh-Pemberton (the governor of the Bank of England) to play a full part in the discussions.

Delors proposed Padoa-Schioppa as the *rapporteur* (secretary) who would draft the text. Pöhl objected that the Italian was too committed to EMU and insisted on Gunter Baer, a German official with the BIS, sharing the job. Pöhl showed his disapproval of Delors being in the chair by reading newspapers throughout the first meeting.

Delors knew that several governors resented his presence and set about winning their confidence. For the first two meetings he limited the agenda to a discussion of basic principles and of what had gone wrong with previous attempts at EMU. The governors began to realise that the chairman was not going to ram a blueprint down their throats. Delors says it made a difference when 'we decided to speak only in English, so they did not have to wear headphones. This speeded up the discussion and put them at ease.'[10]

There were two theories on how to approach EMU. The 'pragmatists' proposed a series of small steps. Jacques de Larosière, the governor of the Banque de France, suggested the immediate creation of a European Reserve Fund. Working together in this forum, the central banks would learn to collaborate on monetary policy. The fund would manage some of the central banks' currency reserves. The presence of this institution would give the goal of EMU credibility, and in the long run it would evolve into the European Central Bank (ECB).

While the pragmatists emphasised the need for action and coordination, the 'fundamentalists' focused on the final shape of the institutions and on the need for a new treaty. They wanted a Bundesbank-style ECB to have sole responsibility for monetary policy. They feared that if the ECB had to share authority with national central banks, chaos and inflation would ensue. The fundamentalists opposed making the ecu a genuinely new currency (as opposed to a basket of existing ones) during the transition to EMU, lest it complicate control of the money supply.

De Larosière and Carlo Azeglio Ciampi, governor of the Bank of Italy, feared that such an 'all or nothing' approach would make the passage to full monetary union hard to achieve. But Pöhl soon made it clear that West Germany would accept nothing less than a fundamentalist model of EMU. And since EMU would get nowhere without German support, the pragmatists realised the report would have to be fundamentalist.

Delors's chairing impressed the governors. De Larosière says:

He summed up debates with extreme skill and objectivity. He did not preside in an authoritarian manner, trying to influence the governors in a particular direction. He became more active when we got down to the details of editing the report.[11]

Even Pöhl says Delors helped to create a good atmosphere:

Delors was more flexible than I expected and my concerns did not fully materialise. The substance of the report came from the governors, not Delors. His contribution was small but we made him famous.[12]

Pass that on to Delors, and he exclaims:

I'm delighted Pöhl says that, because if he'd said: 'It's a scandal, Delors wanted to impose his own project,' we wouldn't have got the report ... One of the great ways to make progress when your own authority is not unquestioned is to get others to promote your ideas.[13]

Delors influenced the report by asking allies such as Ciampi, de Larosière or Thygesen to speak on his behalf, and by working with the two *rapporteurs*. Before each session of the committee, Delors spent a day with Padoa-Schioppa, Baer and Joly Dixon, his adviser on EMU. Together they debated tactics and pored over proposals and drafts.

Padoa-Schioppa's expertise as a monetary economist and central banker gave him a pre-eminent role in shaping Delors's thinking and the report. Once he and Delors saw the committee taking a fundamentalist approach, they sketched the kind of report they wanted and, in the end, were fairly happy with what emerged.

Padoa-Schioppa says:

The governors were inherently suspicious of politicians and the commission. But Delors encouraged their professionalism to get the better of their mistrust. By the end they saw themselves as engineers who had been asked to design a car and were keen to make a good job of it.[14]

Delors contributed to the report's emphasis on 'parallelism' – the need for economic union and monetary union to proceed at the same pace. When the Community had discussed EMU in the early 1970s, the Germans had said that economic convergence should precede monetary union, while the French had claimed that the latter would bring about the former. The Delors Report compromised between these two schools of thought. Delors stressed the importance of convergence in the first phase of EMU, which would, he hoped, allow the problematic transitional phase to be a short one. 'The message of the report is that so long as there is no convergence of economic policies it is impossible to move to the last phase,' says Delors.[15]

But Delors and Padoa-Schioppa did not get it all their own way. Pöhl insisted on 'binding rules' to restrict government budget deficits in the final phase of EMU. The Germans feared that without binding rules a country such as Italy would be free to go on a borrowing binge and force up interest rates throughout the EC. They also feared that such a country could put pressure on the ECB to loosen monetary policy and lessen the burden of its interest payments. Delors thought binding rules would be unenforceable.

At the penultimate meeting of the Delors Committee, in March 1989, Pöhl attacked parts of the draft report which he had already approved and threatened not to sign the final version. He even questioned the need for a revision of the EC treaties. The governors assumed that the Bundesbank council had complained to Pöhl about the draft. To pacify Pöhl the governors agreed on a few changes, including a downgrading of the role foreseen for the ecu.

'It was suspense until the last moment, it was very difficult with Pöhl,' says Delors, who had worried about him throughout the committee's work. 'Sometimes he was intransigent and we wondered if he was going to block, sometimes he was cooperative.' Delors treated Pöhl with kid gloves. 'I didn't try to isolate Pöhl and I took into account what he said, which was sometimes very useful.'[16]

The Delors Report, published on 17 April 1989, proposed a three-stage passage to EMU.

> *The creation of an economic and monetary union must be viewed as a single process. Although this process is set out in stages which guide the progressive movement to the final objective, the decision to enter upon the first stage should be a decision to embark on the entire process.*

The report proposed that stage one should start on 1 July 1990 – the date by which eight governments had promised to liberalise capital flows. Stage one would involve the completion of the internal market and the reinforcing of the EC's competition policy and regional policy. All member-states would join the ERM. The finance ministers would agree on new procedures for coordinating macroeconomic policy and the committee of central bank governors would be strengthened.

Phase two would not start before a new treaty had been agreed and ratified. A European Central Bank would then prepare the ground for the final phase of EMU. Its governing council would consist of EC central bank governors and the full-time members of its board. The bank would issue guidelines on monetary policy but governments would have the last word on interest rates. The ECB would manage some foreign-currency reserves on behalf of its members. Exchange rate adjustments would become increasingly rare. The bands within which ERM currencies fluctuated would narrow. Finance ministers would step up their surveillance of each other's economies.

In phase three exchange rates would be permanently fixed. Soon afterwards a single currency would replace national currencies. An ECB committed to price stability would set interest rates and manage the Community's exchange rate policy. Although independent, the ECB would make regular reports to the European Parliament and to the European Council. The finance ministers would agree on broad economic policies, including a coordinated fiscal stance to balance the ECB's monetary policy. Binding rules would prevent governments from over-borrowing. Much of this EMU blueprint would end up in the Treaty of Maastricht.

Most governments welcomed the Delors Report, although Nigel Lawson, Britain's chancellor of the exchequer, described it as 'totally flawed'. Delors regained the self-confidence which Thatcher's Bruges speech of the previous September had knocked out of him. His vision stretched beyond EMU and he saw no reason to wait for Britain. 'We could have a Europe with concentric circles, with at the centre those who want to go the furthest, that is to say to political union,' he told Le Figaro. Would that be without Britain? 'It's for that country to decide. But there could be a second circle open to those who don't want to go as far as political union.' The first phase of the EC's history, from 1950 to 1982, had been based on Schuman's leitmotif, 'never again war between us'. Since 1984 'there has been my idea that "union is necessary to guarantee survival".' Without that union, 'our countries will turn into museums for the Japanese and Americans to visit.'[17]

Just before the Madrid summit of 26 and 27 June, Spain joined the ERM, leaving only Portugal, Greece and Britain outside. In Madrid Thatcher agreed that the pound would join when a set of conditions – including the completion of the single market and a reduction of Britain's inflation rate – had been met. Only resignation threats from Nigel Lawson and Geoffrey Howe, her two senior ministers, had forced this modest concession from Thatcher. But it won her the goodwill of Kohl, who blocked Mitterrand's bid to set a date for the start of an inter-governmental conference (IGC) on EMU.

The conclusions of the Madrid summit noted that the Delors Report, 'which defined a process designed to lead by stages to EMU, fulfilled the mandate given in Hanover.' The EC's institutions were asked to prepare for stage one, which would start on 1 July 1990. An IGC would lay down the subsequent stages and 'would meet once the first stage had begun and would be preceded by full and adequate preparation.'

The references to an IGC and to EMU's later phases pleased Delors. At his press conference he played on Thatcher's hostility to the principle that accepting phase one implied a commitment to the later phases. 'The political strip-tease includes several stages and there is no automatic link between them.' He meant that Thatcher's would, in the end, reveal her acceptance of EMU. 'The movement has begun and it seems irreversible.'

At her press conference Thatcher declared that when a future summit voted on the holding of an IGC, she would almost certainly vote no, and that she would almost certainly lose the vote. She added that when the conference began she would not leave an empty chair. After the summit she complained to friends that she had agreed to the Delors Committee because the Foreign Office had told her its conclusions would not matter; yet the Foreign Office was now warning that Britain had to take part in further work on EMU lest the others leave it behind.

HISTORY ACCELERATES

During the four years which followed the Milan summit of June 1985, the Community's own agenda – the 1992 programme, the Single Act and plans for EMU – drove it forwards. After the Madrid summit of June 1989, upheavals in the wider world tossed the EC towards the unknown. An orderly and predictable march towards monetary union became confused with a disorganised bolt towards 'political union'.

This ill-defined concept had five ingredients. The plan for EMU would require new institutions and amendments to the EC treaties. Federalists saw a chance to tack on other reforms at the same time.

Concern about a 'democratic deficit' – the idea that the commission and the Council of Ministers were largely unaccountable – provided a second ingredient. National parliaments could not control legislation which the Council of Ministers decided by majority vote, while the powers of the European Parliament remained limited. The West German, Italian, Belgian and Dutch governments thought more power for the European Parliament would solve the problem.

Third, the East European revolutions persuaded several of the 12 that they should improve their coordination of foreign policy. By the summer of 1989 the combination of glasnost and economic failure had undermined the foundations of Soviet communism. Hungary and Poland were becoming democratic but needed Western help to build market economies.

In July President Mitterrand hosted a G7 summit in the newly built Arche de la Défense. George Bush proposed that the European Commission should coordinate the West's aid to Poland and Hungary. So the commission became a clearing house between the 'Group of 24', the rich countries which had pledged help, and the governments which needed it. The Group of 24 extended its aid to each successive East European state which overthrew communism. The commission also managed 'Phare', the EC's own programme of technical assistance for Eastern Europe.

The upheavals in Eastern Europe brought home to Delors, Mitterrand and Kohl, among others, that the EC, although an economic giant, remained a political pigmy. The 12's procedures for coordinating foreign policy seemed ill-suited to the new challenges. The EC covered only the economic side of external relations: trade and aid. European Political Cooperation (EPC) had responsibility for diplomacy. A committee of 'political directors' – senior diplomats based in national capitals – and a six-man Brussels secretariat managed EPC. This shadowy organisation responded to world events by issuing statements – which, since they had to satisfy 12 governments, were invariably of the bland 'the Community and its member-states deplores/welcomes/notes with concern' variety. The commission had the right to take part in meetings of EPC, but not to make proposals.

European Political Cooperation lacked the capacity to react speedily, take initiatives or plan ahead. Its presidency shifted from one member to another every six months, like that of the EC. Governments in other parts of the world found the separation between EPC and the Community confusing, and sometimes complained that they did not know who they were supposed to talk to. If the 12 foreign ministers stopped talking about trade with Hungary, and started talking about its human rights, their legal framework would switch from one body to the other; the EC ambassadors would have to vacate their seats beside each minister to the political directors.

The changes in Eastern Europe made this distinction increasingly anachronistic. By the end of 1989 officials of the EC and EPC were holding joint meetings on Eastern Europe. Britain regarded such pragmatism as proof that the foreign-policy machinery of the 12 was in good order. Delors believed structural reforms to be essential. He thought a greater commission role in diplomacy would help to bind the two sides into a coherent whole. In any case, the Single European Act required a review of EPC in 1992.

Austria applied to join the EC in July 1989. The growing pressure on the 12 to admit new members became a fourth argument for political union. Delors wanted to postpone enlargement, believing there was a contradiction between 'deepening' – the development of federal institutions – and widening. He feared new arrivals would distract the EC from its federal plans and render decision making more difficult. Furthermore, several potential newcomers – Austria, Sweden, Finland and Switzerland – were neutral. Delors worried that neutral members would impede the development of common defence policies (the EC already had one neutral member, but Delors thought the Irish were sufficiently *communautaire* not to create difficulties).

In January 1989, when he had known that membership applications were in the offing, Delors unveiled a scheme which would, he hoped, defer them. Speaking in the European Parliament, he proposed 'a new more structured relationship, with common decision making and administrative institutions' between the EC and the seven countries of the European Free Trade Association (EFTA). They would join the single market but not the Community as a whole.[18] The EFTA countries picked up the challenge and talks on a 'European Economic Area' (EEA) began in December 1989.

Throughout 1989 Delors canvassed the idea of a 'Europe of concentric circles'. He envisaged the 12 – or most of them – at the centre, moving towards a federal government, surrounded by the broader EEA, and a vaguely defined third circle of East Europeans.[19] Delors appeared untroubled that the geographical extent of the 12-nation EC did not correspond to any genuine social, cultural or historical definition of Europe, of the sort which might, in the long term, form the basis of a federation.

The invention of the EEA failed to stop EFTA governments from considering full membership. Most of them thought that if they had to swallow EC rules on the single market, they would be better off with the right to vote on those rules. By the autumn of 1989 Delors realised that even the East Europeans might one day apply. So he thought it urgent to reinforce the EC's institutions before new members joined the club.

The collapse of East Germany gave political union a fifth and decisive push. Without Germany's movement to reunification, political union would have been a more modest enterprise that arrived later. In the summer of 1989, tens of thousands of East Germans fled to West Germany via Hungary. By September it seemed possible that East Germany and perhaps Czechoslovakia would follow the democratic path of Poland and

Hungary. Sooner than most non-German politicians, Delors realised that the Germans might unite, and that if they did, European integration could profit. Some Germans had worried that a closer union in Western Europe would make it harder for the two halves of their country to come together, and had therefore resisted the idea. German unification would remove that objection to a more federal Community.

Delors understood that Germany held the key to the EC's future. Only the Germans could thwart his plans for EMU, for no currency union could be credible without them. Furthermore, Germany provided the link between monetary union and institutional reform. Many Germans said they did not want to give up their monetary sovereignty, by abandoning the D-mark, unless other countries ceded political sovereignty to Community institutions. Kohl had a particular obsession with increasing the powers of the European Parliament. Even the Bundesbank argued that monetary union could not work without political union, on the grounds that it would require central controls on fiscal policy and huge transfers to the EC's poorer regions.

In a series of speeches between October 1989 and January 1990, Delors provoked a debate on the European constitution. In Bonn, on 5 October, Delors praised the Germans for their contributions to the EC, such as monetary stability, the social market economy and the principles of federalism and subsidiarity. The EC offered 'the most realistic framework' for considering the German question. 'Our Community, your Community has a rendezvous with all the Germans.' He called for the coming treaty revision to look beyond EMU:

> There will be no solutions to the problems of economic and monetary union without, in parallel and at the same time, institutional changes which guarantee the democratic and political balance of the Community. This means reducing the democratic deficit of our institutions, which deepens as the Community executive becomes more efficient and stronger.[20]

On 17 October, at the College of Europe in Bruges, Delors delivered a counterblast to the speech Thatcher had made a year earlier in the same place. Thatcher's seven-page speech had been to the point and limited in scope. Delors's discursive and convoluted reply, much of which he wrote himself, ran to 40 pages and contained the essence of his personal and political philosophy. He began by praising Emmanuel Mounier, 'whose stature will grow again as the Europeans become aware that frantic individualism leads to a dead end, just as they have for several years rejected the collectivism of the state which tutors every person and every thing'.

The word history appeared 13 times, usually with a capital H.

> *History doesn't wait. Faced with the huge upheavals which shake the world, and particularly in the other Europe, it is vital that the Community, strong with its rediscovered dynamism, reinforces its cohesion and gives itself objectives which match the scale of the challenges which History has recently thrown at us.*

Delors made an unabashed plea for EC institutions to have more power:

> *Power is not destined to be the opponent of liberty. The Community, and the peoples and nations which compose it, will not truly exist unless it has the means to defend its values and . . . to be generous. Let's be powerful enough to make ourselves respected and to promote our values of liberty and solidarity.*

He soared into a flight of Mounierist dialectics – of the sort guaranteed to put off most Anglo-Saxons. He said that having often linked the concept of power with the demands of necessity, he now wanted

> *to restore it to the service of the ideal. For where will the pressure of necessity lead without a vision of what we want to accomplish? And equally, what bearing would an ideal have without the willpower and the means to act? The moment has come to reconcile explicitly the necessity and the ideal.*

The vision and the willpower had to come from the commission.

> *There's only room in History for those who see far and wide. That's why the founding fathers of Europe are still present today, by their inspiration and by the heritage they've passed down to us . . . Our Community is not only the fruit of history and necessity, but also of willpower.*

The EC should not try and become a United States of Europe on the American model because

> *we have to unite old nations, strong in their tradition and personality. So there's no plot against the nation, no one's being asked to give up a*

legitimate patriotism ... [But] is it sacrilege to wish that each Euro-
pean should have the feeling of belonging to a Community which would
be, to some degree, his second patrie?

The collapse of communism required the 12 to strengthen their bonds, so they could aid economic reform in Eastern Europe and 'at the right moment, deal with the German question.' Delors said that Germany's partners would be less afraid of reunification if the EC's institutions were strengthened. Though he did not say so explicitly, Delors meant that a Germany shackled by common foreign policies would be unable to bully and frighten its neighbours.

How can we prepare the way towards a solution, if not in reinforcing
certain of the Community's federalist traits which can offer everyone a
guarantee of their own existence? There we find the only acceptable and
satisfactory response to the German question.

Delors quoted Genscher saying that Germany should never be an obsta-cle to European prosperity, and that it should behave in ways which appeared beneficial to everyone. That was Delors's way of warning the Germans to sign up for EMU rather than become mesmerised by events in the East.

History is accelerating. So must we ... I have always followed the
politics of small steps ... But now I'm distancing myself from that
because time is running out. A qualitative jump is necessary, in both our
conception of the Community and in how we deal with the outside world.

The existing institutions and procedures were 'insufficient for us to be able to respond to the accelerations of History.'[21]

THE GERMAN QUESTION

On 9 November 1989, the breach of the Berlin Wall signalled the end of East Germany's communist regime. Amid the excitement and uncertainty – would there be two Germanies or one? – Kohl hesitated over committing his country to EMU. On 4 November he had told Mitterrand that he would not let December's Strasbourg summit set a date of autumn 1990 for the start of the inter-governmental conference. With a general election due in November 1990, Kohl worried that the far-right Republicans would cam-paign to save the D-mark if an IGC had already begun.

Influential Germans such as Rudolf Augstein, the editor of *Der Spiegel*, argued that German unity rather than European unity should be the priority. They feared that novelties such as EMU or a common security policy could make it harder for Poland and Hungary to join the EC. Pöhl and Theo Waigel, West Germany's finance minister, opposed setting a date for an IGC. Waigel said that a slower pace would allow the EC to gain experience of EMU's first phase and give Britain time to catch up. The governments of Denmark, Holland and Luxembourg agreed with Waigel.

The French, Italian, Spanish and Belgian governments backed Delors' call for a date to be set. Genscher argued that faster EC integration would calm fears of Germany's reunification and cement its western orientation. The EMU enthusiasts pointed to apparent support from Europe's business people. In September the Association for the Monetary Union of Europe had published a poll of 1428 senior managers in the EC's seven largest economies. Overall, 76 per cent favoured a single currency, while 69 per cent of German managers and 65 per cent of the British did so.

In November John Major, Britain's new Chancellor of the Exchequer, unveiled a plan whereby, after the first phase of EMU, each government would dismantle restrictions on the use of other EC currencies. They would compete to lower inflation in order to discourage their citizens from using other currencies. This 'competing currency' plan won no support, even from cautious Germans such as Pöhl and Waigel, for it was incompatible with fixed exchange rates and therefore EMU.

West German television asked Delors if East Germany's desire to join the EC worried him. '*Ich habe keine Angst* [I have no fear],' he replied in German. But would it matter if there were two Germanies in the EC? Delors said all was possible and it was for the Germans to choose. 'You've done so much for Europe, continue with us. What a beautiful ideal we have to fulfil.'[22] These words made Delors extremely popular in Germany. The Germans noted that while Thatcher, Mitterrand and Andreotti had evident doubts about the desirability of German unification, Delors had none.

Mitterrand, no less worried than Delors by West Germany's wobbling on the IGC, summoned EC leaders to an Elysée dinner on 17 November. He put Eastern Europe on the agenda so that the Strasbourg summit would be free to tackle EMU. Mitterrand launched the idea of a European Bank for Reconstruction and Development, while a billion ecus of aid was approved for Poland and Hungary. The leaders did not discuss German unity but Kohl gave assurances that events in the East would not weaken West Germany's commitment to European integration.

The following week Delors warned the European Parliament that if a 20-member Community kept the same institutions it would be 'paralysed by waffle'. The answer, he suggested, would be weekly meetings in Brussels of deputy prime ministers, or – his personal preference – the transformation of the commission into a stronger political executive with fewer members. 'We need – oh horror! – to centralise more powers on the executive, and we need a stronger democratic control.' The Council of Ministers would become a senate-style revising chamber. He asked the Euro-MPs if there should be one IGC or two – with one for EMU and the other for broader issues. He said if there were two the second should follow the EMU conference by three or four years.[23]

After 28 November, when Kohl unveiled a 10-point plan for German unity, it seemed unlikely that East Germany would remain a separate state. Kohl had neglected to consult his partners about the plan, which said nothing of NATO or the EC and worried both Mitterrand and Thatcher. Charles Powell says:

> From September 1989 until March 1990 there was a Franco-British alliance which tried to slow down German unity. We saw German unity in terms of the balance of power, so we didn't want to tie it down [through political union]. We wanted to construct a framework for containing the dominant power.[24]

In early December, in an apparent bid to slow down German reunification, Mitterrand visited Mikhael Gorbachev in Kiev and Egon Krenze, the East German leader, in East Berlin.

The Strasbourg summit opened on 8 December with the Franco-German relationship under great strain – and Delors warning of a serious crisis if no date was set for the IGC. Over a disputatious dinner at the end of the first day, Kohl refused to promise that he would make an unambiguous statement to respect the Oder-Neisse line, the frontier between East Germany and Poland. Kohl's argument that German public opinion was not yet ready provoked Mitterrand, Thatcher, Lubbers and Andreotti to anger. Delors liked Kohl's pandering to the extreme right no better and, after the dinner, told colleagues that he did not know if he could remain friends with the Chancellor.

The next day Kohl got most of what he wanted in the summit conclusions:

> The German people will gain its unity through free self-determination ... This process should take place freely and democratically, in full respect of the relevant agreements and treaties and all the principles defined by the Helsinki Final Act; it also has to be placed in a context of European integration.

These qualifications meant that Germany would respect the 'Berlin agreements', signed by the four powers which had occupied that city, and the Helsinki accords, with their insistence on the sanctity of frontiers.

In return for that endorsement of German unity, Kohl ceded to Mitterrand on monetary union. An inter-governmental conference on EMU would convene before the end of 1990. The summit also agreed to offer each East European democracy a 'Europe Agreement', which would entail improved access to EC markets.

The Strasbourg air was thick with talk of constitutional change. The Danes wanted stronger social and environmental policies and the Italians more power for the European Parliament. Enrique Baron, that body's president, presented a list of demands for institutional reform. Yet the summit conclusions ignored these ideas – except for the suggestion, inserted at Kohl's insistence, that the parliament elected in 1994 should have more power. This lack of progress annoyed Delors, as did his joint press conference with Mitterrand, who would not let him answer a single question.

The French had kept constitutional change off the agenda. Horst Teltschik, Kohl's diplomatic adviser, says Germany offered Mitterrand a rough plan for 'political union' at the end of October, but that he was only interested in a date for the EMU conference. Teltschik says:

> We knew the French and British were mistrustful of reunification, so we thought the only convincing answer was to accelerate EC integration. I told the French: 'If you're afraid of us, go for deepening, we could not refuse anything you care to propose on integration.' They never got back to us.[25]

At the end of December Mitterrand launched a plan for a European Confederation that would span the continent.

HUBRIS

In the New Year of 1990 the movement to political union gathered momentum, the Strasbourg summit notwithstanding. Delors, like Icarus before him, appeared to believe he had wings. His self-confidence soared to new – and dangerous – heights. He believed the Community capable of a leap towards closer union and no longer thought constitutional reform could wait. In January he told the European Parliament that the IGC should have two halves – one for EMU, the other for institutional questions – under a single presidency.[26] Although he did not say so in public, he let it be known that he would be the ideal person to preside over such a twin conference.

Delors plumped for parallel rather than consecutive IGCs because Kohl insisted that the Germans would not accept EMU without political union, and because German reunification now seemed almost certain. 'I don't want my country to fall back into various temptations,' Kohl confided to Delors, explaining why German and European unification had to go hand in hand. In a coordinated move, Kohl followed Delors's Strasbourg speech with one in Paris in which he called for a second IGC. 'The common German home should be built under a common European roof,' said Kohl. Both Ireland, the EC president in the first half of 1990, and Italy, the following president, welcomed the idea of a second IGC.

On 23 January Delors appeared on *L'Heure de Vérité*, a French television programme, in buoyant form. The programme's own opinion poll revealed that Delors had overtaken Rocard to become the most popular politician in France. Delors hand-picked a studio audience of socialist ministers, trade union leaders and centrist politicians such as Simone Veil and Bernard Bosson. Delors had also invited his fellow commissioners, perhaps to show that he could run a coalition of diverse political families. When Delors said he did not mind being called a Christian democrat, many assumed that he was launching a bid for the presidency, based on an alliance of socialists and centrists.

However Delors spoke mainly about Europe.

> *My objective is that before the end of the millenium [Europe] should have a true federation. [The commission should become] a political executive which can define essential common interests ... responsible before the European Parliamant and before the nation-states represented how you will, by the European Council or by a second chamber of national parliaments.*

For the first time in his life, Delors said, he was using the word federal, because the world was changing so fast and because Mitterrand's broader confederation would only work if the 12 first 'delegated important powers of sovereignty to the centre.' He implied the East Europeans and EFTA countries would be confined to the confederation: 'I don't see how we could build this greater Europe, the European home of Gorbachev, without a solid pier, and this solid pier is the Community of 12.'

When asked what Mitterrand thought of these ideas, Delors became haughty: 'I don't have to consult François Mitterrand before taking an initiative.' He said that would be incompatible with his European role. But he found plenty of fault in Mitterrandian France, criticising the president's '*ni-ni*' rule – that there should be neither nationalisation nor privatisation – for starving enterprises of private capital.

Delors sought to reassure those who feared German unity. 'If Germany's outside Europe, what will become of it? Then our nightmares might really come true.' Letting drop that he was 'with my colleagues in the commission the trustee of European history,' Delors explained that the Treaty of Rome laid down East Germany's right to join the EC. He said that if the French had lost Aquitaine and Midi-Pyrenées during the war, they would have a similar desire for reunification. 'The East Germans are Germans like the West Germans; their case [for joining the EC] is different from the Austrians and the Norwegians.'[27]

Ian Davidson, a *Financial Times* columnist, noted perceptively that Delors was 'virtually going over the heads of the member-states in defining, for Europe's voters, the terms of the agenda and the debate.' Davidson thought this would create problems with the member-states. 'For his own good, Delors is overdoing the vision bit.'[28]

Delors's enemies in the Parti Socialiste snarled at his self-importance. Jean-Pierre Chevènement, the Europhobic defence minister – described by Delors during the programme as 'a desperate case' – declared: 'Jacques Delors expressed himself like a head of government yet he is just a senior civil servant.'[29]

Delors's performance coincided with a growing sentiment in many parts of the French government, including the Elysée, that he had become too cocky. The commission's increasing authority and influence in areas such as the environment, competition policy and the single market, as well as constitutional matters, had annoyed politicians and civil servants in France, as in Britain. During the course of 1990, the French and British governments led a discreet revolt against Delors and the commission.

Scenting the change of climate, Delors became less assertive while governments debated the future of the Community's institutions. He cancelled a commission blueprint for political union that had been due to appear in April. He made no speeches on political union until November 1991.

Delors's intellectual abstinence failed to convince many governments that they should treat the commission more tenderly. But while he lay low others took up the battle for political union. In March the European Parliament approved a report by David Martin, a Labour Euro-MP. This demanded, for the parliament, the right to propose laws (thus depriving the commission of its monopoly of initiative); to have an equal say with the Council of Ministers on legislation ('codecision'); to approve each new set of commissioners, and to sack individual ones; and to veto trade agreements and treaty changes. The Martin Report also called for stronger social and environmental policies and more majority voting in the Council of Ministers.

This report – relatively moderate, given the parliament's tendency to inhabit cloud cuckoo land – influenced several governments. A memorandum from Mark Eyskens, Belgium's foreign minister, which picked up many of the parliamentary demands, added proposals for common foreign policies and an EC role in defence. The Irish announced that a special summit would meet in Dublin, on 28 April, to tackle German unity and political union.

The Martin Report, the Eyskens memorandum and Delors's own thinking focused on the reform of existing institutions, rather than final goals. Kohl sympathised with this institutional approach, but Mitterrand did not.

'The Brussels institutions saw political union as more power for them, but we thought we should begin not with a how, but with what do we want to do together?' says Elizabeth Guigou, then Mitterrand's adviser on Europe.[30] Mitterrand's answer to his own question was common foreign and security policy. As for how, he wanted supranational institutions to have a smaller role.

Kohl had to work hard to gain Mitterrand's support for a joint initiative on political union. He bought Mitterrand's argument that, because of the potential instability of Eastern Europe, the 12 should tighten their bonds and become a strong anchor for the new democracies. Mitterrand accepted Kohl's view that political union should help the European Parliament. He also came round to the argument of Kohl and Delors that it should constrain Germany's freedom. By the spring of 1990, every EC member whose frontiers touched Germany – Denmark, Holland, Belgium, Luxembourg and France – wanted to tie it down.

On 18 April Kohl and Mitterrand published a joint letter, calling for the transformation of relations among the states into a European Union. The letter suggested that a second inter-governmental conference should run parallel to that on EMU and have four tasks: to reinforce the EC's 'democratic legitimacy'; to make the institutions more effective; to ensure the coherence of the union's political, economic and monetary elements; and to define and implement a common foreign and security policy. Political union would take effect at the same time as EMU, on 1 January 1993.

Kohl and Mitterrand had spent three months negotiating a vague text of eight paragraphs. Such was the weight of France and Germany combined, however, that the letter shifted the debate from whether there should be a treaty on political union to what it should say.

At his press conference before the special Dublin summit, Delors called on the 12

> to renew their marriage vows, just as certain couples do after 20 or 30 years of marriage. A greater Europe cannot be built by diluting the Community, by casting into the dustbin of history 30 years of what has been an original experience, when for the first time ever, a number of countries have joined together to pool their sovereignty without being dictated to by the political or military domination of one country over the others.[31]

In Dublin Kohl, Andreotti, Gonzalez and Wilfried Martens, the Belgian prime minister, wanted to set a date for an IGC on political union. Delors said that would be imprudent, for nobody agreed on what the term meant and there had been no preparatory work. Thatcher warned that the loose phrases of the Kohl–Mitterrand letter had made the British worry for the future of their monarchy and 700-year-old parliament. She said the EC had far too much on its agenda – German unity, aid for Eastern Europe, the completion of the single market, the European Economic Area, the GATT trade talks and EMU – for it to take on yet another huge enterprise. The summit concluded by asking the foreign ministers to report to the second Dubin summit that was due in June, 'with a view to a decision on the holding of a second inter-governmental conference to work in parallel with the conference on EMU.'

The British knew they could not block EMU, for the other 11, if they wished, could agree on a treaty to create a European Central Bank. They reckoned they could stop political union if they had to: the 11 could not sign a treaty which covered existing EC institutions. However British morale was poor. Powell says:

> The momentum was unstoppable, it was a constant defensive battle with diversionary tactics. The government was divided – Howe would go along at almost any price rather than be left out – while Thatcher wasn't sure if we should be in the process at all.[32]

The East Germans had voted for reunification in March. The April summit approved Delors's proposals on how to integrate East Germany into the EC. In the interests of speed there would be no amendment to the treaties. Between German monetary union, in June 1990, and full union in October, the two Germanies would consult the commission about changes to East German law. After full union, former East Germany would have derogations (temporary exemptions) from some EC rules, such as those on the environment and farming, for a transitional period.

Before and during the summit, Delors tried to convince Kohl of the need for a special EC fund that would help to pay for the modernisation of East Germany. Delors argued that it would 'give East Germans in particular and all Germans in general a signal of fraternity and solidarity'. Kohl replied that reunification was already frightening Germany's partners, and that asking for economic aid would make it unpopular. If Kohl had not rejected the idea – to Delors's great annoyance – the German government would not have had to borrow so much to finance reunification, and the ERM might have had a different history.

JACQUES AND HELMUT

The president of the commission has few formal means of influencing European politics, other than the right of proposal. His real clout depends on informal links with national politicians, especially the heads of government and the foreign ministers. Delors's personal friendships with, among others, Spain's Felipe Gonzalez, Belgium's Wilfried Martens, Holland's Ruud Lubbers and Italy's Giulio Andreotti served him well at crucial moments. But Helmut Kohl proved by far the most important of his allies.

Delors's handling of German unity turned friendship with Kohl into *Blutbruderschaft* (blood brotherhood). He made sure the EC did not create difficulties for the Germans during their reunification. There were no disputes over how the five East German Länder would join the Community, or over cash questions such as their entitlement to structural funds. In the summer of 1990 the commission prepared 60 directives to deal with the legal and budgetary complications. The Council of Ministers rubber-stamped them, enabling the East German Länder to join both West Germany and the EC on 3 October.

From the fall of the Berlin Wall until the day of reunification, Delors greeted the prospect of German unity with more warmth than any other European politician. In January 1990, at a meeting of foreign ministers in Dublin, Delors proposed three options for linking East Germany to the EC: granting it associate membership; giving it a quick route to full membership; or German reunification. Hans van den Broek, the Dutch foreign minister, attacked Delors for offering the East Germans special treatment,

saying it would fan fears of a greater Germany and anger the East Europeans. The Belgian, British and French foreign ministers sided with Van
den Broek.

Why did Delors welcome reunification when others did not? He divined
sooner than most, in the autumn of 1989, that it would happen, and therefore had little to lose by welcoming the process. He knew that if the EC
opposed reunification the Germans would turn against Brussels and that
Kohl, for one, would be less likely to support EMU. Like Kohl, Delors
saw that German unity could be exploited as an argument for political
union.

But Delors's sympathy for the Germans' cause involved more than
opportunism. 'If I hadn't been carried away by my intuition and my heart,
I wouldn't have reacted so quickly. One had to live with the same rhythm
as the Germans.' Delors had understood how the Germans, more than
most peoples and because of their history, crave to be liked. 'If you like
them – which is sometimes hard – you succeed in establishing a dialogue
with them. There's no other way.' Delors says he had to learn to like the
Germans, and then to feel friendship for them. 'My father never stopped
telling me they were a warrior and imperialist nation.'[33]

There are times when Delors seems to want to make amends for his
father's Germanophobia. On the night the Swiss referendum on the European Economic Area, in December 1992, Delors watched the results with
a group of German diplomats and his own officials. A commission man
remarked that the German-speaking Swiss had voted no because they did
not want to be closer to the Germans. 'No one in the world likes us,' said
Dietrich von Kyaw, the German ambassador. Delors stepped up to him
and exclaimed, with total sincerity: '*Moi, je vous aime!*'

Whatever Delors's motivation for welcoming reunification, the Germans were immensely grateful. 'Here in Bonn we know we have two
friends, Jacques Delors and George Bush, they're the ones who understood what we wanted,' said the same von Kyaw, then head of the foreign
ministry's EC desk, in May 1990.[34] Kohl invited only two foreign politicians to the unity celebrations of 3 October 1990: the European Parliament's Enrique Baron, and Delors.

Kohl will never forget Delors's help over reunification, but the pair had
become friends before anyone imagined that the wall would fall. The
Chancellor had proposed Delors for the commission presidency, in June
1984. Delors then chose Gunter Burghardt, a German with links to Kohl's
Christian Democratic Union, as his deputy *chef de cabinet*. But in the
spring of 1985 *Stern*, a German magazine, quoted Delors as saying that
Kohl was a bad European.

Relations remained frosty until December 1987, when Delors and other commissioners went to meet the German government, which was about to take on the EC presidency. Delors responded to a friendly speech from Kohl by apologising for having described the Germans as 'arrogant' in March 1983. Soon afterwards Kohl invited Delors to his bungalow near Ludwigshafen in the Rhineland-Palatinate. A series of *têtes-à-têtes* on the Delors package and EMU followed. Ever since they have had private meetings about once a month (Delors and Mitterrand have seen each other only three or four times a year).

Delors and Kohl speak through interpreters but enjoy each other's company. Both are inclined to strong emotions and a certain rustic earthiness. They share a caustic sense of humour which often targets other politicians, such as Thatcher. As practising Catholics they discuss the state of their church and their worries about Pope John Paul II. Their political ideas are not far apart: Kohl has often told Delors that if he had been born in Germany he would have become a Christian democrat. They believe in the necessity of Franco-German friendship and in the federal destiny of Europe.

They trust each other not to be tricky, and know how useful the other is. Kohl treats Delors as a kind of consultant on European affairs. He also exploits his French connections. Teltschik says:

> The triangular relationship of Kohl–Delors–Mitterrand was pivotal. Delors mediated between Kohl and Mitterrand, and – never afraid of stating his own views forcefully – tried to influence them while doing so. He understood our domestic problems and helped Mitterrand to do so, such as when we wanted the IGC on monetary union postponed until after the November 1990 elections.[35]

Kohl found it handy having a friend at the head of the commission. 'On many big issues we've worked to defend German interests, rather than French ones – and more often than we have defended British interests,' says one of Delors's (French) aides. Thus when Leon Brittan, then the competition commissioner, tried to cut Germany's subsidies to its coal industry, Delors blunted his attack. Similarly Delors helped to exempt the Treuhand Anstalt (the body responsible for privatising East German industry) from the full force of EC rules on competition. The aide says Delors helped Germany more than other members because 'it served the cause of European construction'.

The pair have their arguments. Kohl upset Delors by failing to consult the commission over the negotiation of the unity treaty that he and Lothar de la Maizière, East Germany's prime minister, signed on 18 May 1990. But they soon make up. Delors knows only too well that many of his achievements have depended on the Chancellor's support. In 1988 Kohl committed the German cash which allowed an agreement on the Delors package, and he installed his friend as chairman of the committee on EMU. The following year, at the Strasbourg summit, Kohl overrode Waigel and Pöhl by agreeing on a date for the EMU conference. In 1990 and 1991, when the commission came under attack in the negotiations on political union, Kohl – some of the time – defended it.

GENIES ON THE LOOSE

No sooner had Delors conjured to life the genies of monetary and political union than they began to escape his control. Some of France's ideas on political union emerged in May, at a meeting of foreign ministers at Parknasilla in Ireland. Roland Dumas, the French minister, talked of changing the European Council from a periodic gathering of heads of government into an institution with its own secretariat. He suggested strengthening the EC presidency by giving it to one country or person for several years, rather than a different country every six months. The inter-governmental slant of these ideas stretched back to the Fouchet plan of 1960 (see Chapter 5).

Delors began to realise that political union might give neither the commission nor the parliament much more power. He feared that any attempt to define the final stage of European construction would lead to inter-governmental architecture. So he talked instead of an '*Acte Unique Bis*' (a Single Act Part Two) which would tackle the EC's most pressing problems and maintain the balance between the institutions. He thought it best to steer clear of defence.

Delors says:

> *The commission had become too important and too feared for them to allow us to be the people who would draw up the treaties, as we had done for the Single European Act. My worry was that there was no preparatory report, no Spaak Report, no Delors Report, nothing at all!*

He still hoped for new foreign-policy procedures which would enhance the commission's role and curb the national veto.

> *At the two Dublin summits [the leaders] took very clear common positions on South Africa, on German reunification, on Eastern Europe . . .*

I asked myself, is that provisional, or is that going to create a climate for a good treaty on political union?[36]

The second Dublin summit, on 25 and 26 June, decided that the two IGCs would start in Rome straight after December's summit. A committee of national officials would carry out preparatory work on political union. Kohl and Mitterrand called for billions of dollars of aid for the Soviet Union, to help Gorbachev. Thatcher argued that aid would be wasted without studies of what help was needed. Delors backed her and the Kohl–Mitterrand plan came to nothing. At Andreotti's suggestion, the commission won the job of carrying out the studies and of preparing assistance for the Soviet economy.

In the summer of 1990 the EC came under growing pressure to admit new members. Cyprus and Malta applied to join in July. The EC's official policy remained that no applications could be considered until after the completion of the single market in 1992. But some commissioners and some governments – notably the Germans and the British – began to argue for a faster timetable. With the East Germans about to join, it seemed unfair to make the Austrians wait. The collapse of communism made neutrality less of a barrier to membership than it had been. The British hoped, as Delors feared, that widening would put a brake on deepening. The Germans had a natural interest in admitting neighbouring countries and, ever optimistic, thought the EC could deepen and widen at the same time. The French and the Spanish shared Delors's caution and disliked the prospect of the EC's centre of gravity shifting northwards and eastwards.

When a country applies to join, the commission must produce a formal opinion before the Council of Ministers can open negotiations. Throughout 1990, Delors prevented commission officials from working on the Austrian opinion. During one meeting of commissioners, Delors argued that the East Europeans would not be ready for membership until they had gone through 15 to 20 years of preparation.

In October 1990 Sweden announced its intention to lodge an application. The negotiations on the European Economic Area had shown the EC to be unwilling to give EFTA countries a say in decision making. They would have to accept the single market on the EC's terms with, at best, some consultation on new laws. The EC's hard line had, for the Swedes, increased the attraction of full membership. The EEA began to look less like an alternative to membership and more like a waiting room. The news from Stockholm made it likely that the EC would have to let in some new members, and Delors began to temper his opposition. He said that a couple of new members could be squeezed in, but added that an EC of 15 or 16 would suffer from institutional paralysis and should therefore await further treaty revisions in mid-decade.

Meanwhile the debates in the committee on political union were making Delors nervous. Pierre de Boissieu, France's brilliant and acerbic representative, shared the belief of his grandfather – General de Gaulle – in a 'Europe des patries'. De Boissieu liked Delors no more than his grandfather had liked Walter Hallstein, the first commission president. De Boissieu proposed depriving the commission of its right to accept or reject parliamentary amendments.

Delors told the author he was convinced of an Anglo-French plot against the commission. Since governments would not give the European Parliament real law-making powers, he believed, they would instead allow it to control the commission. A proposal for the parliament to be able to sack individual commissioners would allow it 'to control their every gesture'. A British plan for the parliament to question commission officials would lead to it 'telling us what to do'. But if the commission was to become a real executive, should not the parliament have real powers of control? Not while the commission's powers remained minimal, he said.[37]

Delors had discerned real trends in the debate on political union but, as is his wont, had exaggerated. He can be like a husband who knows his wife is not having an affair, but, suspecting that she will, accuses her in advance to warn her off. His comments on the parliament revealed his characteristic obsession with the power of the commission. Delors has never demanded more powers without offering strong justifications in terms of efficiency. However several governments thought Delors had asked for too much on too many occasions. Believing him an empire builder, they gave him a rough ride on political union.

The aftermath of the Iraqi invasion of Kuwait, on 2 August, began to colour the debate on political union. The EC had imposed sanctions on Iraq straight after the invasion. In September it had expelled Iraqi diplomats and promised $2 billion of aid to Jordan, Turkey and Egypt, whose economies were suffering from the conflict. The 12 backed the American-led coalition against Iraq but there were Anglo-French tensions over whether, as France wished, the EC should take independent peace initiatives. Most EC members had sent ships to take part in the Gulf naval blockade but only Britain and France had sent troops.

Delors thought the crisis reinforced the case for political union, by showing that the 12 would be more effective with common foreign policies. When the EC foreign ministers met in Venice, on 6 and 7 October, most of them agreed with Delors. Dumas and Genscher proposed that the 12 should decide on common policies for parts of the world – such as the Gulf or Eastern Europe – where they had common interests. Qualified majority voting would determine these policies. Only Douglas Hurd, Britain's foreign secretary, and Uffe Ellemann-Jensen, the Danish minister, argued that such a scheme would not help the 12 to respond more decisively to crises such as the invasion of Kuwait.

Gianni de Michelis, Italy's energetic and loquacious foreign minister, proposed that in 1998 the EC should merge with the Western European Union (WEU), a defence pact of all the EC members bar Ireland, Denmark and Greece. Having lain dormant for many years, the WEU was coordinating Europe's naval blockade in the Gulf. Only a minority backed the de Michelis plan but a majority wanted a beefed-up WEU to work more closely with the EC.

Delors worried about how little these abstract debates meant to ordinary citizens. 'The European project is too elitist and technocratic: we have to reflect on how citizens can have a feeling of participating in a collective adventure,' he told *Le Monde* in October 1990. Delors welcomed Spain's proposals for 'European citizenship' as a step in the right direction: citizens of one EC country would have the right to live in any other, even if they had no job, and to vote in its local and European elections.[38]

The commission published a formal 'opinion' for the political union IGC on 21 October, much of it written by Delors himself. The opinion stressed the importance of a single Community and of the existing balance between the institutions. The European Council would choose certain subjects for common foreign policies, and the Council of Ministers would decide the policies by majority vote. Article five of the WEU treaty – obliging member-states to aid each other if attacked – would be added to the Treaty of Rome.

The commission would maintain its monopoly of the right of initiative, so that the parliament could not propose laws. The parliament would have more say over legislation but the Council of Ministers would retain the last word. The council would vote on all laws by qualified majority. The opinion demanded few new 'competences' but sought to strengthen social policy by adding provisions on working conditions, vocational training and worker consultation.

Delors knew that not all this programme would survive the IGC on political union. His plans for EMU were also under threat. Having accepted the principle of EMU, the Bundesbank spent 1990 fighting to stamp its own mark on the negotiations. Pöhl wanted to weaken the role of the European Central Bank during EMU's second phase, in order to preserve the Bundesbank's authority; and to make economic convergence a strict condition of moving to phase three. Waigel generally followed the Bundesbank's lead.

In April 1990, at Castle Ashford in Galway, the finance ministers and central bank governors had held their first serious debate on the details of EMU. Waigel attacked a paper of Delors's for suggesting that rules on budget deficits should not be rigid. When Delors proposed that the single currency should be called the ecu, Poehl insisted that the D-mark and the other currencies should continue to exist after the fixing of exchange rates. 'We've been badly repaid by the Germans after all we've done for them on their reunification,' said Delors afterwards.

In June, just before the second Dublin summit, Britain launched a diversionary tactic. John Major suggested that in phase two of EMU a European Monetary Fund should issue a new currency, the 'hard ecu' – hard because it would be tied to the strongest currency in the ERM. Phase two would last indefinitely, while people and companies decided if they wanted to use the hard ecu rather than existing currencies. The plan won little support because it was seen as a way of postponing the final phase of EMU.

In August the commission published a formal opinion on EMU, written largely by Delors. The opinion ignored what the Germans had been saying and departed from the Delors Report in three respects. The idea of sanctions on countries which borrowed too much was dropped. It said EMU should involve a single currency called the ecu. And while the Delors Report had not mentioned dates for phases two and three, the opinion said phase two should start in January 1993 and that, because of the risk of free capital flows destabilising the ERM, it should be short.

A furious Pöhl delivered a stinging counterblast in Munich on 3 September. 'In losing the D-mark we would be sacrificing a hard currency on the European altar without knowing what we would get in return.' Pöhl pointed to German monetary union as a salutary example of an over-hasty currency union: unable to devalue, the weaker economy had to adjust through unemployment, while 'ever-increasing transfer payments become inescapable'.

Even the southern members, normally loyal to Delors, were ganging up against his plans for EMU. Unlike Delors, the Spanish and the Portuguese wanted a long second phase of EMU. They knew their economies were far from ready for the final phase and did not want to be left behind when it began. The Iberians, Greeks and Irish wanted an extra slice of regional aid as the price for EMU.

Delors worried that talk of more regional aid would put off the Germans, for they would have to pick up much of the bill. Delors had read the commission's own research on EMU, which had yet to be published. This concluded that fixed exchange rates would – through lower inflation and interest rates, and higher trade and investment – benefit poorer regions more than others. Analysing the growth rates of the 12 over the 15 years to

1988, the commission economists found there was no statistically significant correlation between growth and devaluation. But they noted that the
transitional phase of EMU would strain countries which had to cut budget
deficits and inflation rates substantially. Delors therefore favoured short-
term credits for countries which suffered economic shocks, but refused to
consider expanding the structural funds.

When the finance ministers met in Rome, on 8 September 1990, only the
French, Belgian, Italian and Danish ministers followed Delors's line that
phase two of EMU should start in 1993. They said phase three should start
soon afterwards and that setting deadlines would encourage economic convergence. Waigel, with support from the Dutch and Luxembourg ministers, said the 12 economies should satisfy strict convergence criteria before
they moved to the second and third stages of EMU.

Carlos Solchaga, the Spanish minister, suggested a phase two of five to six
years, starting in January 1994 and involving much more regional aid.
Adapting Major's ideas, he suggested the ECB should issue hard ecus in
phase two and that in phase three the hard ecu should become the single
currency. The Greek and Irish ministers liked Solchaga's plan, which
Delors called 'a hit below the belt'. Delors left the meeting in a state of shock.

On 19 September Pöhl landed another blow by unveiling the Bundesbank's own, deadline-free opinion on EMU. A mere Council of Central
Bank Governors rather than a European Central Bank would hold the reins
in phase two. Only when interest rates had been 'virtually harmonised',
national central banks made independent, budget deficits reduced and
inflation 'very largely eliminated in all countries' would phase three begin.

Such tough conditions led many to question whether the Bundesbank
wanted EMU at all. When the author interviewed Pöhl in October he was, as
always, ambiguous. He said he would favour an EMU which involved just
Germany, France, Denmark and the Benelux countries and that it could
start in 1993. The EC committee of central bank governors, under Pöhl's
chairmanship, had almost completed a set of statutes for the European
Central Bank. Pöhl was proud of these operating rules, which pre-empted
some of the IGC's work, and described them as his contribution to the
construction of Europe. Since the statutes respected the Delors Report's
sketch of the ECB, which had been modelled on the Bundesbank, they
pleased both Delors and Pöhl.[39] The nature of the ECB in phase three was no
longer an issue. The arguments to come would be over phase two and the
transition to phase three.

In the weeks before the Rome summit of 27 October, Delors's mood
brightened. A Dutch compromise proposal, which set dates for the start of
each phase but made them conditional on the fulfilment of convergence

criteria, was gathering support. Delors said dates were essential as 'a test for Germany's commitment to EMU and to bind it into Europe irreversibly.' His campaign for dates had 'obliged Pöhl to reveal his true colours,' and he trusted that, in Rome, Kohl and Genscher would overrule Pöhl and Waigel.[40]

On 5 October Thatcher took Britain into the ERM. On 16 October the commission published its research on EMU, which concluded that a single currency would save the Community 13–19 billion ecus a year of transaction costs (£9–13 billion). At the same time the Association for the Monetary Union of Europe published a poll of 6000 Europeans. Asked if they wanted the ecu to replace their national currencies in the next five to six years, 61 per cent said yes and 39 per cent no. However only 51 per cent of Germans and 37 per cent of Britons approved of the idea.

GLADIATORS IN ROME

Giulio Andreotti, as Italy's foreign minister at the Milan summit of June 1985, had sprung the vote on an inter-governmental conference which ambushed Margaret Thatcher. As prime minister in Rome in October 1990, Andreotti forced a decision on dates for EMU and, once more, enraged Thatcher.

In the run-up to the summit, the Italian government had sent out confusing signals on EMU. Some of them indicated that Andreotti would handle EMU with kid gloves and avoid the question of dates. Yet when the summit began he asked the heads of government to approve a set of instructions for the forthcoming IGC. Eleven of them agreed that phase two of EMU would start in 1994, so long as a fairly easy set of conditions, such as completion of the single market, had been met. A 'new Community institution' would be set up at the start of phase two. The European Council would review the EC's readiness for phase three – which would depend on progress towards economic convergence – within three years of phase two beginning. In phase three the ecu would replace national currencies.

Furious at Andreotti's surprise manoeuvre, Thatcher refused to sign the conclusions on EMU. Nor would she sign another set on political union. She demanded that the GATT trade talks be discussed, for after six meetings EC ministers had failed to agree on a proposal to cut farm subsidies. However Kohl and Mitterrand, whose governments had blocked an agreement, did not want to discuss the matter. Andreotti told Thatcher there was no time to talk about GATT.

Andreotti had pressed for a date on EMU because a few days earlier, at a gathering of Christian Democrats in Venice, Kohl had told him that he was ready to commit Germany. A rash of articles in the British press, critical of the chaotic organisation of the Italian presidency, had increased the eagerness of the Italians to make their summit a historic one. *The Economist* said there was no reason to hold an October summit and quoted an EC ambassador's description of the presidency as 'like a coach trip with the Marx Brothers in the driving seat.' When Andreotti and Delors held their post-summit press conference, the Italian's spokesman announced that 'the bus driven by the Marx Brothers has started to move. One day we hope Mrs Thatcher will catch it.'

Delors declared that the summit conclusions set the stage for a single currency by the year 2000. However, together with Ellemann-Jensen, he expressed regret that no effort had been made to keep Britain on board. The others saw little reason to worry about Thatcher, for they thought she would accept a treaty which allowed Britain to opt out of EMU.

Straight after the press conferences an incandescent Thatcher said on BBC television that the Italians' chairing had been 'a mess' and 'incompetent'. She complained that the presidency had preferred to deal with distant and less keenly contested matters, rather than those which were urgent and difficult. The date of 1994 for phase two of EMU was 'cloud cuckoo land' and she would never put a plan for a single currency before Britain's parliament.

Thatcher picked on Delors as a symbol for everything which had gone wrong in Rome. There was something manic about her mood when, on 30 October, she reported to the House of Commons on the Rome summit. During an attack on the Delors Report, she said it was

> *very ironic indeed that, at a time when Eastern Europe is striving for greater democracy, the commission should be striving to extinguish democracy and to put more and more power into its own hands, or into the hands of non-elected bodies.*

She then criticised Major's hard ecu scheme by saying that the currency would not be used widely in the EC and that it would not lead to EMU (Major had said that it might).

> *Mr Delors said at a press conference the other day that he wanted the European Parliament to be the democratic body of the Community, the commission to be the executive and the Council of Ministers to be the senate. No! No! No!*

Thatcher's speech – and not least the personal attack on Delors – upset Geoffrey Howe, the deputy prime minister. He resigned on 1 November, the same day that the Sun led with: 'UP YOURS DELORS'. On 14 November Howe explained to the House of Commons why he had resigned. He said that staying out of the ERM had damaged the British economy and that Britain would become isolated if it vetoed EMU. The Delors Report was 'an important working document'. Thatcher's stance 'poses serious risks for the future of the nation.'

The unpopularity of the poll tax had weakened Thatcher's premiership. The clashes in Rome over Delors's plan for EMU wounded her. After Howe's speech she teetered. Michael Heseltine's challenge to her leadership administered the *coup de grâce*, and she resigned on 22 November. Delors did not rejoice. He knew that Thatcher had become – for the 11 governments which found her behaviour unacceptable – the greatest unifying force in the Community. He feared for the loss of that force.

The triumphant Italians began to prepare for the second Rome summit, on 14 and 15 December, hoping it would give a decisive push to political union. Italy's own proposals on political union followed Delorist principles but promised much more to the parliament. At the end of November Italy hosted an 'assizes' in Rome, bringing together Euro-MPs and national parliamentarians. They all agreed that the European Parliament should have more power.

France and Germany remained at odds over the content of political union. Mitterrand worried about what he saw as an almost invisible seepage of powers to EC institutions. He wanted national governments and parliaments to play a bigger role when the union encompassed new areas such as foreign policy, EMU and interior-ministry cooperation. In these areas he wanted the European Council to guide policy and a 'congress' of Euro-MPs and national MPs to scrutinise it. Kohl, however, still inclined to Delors's idea of a federal rather than an inter-governmental European union.

This Franco-German divergence reflected two very different histories and constitutions. The Federal Republic of Germany, allergic to any hint of despotism, naturally favoured a multi-layered, federal European constitution. Centralised France, with its powerful presidency, weak government (which normally leaves foreign policy to the president) and feeble parliament, naturally viewed the European Council as a kind of European Presidency, the commission as an executive which should keep away from foreign policy and the European Parliament as a debating chamber.

However much they disagreed, Kohl and Mitterrand always found a compromise. In a joint declaration on 7 December Mitterrand agreed to reinforce the European Parliament. As a quid pro quo, Kohl accepted that the European Council should oversee common foreign and security policies, and that the WEU should become both the EC's defence agency

Presidential control, 1986
(*European Commission*)

Delors's Exocet: Pascal Lamy, 1984

Delors's inspiration: celebrating Jean Monnet's
centenary, 1988 (*European Commission*)

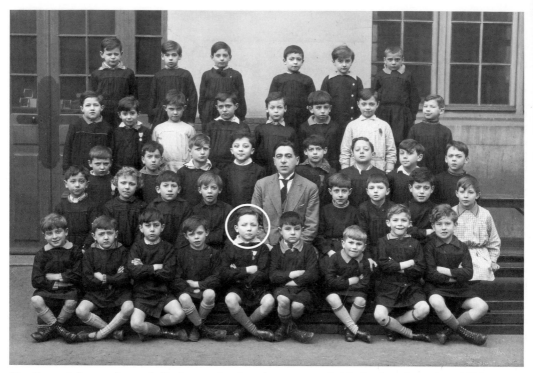

Standing out: Jacques's smock displays a school merit cross, awarded for hard work, in about 1932

Rural roots: hiking in the Auvergne with Marie, Martine and Jean-Paul, 1955

Smart kid: outside the Delors's home, 1934

Two future ministers: Jacques and Martine, about 1958 (*Le Point*)

Tenu de basket: at a basketball tournament, 1949 (*Le Point*)

Down to earth: Marie Delors, 1990 (*European Commission*)

Jacques's flag: unveiling the
12 stars, May 1986
(*European Commission*)

Helmut points to a federal future:
with Chancellor Kohl, February
1990 (*European Commission*)

Dreams dissolve: Dane-struck and
anxious, July 1992 (*Bonn
Sequenz*)

and NATO's European pillar. Three days later, in Berlin, Douglas Hurd signalled a softening of Britain's hard-line Atlanticism. Noting that America was cutting back its military presence in Europe, he called for a 'distinct European role' in defence and suggested that the WEU should represent the Community within NATO.

An optimistic Delors thought the practical difficulties of trying to run common foreign policies with current procedures would lead governments to write a worthwhile treaty. On the eve of the summit he told *The Independent* that after slow beginnings 20 years previously, joint foreign policies were 'suddenly galloping because of events in Eastern Europe and the Gulf, it is like a chemical experiment'. *The Independent* noted that his eyes lit up like a small boy playing with a chemistry set.[41]

The second Rome summit set vague guidelines for the IGC on political union. These included a role for the European Council in defining foreign policy and in discussing security, more powers for the parliament and fresh competences for the EC. The summit approved the commission's plans to give the Soviet Union 1.15 billion ecus of food aid and technical assistance.

Straight after the summit the finance ministers kicked off the inter-governmental conference on EMU. Delors hoped they would welcome a draft treaty just published by the commission. This followed the line of the earlier 'opinion' but added that phase three should start when eight members were in favour, and that no member would be obliged to take part.

The ministers did not like the idea of Delors pre-empting the work of their conference. Waigel savaged the draft, demanded binding rules on budget deficits and insisted that the central bank be set up at the end of phase two rather than the start. Solchaga talked of moving slowly to EMU and, backed by France's Pierre Bérégovoy and Holland's Wim Kok, suddenly found praise for Major's hard ecu plan.

Tired and petulant, Delors told a press conference that 'in all this euphoria [of the IGC's opening] someone has to play Cassandra.' He ridiculed Germany's attempts to define criteria for economic convergence as akin to medieval debates on the sex of angels. He feared that Spain and Britain would spin out the negotiations 'until we all grow white beards'. Of Major and his hard ecu plan, he said: 'I am mistrustful and have good reason to be so.' Talking of the risk that Britain or others could derail EMU, he warned: 'If we need to provoke another crisis then we will do so.'[42]

Delors's outburst against Major – who had tried to behave at his first summit by signing the conclusions on political union – upset Britain's government and excited its media. At the next meeting of the commission Leon Brittan described Delors's criticisms of the British as unjustified and inappropriate. During the shouting which followed Delors said that if a majority of his colleagues disavowed him he was ready to depart. They did not and neither did he.

In an effort to repair the damage, Delors called in the *Financial Times* to explain that Britain had not been his prime target, for it was 'no longer the biggest menace'. He said Waigel's idea of no ECB until the end of phase two was incompatible with the conclusions of the first Rome summit. 'We may see, for the first time in any presidency, decisions of the European Council being reversed.' Delors worried that if EMU was delayed, a war or an economic recession could undermine the whole project.[43]

Delors's rancour was akin to that of a parent who suspects that a beloved child will grow into a strange and hostile adult. He had done as much as anyone to parent the projects of EMU and political union in their early years. He sensed, correctly, that as the inter-governmental conferences got underway, his children would run astray.

CHAPTER EIGHT

TROUBLE WITH THE ANGLO-SAXONS

LIKE HIS intellectual godfather, Emmanuel Mounier, Delors finds the atomistic society of classical liberalism, in which each individual makes rational choices in pursuit of his or her gain, morally repugnant. Against that model Delors stresses the importance of social groups, such as families, clubs, trade unions and associations, which are motivated by fraternity and solidarity.

In his book *Changer* Delors wrote:

> *The production of goods and services has become an end in itself, and the consumer is constantly stimulated, trapped in the gilded prison of marketing. This individualist society puts the growth of material goods before the happiness of man, means before ends, having before being.*

The 'reign of merchandise' gave people 'false needs' and, through demands for higher wages, fuelled inflation.[1]

While Christian personalism is one strong ingredient of Deloronomics, the French tradition of government is another. Ever since the 17th century, when Jean-Baptiste Colbert ran economic policy for Louis XIV, French politicians have inclined to intervention and protection. The French state, more than most in Europe, has sought to manage trade, to promote *grands projets* and to work with companies to develop new technologies and markets. In the decades following the Second World War, many French people, including Delors, understood that Colbertism no longer suited a country whose economy had grown inextricably intertwined with those of its neighbours. They looked to the European Community to take over some of the tasks of the French state. During his presidency of the European Commission, Delors has sometimes leaned towards 'Euro-Colbertism'.

Some of Delors's most formidable political opponents have had more faith in markets than he does. Many of them – such as Margaret Thatcher, George Bush, Leon Brittan and John Major – have been 'Anglo-Saxon', as the French call people from Britain and America. Those countries invented economic liberalism and remain more influenced by it than continental Europe. That is one reason why Delors and the Anglo-Saxons often find it hard to understand each other.

Yet despite ten years of a French, socialist and personalist commission president, the EC has become – across the whole range of its economic policies – more of a force for than against economic liberalism. The commission pulled back from *dirigiste* industrial policies. A strengthened competition policy curbed state aid to industry. The EC built a few outlying ramparts, but never a Fortress Europe.

Deloronomics is an ambiguous ideological brew of variable flavour. Delors's intellect or pragmatism may convince him of the need for market-orientated policies. Then his deeper instincts may tug him the other way. There were moments – for instance when he tried to block a GATT deal in November 1992 – when Delors's inability to resolve the conflict between his head and his heart proved disastrous for his reputation. He has often tried to reconcile the two by declaring his support for three principles of EC economic policy: competition which stimulates, cooperation which strengthens and solidarity which unites.

Delors is suspicious of consumerism and the consumer movement, which have always been stronger in Anglo-Saxon countries than in France. 'There is a conception of competition which aims to privilege only consumption, which can be destructive of production,' he says. 'That's what Leon Brittan [who held the job of competition commissioner from 1989 to 1992] and I disagree about.'[2]

Delors has never championed EC action on consumer rights. During his presidency only one major directive in this area, that of 1991 on product safety, became law. Delors decided not to upgrade the commission's consumer policy unit into a full directorate-general. He tried and failed to cut the chapter on consumer rights out of the Maastricht treaty.

In March 1991, speaking to a group of French farmers, Delors defended tight restrictions on the use of marks of origin (Champagne, Camembert and so on) for food and drink: 'We have to resist this tendency we find in Europe, according to which the consumer is king and so intelligent that he can choose himself between different products.'[3]

When discussing the Common Agricultural Policy (CAP) or the GATT trade talks, Delors has seldom mentioned that lower prices for food or goods would benefit consumers. In October 1986 the *Financial Times* asked Delors why the EC had imposed anti-dumping duties (penalties on imports that are considered 'unfairly' cheap) on Japanese photocopiers. Delors answered, in Colbertian style, that if everyone bought at the cheapest prices, Europe would have a trade deficit. 'That would lead to dependency, and then Europe would not exist – why bother to have an independent foreign policy? We don't have much in the way of gold, oil or primary products, so we have to get organised.'[4]

Europe's economic decline, relative to Japan and America, has obsessed Delors since the early 1970s. In his first month as commission president he told the European Parliament that he saw two remedies: the 1992 programme, to encourage competition; and a stronger Community industrial policy, to promote research on new technologies, collaboration among European companies and better training.[5] But while the 1992 programme sailed ahead, Delors's ambitious plans for industrial policy made little progress. At the Milan summit of June 1985, when Delors proposed the creation of a Technology Community and a doubling of spending on R&D, no one listened.

In November 1990 the commission approved a new strategy for industrial policy, set out in a paper by Martin Bangemann, the industry commissioner. This signalled an end to 'vertical' industrial policies, which had channelled aid to particular sectors. The paper pointed out that companies which received such aid sometimes lost their competitive edge, while those which did not suffered unfair discrimination. Industrial policy would henceforth be 'horizontal', which meant spending money on training, infrastructure and research, to the benefit – in theory – of the whole economy.

Delors supported this new strategy and the commission has, for the most part, kept to it. But the economic downturn which began in 1991 revealed that many European industries had lagged behind their American and Japanese counterparts. Delors renewed his interest in industrial policy and the idea that Europe needed fewer, larger companies if it was to hold its own in world markets. 'Whatever some may say, I say long live Euro-champions,' he blurted out in August 1991.[6]

In the spring of 1991 Delors invited the chief executives of Olivetti, Siemens, Bull, Thomson and Philips to a restaurant in the Burgundian town of Saulieu. He urged them to create an Airbus-type venture for semiconductor research and production, adding that if they collaborated the EC could provide $5 billion of aid over 10 years. Delors's guests claimed to be interested in European cooperation. In the long run, however, they preferred to make global alliances with Japanese and American firms.

The Treaty of Maastricht, agreed in December 1991, contained a new chapter on industrial policy, but its thin contents left Delors disappointed. Two months later Delors unveiled a five-year budgetary plan for the years 1993 to 1997, including 3.5 billion ecus (£2.5 billion) a year for 'industrial competitiveness'. Under that new heading Delors proposed to target the EC's social fund on retraining workers in declining industries; to redirect R&D money from basic research towards high-tech projects which were almost ready for commercial marketing; and to get tough with countries which closed their markets to EC firms.

Strictly, these proposals did not renege on the Bangemann paper. However, Leon Brittan worried that individual firms might gain if the EC funded retraining programmes or handed out R&D money to projects which were close to the market. Delors did not allay such fears when, in an early draft of his plan, he wrote that it would be desirable if horizontal benefits applied to the car, textile, defence and electronics industries – which happened to be France's problem sectors at the time. The Edinburgh summit of December 1992 squashed the proposal to spend more money on 'industrial competitiveness', but left Delors's ideas for reforming the social fund and R&D spending on the agenda.

Delors admits to being 'greatly disappointed' with what he has achieved on industrial policy in his time as president. He says he never wanted a *dirigiste* policy, with the commission picking winners. 'I'm asking that firms cooperate together and that Community policies support them – either through an R&D effort or through training people to adapt to new methods of work.'[7] He says that unless European firms learn to cooperate as the Japanese do, 'I will die of chagrin and in 2010 one will see that I was right.'[8]

Delors is bitter about the failure of the commission's plans for a European HDTV (high-definition television) industry – a very vertical exception to the philosophy of horizontal industrial policy. The commission sponsored HDMAC, a new satellite-broadcasting standard which, when combined with specially designed wide-screen televisions, would provide cinema-quality pictures. Delors's enthusiasm for this *grand projet* transcended economics. In January 1989 he told the parliament that HDTV was needed 'in the name of competitiveness, but also in the name of cultural defence; the Community refuses to leave the monopoly of audiovisual techniques to the Japanese and that of programmes to the Americans.'[9]

The Council of Ministers passed directives which set HDMAC as Europe's future standard. But programme makers and satellite broadcasters – including Rupert Murdoch's News Corporation – refused to accept the new standard without EC money. Britain vetoed the use of Community funds. While Europe procrastinated, America leaped ahead with digital HDTV technology. By 1993 European and Japanese HDTV standards looked redundant. Having spent about 200 million ecus on the project, all that the EC and its governments had to show were some advances in screen and studio technology.

Even the EC's horizontal research effort disappointed. In 1993 the commission's internal auditors concluded that Esprit, its flagship programme for information technology, had become ineffective. They criticised Esprit's 'top-down' philosophy: companies had got together and decided which technologies to develop. Not enough of the Community's R&D has been 'bottom-up' or consumer driven.

Like Delors himself, the commission houses competing schools of thought on industrial policy. The directorate-general for information technology, which has close links to that industry, favours direct aid for 'strategic' sectors such as its own. The directorate-general for industry, which believes in a hard-line horizontal approach, has had allies in Bangemann and Brittan. One of Delors's advisers notes that he has allowed the commission's philosophy to evolve towards horizontal policies. 'His intelligence has grasped the new thinking, but the old ideas keep coming back. So the evolution has been slower than it might have been under another president.'

In 1992 Delors approved an article by two of the commission's top economists which lashed 'Euro-Colbertist' industrial policies. The article described ideas such as European champions and strategic industries as meaningless. The economists argued that the globalisation of markets and companies made any link between the interests of a government and the nationality of a firm highly tenuous. States which wanted to be competitive, they wrote, needed to have people, of whatever nationality, carrying out R&D on their territory, rather than companies of the same nationality carrying out R&D anywhere. The article concluded with a plea for EC industrial policy to focus on investing in 'generic' technologies, which benefit all sectors, and in human resources.[10]

Delors often refers to the globalisation of economics, and his intellect understands that the EC can no longer be viewed as a self-contained economic unit. Yet his intuition has continued to see Europe as an embryonic nation in need of protection. He asked a meeting of socialists in February 1993:

> *Should the EC let itself be undercut by competitors with sweatshop labour conditions? We should distinguish between countries which share the fruits of their trade and those which exploit their workers.*[11]

Delors says he does not mind European companies collaborating with the Japanese or the Americans in areas where they've fallen behind. However, 'there will be no political Europe without a certain economic autonomy. One can't be a political power with the biggest 50 firms in this land having flags from America, Japan, Korea and so on.'[12]

Hard facts sometimes lead Delors closer to Adam Smith than to Colbert. One achievement of his presidency has been the progressive liberalisation of trade between the EC and Eastern Europe. The collapse of Comecon's system of planned commerce deprived the East European countries of their traditional markets. They signed trade agreements with the EC in 1989 and 1990, which removed many tariffs and quotas on their exports.

In 1991 the commission negotiated wider-ranging 'Europe Agreements' with Poland, Hungary and Czechoslovakia. The more protectionist member-states, led by France, tried to minimise the extension of access to EC markets. In May Delors went on French television to argue that the East Europeans needed trade more than aid and that the EC should open its frontiers. However, the French government maintained a hard line and the East Europeans refused to accept what the EC was offering. Delors's lobbying of his compatriots eventually led to an improved EC offer and, in December 1991, to the signing of Europe Agreements with Poland, Hungary and Czechoslovakia. Similar deals followed with Romania and Bulgaria. 'Delors deserves credit for getting the French on board for the Europe agreements,' says Uffe Ellemann-Jensen, a fervent liberal who was then Denmark's foreign minister.[13]

The Europe Agreements set out procedures for regular discussions between the EC and the 'associate' members (as the East Europeans became). They committed both sides to free trade in industrial goods but allowed the East Europeans to keep tariffs for 10 years. The Community could keep tariffs on 'sensitive' items for five years and restrict import surges which caused 'serious injury' (in 1993 the EC used this provision to curb imports of some types of East European steel). Farm trade remained regulated, but associate members could increase many sorts of food export by 10 per cent a year for five years.

No sooner had the East Europeans signed the Europe Agreements than they demanded a better deal. Early in 1993, with Delors's approval, Leon Brittan and Hans van den Broek – the commissioners responsible for external policy – proposed revisions. As a result, the Copenhagen summit of June 1993 decided to speed up the timetable for trade liberalisation; to establish regular meetings between EC prime ministers and their East European counterparts; and to accept the principle that those associate members which wished 'shall become members of the European Union'. For all their imperfections, the Europe Agreements and the earlier trade agreements have made an impact. The value of EC imports from Poland, Hungary, Czechoslovakia, Bulgaria, Romania and Albania grew from 12.2 billion ecus in 1989 to 19.5 billion ecus in 1993 (in current prices).

Delors accepts that open trade is a necessity, but criticises liberals for underestimating the social and environmental costs. So he opposes 'big bang' liberalisations and argues that groups which are adversely affected should be helped. Delors has never shown much interest in the economic theory of trade. He tends to see an economy as a self-contained system, rather than one influenced by a significant external sector. He once asked a colleague why the 1992 programme had failed to protect Europe from the effects of America's recession.

Delors has never accepted that free-wheeling financial markets are a necessity. 'We are living in a state of turmoil, because we have mistaken incidentals for essentials,' he told the European Parliament just after the stockmarket crash of October 1987. 'Finance is incidental, the essential is the creation of wealth and the creation of employment.' He said he would refuse to 'follow the current fashion of raving about futures markets,' which, having been designed to stabilise spot markets, had begun to destabilise them.[14]

Economists who work with Delors note big gaps in his knowledge of macroeconomics, yet are impressed by his facility in other areas. 'He's good at the economics of institutions, such as central banks, and of labour markets, such as benefits and wages,' says one. Since the late 1950s Delors has argued that every worker's remuneration should consist of three elements: a basic salary, a profit-share linked to his or her company, and a bonus related to macroeconomic performance.

Delors finds the interaction of institutions and economic variables fascinating. He has never been the kind of socialist to argue that unemployment can be solved merely by increasing demand. He has long emphasised the need to improve the agencies which train and place the unemployed – a theme of his 1993 white paper on employment and competitiveness (see Chapter 12).

Delors can be obsessive about institutions. Like a number of his compatriots, he sometimes appears to believe that the creation of an institution can solve any problem. In August 1993, speaking to his political club Témoin, Delors proposed the creation of an 'Economic Security Council'. This would consist of America, the EC, Japan, Russia and China, plus one country from each of Africa, Latin America, Asia and the Pacific, plus the IMF, the World Bank, the GATT and the International Labour Organisation. The job of this council – a kind of embryo world federation – would be to recommend solutions to global economic problems.

COMPETITIVE COMMISSIONERS

Several of Delors's most influential colleagues in the European Commission have been ardent free-marketeers. In Delors's first term as president (1985 to 1988) Peter Sutherland, the Irishman in charge of competition, was one of the few commissioners who stood up to him. Sir Leon Brittan, competition commissioner in Delors's second term (1989 to 1992), proved just as liberal and forceful. Surrounded by such colleagues, Delors sometimes had to accept more liberal policies than he would have liked.

The 1992 programme removed hidden forms of protection, thereby increasing the risk that companies would seek government handouts, cosy cartels or monopolistic mergers. Thus an effective single market required a tougher competition policy, which meant common rules on state aid, price-fixing and takeovers. For instance, a German steelmaker could not compete fairly against a Spanish steelmaker which received much higher levels of subsidy.

Sutherland asked Delors for the competition job because of its economic importance, and because a close reading of the Treaty of Rome had shown him that, in theory, the commission had more power in this field than any other. Before Sutherland, the commission had seldom used the considerable powers which lay in the treaty.

With the combative spirit of the rugby player he had once been, Sutherland began to apply article 92, which allows the commission to ban state aid which distorts competition. He hauled before the European Court any government that resisted. The task facing Sutherland was huge. A commission inquiry found the annual average level of state aid in the mid-1980s, in the EC's then 10 members, to be 82 billion ecus, or 3 per cent of Community GDP.

Sutherland and Delors held contrasting political philosophies. Sutherland recalls:

> *True to French traditions, Delors opposed the idea of a* gouvernement des juges *– he didn't like the idea of a supreme court having a political role. I saw the law as a way of promoting federalism and the Court of Justice as the most important EC institution. Delors argued back that even if you win in court you still have to win the hearts and minds of the people. He preferred the political process and institutional reform.*[15]

Delors agreed with the principle that the single market required a tough line on state aid, but tended to object to Sutherland's zeal on particular cases. Delors branded Sutherland '*le petit sheriff*' and on one occasion complained that Versailles would never have been built if DG4 (the directorate-general for competition) had been around. The two men clashed frequently, and sometimes explosively, in commission meetings (see Chapter 6).

Sutherland sought to lower the tension by arranging a weekend seminar for the president and his officials on the economic, political and philosophical basis of competition policy. This did not prevent future disagreements but by 1987 Delors and Sutherland had reached a *modus vivendi*: Delors would allow his cabinet to fight the Irishman's policies but usually left him a free hand in commission meetings.

Sutherland extended the commission's sway in many areas other than state aid. Companies suspected of price-fixing suffered dawn raids from commission officials, and those found guilty were punished. For instance, the commission fined 15 polypropylene manufacturers 60 million ecus (£40 million) in April 1986. Sutherland dusted off article 90 of the Treaty of Rome, which allows the commission to bypass the Council of Ministers and to break up some kinds of public monopoly by decree. In 1988 Sutherland used this draconian power to liberalise the market for telecommunications equipment.

No treaty article gave the commission a clear right to control corporate takeovers, and its own proposal for a merger regulation had languished in the Council of Ministers since 1973. But Sutherland was not deterred. He used article 85, which bans anti-competitive agreements, and article 86, which bans the abuse of dominant market positions, to nose his way into merger control. In March 1988, when British Airways bought British Caledonian, Sutherland brandished those two articles and the threat of the European Court. British Airways agreed to give up some of the acquired routes, allowing Sutherland to establish the principle that the commission had a say in mergers.

Industrialists began to grumble about the double hurdle of national and EC controls, especially since the latter were so ill-defined. Governments came round to the view that the single market required an EC level of merger control and a clear definition of when it should apply. In 1989, after Brittan had replaced Sutherland, the Council of Ministers passed the long-blocked merger regulation. Henceforth the commission rather than national authorities would vet any merger worth more than 5 billion ecus ($5.65 billion), so long as not more than two-thirds of the merged business was based in one member-state, and so long as at least 250 million ecus of each company's business was within the EC.

During Delors's 10 years as president, the commission has increased its powers over competition policy more than any other area. The firmness of Sutherland and Brittan on mergers and state aid contributed to the anti-commission sentiment of the early 1990s. Delors thought them doctrinaire and sometimes blanched when they targeted French firms. But in general he supported their efforts to establish a strong competition policy.

By the end of his first commission, Delors had grown as close to Sutherland as to any of the commissioners. They enjoyed chatting about their common passion for sport. 'I liked Delors above all for his intellect: he had the most formidable brain that I ever encountered,' says Sutherland. 'But he was extremely tense, like a coiled spring.'[16] They remained friends and in May 1993 Delors was instrumental in persuading Sutherland to take the job of GATT director-general.

In Delors's second commission Brittan, Bangemann and Frans Andriessen, who had the external relations portfolio, led the camp of the free-marketeers. Whether the commission argued over increased spending on 'industrial competitiveness', the imposition of 'anti-dumping' duties or the volume of Japanese car imports, Delors could be sure that Brittan would prove his most consistently liberal opponent.

When their disputes threatened to become disruptive, they would often hold a quiet lunch. On such occasions they would avoid ideology, and their strong sense of pragmatism usually allowed a compromise to be found. For instance in 1991 Brittan tried to make Renault pay back FFr12 billion of aid to the French government; Delors sought a minimal sum and in the end they agreed on FFr6 billion.

Delors appreciated Brittan's interest in a wide range of policies, his application and his negotiating skills. He had more respect for Brittan than any other member of his second and third commissions and describes him as 'one of the most brilliant men I have met.'[17] The Englishman's qualities, reinforced by an impressive cabinet, made him the most influential commissioner other than Delors.

Lord Cockfield had come to Brussels with the reputation of a Thatcherite poodle, but soon 'went native' and accepted Delors's authority. Brittan came to Brussels with the same reputation. He too went native, in that he came to believe in a tighter union. But he guarded his independence and never became the loyal supporter of Delors that Cockfield had been. In that Brittan resembled Sutherland. Yet while Delors ultimately warmed to Sutherland he remained suspicious of Brittan. Delors says: 'There are moments when he's not entirely above board. He never misses an occasion to rough me up in the British newspapers.'[18] Brittan's team say they have asked Delors's team for proof of the Englishman turning the press against the Frenchman, and that none was forthcoming.

The other commissioners have a great deal of respect for Brittan but, although he can be charming, few of them warm to him. He becomes absorbed in ideas but – unlike Sutherland – is less interested in people. When Brittan argues a point, his advocate's training may lead him to drive it home more relentlessly than is necessary in order to win. He may not notice how much he has bruised the ego of his opponent. Brittan's political antennae are weak; he sometimes wastes time, energy and political capital in pressing a case that the other commissioners can see he will lose.

Brittan and Delors have little in common. Brittan is an urbane Jewish barrister who seldom expresses emotion. More than Delors, he is inclined to pomposity and to exaggerate his triumphs. Deep down Delors has as much pride as Brittan, but he carries a veneer of Catholic humility. Delors complains that while he often gives Brittan little bits of help, or makes concessions, the favours are seldom returned.

For his part, Brittan complains that if Delors does offer a concession, his cabinet may claw it back, for instance by doctoring the minutes of a meeting. Brittan has made several formal complaints to Delors about supposedly dubious behaviour by his cabinet (see Chapter 6). Brittan's team also complain of Delors's slipperiness: in early 1993, when Brittan and Van den Broek were battling over the division of the external relations portfolio, Delors promised each of them the same bit of territory (they say). Brittan's officials blame such tangles on Delors's dislike of confrontation. Although hard on subordinates, he tries to avoid rows with peers.

YELLOW PERIL AND BIG BROTHER

When Delors talks of the need for a European Union industrial policy, he invariably refers to Japan and America. He defines his sense of European patriotism in relation to those two powers.

> *The European identity is a sense of the universal, the world started out from chez nous, let's be proud of it. We don't want to be brutally Japanified, Americanised or globalised ... My dream is that Europe should shine forth, without dominating, and that it should give the example of a certain fraternity.*[19]

Delors is more suspicious of the Japanese than the Americans, for he thinks they do not play fair or stick to the rules. In private he has complained of the Japanese waging the third world war by other means. Delors sometimes implies that because the Japanese way of life is different, Europe cannot compete on fair terms without a measure of protection.

Delors is probably no more or less anti-Japanese than the average Frenchman – which means that, to the average Anglo-Saxon, he is anti-Japanese. He thinks Europeans too relaxed about the success of Japanese companies. He says: 'They continue to pedal ahead and to establish their power. China and Korea are mistrustful, they fear Japanese domination more than Europeans do.'[20] He says nations wishing to play a role in the world must be 'powerful, generous and open – the Japanese have not yet passed this test. We must be strong with them.'[21]

The success of the 1992 programme led the Japanese government to take the commission seriously. On a visit to Tokyo in May 1991, Delors was treated like a head of state and given an interview with the Emperor. Prompted by Pascal Lamy, Delors proposed that Japan and the EC should broaden their relationship, to discuss politics as well as commerce. Delors hoped that a more rounded relationship might induce the Japanese to greater flexibility in trade disputes. This initiative resulted in the EC–Japan declaration of July 1991, which set down procedures for regular meetings.

A few days before signing this declaration, Delors drank beer with a group of French journalists. He told them he had been 'cuckolded' by the Japanese negotiators and played on yellow being (in France) the colour of cuckolds. Just after the signing, Delors told the *Financial Times* that the point of the declaration was to show the Japanese that they were not ants or outcasts (as his friend Edith Cresson had recently called them). But he complained that 'behind the politicians is an infrastructure, which governs, whose motives are not always the best in the world.'[22]

Delors is disappointed with the results of the declaration. He says that although one must be careful with Americans,

> *it's a clear enough game and we understand each other. But with the Japanese there is no [real] dialogue. Many of my colleagues are content to have obtained Japanese concessions on whisky exports. But I consider that while we fought three years for those concessions they ate up a third of our industry.*

He says he is not a protectionist, but that he just wants to 'defend our interests vigorously.'[23]

Delors's feelings towards America are more ambiguous. He enthuses about American popular culture. He owns thousands of records of American jazz musicians and hundreds of books on American films. An original poster of Citizen Kane hangs on the wall behind his desk. He can recite long passages from Marx Brothers films, and talk knowledgeably about American basketball.

But like most French politicians, Delors dislikes America's *laissez-faire* individualism and its tendency, as he sees it, to bully and to patronise. In October 1992, in the thick of the transatlantic dispute on farm subsidies, he declared: 'If Europe wants to be adult, it must learn to say no to its big brother.'[24]

America's go-getting entrepreneurial culture is alien to Delors. When Delors toured Silicon Valley in 1985, David Packard (of Hewlett-Packard) told him he had started his business with $500 and a garage. Delors asked what he did when he needed more money. Packard said he went to Bank of America, but they gave him 60 forms so he binned them. Delors was concerned: how had Packard got the money? 'I borrowed $2000 from a friend next door.' Delors appeared worried and asked: 'With what formalities?'

There was little love lost between the Reagan administration and Delors. In April 1985 Malcolm Baldridge, America's commerce secretary, declared that Europe should learn from the example of Reaganomics. 'We in Europe don't want *une economie sauvage*,' replied Delors in a speech in Venice. 'We can't take lessons from a country which finances its development with military spending and a budget deficit.' The following year James Baker, then America's Treasury Secretary, intervened personally to prevent Delors taking part in a meeting of the Group of Seven finance ministers in Tokyo.

In 1988 and early 1989, Americans became worried that the 1992 programme would lead to a Fortress Europe. A banking directive threatened to exclude American banks from the European market, in retaliation for American restrictions on foreign banks. The EC also banned American beef because of its hormone content. However, fears of EC protectionism diminished when Leon Brittan moderated the banking directive.

Delors wanted America to treat the EC as an equal partner. In February 1989, shortly after George Bush had moved into the White House (with Baker as his Secretary of State), Delors proposed a new partnership between the EC and America. He said they should collaborate more on economic and political issues, such as how to help Eastern Europe and the Soviet Union. The new administration did not reply and a hurt Delors declined a subsequent invitation to visit Washington.

Then in May, speaking at Boston University, Bush announced a shift in America's EC policy: 'A strong united Europe means a strong America.'[25] Robert Zoellick, Baker's chief adviser, had helped to convince Bush and Baker that America should abandon its old suspicion of the EC. Zoellick argued that since both shared similar values, a stronger EC could help America shoulder the burden of maintaining order around the world. Since America could not stop EC integration, it might as well gain goodwill by welcoming the process. This new line meant the commission and its president had to be taken seriously.

At the end of May 1989, when Bush passed through Brussels, he asked the commission president to lunch in Washington. He rightly assumed that Delors would not refuse a personal invitation. In June, over lunch in the White House, they discussed Eastern Europe. One consequence was

Bush's suggestion that the commission should coordinate the West's aid to the region. Zoellick explains: 'EC officials tend to be insular, as they spend so much time trying to make their Byzantine institutions work. We thought this new role would make them broaden their horizons.'[26]

Bush's reaction to the rapid changes in Germany echoed that of Delors. 'More than most Europeans, we thought the proper response to reunification was deeper European integration, to anchor Germany,' says James Dobbins, one of Bush's EC ambassadors. He claims the EC's move to closer union did, in the event, make it easier for the four occupying powers (America, the Soviet Union, France and Britain) to accept German unity, and for the Soviet Union to withdraw its troops from East Germany. 'Germany and its neighbours could adjust to its reunification with more confidence.'[27]

In December 1989, in Berlin, Baker called for new institutional links between the EC and America. He reaffirmed American support for the European union that Schuman and Monnet had dreamed of, and for German unity.

> We see no conflict between the process of European integration and the experience of cooperation between the EC and its neighbours: the attraction of the EC for countries in the east depended most on its continual vitality.[28]

Such words delighted Delors as much as they made Thatcher feel uneasy.

Baker's speech bore fruit the following September, when the EC and America agreed to a 'Transatlantic Declaration'. Henceforth the American president would meet the president of the commission and the president of the Community (the prime minister who happened to hold that rotating job) twice a year. America's secretary of state would also meet the 12 foreign ministers and the president of the commission twice a year.

Delors seemed to have won the equal treatment he desired. Yet the relationship between the commission and the Bush administration never became genuinely warm. The pragmatic Baker understood the importance of getting on with Delors. But Bush never felt comfortable with Delors and sometimes saw the EC as a mere trade club. Some of those who had Bush's ear liked neither Delors nor his organisation. Brent Scowcroft, the national security adviser, thought Delors anti-NATO; Carla Hills, the trade representative, saw him as a French agent; and James Brady, the treasury secretary, viewed EMU as a threat to the dollar.

When Delors met Bush he spoke his language, out of politeness. Delors learned to speak English after becoming commission president and, despite a strong accent, makes himself understood. However Delors's wit, charm and intelligence are lost when he speaks English. Thus Bush found Delors less impressive than did many of the State Department's francophone officials.

Several of those officials believe the Bush administration did not handle Delors well. 'His institution was on the make and he was looking for respect,' says one of them. 'We said the right things but Delors felt that when they came from the White House or the Treasury they were not sincere – which was true.'

Zoellick notes, with some regret, that senior figures like Bush, Baker and Scowcroft were all problem-solvers rather than strategists. 'We didn't have anyone at that level who could engage with Delors on strategy.' Zoellick thinks Delors underestimated the risk of damaging the transatlantic defence link, and points to his lack of expertise on military matters. But he admires Delors and says no-one so attached to popular American culture could be called anti-American.[29]

During 1992 Americans became disillusioned with the EC. European attempts to mediate in the Yugoslav conflict failed dismally. The Community proved a shambolic and incoherent negotiating partner in the GATT talks. When Delors tried to stop a deal on farm subsidies, in November, he lost Bush's goodwill. The White House blamed the episode on Delors's ambitions for the French presidency, and complained that its support for European union had been poorly repaid.

Bill Clinton's administration, which took office in January 1993, continued the policy of favouring European integration. Although Clinton showed less interest in Europe than Bush had done, he got on much better with Delors. Clinton found a kindred spirit who shared his eclectic approach to economic policy and his enjoyment of intellectual debate. In January 1994, when he visited the commission president in Brussels, they spent nearly an hour and a half of a four-hour meeting discussing Delors's white paper on competitiveness. Both enthused about the potential of multimedia 'information highways'. They agreed that Europe needed to learn from America's labour market and that America needed to learn from Europe's social safety net.

MAJOR PROBLEMS

Any Frenchman with a Gallic perspective and limited international experience is liable to be described by his compatriots as *hexagonal*. The origin of the term is that France, on a map, looks like a hexagon. The author has never seen Delors angrier than when informed that a close friend thought him '*très hexagonal*'. 'Really, if I'm hexagonal, what can one say about the rest of the French? That hurts. For the past 30 years I've been the one saying to the French: look what's happening abroad. I've studied the English since 1950.'[30]

Delors is both right and wrong. He has read copiously on the politics, economics and social systems of many countries. But his knowledge of foreign climes, such as Britain, is more theoretical than practical. Apart from meetings and conferences Delors has travelled little outside France. In the 1950s and 1960s, like most Frenchmen of his generation, he spent half his holidays with his parents (in Corrèze) and the other half with his in-laws (in the French Basque country). Delors's understanding of how other Europeans think and behave is, on occasion, limited – but much less so than when he arrived in Brussels.

Delors often expresses admiration for Westminster democracy. In February 1992 he said on French television:

> *You have to keep the British in the EC for their democratic tradition if nothing else. They have the best journalistic debate, the best parliamentary committees, the best quizzing of prime ministers after a summit.*[31]

Some of Delors's close personal friends are British, and he is not anti-British in the way that he can be anti-American.

Yet a sizeable minority of the English detests Delors. His federalist prescriptions infuriate Thatcherites and their many friends in the press. His success in increasing the sway of 'Brussels' in British life has grated against a proud tradition of national independence. Sounding, thinking and looking like a Frenchman has not helped Delors's image. His abstract and complex style of argument is inimical to many Anglo-Saxons. His tendency to be arrogant and self-important proved a boon to those who wished to caricature him as the Napoleon of Brussels. Although Delors wears the smartest suits, his stocky build, stiff gait and erect posture give him a faintly Napoleonic appearance.

Even pro-European Conservatives found that attacking Delors was the easiest way to win a loud cheer at their annual conference. 'How dare a jumped-up French bureaucrat like Jacques Delors tell John Major what to do?' asked David Hunt, the employment secretary, in October 1993. The Foreign Office remained a rare outpost of British Delorophilia. Geoffrey Howe and Douglas Hurd, two foreign secretaries, enjoyed Delors's company. David Hannay and John Kerr, two EC ambassadors, speak fondly of Delors.

Delors has a particular problem with British prime ministers. He is intolerant of what he sees as Major's obsession with the short-term tactics of party politics. They got off to a bad start in October 1990, when the Chancellor of the Exchequer, as he then was, took sterling into the ERM. Delors told Major the rate of DM2.95 was too high, and that by acting unilaterally, rather than discussing the pound's entry at a meeting of finance ministers, he had broken EC rules. Major did not take kindly to this ticking off. 'He later explained to me that the rate of 2.95 was the concession he had had to make to Mrs Thatcher,' says Delors.[32]

Four months after Major became prime minister, in March 1991, Delors delivered a lecture on defence policy at the International Institute for Strategic Studies in London. Afterwards, over dinner at 10 Downing Street, Major tried to be friendly and asked Delors about his speech. Delors explained his ideas in more detail than was necessary and Major argued back. They spent the whole evening squabbling about defence policy, which is not Delors's strongest suit. Major did not realise Delors could not understand all of his English. Delors did not appear interested in trying to find common ground with Major.

Delors's tendency to shoot from the hip upsets Major. At the end of September 1992, Major prevaricated over ratifying the Maastricht treaty. In a speech in Brussels, Delors complained of a 'deficit of behaviour' among some politicians, and made it clear whom he had in mind. Referring to Major's comments after the Maastricht summit, Delors said that when a leader 'goes back home and says "game, set and match", and then says "I'm going to work for Europe with the others", one understands the stupor of the citizens of this country.' The EC risked damage from 'nationalistic vanity.'[33]

Six weeks later, in the middle of the crisis which followed Ray MacSharry's resignation as EC negotiator in the GATT talks, Delors visited the London School of Economics. He received a message that the prime minister wanted to see him. Angry at being summoned, and at comments from Michael Heseltine, the trade and industry secretary, that he had acted for France in the GATT talks, Delors drove to 10 Downing St.

Delors told Major that Heseltine's comments were unacceptable. A polite Major said that he wanted to talk about the future, not the past, and that it was essential to get the GATT talks moving. Delors argued against making further concessions to America, but Major urged him to get a deal at any price. When Delors said one or two EC members would not give further ground, Major raised his voice: 'We have to get the talks started to help the unemployed!'

Delors shouted back: 'We have to think of the 12 million farmers, many of whom are struggling to grow oilseeds and to export cereals!' Delors implored Major to consider 'questions of society'. Neither appeared to understand the other's arguments.

Major asked Delors to have some understanding of his domestic difficulties. He said a recent speech by Martin Bangemann, the senior German commissioner, which had described the Maastricht treaty as a stepping-stone to a federal Europe, had almost destroyed his government; just after that speech he had scraped through a House of Commons vote on Maastricht with a majority of three.

They agreed on a communiqué on the need for a GATT deal. Major then suggested they shake hands on the doorstep. Still in a huff, Delors did not reply. As they walked down the corridor towards the front door, Major repeated his suggestion. Delors gave an affirmative grunt, so they went outside, smiled for the cameras and shook hands. Delors recalls of the meeting: 'Major lost control of himself. That I will never forget, one doesn't treat people like that.'[34]

During the Edinburgh summit of December 1992, Delors thought Major had promised to remove Britain's veto on funding for HDTV. The British say Major had merely agreed to another meeting on the matter. After the summit Delors and Major shared a flight to Washington. Delors complained to journalists that Major had not kept his word on HDTV. This got back to Major, who walked to where Delors was seated and, in front of several journalists, harangued him. 'He insulted me in saying, "I won't give a penny, I'll oppose everything, it's scandalous",' says Delors. 'All that with such a tone of command, treating me like a farmer's boy! For the second time in a month!'[35]

The following month Hoover closed a factory in Dijon and, attracted by lower wages and social charges, shifted production to Cambuslang in Scotland. France's labour minister, Martine Aubry, and her father were furious. 'The controversy on social dumping: M Delors et Mme Aubry condemn the transfer of Hoover in Scotland', Le Monde headlined on 29 January. Delors said it was outrageous that countries were competing against each other to lower social standards. He added that if the commission's directive on workers' councils – blocked by Britain – had been in force, Hoover would have found it harder to play off one group of workers against another. Major crowed: 'Europe can have the Social Charter, we can have the jobs.' Delors replied that if the prime minister said such things, 'how can the British people believe that we're trying to build a family?'[36]

Relations between Major and Delors remained fraught, yet Major respected Delors's ability as an economic analyst. At the Copenhagen summit, in June 1993, Delors produced a paper on Europe's declining competitiveness and made a verbal presentation on the same subject. British officials thought the paper full of unsound economics. Yet Major so liked the verbal presentation that he ordered his officials to distribute the paper to the press.

'Delors is sometimes unfair to the prime minister, when he expresses impatience,' says one of Major's senior ministers. 'Delors is fine with Britons who are interested in the EC, but makes little effort with those who are not.'

DELORS'S NEMESIS

From its birth in the Uruguayan resort of Punta del Este, in September 1986, a nemesis haunted Delors's presidency. The 'Uruguay Round' of the General Agreement on Tariffs and Trade (GATT) often brought out the worst in Delors – uncontrollable emotion, a Gallic view of the world and deep mistrust of the Anglo-Saxons.

The Uruguay Round aimed to lower tariffs on industrial goods further than earlier GATT rounds, and to liberalise new areas such as services and agriculture. GATT's members agreed to complete the round in December 1990, at a grand meeting in Brussels' Heysel stadium.

The technicalities of these negotiations were mind-bogglingly complex, but huge issues were at stake. The Uruguay Round was rather like a 1992 programme for the world economy: it promised to boost trade and thus to increase global wealth by several hundred billion dollars. However any liberalisation creates losers as well as winners. Some French farmers believed they would suffer from the Uruguay Round, which is why it proved so difficult to negotiate.

When the EC takes part in trade talks, the Council of Ministers gives the commission a mandate, the commission negotiates on behalf of the Community, and the council must approve any ensuing deal. Throughout the Uruguay Round, both the council and the commission suffered sharp internal divisions. On the council, ministers from Britain, Germany, Holland and Denmark usually wanted more liberalisation, and the others less. On Delors's 1989 to 1992 commission, Frans Andriessen, the Dutchman who had overall responsibility for GATT, often wanted to make concessions, while Ray MacSharry, the Irish agriculture commissioner, took a tougher line. Public rowing between Andriessen and MacSharry weakened the commission's negotiating hand, but Delors did little to end it.

By the summer of 1990 arguments between America and the EC on farm subsidies were holding up progress on the rest of the Uruguay Round. America demanded cuts of 70 to 90 per cent in farm subsidies, over 10 years. The EC described that as ridiculous and unrealistic but made no counter-offer. Visiting Delors in July, James Baker asked if he could accept the GATT secretariat's latest proposal for lowering food prices, tariffs and export subsidies. To the surprise of the Americans – and his own staff – Delors said he would resign rather than accept that proposal.

In the autumn of 1990 EC ministers met six times to consider an offer on farm subsidies but, partly because of French intransigence, could not agree. Delors kept quiet and did nothing to break the deadlock. Finally, in November – just a month before the round was scheduled to end – the council proposed a 30 per cent cut in subsidies. However that cut would be over the 10 years which began in 1986, which meant a real reduction of about 15 per cent.

The lateness and the meagreness of this offer was the principal cause of the Heysel meeting's breakdown in December. Delors avoided the occasion while Andriessen and MacSharry contradicted each other in public. Carla Hills, the American negotiator, made over-the-top demands and provocatively called for the abolition of the CAP, which did nothing to increase the chances of an agreement. But the world blamed the breakdown on the Community.

A week later, at Delors's Rome summit press conference, a question on the GATT triggered an explosive response.

> *The Americans should stop insulting us, I'm not going to be an accomplice to the depopulation of the land. It's not up to the Americans to tell us how to organise our farm policy and the balance of our society. Their attitude is to treat the EC as if it had the plague and then encourage the rest of the world to join in.*[37]

The chances of a GATT deal improved in July 1991, when the commission approved a plan from Delors and MacSharry to reform the CAP. They hoped to control overproduction by decoupling the income of farmers from their output. Lower guaranteed prices would allow the EC to spend less on buying up surplus production and on subsidising exports. Small farmers would receive compensatory cash payments, based on the area of their land, so that they would not lose income. Bigger farmers would receive partial compensation so long as they set aside some land.

By lowering subsidies, the plan would bridge some of the gap between Europe and America in the negotiations on the farm trade. However, Delors and MacSharry denied their proposals had anything to do with GATT, lest the French accuse them of giving in to American pressure. When the Council of Ministers passed the CAP reform, in May 1992,

France, Britain and Germany insisted that large arable farmers receive full compensation for lower prices. Even modified, however, the CAP reform cut prices (by 29 per cent for cereals) and thus discouraged overproduction.

French farmers never liked the reform, since cash payments implied they were pensioners rather than productive workers. Delors worked hard to sell the scheme, telling farmers they should treat the payments as a salary for looking after the countryside. But he also sought to reassure them he had not forgotten his Corrèzian roots: 'The rural world has developed around farmers, who are, at the same time, producers of goods, creators of civilisation and gardeners of nature.'[38] In another speech he asserted that 'Europe is and must remain a "green power". If the Uruguay Round means giving up the right to export, it will fail.'[39] Yet French farmers attacked Delors's cottage in Burgundy, pumping defoliant into the garden and cattle feed into the living room.

The CAP reform offered a chance to revive the Uruguay Round. The commission delegated responsibility for GATT to four commissioners: Andriessen and Bangemann, who favoured flexibility, and Delors and MacSharry, who wanted to be tough with the Americans. A senior commission official recalls: 'Delors did not discourage a deal: he was happy to let Andriessen tackle GATT and make a mess of it. Delors never seemed to make GATT a priority.'

The multilateral negotiations could not advance until the EC and America settled their differences. George Bush did nothing to help when, in September 1992 – and in mid-election campaign – he announced a doubling of America's subsidised cereals exports. Delors's reply on French radio helped even less:

> *The imperial power won't always be able to mock the others. One should not believe that because America has friends in Europe, and some get rather frightened when it raises its voice, that we are going to let ourselves be trampled on.*[40]

By early October two major issues were keeping the EC and America apart. First, the EC had ignored two rulings from GATT panels that its oilseed subsidies were too high. America wanted the EC to accept a ceiling on oilseed production. Second, America had proposed cutting the volume of subsidised farm exports by 24 per cent over six years. The EC would not go beyond 18 per cent, although both sides agreed to cut the value of these exports by 36 per cent, and internal subsidies by 20 per cent, over six years.

Suddenly, three weeks before the American election, Bush made a personal bid to wind up the Uruguay Round. In Brussels on 11 and 12 October, American negotiators gave ground on the liberalisation of services and proposed a 22 per cent cut in the volume of farm exports. MacSharry saw a chance to clinch a deal before he retired from the commission at the end of the year.

Having left school at 16, MacSharry had run a road-haulage business before becoming a Fianna Fàil Minister of Finance. After becoming agriculture commissioner in 1989, MacSharry revealed a canny understanding of farmers. He lacked Sutherland's gregariousness and intellect, but had all of his pugnacity.

MacSharry, Andriessen and Bangemann wanted to go half way to meet the Americans, but Delors did not. MacSharry claims that Delors's main concern was the timing of a deal rather than its substance. 'Delors told me he did not want a deal before the French elections [due in March 1993] because of the upheaval it would cause in France.'[41] Delors denies ever saying that. MacSharry made arrangements to meet Edward Madigan, America's agriculture secretary, in Chicago. Delors says he did not try to prevent MacSharry from going because Andriessen had assured him of American concessions in other areas of the GATT which later turned out to be fictitious.[42]

In Chicago on 3 November, America's election day, MacSharry and Madigan came close to striking a deal. John Major, eager for an agreement, took the unusual step of sending John Gummer, then president of the council of farm ministers, to Chicago. Ministers are supposed to leave the commission a free hand on such occasions. Gummer did not enter the negotiating chamber but sent in his own proposals.

'We knew they wanted an accord, but that we would have to move,' says MacSharry. 'There was talk of a 21 per cent cut in export volumes, and we might have agreed on that.[43] But other issues prevented a deal. Madigan wanted a 10 million tonne annual ceiling on EC oilseed output. MacSharry refused any ceiling and suggested a formula linked to the area of crops. Nor could the two sides agree on a 'peace clause': MacSharry wanted both sides to renounce the right to challenge the other's trade regime before a GATT panel.

Madigan left the room in order to vote. MacSharry then took a series of telephone calls – from Jean-Pierre Soisson, the French farm minister; from Pascal Lamy, who was in New York to run a marathon; and from Delors, twice. Delors told MacSharry that a figure of 21 per cent would mean cutting output by even more than the CAP reform already required – and would therefore exceed the commission's negotiating mandate.

Delors said he would oppose such a deal, that the commission would vote it down, and that if it went to the Council of Ministers France would wield the 'Luxembourg Compromise' (a veto).

MacSharry says he had gone to Chicago assuming that 21 per cent would be acceptable; Delors's calls therefore seemed to change the commission line. He told Delors he had no intention of going beyond the CAP reform, because a 21 per cent cut would, in his view, fit within it. MacSharry says:

> *The Americans heard some of the calls, and understood we were under pressure. They thought, what is the point if the EC can't deliver on the figure [of 21 per cent]? So the Americans became more demanding on the peace clause.*[44]

The phone calls left MacSharry tense and upset, and undoubtedly made it harder for him to negotiate. 'Without the pressure perhaps there would have been a deal,' he says, adding that if there had been, a majority of both the commissioners and the farm ministers would have backed it. 'If the peace clause had been all right I might have done a deal and told Delors to stuff it. This was very important for the EC's image: for three years the world had accused the EC of stopping a deal on farm trade.'[45]

The American line stiffened with Madigan's return from voting, and the talks broke down. During his flight from Chicago to Brussels, MacSharry watched *The Sting*. When he landed he told friends that 'The Sting II' would be even better. MacSharry delivered it on 4 November, in the form of a letter to the commission president. He said he was resigning his responsibilities in the GATT talks because Delors had undermined the negotiations. MacSharry told a few journalists of the letter's contents.

Newspapers from many countries – although not France – led with the story that Delors had tried to wreck the GATT talks. Delors's demonisation spread beyond Britain. Michael Fuchs, president of Germany's foreign trade association, said: 'Delors equals chauvinism, protectionism and selfishness. We don't need another Sun King in Brussels – one in Paris was enough.'

In complete disarray, the commission could not say who was responsible for negotiating on agriculture. Andriessen said on Dutch television that Delors's point of view did not and should not prevail in the commission. The 'Cairns group', which linked agricultural exporting countries, blamed the commission for disrupting world trade, promoting unemployment and harming the third world.

Delors's aides struggled to minimise the damage. They claimed MacSharry was overoptimistic on the impact of the CAP reform, and that a further cut of 2 million tonnes of cereals would be needed to satisfy the 21 per cent figure (the EC produced about 180 million tonnes of grain a year). They said the president had a duty to help any member-state which risked isolation, and that in the past he had, for instance, helped Germany on coal subsidies. They added that Delors sympathised with small peasants because of the memory of his grandfather, and that he tended to overreact to American bullying. Thus the assumption of many Anglo-Saxons – that Delors had put his ambition for the French presidency before a GATT deal – was entirely false, according to the aides.

MacSharry is dismissive of these excuses.

> *How is the small farmer affected by agricultural exports? He feeds grain to cattle or sells it to cooperatives. The export subsidies go to the big farms of the Paris basin. There was no American bullying in Chicago: we were the ones who were doing the bullying.*[16]

Delors now describes the near deal of Chicago as 'scandalous and unbalanced'. What he said to MacSharry during those phone calls represented

> *my opinion, I didn't do it for France. I took no instructions from the French government, I can swear to you on my mother's life. We never had meetings with the French, saying what should we do, what do you want?*[17]

In the week after the Chicago talks, MacSharry planned a routine trip to Ireland. When he applied for travel expenses the financial controller told him he had exceeded his annual limit and that he could have no more. MacSharry says: 'When I queried this I found the blocking order had come from the president's cabinet. So I paid for the trip myself. The timing of this episode was not a coincidence.'[48] The president's men say it was a coincidence, that MacSharry had the highest expenses of any commissioner and that he should not have used EC funds to pay for private trips home.

Spain, Portugal, Belgium and Greece offered France moderate support in its opposition to the near deal of Chicago. The other member-states were keen for an accord. The German and British governments told Delors bluntly that he must restart negotiations. Delors faced a simple choice: either bow to the wishes of most member-states, try to reach an agreement with the Americans and hope to salvage his reputation; or resign, wrap himself in the Tricolour and campaign against the Uruguay Round.

Delors's head proved stronger than his heart. On 11 November he met MacSharry, Andriessen and Bangemann. The four of them decided that the Irishman should take back his job. MacSharry flew to Washington on the understanding that he would negotiate on his terms. In Blair House he agreed on a 21 per cent cut in export volumes over six years and a peace clause which would last six years. However, Madigan rejected MacSharry's offer of a 5.13 million hectare limit on oilseed production. MacSharry flew home, but before he reached his office Bush had overruled Madigan. The 'Blair House accord' was sealed on 20 November.

In private Delors said the deal was a bad deal but that he could live with it. In public he accepted it with grace and ensured the commission gave it unanimous support. He approved a commission study which judged the deal compatible – beef exports excepted – with the CAP reform. 'As I was president I affirmed my solidarity [with the other commissioners] and from that moment on anyone who has a little understanding for me knows I spoilt my political career in France,' he says, ignoring that the episode failed to dent his opinion poll ratings.[49]

Delors recalls a letter from an official, which told him he was a great president because he had put the interests of the commission before his own. 'That's what I did . . . but on that day I lost authority in the commission, and in France people attacked me [for accepting the accord] throughout the electoral campaign of March 1993.' Delors says he could easily have rejected the accord, resigned from the commission and urged Europe to stand firm against America.[50]

Delors set about selling the agreement on farm subsidies in France. In December, during a television interview, he said that triumphant protectionism was messing up the world economy and that a GATT deal would help to prevent it.

> *What is the aim of GATT on agriculture? It's that the two elephants who monopolise the market, the United States and the Community, leave some space for the developing countries. So many politicians make us cry with their Sunday speeches on these countries, but do they think about them in the week, when they stir up French farmers and lie to them? Not at all.*[51]

Such arguments were a rarity in France. Neither employers' lobbies nor political leaders had dared to speak in favour of the Uruguay Round, for fear of being thought anti-peasant. The socialist government of Pierre Bérégovoy, plumbing the depths of unpopularity, threatened to wield the Luxembourg Compromise against the Blair House accord. Delors warned that a French veto would damage the influence and image of France and that 'at that moment the position of the two French commissioners would become difficult.'[52]

Delors's intervention failed to soften French attitudes. In the run-up to the general election of March 1993, French politicians of all persuasions denounced America and the Blair House accord. The uncertain standing of that accord and the inexperience of the Clinton administration held up progress on the rest of the GATT round. Edouard Balladur's centre-right government, formed in March, demanded that the farm subsidy agreement be renegotiated. America's new trade negotiator, Mickey Kantor, refused. Like many other EC members, Germany wanted the Blair House accord but was not prepared to force it on the French.

Delors told friends that America was using GATT as a means of prising the 12 apart. But he gave a free hand to Leon Brittan, who had become the trade commissioner in January 1993. Brittan sought 'clarifications' and 'interpretations' of the Blair House accord so that France could export a bit more grain. Balladur insisted that nothing short of a completely new agreement would suffice. For most of the year Delors – in common with the rest of France's politicians – said nothing in favour of a GATT deal.

Peter Sutherland became GATT director-general in July and injected new urgency into the talks. He persuaded GATT's 116 members to aim for a 15 December conclusion of the Uruguay Round. However by September, with the talks between the EC and America still deadlocked, the deadline began to look unrealistic.

Behind the scenes Delors started to play an active role, urging Balladur – with immediate success – to soften his government's bellicose rhetoric. Then on 17 October, to the great relief of his closest advisers, Delors said on French television that it was urgent to reach a GATT agreement. He pointed out that French exporters of goods and services would benefit to the tune of FFr5–6 billion a year. He criticised entrepreneurs for saying only in private, and never in public that they wanted a GATT deal.

> *France is in the process of inventing a Maginot line and getting itself a bad reputation in 80 countries. A kind of collective trauma has seized our country and is damaging to the most profound interests of France.*[53]

In Brussels on 7 December, Kantor and Brittan finally stuck a deal on farm subsidies. The Blair House accord would stand, but Kantor agreed to 'interpretations' which would allow EC farmers to export an extra 8 million tonnes of grain over six years. The 21 per cent cut in the volume of exports would be based on 1991 and 1992, rather than 1986 to 1989, when output had been lower. Grain already in storage would be exempt from the cuts.

This cleared the way for the rest of the world to complete the Uruguay Round at GATT's Geneva headquarters, on 15 December 1993. The agreement cut industrial tariffs by an average of 40 per cent and phased out quotas on textiles. It extended GATT rules to some service industries, to public procurement, to intellectual property and to agriculture. It also covered new procedures for settling trade disputes, the replacement of GATT by a stronger 'World Trade Organisation' and much else. The World Bank, the OECD and the GATT secretariat estimated that the direct benefit of the Uruguay Round would be $210 to $270 billion of extra global output, by 2002 in 1992 prices, and that indirect gains would be much greater.

After seven years Delors's nemesis had been laid to rest. But it lived long enough to inflict lasting damage on his international reputation. Delors is still bitter about the behaviour of Andriessen and MacSharry in November 1992. 'If I had followed my feelings I would have hit them hard, because they demolished me before the press. Since I've been at the commission I've never used the press against someone like that'.

He may be right, but his cabinet has sometimes thrown mud at other commissioners via journalists. Delors believes that he is an innocent compared with skilled media manipulators. 'It's a matter for everyone's conscience: perhaps Carla Hills and Leon Brittan would say to me: "Jacques, you don't know anything about politics".'[54]

At various times during the Uruguay Round, Lamy counselled Delors to show more flexibility. However he backed his boss to the hilt during the Chicago episode and now claims that events have proved Delors right. By forcing MacSharry to get a better oilseed deal in Washington, says Lamy, Delors increased the chance of France accepting the cut in farm exports. 'Delors reacted with a French sensibility, but if this sensibility hadn't been strongly represented, the Community crisis would have been immediate.' He means that France would have used the Luxembourg Compromise straight away, rather than just threaten it.[55]

Many who observed Delors during the GATT talks were struck by his ambivalence. Zygmunt Tyszkiewicz, secretary-general of Unice, the European employers' lobby, says: 'We often told Delors he should put his weight and prestige behind GATT. He would always tell us he was just off to see Bush or Clinton, but he never put "Delors" into GATT, as he had into social policy.'[56]

An American ambassador judges Delors badly informed on farm trade, noting that he sometimes got his numbers wrong and that he never seemed to understand that lower export subsidies would not hurt small farmers.

> *Despite being so well-informed on most issues, and despite his extraordinary intelligence, the farm trade was a blindspot. On all other GATT issues – industrial policy, Airbus, even television – he was rational, but on agriculture he would raise his voice and talk emotionally of Corrèze and rural depopulation.*

The ambassador's conclusion sums up Delors's attitude to GATT: 'His head said the Uruguay Round was essential, his heart said stand firm on agriculture.'

CHAPTER NINE

THE ROAD TO MAASTRICHT

A YEAR OF tortuous, ill-tempered and often tedious negotiations culminated in the Dutch town of Maastricht, on 10 December 1991, with an agreement on a new European constitution. The two inter-governmental conferences, on EMU and political union, had progressed through monthly meetings of foreign ministers and of finance ministers, weekly meetings of officials, 'informal' ministerial gatherings at weekends, working parties, position papers and draft treaties – all of which, to the lay person, appeared almost incomprehensible.

But behind the sub-clauses, the legalistic jargon and the procedural wrangles, important principles were at stake. Would the Community evolve along the federal path set out by Monnet, or towards de Gaulle's *'Europe des patries'*? Should there be one Community or several different bodies? Would the commission gain or lose power? What role would the EC have in social policy? How would the treaty attempt to fill the 'democratic deficit'? How much should common foreign policies constrain member-states? Should the 12 agree on European defence arrangements or continue to rely on NATO? When would monetary union begin?

Looking back on the two IGCs, Delors remembers them as 'a real nightmare'.[1] By pursuing an overambitious strategy in the conference on political union, he lost control of its direction. The successes of 1988 and 1989 – the implementation of the 1992 programme, the Delors package and the Delors Committee – had made him over-confident. In 1990 Delors had shown signs of hubris, but his influence remained near its peak. In 1991 he pushed a federal agenda, apparently oblivious to the growing tide of anti-commission sentiment in national capitals.

Delors's support for a model of political union that had no chance of being adopted undermined his authority. His judgement appears to have been weakened by the strength of his own convictions. He believed passionately that what was at stake was whether Europe would flourish or decline. That was an issue on which, against his normal nature, he would not compromise.

The sheer volume of EC business may have contributed to tactical errors: the negotiation of the European Economic Area, talks with Poland,

Hungary and Czechoslovakia on 'Europe Agreements', efforts to restart the GATT talks and reform of the Common Agricultural Policy all competed for his time and energy. In the commission's work programme for 1991, Delors had listed no less than 11 priorities. Wars in the Gulf and Yugoslavia added to the difficulties: they harmed the standing of the EC and therefore of Delors.

Nevertheless Delors proved a powerful influence in the IGC on monetary union. That conference had already been well prepared and ran more smoothly than the one on political union. The nub of the argument concerned the transitional phase of EMU: what would the central institution do, when would it be set up and how would the EC decide to start the final phase? Delors, the French and a majority of governments wanted to do as much as possible, as soon as possible. The Germans and the Dutch wanted to do as little as possible for as long as possible.

The British spent much of the conference on the sidelines. Their draft treaty, which revived the idea of a monetary fund to issue 'hard ecus' during phase two of EMU, gathered dust. Norman Lamont, the Chancellor of the Exchequer, showed little interest in the principal arguments of the IGC and focused on the nature of Britain's opt-out.

Draft treaties from the commission and France called for the European Central Bank (ECB) to be set up at the start of phase two, in 1994. Phase three of EMU would begin when a qualified majority of governments was in favour. Germany's draft, which hit the conference table with a thud in March, proposed a mere Council of Central Bank Governors in the second phase. There would be no ECB until the European Council had decided, by unanimity, that phase three would start. The German draft left no doubt that national central banks (or rather one in particular) would run monetary policy during phase two.

Delors authorised his spokesman, Bruno Dethomas, to say the Germans had reneged on the conclusions of the first Rome summit. 'Jacques Delors is far too intelligent to have made such a foolish statement,' said Helmut Kohl, who described the accusation as 'absurd'. The Chancellor was right, for the Rome conclusions had referred to the creation of a 'new institution' rather than a central bank.

Luxembourg held the EC presidency and so chaired the conference in the first half of the year. In May Luxembourg published a draft treaty which split the difference between the French and the Germans: a council of governors would be created in 1994 and an ECB in 1996. Meeting in Luxembourg in May, ministers agreed on three principles to govern the passage of countries to the third phase: no coercion, no veto, and no arbitrary exclusion. These principles meant that the other countries could not force Britain to go forward, that Britain could not stop the others going forward, and that no country which had achieved economic convergence could be prevented from going forward.

When the Dutch took over the presidency in July, they – with some help from the Germans – prepared a new draft treaty. Earlier drafts had assumed the EC as a whole would decide when to start phase three, and that members which did not make the grade would have derogations (temporary exemptions) from the monetary union. But the Dutch proposed that at the end of 1996, if six or more countries wanted to move ahead and had satisfied convergence criteria over a two-year period, they could start a currency union among themselves. The criteria would be rates of interest and inflation at the lowest EC levels, no excessive budget deficit, and no devaluation within the ERM. Those in the advance guard could veto any other country from joining them, if they judged that it did not meet the criteria. Laggards would not even have the comfort of a derogation.

When the finance ministers debated this draft on 9 September, Delors launched a furious attack. He said a 'two-speed' EMU went against the Community principle that all members shared the same goals – even if some needed derogations. Delors also wanted unemployment to be added to the list of convergence criteria.

Only the Germans defended the idea of two speeds, so Wim Kok, the Dutch minister, had to offer revisions. He suggested that the European Council as a whole should decide when to start phase three, that seven or eight countries would have to meet convergence criteria before it could begin, and that those which did not would have derogations. These changes were as much symbolic as substantive, but they mattered a great deal to countries such as Spain, Portugal and Italy, which suspected they would not be in the first group. Other parts of the Dutch draft won general approval. A European Monetary Institute (EMI) would be set up in 1994, becoming the ECB before the start of phase three.

Germany's arguments carried the most weight in these debates, for the other members still worried about its commitment to EMU. For three months (until September) Theo Waigel, the German minister, had been 'too busy' to attend ministerial sessions of the IGC. The Germans continued to argue for sanctions against countries with 'excessive deficits'. Only the strange alliance of Delors and Lamont argued against the centralisation of fiscal policy. Delors claimed that EC sanctions would breach subsidiarity and be unnecessary: any government in difficulties would need an EC loan, and that would have conditions, such as budget cuts, attached. Lamont argued that markets would discipline profligate governments by demanding higher rates of interest.

Waigel replied that the markets could not be trusted: they would never believe the rule – agreed by all – that the EC would not bail out bankrupt governments, and would therefore lend to the most spendthrift of them. Pierre Bérégovoy, the French finance minister, favoured binding rules for a different reason. He wanted an EC fiscal policy as a counterweight to the ECB's monetary policy, and thought rules on borrowing a step in that direction. In October Delors and Lamont conceded defeat: governments which continued to run 'excessive deficits' would, after public warnings from the EC, face financial penalties.

In November ministers argued over the nature of the EMI. The French wanted a substantial institute and the Germans a flimsy one. The final compromise pleased the French by giving the EMI its own capital and the ability to manage members' foreign currency reserves, if they wished. It pleased the Germans by giving the EMI the right to coordinate but not to control members' monetary policies.

Many of the finance ministers treated the subject of EMU with scepticism, perhaps because it would curb their own power. But in the weeks before the summit, Delors and the French started to win more arguments. The less sceptical prime ministers and foreign ministers put pressure on the finance ministers to minimise the risk of a country blocking the start of the final phase.

The last finance ministers' meeting before the summit began at the Dutch resort of Scheveningen, on 1 December, and ended in Brussels after three days and nights of continuous negotiation. Delors criticised the current Dutch draft for giving any member the right to opt out of phase three. Although he did not say so directly, he feared Germany might use a provision that had been put in the treaty to please Britain. Delors proposed a legally binding protocol which gave only Britain the right to opt out. Lamont, anxious that Britain should not appear a special case, demanded that everyone have that right. Delors retorted that 'a generalised opt-out would hang over EMU like a sword of Damocles.' The Danish minister wanted the right to opt out of EMU and began the meeting by backing Lamont. Later on, however, he said he would prefer a customised protocol for Denmark. That left 11 ministers against Lamont. Kok, in the chair, deleted the generalised opt-out.

Bérégovoy proposed a vote in 1996 on whether at least seven countries met the convergence criteria. If there was unanimity that they did so, phase three would begin. A negative result would lead to another vote in 1998, when a simple majority would suffice to start phase three. The Bérégovoy plan proved popular, for it would ensure that Britain could not veto fixed exchange rates. By the time the Maastricht summit began, almost all the arguments over EMU had been resolved. The treaty which emerged from that summit blended the Delors Report with German priorities.

DELORS'S DESIGN

While the 12 laboured over draft treaties they had to cope with the war against Saddam Hussein, the onset of fighting in Yugoslavia and the break-up of the Soviet Union. The 12 struggled to maintain a common line and to respond effectively to these challenges, but their embarrassing perform-ance lowered expectations of what political union could achieve.

By the first week of 1991 the EC's united front on the Gulf had begun to crumble. France wanted a European peace initiative before the United Nations' deadline for Iraq to leave Kuwait expired on 15 January. Roland Dumas, France's foreign minister, persuaded his EC colleagues to invite Tariq Aziz to a meeting in Luxembourg – but the Iraqi foreign minister turned them down. Mitterrand then sent Claude Cheysson on a mission to Iraq which proved fruitless. Delors complained to Rocard, the French prime minister, that solo diplomacy was damaging the EC.

On 14 January EC foreign ministers decided that further peace initia-tives would be pointless. However French diplomats grumbled that Brit-ain had disabled the EC by preventing it from acting independently of America. France put a plan to the UN security council which linked Iraqi withdrawal from Kuwait to a peace conference on the Middle East. Britain and America blocked the French plan and the deadline expired with the allies rowing. When operation Desert Storm began, on 17 January, Jordan, Egypt and Turkey had not received the $2 billion that the EC had promised them the previous September (the money arrived in February).

Strictly, most of this embarrassing performance could not be blamed on the Community, since diplomacy was the preserve of European Political Cooperation. The more federalist governments argued that the disarray reinforced the need for common foreign policies. But Delors knew that damage had been done. 'Being brutally honest, public opinion sensed that Europe was rather ineffectual,' he told the European Parliament on 23 January. Divergent responses had 'highlighted Europe's shortcomings'.[2]

The Gulf War appeared to turn the European nations away from a united future and back to their historical differences: Britain to unswerving Atlanticism, France to de Gaulle's fixation on influence in the Arab world and on independence from America, and Germany to a pacifistic reaction against Nazism. Public opinion polls showed that about 80 per cent of the British thought the war justified, as did 65 per cent of the French, but that 80 per cent of Germans thought it unjustified. Germans demonstrated outside America's embassy in Bonn, but not outside that of Iraq. A majority of the Dutch, Danes, Spaniards and Greeks opposed the war. Belgium refused to sell ammunition to British forces in the Gulf.

By the time the fighting in the Gulf ended, on 28 February, Delors was morose. The IGC on political union had not begun well. Governments had thrown about 50 proposals onto the conference table but had yet to make any meaningful concessions. He told the *Wall Street Journal*:

> *If we want to become a great world power, in partnership with the Americans, then we have to pay the price. I will judge the Europeans by the degree of their ambition. If their ambition is only mediocre I'll shut the door.*

He said he was less optimistic than he had been a year previously.

> *Over 34 years of history the EC has had 18 years of stagnation, six of crisis and ten of dynamism – I keep asking myself, where is the next stagnation and where will the next crisis come from?[3]*

In March Delors delivered his first ever speech on security policy at the International Institute for Strategic Studies in London. He called on the EC to 'shoulder its share of the political and military responsibilities of our old nations.' He wanted the Western European Union (WEU) to have its own multilateral forces and to come under the EC's wing.[4] The contents of the speech were hardly shocking, but many diplomats – unaccustomed to hearing commissioners use military terms such as 'command structures' – complained of Delors dabbling in matters beyond his ken.

The argument over defence became one of the bitterest of the IGC. A Franco-German paper in February had called for the European Council to guide the common defence policies of the WEU. That institution would become the European pillar of NATO and grow 'organic links' with the EC. A decision would be taken in 1996 or 1997 on whether to merge the WEU and the EC. Delors liked this scheme, as did the Spanish, Italian, Portuguese, Greek, Belgian and Luxembourg foreign ministers. Neutral Ireland and pacifistic Denmark did not belong to the WEU and opposed linking it to the Community. Britain and Holland did not mind loose ties between the WEU and the Community, but thought the Franco-German plan would push those organisations too close and therefore endanger NATO.

France scored points in the defence debate on 8 April, at an EC summit in Luxembourg. When everyone had agreed to send aid to the Kurds in

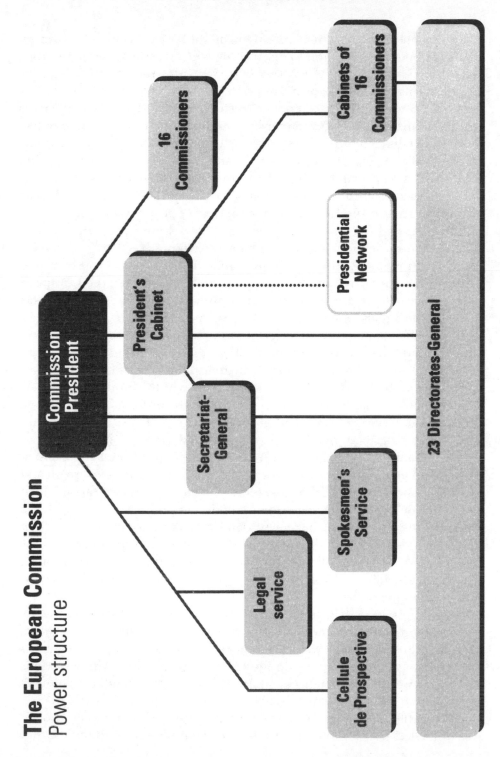

The European Commission
Power structure

Commission President

16 Commissioners

Cabinets of 16 Commissioners

President's Cabinet

Presidential Network

Secretariat-General

Spokesmen's Service

Legal service

Cellule de Prospective

23 Directorates-General

Northern Iraq, France, then president of the WEU, convened a short meeting of that organisation to discuss an airlift. Major consented to that demonstration of 'organic links' in return for Mitterrand backing his own idea of safe havens for Kurds in Iraq.

Shortly afterwards James Baker, President Bush's Secretary of State, sent EC ministers a warning: America would take its troops home if an EC caucus excluded it from discussions on European security. Any European defence 'pillar' should be inside NATO and include members of that alliance which were not in the WEU. Delors replied that when NATO should have been worrying about its own strategic review, it was 'too busy ogling at the political union IGC as if it were some kind of pornographic show.'

The IGC had become a show which Delors found increasingly distasteful. Pierre de Boissieu, the French representative, had proposed a model for European Union which resembled the façade of a Greek temple. Three pillars supported the entablature, which represented the European Council. One pillar, the European Community, included EMU and was based on the Treaty of Rome. A second consisted of common foreign and security policy, and a third of interior-ministry cooperation on immigration, visas, asylum and police matters. The commission and the European Parliament would play lesser roles in the new pillars than in the EC.

This French plan set off deep historical echoes in EC foreign ministries. Delors and Hans van den Broek, the Dutch foreign minister, claimed that de Boissieu was seeking to revive his grandfather's anti-EEC 'Fouchet plan'. The British described the temple as a beautiful design.

Luxembourg's draft treaty for European Union, published at the end of April, adopted de Boissieu's pillars. The sections on common foreign and security policy followed Franco-German ideas: the European Council would decide which areas were ripe for common policies, and the WEU's links with the union would be reviewed in 1996. The parliament would win 'codecision' – the right to block laws – in a limited number of areas. The Luxembourg draft was hard on the commission, proposing, for instance, that it should have no role in the preparation and implementation of common foreign policies.

The commission's own draft treaty on political union had been ignored by Luxembourg. This document sought to shift the EC's institutional balance in a federal direction – just when a number of governments wanted to push it the other way. Delors made a huge tactical mistake in authorising this document, which reflected his own, personal priorities. Few governments took the draft seriously, which left Delors on the sidelines of the IGC.

Much of the draft – such as the sections on majority voting, social policy and mutual defence – followed the earlier commission 'opinion'. Other sections went further. The draft proposed a new legislative system. Instead of detailed directives, the Council of Ministers and the European Parliament would agree on 'laws' which laid down general principles. Thus a law might say that drinking water should not contain certain pollutants. The commission would then write a regulation to fill in the details – specifying, for instance, the permitted number of parts per million of each pollutant. Both the European Parliament and the Council of Ministers could veto a regulation before it entered into force. National governments would write the regulations for EC laws which did not require every member to follow identical rules.

Delors argued that this scheme would free the European Parliament from needless discussion of technical detail, and promote subsidiarity, by allowing national parliaments to do more. The scheme would probably have made the law-making process more efficient, but it ignored some members' growing hostility to the power of the commission.

Much else in the draft annoyed governments. The commission would replace member-states in international organisations such as the IMF. In the committees which managed the single market, the commission would have more say and the governments less. An article would allow the EC to raise its own taxes.

The section on foreign policy proved the most provocative. The right of initiative would lie either with the commission, or the EC presidency, or at least six member-states but not with individual governments. The commission, the Council of Ministers' secretariat and the EC ambassadors (rather than the political directors who are based in national capitals) would prepare and implement the common policies.

'The commission's chief concern seems to have been to give themselves more power,' said Carlos Westendorp, Spain's minister for Europe, in a typical reaction. 'The commission's role should be to search for common ground, but in taking an extreme position it has behaved like a 13th member.'[5]

Contents apart, the late arrival of the commission draft lessened its impact. Promised for January, the document appeared in sections between February and June. François Lamoureux, who wrote large parts of the document, says the other commissioners held it up with a line-by-line examination. Frans Andriessen tried to increase the document's federalist slant, while Leon Brittan sought to tone it down. Delors's colleagues would not give him the kind of *carte blanche* he had had during the negotiation of the Single European Act.[6]

In 1985 Delors and his advisers had worked closely with the presidency (Luxembourg, again) and Niels Ersboll, the secretary-general of the Council of Ministers, in preparing drafts for the IGC. In 1991 Joseph Weyland, Luxembourg's EC ambassador and chairman of the IGC, worked with Ersboll, but – after the first few months – without the commission. 'The commission didn't show up when we and the council secretariat invited them round,' says Weyland. 'We supposed that Delors did not want to get tangled up in the presidency text.'[7]

Delors's memory is that 'the Luxembourgers refused to work with us, it was not we who refused to work with them.'[8] Relations between the presidency and the commission became poisonous. Delors's officials say that when Luxembourg adopted the pillars he told David Williamson, the commission's delegate to the IGC, to avoid contact with the presidency. By then, according to Lamoureux, Luxembourg was 'in the pocket of the French and the council secretariat,' meaning de Boissieu and Ersboll, both able and wily, and both keen to contain the commission's power.[9]

DRESDEN AND BELGRADE

Delors concentrated his energies on undermining Luxembourg's draft treaty on political union. He visited several heads of government, including Kohl, and circulated a memorandum. This said:

> The IGC should be guided by the basic thinking which has been behind the construction of Europe for 40 years now, namely that all progress made towards economic, monetary, social or political integration should gradually be brought together in a single Community as the precursor of a European Union.

The pillars 'would break the existing model.' The memorandum suggested adding an introductory section or *chapeau* to the draft which, rather than overturn the pillars, would bind them together. A further amendment would allow the commission to 'participate fully' in foreign policy.

In June the foreign ministers gathered in Dresden for the first EC meeting in former East Germany. Delors's diplomacy paid off: during the 'Battle of Dresden', as it became known, Holland, Belgium, Greece, Spain, Italy, Portugal and Germany backed his critique of the Luxembourg draft. Mark Eyskens, the Belgian minister, said the EC needed not a temple with pillars but a tree with branches.

Dumas defended the temple, stressing how complicated it would be for the EC to cover foreign policy since – even Delors agreed – its normal decision-making procedures could not apply. He warned of a treaty with multiple 'exceptions, special regimes and derogatory clauses from EC mechanisms – thus a judicial imbroglio.' Only Britain's Hurd and Denmark's Ellemann-Jensen backed Dumas and the Luxembourg draft.

Shellshocked, the Luxembourgers promised to revise their text. Delors left the battlefield elated, believing that seven or eight countries had supported the idea of a single community and that he had fought his way back into the heart of the negotiations. Hurd left Dresden depressed, fearing the temple design under threat. However neither Delors nor Hurd had realised that some governments would abandon the tree if they thought it would harm the prospects of an overall agreement.

Weyland asked Delors to help him write a new introductory section for the treaty. The result referred to 'a process leading gradually to a union with a federal goal.' Any country joining the union would have to join all its parts. 'A single institutional framework [would] ensure continuity and consistency.' A future IGC would 'strengthen the federal character of the union.'

Most countries welcomed the revised Luxembourg draft. Eyskens and Van den Broek, however, said the *chapeau* was not enough and that the 12 still needed a tree rather than a temple. Hurd complained that a British parliament would never accept the word federal. Delors retorted – with a reference to Britain's pre-election period – that some ministers were more preoccupied with forthcoming elections than with the long-term interests of the Community.

The real world gave the conference on political union little respite. No sooner had fighting in the Gulf died down than the Yugoslav federation began to break apart. Delors believed that if the West supported the economic reforms of Ante Markovic, the prime minister, with enough aid, the federation could survive. But when Delors visited Yugoslavia in May 1991 he found that the leaders of the republics did not want to work with Markovic. They seemed blind to the benefits of staying in an economic union. The trip left Delors pessimistic about the EC's chances of sorting out the problem (Delors had a similar experience in the Soviet Union in June, when only Gorbachev listened to his message that the republics needed an economic and monetary union).

The Slovene and Croat declarations of independence, on 25 June, provoked the Serb-controlled federal army to take military action. At the second Luxembourg summit of 1991, on 28 and 29 June, Kohl spoke in favour of self-determination for Slovenia and Croatia. Gonzales, Mitterrand and Major stressed the need to preserve the integrity of the Yugoslav state. In mid-summit the heads of government dispatched the 'troika' – the foreign ministers of the past, present and future presidencies – on an instant peace mission to Yugoslavia.

Armed with no more than a threat to suspend EC aid, Italy's Gianni de
Michelis, Luxembourg's Jacques Poos and Holland's Hans van den Broek
persuaded the Yugoslav factions to accept their peace plan. A Croat would
succeed to the federal presidency, Yugoslav troops would withdraw to
barracks, the declarations of independence would be suspended and constitutional talks would begin. When a triumphant troika returned to the
Luxembourg summit, less than 24 hours after they had left, de Michelis said
that America had been informed but not consulted. Poos declared that 'this
is the hour of Europe, not of America.'

None of the Yugoslav parties respected their engagements. Yet on 7 July,
after two more troika visits, all parties gathered on the island of Brioni
agreed to a peace plan. The Community postponed the question of whether
to recognise Croatia and Slovenia and sent 200 observers (including some
from the commission) to monitor the agreements. For several weeks it
looked as though the EC had solved the Yugoslav problem.

However by August Serbs and Croats had begun a war and the EC was
finding it hard to maintain a united front. Britain opposed any kind of
military involvement and, in September, thwarted a French, German and
Italian plan to send a WEU peacekeeping force. In the same month an EC
peace conference, chaired by Lord Carrington, opened in the Hague. The
Serbs continued to conquer territory, leading the EC, in November, to
suspend the peace conference and to impose sanctions on the rump of
Yugoslavia. The German campaign for the recognition of Slovenia and
Croatia (which had historical ties with Germany) led to accusations in
France (which had links with Serbia) that Germany was trying to create an
Austro-German sphere of influence in the Balkans.

When EC foreign ministers discussed Yugoslavia on 17 December,
Hurd, Van den Broek and Lord Carrington warned that recognising
Slovenia and Croatia could spread the conflict into Macedonia and Bosnia.
Genscher dismissed these warnings and, against the advice of his officials,
said Germany would recognise the republics come what may. The others,
believing that the 12 should, in the spirit of the recent Maastricht summit,
hold a common line, ceded to German bullying. The 12 agreed to recognise
any Yugoslav republic which met certain conditions, including respect for
minority rights, on 15 January 1992.

Two days later Genscher announced that Germany would recognise
Slovenia and Croatia, although the latter had failed to guarantee the rights of
its Serb minority. The EC could no longer avoid the question of recognising
Bosnia. On 15 January ministers made the fateful announcement that they
would recognise Bosnia once that republic had held a referendum on its
independence.

Throughout the IGC on political union, France and Germany led the campaign for common foreign policies. Yet France, with its Gulf diplomacy in January, and Germany, with the recognition of Slovenia and Croatia in December, undermined the prospect of common policies by showing that, when vital interests were at stake, they would act without regard to their partners.

On Yugoslavia, EMU and political union, united Germany was proving a powerful and influential voice. In the EMU negotiations Delors needed French support against German foot-dragging, but on political union he depended on the Germans to soften France's inter-governmental stance. Kohl never ceased to remind his partners that Germany would not swallow monetary union without a potent dose of political union. German politicians talked of a 'window of opportunity', a limited time in which other Europeans could exploit their fears of the Germans and the Germans' Euro-enthusiasm by binding them in to a deeper union. Germany's political elite had long believed that German self-interest required European integration. The Community offered an acceptable and non-nationalistic vehicle through which Germany could exercise power.[10]

Kohl announced new German priorities at the Luxembourg summit of June 1991. A wave of asylum-seekers, fleeing the chaos in Eastern Europe and the Balkans, had arrived in Germany. A liberal constitution prevented Germany from excluding them, so Kohl looked to the EC for a solution. He called for common policies on asylum, visas and immigration, and launched a plan for 'Europol', a joint European police force.

In July 1991 Sweden applied for EC membership, and the commission published its long-delayed opinion on Austria's application. Although generally favourable, the opinion warned that letting in Austria would mean letting in others, which made further constitutional reforms – beyond the current round of political union – essential.

In August, before retreating to his cottage in Burgundy, Delors told the *Financial Times* that he had changed his mind on the desirability of enlargement. He said it was the EC's responsibility to organise Europe, even if that meant, one day, taking in the East Europeans. He would spend his holidays reading about Mitteleuropa since 1900, so that he could reflect on whether these countries should be allowed to join.[11] On 20 August the abortive coup against Gorbachev interrupted Delors's reading.

DUTCH COURAGE

Cheered by the results of his Dresden offensive, Delors hoped the conference on political union would swing his way. The Dutch government, the most federalist of the 12, had taken over the EC presidency. Like most of the EC's smaller states, the Dutch had traditionally favoured a strong commission as a counterweight to the big powers. Busy with Yugoslavia, Van den Broek had left Piet Dankert, the minister for Europe, in charge of the IGC. This chain-smoking socialist and former president of the European Parliament had been a friend of Delors's since their days in that assembly.

But despite these favourable omens, Delors fared no better with the Dutch in command than he had under the Luxembourg presidency. He continued to make unrealistic demands and failed to play the central role which he had done in the negotiation of the Single European Act.

With the support of Lubbers, Dankert embarked on a brave and, ultimately, foolhardy strategy. He binned Luxembourg's draft treaty on political union and, to Delors's delight, proposed a single community rather than pillars. Dankert's draft was generous to the commission and to the parliament.

Countries holding the presidency are supposed to act as unbiased umpires. Dankert's draft, however, promoted Holland's own priorities – federalist, pro-NATO and against huge financial transfers to southern Europe. Spain and the poorer members complained that the new draft promised them no cash. France, Germany, Spain, Italy and Belgium criticised its vagueness on security policy. The British, French, Danes and Portuguese were appalled that a tree had replaced the temple.

The Dutch said they could not understand what all the fuss was about. In the single community they were proposing, the commission and the parliament would have only a limited role in foreign policy and in interior-ministry cooperation. For instance, only governments would have the right of initiative on police work and customs collaboration. The British replied that once the EC had touched foreign policy there would be a presumption that, in the long run, its normal institutional framework would apply. Thus the question of whether the union resembled a temple or a tree was of more than metaphysical interest.

Dankert strengthened the draft's provisions on common security policy, in a bid to win allies. But when, on 30 September, the foreign ministers reviewed the text, every country except Belgium spoke against it. De Michelis and Genscher said that although they favoured a single community, introducing that idea at such a late stage could endanger an agreement at Maastricht. Delors praised the text but said he would follow the majority. Van den Broek had to promise he would prepare a new draft with pillars.

Two months of the IGC had been wasted while the Dutch wrote and defended their treaty. With only 10 weeks left before the Maastricht summit, some governments feared there would not be enough time to untangle the many knots of political union. Several of them blamed Delors for pushing the Dutch into their disastrous draft. One senior Luxembourg diplomat claims that commission officials helped the Dutch to write sections and that Delors discussed the draft in the Hague in August. A top French official says that when he read the Dutch draft he recognised the unusual typeface of commission printers.

Delors admits he supported the Dutch treaty but denies travelling to the Hague or helping to write it.[12] Delors's staff say that he and Lubbers discussed the draft on the telephone but that the Dutch prime minister did not follow Delors's advice. Dankert showed Delors the Dutch text in early September, 10 days before it was published. Delors persuaded him to moderate some sections, for instance by lessening the role of the Court of Justice. Delors's staff admit that parts of the draft recycled earlier commission texts.

Why did Delors support Dankert's doomed attempt to scrap the Luxembourg draft, when, after the Battle of Dresden, he had succeeded in adding an introductory *chapeau*? 'The Dutch philosophy was close to that of the commission, so it would have been very hard for us not to support their project.'[13]

In October, at Harzuilen in Holland, Hurd and de Michelis unveiled – to the surprise of their fellow foreign ministers – a joint plan for European security. Hurd accepted 'the longer-term perspective of a common defence policy'. The plan left the WEU half-way between NATO and the European Union but its links with the latter would be reviewed in 1998. The WEU would command a 'rapid reaction force' to serve outside the NATO area.

The British had not moved far enough to satisfy Dumas and Genscher who, furious at being upstaged, announced a meeting in Paris later in the week 'for all those colleagues on the same wavelength.' Delors's suggestion that the Anglo-Italian plan would be good for the short term and the Franco-German approach viable in the long term failed to calm tempers. Van den Broek accused the French and the Germans of trying to usurp the presidency, which alone had the right to call meetings. The French said the Dutch had made such a mess of their draft treaty that they could not be trusted to run the IGC.

Only the Spanish minister joined Dumas and Genscher at their meeting in Paris. Two days later, however, a Kohl–Mitterrand letter announced the creation of a Eurocorps under WEU command. They invited other members to contribute to the force which – unlike that proposed in the Anglo-Italian plan – would operate inside the NATO area. The WEU would become an 'integral part' of the European Union.

On 8 November NATO concluded its strategic review at a summit in Rome. Major and Mitterrand used the occasion to agree on a form of words which left the WEU somewhere between the European Union and NATO. The Europeans reassured George Bush, who had been troubled by the announcement of the Eurocorps, that the Atlantic Alliance was safe. The NATO summit left just one defence argument to be settled at Maastricht, and that was more semantic than substantive. Britain wanted the treaty to refer to 'common defence policies', while the French favoured the apparently stronger 'common defence'.

Social policy, by contrast, was becoming the most intractable problem of political union. All through the year, Delors had argued vigorously for qualified majority voting on labour law. In May Hurd had protested that majority voting would lead to higher costs for industry. Delors replied that he felt like 'someone at the start of the century who heard people say that the abolition of child labour would cause the general collapse of the economy.'

In October the Dutch published a new draft, reviving the Luxembourg design of a European Union with pillars. The social chapter extended EC competence to equal opportunities in the labour market, to information and consultation for workers and to 'working conditions'. Qualified majority voting would apply in all these areas. The social chapter picked up an idea from Delors's own draft treaty: if employers and unions reached EC-wide agreements on these matters, the Council of Ministers could convert them into EC law.

John Major decided that labour law was the one area where Britain would not compromise.[14] Sir John Kerr, Britain's negotiator in the IGC on political union, refused to discuss any amendment to the social policy provisions of the existing treaties. Other delegations found British tactics infuriating: defence policy apart, Britain had offered no compromises since the IGC had begun.

Major wanted to fight the following spring's general election with a united party. That meant his government had to appease Conservative Eurosceptics. Hurd attacked the commission for 'inserting itself into the nooks and crannies of everyday life.'[15] Peter Lilley, the trade and industry secretary, said that 'like the car, Delorean economics is flashy, expensive and fundamentally fraudulent.'[16]

The Spanish were proving almost as truculent and stubborn as the British. They had begun the conference by demanding larger EC structural funds, direct cash transfers from rich governments to poor ones, and a special fund to help poorer members pay for higher environmental standards. Luxembourg's and Holland's draft treaties had ignored these requests – prompting Carlos Westendorp to threaten a veto at Maastricht. By November the Spaniards had focused their energy on one demand: a treaty article to specify that budget contributions should reflect members' wealth (the bulk of the EC's revenues came from a share of VAT receipts, which put the high-spending Spaniards at a disadvantage). Seeking to mollify the Spanish, Delors backed their demands for a treaty article and proposed a 'cohesion fund' to finance environmental and transport projects in poorer states.

Delors disliked the new Dutch draft as much as he had liked its predecessor. When the foreign ministers met at the Dutch town of Noordwijk, on 12 November, Delors succeeded in making several changes. He restored the commission's right to withdraw a law that had been amended in ways it did not like. He deprived the parliament of the right to propose legislation and switched environmental law to majority voting.

Delors joined Hurd in criticising the numerous new 'competences'. Delors suggested keeping the chapters on 'Trans-European Networks' (infrastructure projects) and industry but scrapping those on tourism, energy, disaster relief, consumer rights, health, education and culture. He said the new treaty should follow the example of the Single European Act, which had a limited number of precise competences, rather than the Treaty of Rome, which had many vague competences that had seldom been used. The chapters on tourism, disaster relief and energy were excised.

However the ministers ignored Delors on the the treaty's overall structure and on its foreign policy provisions. Kohl shared Delors's hostility to the Dutch draft. Together, at the end of November, they launched a federalist offensive. Kohl demanded a set of 'evolutionary clauses'. One would extend the European Parliament's powers of codecision in 1996; another would shift asylum policy from its inter-governmental pillar into the EC in 1994. The British said that postponing federalism for a few years did not make it any more palatable. Kohl failed to win evolutionary clauses but gained others which specified that certain issues – including the parliament's powers – would be reviewed in 1996.

On 21 November Delors described the Dutch text as 'inapplicable and crippling' in the European Parliament. Because of the 'likelihood of politicians and bureaucrats striking deals behind closed doors, the inter-governmental will pollute the European Community and roll it back. [There was] not one example of a grouping of nations which has survived on the basis of inter-governmental cooperation.' The plan for the EC to manage external economic relations and for the member-states to run foreign policy would lead to 'organised schizophrenia'. As soon as the Maastricht treaty was signed, he urged, work should start on preparing 'our institutions for a Community which will perhaps consist of 15, 20 or 25 members.'[17] On the same day, in the British House of Lords, Lady Thatcher, as she had become, called on Major to halt the 'conveyor belt to federalism' at Maastricht.

In private Delors pointed to Greece's veto of an oil blockade against the rump Yugoslavia as proof that common policies would be feeble without majority voting. On 27 November the commission published a declaration, written by Delors, on political union.

> *As matters stand, the Union is to develop alongside the Community without there being an explicit restatement, as there was in the Single European Act, of the determination to bring together in a single entity all the powers which the member-states plan to exercise jointly in political and economic matters.*

The European Union's lack of a legal personality (international treaties would have to be signed by the member-states and/or the EC) would breed confusion on who represented the Union and who implemented its policies. The proposal that those tasks should be carried out by the EC president 'in association with the commission' would fail to ensure the coherence of the Union's various external policies.

Delors's obsession with the treaty's foreign-policy provisions was hard to fathom, even for some of his officials. The Dutch draft had retained much of the June *chapeau*, such as references to a 'single institutional framework' which would, supposedly, stop the pillars falling apart. However in February 1994 one of those officials commented that if the 12 had listened to Delors, and there had been a central authority telling the Union what it should do, the siege of Sarajevo would not have endured so long.

Many governments thought Delors's arguments on foreign policy amounted to a simple bid for more commission power. On 6 December Delors visited Mitterrand in search of support, but found none. 'Elysée sources' told *Le Monde* that the lesson of the EC's founding fathers was the importance of Franco-German friendship, rather than of federalism. They said the commission interfered too much in domestic policy and that it would lose its right of initiative if the EC was to be redesigned from scratch.[18]

The mood in Germany was no more congenial for Delors. Having shown little interest in the IGCs for most of the year, the Germans had suddenly woken up to their importance. A plethora of newspaper articles urged the EC's leaders to abandon their plans for EMU. Karl Schiller, a former finance minister, wrote in *Der Spiegel* that a lesson had been learned from

German monetary union: EMU would not work unless Germany transferred huge sums of money to its partners. An opinion poll in *Bild* found that only 17 per cent of Germans favoured EMU, and on 9 December, as the Maastricht summit opened, 'HANDS OFF OUR CURRENCY' led that newspaper's front page.

The Dutch ignored Delors's strictures on foreign policy when they revised their draft treaty for the last time. At his pre-summit press conference, Delors ridiculed the provision for implementing details to be settled by majority vote, so long as there was unanimity to do so. If the EC ministers were due to meet their East European counterparts,

> *first we would have to decide, unanimously, whether the meeting was to be in Warsaw, Budapest or Prague. Then we would have to agree whether we were going by plane. Lunch? We would need an opt-out for vegetarians. No doubt we could use majority voting to decide where the smoking and non-smoking sections should be.*[19]

Delors's advisers said he might resign if a 'bad' treaty was agreed in Maastricht. But it was far from certain that there would be an agreement. Arguments on the social chapter, the powers of the parliament, the form of words for defence policy, voting rules on visas, Spain's budgetary demands and much else would have to be resolved.

THE BIRTH OF THE BEAST

What better place than Maastricht to negotiate a Treaty on European Union? The market town, whose name means the bridge over the River Maas, lies in a narrow tongue of Dutch land between Germany and Belgium. Charlemagne's capital of Aachen, in Germany, and Liège, in Belgium, are close neighbours, while France and Luxembourg are only 100 kilometres distant. Verdun, where Louis Delors had fought, is 200 kilometres further up the Maas (known as the Meuse in France). Maastricht straddles the frontier between Europe's Latin and Germanic cultures, as well as the border between its Protestant and Catholic religions.

Although in the heart of the European Union, Maastricht is far from the centre of the European continent. The town gave birth to a treaty which embodies a 40-year-old vision of union among the West European states. Whether that vision is relevant to the half of Europe which shook off communism during the treaty's gestation is a moot point. Coincidentally, while the EC's leaders concluded their treaty on 9 and 10 December, Mikhael Gorbachev lost his grip on the Soviet Union and prepared to resign.

On the eve of the summit Delors addressed a thousand flag-waving, foot-stamping federalists in Maastricht's town square. 'Federalism is a guideline, not a pornographic word, you can speak it out loud!' he exclaimed, referring to the word which everyone expected to be struck out of the Dutch draft. 'We have focused too much on a country which has said no, no, no!' He hoped that the EC's leaders, who would 'shamefacedly hide the word under the table, will at least maintain their federal aspirations.'

The following morning 12 heads of government and their foreign ministers sat down at a round table in Province House, the seat of the Limburg government. This circular structure of stone and marble, built in 1986, lies on Government Island in the River Maas. A bridge links the island to the mainland where, in a nearby conference centre, several thousand journalists waited. Every few hours, throughout the summit, spokesmen and spokeswomen for the 12 delegations would appear in briefing rooms to feed the press information. Each would carry essentially the same message: his or her government was winning all the important arguments.

When the summit began Mitterrand and Andreotti unveiled a plan they had concocted over dinner the previous evening which would, they hoped, make the move to a single currency irreversible. The two septuagenarians proposed that if EMU did not start in 1997, because a majority of members could not meet the convergence criteria, it would begin in 1999 with as many as were ready. Kohl agreed, to Delors's delight – and, when it heard, to the Bundesbank's horror (at that time only Denmark, France and Luxembourg could satisfy the treaty's five criteria).

John Major won a series of symbolic victories. 'An ever closer union among the peoples of Europe' replaced the 'federal goal'. The plan for a treaty revision in 1996 'to strengthen the federal character of the union' lost the reference to federalism. On the more substantive arguments, however, Major made concessions: the European Parliament won wide-ranging new powers, 'joint actions' in foreign policy would bind members and visa policy would be settled by majority vote.

Gonzalez failed to win a treaty article on the financing of the EC budget. But he won a protocol – drafted by himself, Delors and Kohl – which spelt out how the budget would, in future, be funded more fairly. Lubbers proved a cool and competent chairman. He often interrupted the debate and asked Delors to explain a problem and to summarise the position of each country. Delors would respond with an off-the-cuff and unbiased speech of three or four minutes. Major remarked to an aide that Delors was playing the role of a consultant to the Community's heads of government.

On the evening of the first day, in an effort to soften Major's opposition to the social chapter, Lubbers produced a watered-down version. This proposed a modest extension of qualified majority voting to the right of information (but not consultation) for workers, and to the health and safety aspects of working conditions. It retained the provision for the 'social partners' – employers and trade unions – to make agreements which could become EC law.

Arguments on the social chapter dominated the summit's second day. Mitterrand, Andreotti and Wilfried Martens, the Belgian prime minister, declared they could not accept the watered-down social chapter. Sir John Kerr suggested to Major that he accept the watered-down chapter, but that he try to get it diluted a little further. Had Major followed this Foreign Office advice, France, Italy and Belgium would have probably accepted the watered-down chapter. Major spoke on the telephone to Michael Howard, Britain's Thatcherite employment minister, who advised him to give no ground. Major believed that Howard and other Thatcherite ministers might resign if he accepted any kind of social chapter. After much pondering, Major told Lubbers he would not accept the watered-down chapter.

Delors tried to break the deadlock with a proposal which would allow Britain to opt out of particular social laws and then – if it wished – to opt back in. Mitterrand suggested a general opt-out on social policy for the British. But by mid-afternoon Major had rejected all these varieties of opt-out. Off-stage, Pascal Lamy speculated that if the British would not take a one-country opt-out, because of the negative connotations, they might buy the idea of 11 countries opting in to the social chapter. Lamy and his team worked on this idea and prepared some documents. Their concern was to safeguard the role of EC institutions, and notably the commission, in any social-policy club of 11 members.

Meanwhile on-stage, the argument on the social chapter had run on for six hours and seemed likely to wreck the summit. Mitterrand announced that he was about to fly back to Paris. At 7 pm Lubbers suspended the session. In a bilateral meeting, Major sounded out Lubbers on whether a greatly diluted version of the watered-down chapter might break the deadlock – while stressing that he would not necessarily accept such a version. Lubbers said no.

Kohl called Delors over and suggested postponing the application of the social chapter for a few years. Delors convinced Kohl that to put off an agreement on social policy would damage the EC, and that an 11-country opt-in would be a better idea. Kohl joined Lubbers and Major in a trilateral meeting which ended in them all agreeing that Delors's idea was a possible way forward. Major still had doubts about the plan and worried about the Labour Party attacking him for leaving Britain on the outside. Kerr told him Britain would not get a better deal.

In a series of bilaterals and trilaterals, Delors, Lubbers and Kohl saw Major several times. 'By then there were only four people alive around the table: Lubbers, Major, Kohl and myself,' says Delors. He claims that in the end his own powers of persuasion brought Major round to the 11-country opt-in.[20]

Lubbers reconvened the summit and Delors explained the plan. He stressed that EC institutions would play their normal role in the new arrangements. Kohl, Mitterrand and de Michelis spoke in favour of the scheme. No one argued against, for a dispute at that late hour would have led to a breakdown. Lubbers asked Delors to draw up the necessary documents.

Lamy had papers already prepared. Kerr and Jean-Claude Piris, legal officer of the Council of Ministers' secretariat, went into a huddle with Lamy and edited the texts. The social chapter, now excised from the body of the treaty and called an 'agreement', would be signed by 11 governments. A protocol appended to the treaty noted that the 11 would make social policy according to the rules of the 'agreement', and authorised them to use EC institutions and procedures while doing so. The protocol modified normal voting rules to take account of Britain's absence. The protocol had some bizarre consequences: British commissioners would help to draft laws for the 11-country social community, and British Euro-MPs would vote on them; but British ministers would not.

Delors brought these documents to the table, and at 1 am, after 31 hours of negotiation, the 12 approved the treaty. Many thought the 'social beast' – as the new arrangements came to be called – would have a limited lifespan. If the Labour Party won the general election, Britain would opt back in and make the scheme redundant. 'History teaches us that if one or two members lag behind, they always follow,' said Lubbers, sitting beside Delors at their 2 am press conference.

Others who observed the birth of the beast feared that it would end up biting those who had conceived it. Anyone aggrieved to see Britain winning investment through the lightness of its labour laws might complain to the Court of Justice that the protocol distorted the single market. However nobody present that night, and least of all John Major, suspected that the beast would come within a hair's breadth of bringing down his government in July 1993.

MAASTRICHT AT A GLANCE

The Treaty of Maastricht establishes a European Union of three parts or 'pillars'. One part, based on an amended Treaty of Rome, covers the European Community and includes EMU. Two new pillars cover common foreign and security policy, and cooperation on justice and home affairs. The European Commission, the European Parliament and the Court of Justice have less say in the new pillars than in the EC. The European Council gives the Union 'the impetus for its development' and defines its general policy.

Citizenship of the European Union confers the right to diplomatic and consular help from any of its governments, and to live and work in any member-state. A citizen may vote or be a candidate in any municipal or European election. He or she may petition the European Parliament and appeal to an ombudsman to investigate maladminstration.

The principle of subsidiarity means that, in areas which do not fall within the EC's exclusive competence, it

> *shall take action only if and in so far as the objectives of the proposed action cannot be sufficiently achieved by the member-states and can therefore, by reason of the scale or of the effects of the proposed action, be better achieved by the Community.*

Every three years the commission reviews the economic disparities between richer and poorer members and, if necessary, proposes measures to reduce them. A 'cohesion fund' finances environmental and infrastructure projects in member-states whose per capita GDP is less than 90 per cent of the Union's average. A consultative committee of the regions is created. The European Court of Justice gains the power to fine any government which ignores its rulings.

The treaty extends the EC's field of action to education, health and culture. It cannot legislate in these areas but may promote cross-border cooperation such as student exchanges or health education programmes. The EC gains the right to make proposals on consumer protection; and on 'trans-European networks' – transport, telecommunications and energy projects – which may receive loan guarantees, interest-rate subsidies or money from the cohesion fund. In all these matters ministers will vote by qualified majority.

The new chapter on industry allows the EC to encourage small businesses, to help industry cope with structural change and to promote the exploitation of innovation – so long as it does not harm competition. Decisions on industry require unanimity. Voting on capital controls and transport switches from unanimity to qualified majority, as does environmental law – unless it concerns taxation, town and country planning or choice of energy source.

The treaty establishes a 'codecision procedure' in the European Parliament. If the Euro-MPs reject a legislative text from the Council of Ministers, or if ministers reject parliamentary amendments, the two sides form a conciliation committee. If the committee cannot find a compromise the proposal cannot pass; if a compromise does emerge, both the parliament and the council must vote in favour for it to pass. Codecision applies to measures on the single market, education, health, culture and consumer protection, as well as to programmes for the environment, research and trans-European networks.

Any international agreement of the EC which has institutional or budgetary implications, or which affects an area covered by the codecision procedure, requires parliamentary assent. The parliament must vote in favour of the new commission president before he or she may take office, and must then approve the new college of commissioners. Each commission serves a five-year term (instead of four), to match the parliament's five-year timespan.

The social chapter applies to every member except Britain. Laws on working conditions, on information and consultation of workers and on equal employment rights for men and women are decided by qualified majority. Decisions on other subjects, such as social security or minimum wages, require unanimity. If employers and trade unions can reach EC-wide agreements, the Council of Ministers may turn them into law.

A transitional phase to economic and monetary union began in January 1994, with the creation of a European Monetary Institute (EMI), sited in Frankfurt. This coordinates members' monetary policies, oversees the development of the ecu and prepares for the final phase. Member-states retain monetary sovereignty but must make their central banks independent by the end of the transitional phase. The institute will become the European Central Bank (ECB) shortly before the final phase of EMU begins.

That will be in 1997 if the European Council decides, by qualified majority, that a majority of EC members meets five criteria: inflation within 1.5 per cent and interest rates within 2 per cent of the three best-performing states; a budget deficit of less than 3 per cent and a national debt of less than 60 per cent of GDP; and no devaluation within the ERM for the past two years. Otherwise EMU will start in 1999 with as many members as can meet the criteria.

Participants in the final phase will lock their exchange rates irrevocably. Later on the ecu will replace national currencies. The ECB will set interest rates in line with its goal of price stability – although without prejudice to that commitment it should also support the EC's economic policies and its objectives such as a high level of employment and sustainable growth. The bank's council, consisting of national central bank governors and an executive board, will be independent of national or EC institutions. Its president will report regularly to, and face questions from the Council of Finance Ministers (Ecofin) and the European Parliament.

Ecofin will define exchange-rate policy for the ecu, in consultation with the ECB. It will issue broad guidelines for the Community's economic policy and may, if it considers a government's policy inconsistent with EMU, recommend changes. Bankrupt governments will not be bailed out. If Ecofin judges a country's budget deficit 'excessive' it may demand cuts. If, after a public warning from Ecofin, a government takes no action, ministers may insist that it publish financial information with its bond issues; or block credits from the European Investment Bank; or impose a fine.

In the new pillar for foreign and security policy the commission shares the right of initiative with governments. The Union's foreign ministers decide which areas merit 'joint action'. For each of these areas the ministers decide, by unanimity, what the common line should be, what action should be taken and which details of implementing the policy, if any, should be settled by qualified majority.

The presidency is responsible for representing the Union in matters concerning common foreign and security policy, and for implementing common measures (in practice it leaves much of that work to the Council of Ministers' secretariat, which has subsumed the former European Political Cooperation secretariat). The commission 'shall be fully associated' in the representation and the implementation. Governments must follow the common line and support it in international organisations. That obligation is political, not legal, for the Court of Justice has no role in foreign policy.

Similar procedures (but without any majority voting) apply to the 'eventual framing of a common defence policy, which may in time lead to common defence.' The European Union will ask the Western European Union (WEU), 'an integral part of the development of the Union', to implement decisions with defence implications. A strengthened WEU will become the European pillar of the Atlantic alliance, without prejudice to that alliance.

The other new pillar covers interior-ministry cooperation. The commission and governments share the right of proposal on asylum, immigration and rules for frontiers. Ministers may decide, by unanimity, to shift any of these subjects into the EC. Only governments may take initiatives on police work, customs and the fight against terrorism and drugs. A committee of senior interior-ministry officials coordinates the work of this pillar and prepares ministerial meetings. All decisions require unanimity.

Confusingly, the treaty places visa policy inside the EC. Ministers decide rules on short-term visas and on visa formats by qualified majority. From January 1996, all visa policy will be settled by qualified majority.

A 'single institutional framework' applies to all pillars. The Council of Ministers and the commission are charged with ensuring that the Union's external policies – whether they concern security, economics or development – are consistent. Any applicant for membership must join the whole Union. An inter-governmental conference in 1996 will review, in particular, defence policy and the parliament's powers.

Appended to the treaty are 17 protocols, which are legally binding, and 33 declarations, which are not. One protocol contains the statutes of the European Central Bank, and another those of the European Monetary Institute. Spain won a protocol saying that the system of budgetary finance would be reformed so that contributions better reflected members' ability to pay. Separate protocols allow Britain and Denmark not to participate in the third and final phase of EMU. Other appendices are less weighty: one protocol effectively bans Germans from buying holiday homes on the Danish coast, while a declaration – inserted at Britain's insistence – requires the EC 'to pay full regard to the welfare requirements of animals.'

THE MEANING OF MAASTRICHT

The essence of the deal in Maastricht – like so much in the history of the EC – was a Franco-German bargain. Mitterrand persuaded Germany to agree to a single currency and to the goal of a common security policy. Kohl persuaded France to agree to a German model of EMU and to more power for the European Parliament.

The federalist camp, which included Italy, Holland, Belgium and Luxembourg, was able to claim that the treaty laid the foundations of a future European state: a parliament with teeth, common citizenship, common foreign and defence policies and a single currency. The poor four – Spain, Portugal, Greece and Ireland – received promises of cash.

Little in the treaty appealed directly to the EC's northern pragmatists, the British and the Danes. The more pro-European among them could view the document as a collection of sensible reforms: EMU would reinforce the single market, while new foreign-policy procedures would allow a more coherent response to events in central and eastern Europe. Denmark had been keen to strengthen the EC's social and environmental policy, but Britain spent most of the coach trip to Maastricht in a passenger seat.

British and Danish stubborness imposed 'variable geometry' on the Community treaties for the first time. Their opt-outs established the principle that members did not have to subscribe to all aspects of the Union. The Western European Union, the ERM and the 'Schengen agreement' on frontiers – each a club with less than 12 members – had existed before Maastricht, but had not been covered in the treaties.

Any document so long and unreadable – many of the articles in its 253 pages make no sense unless the reader understands their cross-references to other parts of the treaty or to earlier treaties – was likely to be unloved. The fact that almost none of the EC's leaders championed the treaty or made an effort to sell it to their electorates (except in Denmark and Ireland and, ultimately, France, which held referendums) did not help its popularity. The text was so open to conflicting interpretations that few politicians warmed to many of its sections. The complexities and ambiguities, born of the need to attract 12 signatures, made the document hard to defend.

Jacques Delors has never been enthusiastic about the Treaty of Maastricht. He is fairly content with the provisions for EMU, but describes the agreement on political union as 'ungodly'. He says that 'the ambition paraded is huge, compared with the mediocre text.' He compares it to 'a beautiful racing car with a Deux Chevaux engine inside.' By the summer of 1993, Delors had distilled his criticisms of the treaty down to five points.[21]

One, 'that there should be divergent paths which one day come together, fine. But not the three pillars.' Two, 'excessive ambition. People wanted to put every aspect of internal security and justice into the treaty – we could have kept that for later.' Foreign and security policy should have been tackled at a later date. Three, 'the decision-making process in foreign policy is impotent and stupid.' In 1990 he had thought the outlook for foreign policy promising. Yet in 1991, he says, governments forgot about it and become obsessed with defence.[22] Four, 'the diplomats couldn't agree on defence, so they arrived at a pure literary compromise.' He describes the treaty's words – 'the eventual framing of a common defence policy, which may lead in time to common defence' – as 'a load of ****.' Five, the provisions for the parliament are 'lamentable, from a technical point of view, since there are now seven procedures governing relations between the council and the parliament.'[23]

All this leads Delors to a hindsightful conclusion.

We shouldn't have made a treaty on political union, it was too soon. My
profound intuition is that we were not ripe for that. We should have
made a treaty on EMU and perhaps added a small treaty, something
very simple, on the triangle council–parliament–commission, to simplify
procedures, and on transparency and democratisation. But because of
the governments' excessive ambition, they wanted to go further.

He didn't resign at Maastricht because that would have only helped the
Thatchers, Le Pens and Chevènements. However, 'from the point of view
of institutional logic, I always thought it a bad treaty. I shut up because we
had to get it ratified.'[24]

In fact the Treaty of Maastricht is less of a setback for the commission
than Delors would have one believe. In relative terms, the procedures in
the new pillars shift the balance of power within the Union from EC
institutions to governments. But in absolute terms the commission gains a
wide range of new powers. These include a formal role in foreign policy; in
the economic surveillance mechanisms of monetary union; and in cooperation on asylum, immigration and rules at frontiers. The EC's many new
competences (industrial, consumer and visa policy, for instance) and
expanded competences (such as social and environmental policy) offer the
commission new scope for initiatives. The spread of qualified majority
voting means that more of the commission's proposals will pass the Council of Ministers.

The treaty melds inter-governmental and federal elements, and by no
means suppresses the latter. As Lamoureux says, with some hyperbole:
'Two things matter in the history of the EC: the introduction of qualified
majority voting in the Single European Act, and phase three of EMU in the
Maastricht treaty.'[25]

The British and French, who imposed the design of the Greek temple on
their partners, recognise the treaty's hybrid nature. John Kerr sees the
European Parliament as the biggest winner, for the treaty could mark a step
towards it setting the EC's agenda and electing the commission. But he
adds: 'The pillars are important and could prove to be a turning point: for
the first time in the treaties we have an alternative to the Monnet structure
[the commission–council–parliament triangle].' He also believes the article
on subsidiarity will make the commission less intrusive.[26]

François Scheer, secretary-general of the French foreign ministry
during the IGCs, says:

Maastricht allows us to leave behind the old theological quarrels
between the Europe of Monnet and the Europe of de Gaulle. Maastricht

*is a baroque treaty but we needed it to give a 10–20 year perspective to
European integration.*

Scheer believes that the Union, like a bicycle, must move forwards or fall
over – and that the treaty gave it momentum.[27]

Although the agreement on political union is kinder to the commission
than Delors admits, he badly misjudged the mood of the IGC. Only Belgium supported the commission through thick and thin. Delors's draft
treaty, too federalist to be taken seriously by many governments, distanced
him from the heart of the negotiation. Then, having staged a successful
comeback at Dresden, he lost further credibility by supporting the ill-
starred Dutch draft.

Ersboll, who had a big hand in the Luxembourg drafts and in the final
Dutch draft, says:

> *Delors made the mistake of thinking the commission could write the
> treaty, when that is the business of governments – though the commission
> can be a useful assistant. He didn't understand that the governments
> didn't want the commission to play a big role in foreign policy.*[28]

Was Delors badly advised? Some of the president's friends blame his
mistakes on Lamoureux, who wrote substantial sections of the commission's draft treaty. When Lamoureux went to work for Edith Cresson, the
French prime minister, in July 1991, the cooler and more technocratic
Michel Petite replaced him as Delors's adviser on political union. Others
blame David Williamson, the commission's official representative in the
IGC. As commission secretary-general, he had so many other responsibilities that he did not have time to immerse himself in all the details of
political union. Williamson complained to friends of 'the KGB looking
over my shoulder', meaning Lamoureux, and had to defend proposals
which he thought too federalist. His powers of persuasion could not match
those of some other conference participants, such as Britain's Kerr or
France's de Boissieu.

Yet it was not Lamoureux, or Williamson, but Delors – and the other
members of the college – who approved the commission's draft treaty and
must take responsibility for its strategy. Delors wrote parts of the draft
himself. When Delors reflected on the best design for a political union, his
own logic – asking questions like, what would be most efficient? – got the
better of his normally strong sense of the possible. 'Why this mistrust
towards the commission?,' asks a perplexed Delors. 'Because we made
mistakes? Because we became too powerful? Because people personalised
the resurrection of Europe around my modest person?'[29]

However much Delors disdains the Treaty of Maastricht, public opinion has rightly tied the two together. Delors pushed the Community towards monetary union, while much of political union is, in essence, what member-states demanded in return for accepting EMU. There would have been no Treaty of Maastricht without Delors's 'modest person'.

CHAPTER TEN

THE DEMONS RETURN

THE THEORY of chaos, in natural science, explains how a butterfly beating its wings over the Amazon can set off a hurricane in the Caribbean. Denmark's 50.7 per cent rejection of the Treaty of Maastricht, on 2 June 1992 – by a margin of just 45,000 votes – showed chaos theory at work in politics. The Danish referendum could not have unleashed a political hurricane if ominous clouds had not already gathered over Europe. An economic depression was biting and many people had become fed up with politicians in general and the EC in particular. To the east old nationalisms were reviving.

Jacques Delors could not control the turbulent events of 1992 any better than a butterfly could change the course of a hurricane into which it had been sucked. Delors began the year with plans to push post-Maastricht Europe further towards federalism. He overbid – just when the political climate was turning sharply against European integration. Like the 12 governments, Delors assumed that the treaty of Maastricht would come into force at the end of 1992, after ratification by referendum in Denmark and Ireland and by parliamentary vote in the other members.

In February 1992 the commission president unveiled the 'second Delors package', an EC budgetary plan for the years 1993 to 1997. He had viewed the first package, covering the years 1988 to 1992, as the twin of the Single European Act. He described the second, entitled 'The Means of our Ambitions', as the bill for the Maastricht treaty. Delors's plan would increase the ceiling on the EC budget from 1.2 per cent of Community GDP in 1992 to 1.37 per cent in 1997 – from 66.5 billion ecus to 87.5 billion (at 1992 prices, assuming economic growth of 2.5 per cent a year). The extra spending would go on larger structural funds and the new cohesion fund; on 'foreign policy', meaning aid for neighbours and friends; and on 'industrial competitiveness', meaning aid for industry.

Delors had favoured a 1997 ceiling of 1.32 per cent of GDP, but had been overruled by other commissioners. He should have fought harder on the ceiling, for the economic downturn was straining every member's budget. Eight of them attacked the commission's proposal as overambitious. Only Spain, Portugal, Ireland and Greece, which would benefit from the larger structural funds, supported it.

The long-running negotiations on the European Economic Area came to an end in February. The seven countries of EFTA and the 12 of the EC had agreed on a treaty in October 1991. But two months later the judges of the European Court of Justice had annulled the agreement, on the grounds that the proposed EEA Court would infringe their autonomy. The commission's legal service had failed to check the Court of Justice's view in advance and had ignored the warnings of many legal experts that the EEA Court was a flawed concept.

The entire 1000-page treaty had to be renegotiated to satisfy the jealous judges of Luxembourg. The result offered less to the EFTA countries: some disputes within the EEA would be settled by arbitration, and others by the Court of Justice. The unbalanced nature of the agreement was one reason for 50.3 per cent of the Swiss voting against it in December 1992. Switzerland's No Forced Liechtenstein to abandon the EEA.

But although Switzerland dropped out and the EEA did not, as Delors had once hoped, postpone membership applications from EFTA countries, it proved one of his more worthwhile ideas. Coming into force in January 1994, the EEA allowed the free flow of goods, capital, services and people in a market of 372 million consumers. The EEA's economic output of $7500 billion (in 1992 prices) outscored the North American Free Trade Agreement's $6800 billion. The EEA established common rules on the single market, the environment, R&D, mergers and state aid. Five EFTA countries had accepted 12,000 pages of EC legislation, and covered much of the ground towards becoming full members.

Finland applied for EC membership in February 1992, followed by Switzerland in May (its later referendum on the EEA rendered that meaningless) and Norway in November. The Hungarian government talked of applying in 1994. The Maastricht summit had asked Delors to present the Lisbon summit of June 1992 with a report on the implications of enlargement. He decided to use the opportunity to argue for a deeper political union than the one just agreed at Maastricht. He believed that without further institutional reform, a wider EC would degenerate into a mere free-trade area.

Delors said on French television that if the EC's nations were really going to come together to run a common foreign policy, 'at that moment France's nuclear deterrent should, in my view, be put at the service of this common policy.' He suggested that, instead of the commission and a rotating presidency, a single body should run the EC.

You could have the 25 heads of state meeting and saying, 'voilà, M Dupont is named president of the European executive for three years.'

He'll choose his own ministers and could be sacked by either the Euro-
pean Parliament or the European Council.[1]

Delors asked a group of commission officials to study the institutional
consequences of Austria, Sweden, Finland, Switzerland and Norway
becoming members. The problem was not only that, by definition, a larger
EC would find it harder to reach decisions. The newcomers were small
countries and would therefore exacerbate the problem of small members
being over-represented in the Council of Ministers. Germany, Britain,
France and Italy had 10 votes each (and Spain eight), while six of the small
members, with populations of a quarter to a tenth as large, had three or five
votes (Luxembourg, exceptionally, had two).

A paper from the commission's secretariat-general discussed several
innovations: giving smaller countries fewer votes; allowing ministers to
pass all laws by qualified or simple majorities; reforming the presidency so
that smaller countries could not hold it except in tandem with a larger
country; and cutting the number of commissioners, so that some countries
would have none.

Frans Andriessen, the commissioner responsible for enlargement, suggested a 'mini inter-governmental conference' in 1993, to run parallel with
the EFTA countries' membership talks. This would tackle immediate
problems such as reform of the voting rules, and leave wider issues, such as
common defence, for the IGC due in 1996.

Delors encouraged this debate. He told the European Parliament in
April: "There's an objective contradiction between deepening and widening. Political imperatives may lead us to say, we must enlarge, but then we
have to draw the consequences.' He promised that the commission's report
to the Lisbon summit would

> *certainly be a political, institutional and intellectual shock for the 12*
> *member-states, which have not yet reflected enough on what, for exam-*
> *ple, a Community of 35 members would be like.*

In the same speech Delors showed some insight into the problems which
lay ahead.

> *More and more, our adventure is too elitist and technocratic, and people*
> *are not comfortable with it. All and each of us must examine our con-*
> *sciences. We have too many complicated procedures, Byzantine quar-*
> *rels and sophisticated rules – hence the distance and the disinterest of*
> *citizens.*

213

The principle of subsidiarity, he said, offered a remedy. He wanted the EC to 'concentrate on the essentials, I'm in favour of sending back some competences to the national states.'[2]

Delors saw no contradiction between the two ideas of this speech. He thought enlargement required more federal institutions, but recognised that the result, sooner or later, would be an anti-EC backlash. He hoped to forestall it by returning some less essential business to the member-states.

The Strasbourg speech acted as a red rag to the British bull. Major's government had hoped that the agreement in Maastricht would allow political union to be forgotten for several years. When the foreign ministers gathered at Guimaraes in Portugal, on 3 May, Douglas Hurd ticked off Delors. However Hans-Dietrich Genscher and Roland Dumas defended the commission president, saying that institutional questions could not wait until 1996.

The next day Britain's *Sunday Telegraph* carried an article which may have changed the course of European history, 'Delors Plan to rule Europe'. Boris Johnson, the paper's Brussels correspondent, reported that Delors wanted to scrap the rotation of the EC presidency and to centralise power in Brussels. The member-states would lose their remaining veto-rights and the European Parliament would appoint an EC president who would replace the commission president. Johnson's article was not the first to pick up the institutional ideas which were floating around the commission, but it was the first to brand them as Delors' own.[3]

Meanwhile Denmark was in the thick of a keenly fought referendum campaign on the Maastricht treaty. The *Sunday Telegraph* article, widely reprinted in Denmark's newspapers, had a huge impact. The *Nej* campaign, which had argued that the new treaty would centralise power in Brussels and deprive small states of their rights, claimed vindication. Before the article opinion polls had suggested a narrow vote in favour of the Maastricht treaty on 2 June; afterwards they pointed to a narrow vote against.

The Danish government was furious with Delors. Uffe Ellemann-Jensen, the foreign minister, said that unless he disowned his reported opinions, Denmark would veto his reappointment to the commission presidency (the Lisbon summit would decide whether Delors should serve a further two years, starting in January 1993).

Delors waited a couple of weeks before briefing Danish journalists in Brussels. He denied that he wanted to deprive small countries of the right to hold the EC presidency. He insisted that there was no 'Delors plan' and that the ideas circulating in the commission were for 10 or 15 years hence. He said he had not seen the paper from the secretariat-general which had fallen into the hands of journalists. But the damage had been done. Many of the Danish politicians, academics and journalists who observed the referendum judge the 'Delors plan' to have been one of several factors which determined the result.

Delors accepts no blame for the referendum result, pointing out that he never put his name to the ideas which the press seized on and exaggerated. Yet once Delors had launched the constitutional debate, articles such as Johnson's were likely to appear. Because the commission is the world's most open bureaucracy, journalists invariably hear of new papers or initiatives. Delors's own staff had briefed journalists, including Johnson, on their ideas for constitutional reform. Delors himself had promised a shock to the heads of government; yet when he entered the commission press room on the morning after 2 June, the pallor of his skin suggested he had received an electric shock.

Much else had boosted the anti-Maastricht forces in Denmark. Some Danes blamed rising unemployment on the EC. Although supported by most political and business leaders, the pro-Maastricht camp ran a desultory campaign. The opposition social democrats, paralysed by a leadership contest, took little part in the debate. The 'June Movement', a well-organised group of non-party academics, presented slick arguments against the treaty and made voting *Nej* respectable. The government was unwise enough to distribute 300,000 copies of the treaty, without explanations or summaries, through post offices; some found the unreadable document frightening. Traditionally, the Danes have never held their leaders in great esteem; after 2 June many of them admitted to voting no because the establishment had said vote yes.

Even before 2 June, there were signs of an anti-government *fronde* in the EC. This was hardly surprising, for every member-state except Greece and Ireland had had the same group of rulers for most of the previous 10 years. François Mitterrand changed his prime minister after the socialists won only 18 per cent in March's local and regional elections; but the ruling party remained unpopular. In April, in a parliamentary election, the Italians shook their governing classes by voting for opposition groups like the Lombard League. In the same month Britain's general election cut John Major's majority to 20 seats, giving Conservative backbenchers – many of them anti-EC – a hold on his government.

Helmut Kohl's mismanagement of German unity had eroded his popularity. With inflation touching 5 per cent, an atmosphere of economic malaise made Germans unwilling to sacrifice the D-mark. Peter Gauweiler, Bavaria's environment minister, described the ecu as 'esperanto money', while *Der Spiegel* and *Bild* continued to attack EMU and anything else that came out of Brussels.

Opinion polls showed that most Germans opposed EMU (although a small majority favoured the Maastricht treaty). Germany's political elite responded to the new, Eurosceptical mood. In March the social democrats said they would not support ratification unless the German parliament could vote on the final phase of EMU before it began (the government later agreed). In May Volker Ruhe, the defence minister, argued that it was more important to widen the EC than to deepen it. Then Theo Waigel, the finance minister, proposed calling the single currency the frank rather than the ecu. He claimed this would not contradict the Maastricht treaty which, in its German translation, referred to the ECU, as in European Currency Unit; most other versions spelt the word ecu, which implied the currency had to be called those three letters (by September Waigel was canvassing for the 'Euro-mark').

Since the treaty could not come into force until ratified by all 12 members, the 2 June referendum – in theory – killed it. However EC governments were loath to abandon the document they had painstakingly crafted. They feared that any renegotiation would open Pandora's box and deprive them of the prizes they had won at Maastricht. So on 5 June, when EC foreign ministers gathered in Oslo (in the margins of a NATO meeting) they turned down a Danish request to renegotiate the treaty. The ministers declared they would press ahead with ratification – in effect telling the Danes to think again or face the consequences.

The French and German governments – although not the British – argued that if the Danes did not reverse their decision, they would have to be kicked out of the EC by one means or another. The easiest method would be to amend the Maastricht treaty so that it covered 11 instead of 12 countries. That would require Denmark to agree to leave the EC. If the Danes did not cooperate the 11 would have to renounce the Treaty of Rome, replace it with an agreement among themselves and leave Denmark alone in the old EC. 'We're not going to let 45,000 peculiar people stop Europe's momentum. Legal solutions can always be found,' said one top German official. Delors also took a hard line. He said on French television that unless the Danes swallowed Maastricht they would have to quit the EC for the EEA, and that they might well lose the benefits of the Common Agricultural Policy.[4]

On 10 June a chastened Delors addressed the European Parliament. He called for greater transparency in the EC's decision-making processes; for a better effort by governments, parliaments and the commission to explain what the EC did; and for a debate on subsidiarity. He promised that the commission would propose fewer laws and suggested that it and the council should simplify their legal texts.[5] Delors knew that the Danes had pushed institutional reform off the Community's agenda. The paper on enlargement that he prepared for the Lisbon summit turned out as mild as Vinho Verde.

The Danish *Nej* reinvigorated nationalists throughout northern Europe. All of a sudden, Maastricht and a federal future no longer appeared inevitable. With the Lisbon summit of 26 and 27 June due to decide on Delors's future, English newspapers bayed for his blood. A *Sunday Times* editorial said of the 'Napoleonic' Delors that 'his goal is a nuclear-armed, pan-European, socialist superstate, commanded from Brussels ... with his own finger presumably on the trigger.' The paper accused Delors (falsely, for the story was an invention) of trying to harmonise specifications for condoms.[6] Even pro-European newspapers such as the *Financial Times* and *The Economist* joined the bandwagon and called for his sacking.

In the week before the summit Major made Delors sweat by refusing to say whether he would veto his reappointment. But on the summit's first day all agreed that Delors should serve a third term, until December 1994. The heads of government avoided rows and, buoyed by Ireland's referendum – a 67 per cent vote for Maastricht on 18 June – tried to convince each other that it was business as usual. They decided to start membership talks with EFTA applicants as soon as the Maastricht treaty had been ratified and the second Delors package agreed. Mitterrand, previously hostile to enlargement, had come round to the view that it would help to maintain the EC's faltering momentum. In any case, France would gain nothing by resisting a seemingly inevitable process.

On Yugoslavia, as usual, the EC appeared ridiculous. The Bosnians had voted for independence in a referendum in March, although the Serb community had not taken part. The EC's recognition of the Bosnian republic provoked fighting among its Muslims, Serbs and Croats, and in April Sarajevo came under siege. In Lisbon the 12 issued a hollow-sounding declaration that they would not exclude the use of force in pursuit of humanitarian objectives. Constantin Mitsotakis, Greece's prime minister, vetoed EC recognition of the former Yugoslav republic of Macedonia; many Greeks thought its name implied a territorial claim on part of their country.

Delors delivered a long speech to the heads of government on the importance of subsidiarity. Kohl and Major said the best way to reassure public opinion that there never would be a centralised superstate was to apply that principle. Nobody demurred: opposition to subsidiarity had, since 2 June, become no more acceptable than the slaughter of baby seals. Delors had decided to make subsidiarity his Big Idea of 1992.

NICE IDEA, SHAME ABOUT THE WORD

Delors's championing of subsidiarity appeared to cynics as mere opportunism. What better way to fend off those who claimed the commission had become over-mighty? Delors undoubtedly recognised the tactical benefits of promoting the principle in the aftermath of the Danish referendum. His attachment to subsidiarity, however, had been longstanding.[7]

In his 1975 book *Changer*, Delors described subsidiarity while criticising the centralisation of the French state – although he did not use the word. Delors spoke of the need for subsidiarity in January 1985, in his first presidential speech to the European Parliament. Later in that year he inserted the principle into the environmental chapter of the Single European Act.

Two events in 1988 prompted Delors to renew his interest in the idea. In May, while attending a conference organised by the German Länder, he learned of their fear that the EC had, since the Single European Act, begun to encroach on their powers. He told the Länder that subsidiarity would prevent the EC from getting involved in decisions that were better handled at national or regional level. In September, after Margaret Thatcher's Bruges speech, Delors saw subsidiarity as a means of deflecting criticism of the EC. He appointed a group of officials to weed out unnecessary commission proposals.

In 1989 Delors pushed subsidiarity into the Delors Report on EMU, and into his own Bruges speech, where it made 12 appearances. During the IGC on political union Delors fought for subsidiarity to become an article in the treaty and, thanks to British and German support, got his way.

In January 1992 Michael Heseltine, then Britain's environment minister, visited Delors in Brussels. Heseltine proposed that an EC environmental inspectorate should monitor the work of national inspectors. Heseltine hoped that such an inspectorate would force southern Europeans to respect the EC's green rules. Delors said he was against the idea. Heseltine thought Delors had not understood his English and repeated the proposal slowly, clearly and loudly. Delors repeated that he did not like the idea and said it clashed with the British government's policy of subsidiarity. A flabbergasted Heseltine had to turn to officials for help.

In February Delors received a paper from the Cellule de Prospective (the commission think tank) on 'The philosophical history of the concept of subsidiarity'. This concluded that Calvinist theologians had invented the idea in the 1570s, to show how their church differed from the centralising papacy. Leo XIII borrowed the principle for his 1891 encyclical, *Rerum Novarum*, to guide relations between society and the individual, and between social groups of different levels. The idea became one of the foundations of the social teaching of the Catholic church. It meant not only that society should respect the autonomy of the person, but also that it should create the conditions which allowed the person to flourish. Pius XI put subsidiarity into *Quadrogesimo Anno*, an encyclical of 1931, to stress the domain of the individual and of the family against the totalitarian state.

Speaking in Maastricht, in March 1992, Delors praised the European Parliament's definition of the idea, contained in its 1984 draft treaty on European Union: 'The union acts only to lead tasks which can be undertaken more efficiently in common than by the states working separately.' He said that he would add: 'In particular, because the dimensions or the effects of the action do not allow national or regional authorities better to realise the objectives.' Subsidiarity was not only about limiting the intervention of a superior authority, but also 'an obligation on this authority, *vis-à-vis* the persons or collective organisations [at a lower level], to provide the means for their self-fulfilment.'[8]

Thus the higher levels of government should take a paternal interest in those below them. Delors's definitions of subsidiarity sometimes resemble his descriptions of personalism. He tends to make his favourite ideas – subsidiarity, personalism, federalism, the European model of society – sound like different manifestations of the same underlying principle.

Thus he defines federalism as 'a clear distinction between the levels of power'. The virtue of federalism is to

> *allow people to live together, while retaining their diversity, because the division of powers is clear. I'm for a federal Europe not to increase the powers of the Community but because one knows who does what.*

One of the paradoxes of 1992 was that John Major championed subsidiarity to rein back the powers of the commission, while Delors praised the principle as a means of bringing about federalism.[9]

In the spring of 1992 Delors decided that environmental policy was ripe for the application of subsidiarity. He complained that EC directives on bathing water and drinking water were too detailed. 'We must lay down some general environmental principles and leave the national states to implement the details in good faith,' he told *The Guardian*.[10] In June he suggested that policing the single market could be left to national governments and courts.

Yet Delors never came up with a list of competences for the EC to hand back to member-states. And it proved difficult to find specific examples of EC laws that were redundant. The directive on the hunting of wild birds, for instance, had provoked enormous hostility to the EC in south-west France. Clashes between environmentalists and ring-dove hunters, who ignored the directive, were frequent and fierce. Delors had gone on record as saying that the law breached subsidiarity. But when he examined the problem in the summer of 1992, he found the directive to be a model of subsidiarity: it laid down the principle that certain species should not be shot while nesting or migrating, and left each government to set dates for the hunting season. Delors learned that the Danes became angry when the French shot ring doves on their way from North Africa to Denmark.

Delors admitted that the commission had abused subsidiarity but argued that governments were also guilty. He pointed out that most commission proposals originated with governments or lobbies which, disliking a member-state's rules, demanded EC legislation. For instance, a German law required mineral water companies to collect used containers. That suited German companies, which use glass bottles, but made it hard for French and Belgian firms, which use plastic bottles, to compete in Germany. So France and Belgium asked the commission to write EC rules on mineral water bottles. After analysing the 535 proposals that it had made in 1991, the commission concluded that only 30 had been its own ideas (however those 30 included controversial measures on maternity leave, working time and the liberalisation of electricity markets).

In October 1992, before the Birmingham summit, Delors sent governments a 20-page paper on the application of subsidiarity. That principle, Delors argued, implied that every Community action should satisfy two tests. In areas where the EC and the member-states shared competence (such as labour law or R&D), was EC action necessary? And then, in all areas of EC activity, including those of exclusive competence (such as agriculture or trade), was the intensity of the action proportional to the objective pursued? In line with this idea of 'proportionality', Delors suggested greater use of non-binding recommendations or of programmes which supported national initiatives. If measures had to be binding, Delors proposed 'framework laws' which would set objectives and leave national parliaments to decide how to achieve them.

Delors picked an example of what he considered 'over-intense' EC law.

The campaign for clean beaches would probably have been just as effective if the EC had opted for recommendations, in combination with a system of awards for clean beaches, rather than having to commence dozens of infringement proceedings for failure to meet the various technical standards laid down by EC legislation.

Henceforth, Delors promised, each commission proposal would include an explanation of how it conformed to subsidiarity.

Worthy stuff, but was Delors wise to devote so much energy to an inherently technocratic concept? The problem with subsidiarity is its subjectivity. One country's bureaucratic interference is another's urgently needed EC action. Germany regards exacting EC rules on the purity of beer and food as essential rather than a breach of subsidiarity. Britain says the same of detailed regulations on the transport of animals. Germany and Britain do not agree on which EC laws are necessary.

In the European Parliament, just after the Danish referendum, Delors had offered subsidiarity, explanation and transparency as the answers to the EC's problems. He should have devoted more attention to the second and third ideas. The Council of Ministers was the only democratic law-making body in the world which deliberated in secret. To find out what ministers said and how they voted, journalists had to ask national spokesmen and spokeswomen – whose reports were always slanted and sometimes mendacious. In the summer of 1992 the Danish government suggested opening up the council's legislative debates. It thought that people who watched their ministers perform on television might feel less alienated from the EC.

However Delors the bureaucrat worried that televising proceedings would impair efficiency. 'The actors would have one eye on the subject and the other on the media,' he said in September.[11] 'Dynamic compromises would be harder to find,' he added a month later, meaning that horse-trading would be less easy.[12] Perhaps, but if Delors had championed transparency he would have seemed ahead of the times rather than behind them. Subsidiarity was too arcane an idea and too ugly a word to capture the public imagination.

CHAIN REACTION

On 3 July François Mitterrand announced a referendum on the Treaty of Maastricht. He was not obliged to do so, for the French constitution would have allowed ratification through a parliamentary vote. Mitterrand chose a referendum to dispel the doubts over Europe's future which had arisen since 2 June. He also wanted to embarrass the French right, which was divided on Maastricht. The risks seemed small, for opinion polls showed 70 per cent of the French to favour the treaty.

Most of France's political establishment campaigned for a *Oui*, against the National Front, the Communists, some Greens, dissident Socialists (led by Jean-Pierre Chevènement) and a wing of the Gaullist RPR (led by Charles Pasqua and Philippe Seguin). Delors thought Mitterrand mistaken to call a referendum. The anti-Maastricht camp depicted Delors as the chief of an overweening bureaucracy. They taunted him with the 1988 comment that in 10 years' time 80 per cent of economic laws would be made in Brussels. An indignant Delors complained that ministers did nothing to defend him or the commission. Yet he remained aloof from the campaign. He said it would be improper for a commission president to become involved in a domestic political conflict. His close aides knew there was another reason for his absence: in his heart he did not believe in the Maastricht treaty.

Mitterrand had failed to appreciate that the French were fed up with their political leaders, who had scarcely changed in 20 years. The socialists, especially, had been tainted by a series of financial scandals and by unemployment of over 10 per cent. Some remembered how a referendum defeat had made de Gaulle resign in 1969 and hoped for a repeat with another unpopular septuagenarian. As the summer wore on the French turned against Maastricht, for their own, Gallic reasons. British and Danish opponents worried most about losing sovereignty to over-mighty bureaucrats, while Germans feared inflation and the loss of the D-mark. Some of the French (like some of the Danes) feared domination by Germans in a more united Europe. However the principal theme uniting French critics was that the treaty stood for economic liberalism. Farmers who thought the reform of the CAP would shrink their incomes, industrial workers who worried about foreign competition and *petits commerçants* who did not want a single market drove the *Non* campaign.

What the EC had done, what it was doing and what it stood for counted for as much as the contents of the new treaty. The anti-Maastricht campaign branded the treaty as a boon to the bourgeois, the bankers and the bureaucrats, and rallied all those who feared for their future. The referendum results would show a near-perfect match between areas of below-average wealth and areas voting no.

In late August several opinion polls pointed to a victory for the *Nons*, which shook the currency markets. The exchange rate mechanism (ERM) had not experienced a realignment since 1987. The markets had assumed that the EC's political commitment to monetary union meant that ERM parities were more or less fixed – until the Danish referendum cast doubts over the Maastricht treaty. The Bundesbank's hike of its discount rate, to 8.75 per cent on 16 July, further unsettled the markets. Speculators started to believe that governments with stagnant economies would rather devalue against the D-mark than continue to match the Bundesbank's high interest rates. By early September they were selling lire, pounds and pesetas. A weak dollar added to the strains by encouraging investors to buy D-marks.

At an 'informal' meeting in Bath on 5 September, EC finance ministers put heavy pressure on Helmut Schlesinger, who had just replaced Karl Otto Pöhl as Bundesbank president, to cut interest rates. He ruled that out but hinted that a realignment would change the situation. Norman Lamont, the British minister who had the chair, would not allow any discussion of a realignment. He and John Major had staked their credibility on refusing a devaluation.

On 14 September the markets forced a 7 per cent devaluation of the lira. The Bundesbank cut its Lombard rate by 0.25 per cent, but no more, because Britain and Spain refused to join the devaluation. Schlesinger weakened the pound by telling *Handelsblatt* that a further ERM realignment would be in order. Two days later Lamont raised short-term interest rates by 5 per cent in a bid to protect the pound. The Bundesbank and the Bank of England hurled their reserves onto the markets (the latter spending £12 billion during the crisis). But a speculative hurricane, the like of which the currency markets had never seen, forced Major into the humiliation of taking the pound out of the ERM on the evening of Black Wednesday, 16 September. The cornerstone of the British government's economic policy had disappeared. That night, after a meeting of the EC's monetary committee in Brussels, the lira left the ERM and the peseta devalued by 5 per cent. Britons and Germans blamed each other for the pound's fate.

Meanwhile the success of the *Non* campaign had persuaded Delors to become involved in the French referendum. On 28 August, addressing a summer school of Rocardians in Quimper, he could not control his anger.

> There's no place in a democracy for people who call for a Non, for the sorcerer's apprentices, for those who awaken phantoms. I will say to them they should get out of politics.[13]

That outburst allowed Delors's opponents to portray him as malicious and unbalanced. A close aide admits that the surge of anti-Maastricht sentiment unhinged Delors for some of the referendum campaign. 'In Quimper he skidded off the track because he was trying to please his audience – which was a great error.'

The next day Delors ran into a barrage of hostile questions at a conference of the Green Party in Saint-Nazaire. Militant ecologists blamed the commission for unemployment and nuclear power. He told them:

Don't do what I did when I was 20, when I went round in circles in my
bedroom telling myself I was right and the world was wrong, for I wasn't
useful. It's not enough to feel good, you should be responsible politicians
who try to be useful.[14]

On 31 August Delors said on the radio that he would resign if the *Non* campaign won, 'for I don't see how I could compensate for the handicap of the loss of influence of France and her representatives in European institutions.' Two days later he told *Le Monde* that the Maastricht treaty would curb the 'soft tyranny' of the commission, which had been necessary during the first phase of the EC's history. 'All those who want to take Jacques Delors and the Brussels technocracy down a peg should vote *Oui*.' He admitted to being 'panicked' by the gulf between the political class and society in every European country.[15]

Delors appeared traumatised to see his own people – for so long in the vanguard of building the European edifice – on the brink of inflicting more damage than Mrs Thatcher's handbag ever had. He looked lifeless and tired during television appearances. He seemed ill at ease defending the treaty, although he had not lost his skill for metaphor. He told *La Croix*:

We must abandon our rather too rationalist French mentality, and
realise that Europe is more of an English garden than a French garden.
It's rather messy, but that's how we make progress.[16]

Delors suppressed his true opinion of the Maastricht agreement (see Chapter 9) lest it damage the prospect of a *Oui*. He feared that a *Non* would destroy not only the treaty and the ERM, but also the 'Community method'. He had written earlier in the year that the method involved

progressively creating positive links of interdependence among coun-
tries, which certainly doesn't prevent each one affirming its personality
and aspirations, and which does not exclude differences and arguments.
But – and that's the fundamental change – what has been gained is so
precious that the willpower exists, in the last resort, to find positive
compromises.[17]

Delors thought that if the goals of the Maastricht treaty disappeared, member-states would have little incentive to restrain their immediate self-interest.

Delors knew that a French *Non* would feed the phantoms of nationalism. Without the 'deepening' of the treaty's provisions for political union,

France and Spain would veto any further widening. Germany would devote more attention to Eastern Europe, while France would be less willing to compromise in the GATT talks. The commission would lack the clout to extend the single market into new areas such as telecommunications and energy. Most member-states would try to draft a new treaty, while Denmark and Britain would probably stand aloof.

No one doubted that relations among the EC's members would reach unprecedented levels of rancour, paranoia and bitterness. The final opinion polls showed no statistically significant difference between the *Ouis* and the *Nons*. On Sunday 20 September, Delors waited for the French electors to determine his and the EC's future.

France's *'petit oui'* of 51.05 per cent failed to banish the demons of disintegration. Britain's Thatcherites, jubilant that the pound was floating (or rather sinking) free, argued that if so many of the normally *communautaires* French opposed the treaty, the British should ditch it. That evening Major said on television that Britain would ratify the treaty on three conditions: popular concerns about EC bureaucracy would have to be addressed; the ERM would have to be reformed; and a solution to the Danish problem would have to be found. As the prime minister of the country which held the EC presidency, Major announced a special summit to tackle these issues.

Later on Major let it be known that he would not push the Maastricht ratification bill through parliament until the Danes had decided what kind of special deal they wanted from the EC. Such prevarication made EMU appear less likely and delighted currency speculators. They picked on the franc and, on 23 September, only FFr160 billion of Franco-German intervention spared it from devaluation.

Major's wobbling isolated Britain from its partners. Several French and German politicians held out the prospect of a two-speed Europe. If Britain or Denmark blocked Maastricht, they said, an inner core should go ahead in areas such as EMU, defence and immigration. Speaking in Brussels on 25 September, Delors warned the British not to link their ratification to sorting out the Danish problem.

> *If anyone is looking for pretexts to delay implementing the treaty ... I wouldn't rule out the possibility that some countries would take initiatives, given that we must not delay.*

Two days earlier Kohl had pandered to fashion by describing the commission as 'too powerful, constantly expanding and exterminating national identities.' Delors said that excessive criticism would destroy the morale of civil servants and cripple the EC's institutions. 'I'd like it if Chancellor Kohl would think a little about that.' He called for the EC to accelerate moves to EMU, as soon as currency markets were stable.

> *Without a united EC front, America and Japan will be free to exploit the divisions of the European nations. In the past, competing European nationalisms have led to decline, regression and ridicule. The question for Europe's leaders is, will you let Europe decline or not?*[18]

Delors believed that a two-tier Europe would be the best response to British foot-dragging. But he also saw the tactical benefits of frightening the British with such talk. All the discussion of two speeds seemed to have some effect, for Major soon promised that Britain would ratify the treaty by early 1993.

Before and during the Birmingham summit of 16 October, Delors and the British clashed over new procedures for enforcing subsidiarity. Delors claimed that British proposals, which gathered some support from France and Germany, would circumscribe the commission's right of initiative. However the small states, which view the commission as their protector, and the 'poor four', which believe a strong commission is good for regional aid, stood by Delors. As a result the 'Birmingham Declaration' on subsidiarity and openness left the commission unharmed and included several of Delors's own ideas.

During a summit tea-break, Uffe Ellemann-Jensen, the Danish foreign minister, presented Delors with that day's *Sun*. The front page consisted of a 'cut out and burn' mask of Jacques Delors, under the heading 'Tell Delors to Fawk Off'. The *Sun* said that since Delors, like Guy Fawkes, had plotted to destroy parliament, he too should be burnt on 5 November. When the Dane explained who Guy Fawkes was Delors laughed and filed the article for his archives.

John Major's decision to allow British Coal to sack 30,000 miners overshadowed the summit, while his retreat of a few days later revealed the weakness of his government. Major announced a House of Commons 'paving motion' on the Maastricht treaty for 4 November. Strictly, the success or failure of such a motion would have no effect on the ratification process. But Major let it be known that a defeat would lead to his resignation. The Labour Party's desire to embarrass the government proved stronger than its support for the treaty, and it joined the Thatcherites in voting against the motion. Major won by three votes – but only after promising Conservative waverers that Britain would not ratify until the Danes had held a second referendum.

That delay maddened Britain's partners. 'Incomprehensible', said Lubbers. 'Unacceptable', said Mitterrand. 'Regrettable', said Kohl. They feared the delay would worsen already strained relations and thus make the GATT talks harder to resolve; the enlargement negotiations slower, for the EFTA countries would not know the nature of the body they were seeking to join; and the Danes more awkward, for they would be less willing to accept Maastricht if they thought the British might not.

The Danes were already being difficult. On 30 October their parliament had decided not to hold another referendum unless Denmark won legally binding opt-outs from the treaty's provisions on EMU, common defence, citizenship and judicial affairs. In other words, the Danes would not accept four of the five objectives set out at the start of the treaty. Many of Denmark's partners complained that it was asking for an effective renegotiation of the Maastricht treaty. Delors worried that so many opt-outs would set a precedent for countries which sought to join the EC. He feared that if opting out became endemic, the Community's coherence would suffer.

The British were more sympathetic to Danish demands. They urged the other members to bend over backwards to ensure that a second referendum did not say *Nej*. The others professed to be untroubled by such a prospect, saying that it would merely lead to Denmark's departure from the EC. The British insisted that they would oppose any move to expel the Danes.

The other members accused Britain of using the EC presidency for the blatant promotion of its own interests. They claimed that Britain was exploiting Denmark's desire for opt-outs to weaken the Maastricht treaty's objectives. They pointed to Britain blocking the funding of HDTV, trying to shackle the commission with new procedures on subsidiarity and refusing a larger EC budget in the talks on the second Delors package.

In November the inter-governmental wrangling reached levels of acrimony unseen since de Gaulle had left an empty chair in 1965. In the long-running GATT saga (see Chapter 8), Delors tried to prevent Ray MacSharry, the agriculture commissioner, from striking a deal with the Americans on farm subsidies. France warned that it would use the Luxembourg Compromise against a GATT agreement – becoming the first country to threaten that veto since the signing of the Single European Act. French hostility to the GATT talks shook the Franco-German alliance and left the Anglo-French relationship in tatters.

Currency speculators fed on these tensions. They suspected that the Spanish, Danish, Portuguese, Irish and French currencies would cut free from the D-mark and its high interest rates. Such suspicions have a tendency to become self-fulfilling. On 22 November the Spanish peseta and the Portuguese escudo devalued, while the Danish krone, the Irish punt and the French franc narrowly escaped that fate. The Bundesbank's Schlesinger added to the markets' uncertainty by attacking the Maastricht convergence criteria as over-lax. He complained that the Bundesbank had to intervene too often to help weaker ERM currencies (it had spent DM92 billion on supporting other ERM currencies in August and September).

When the Community had been a success story, in the late 1980s, the commission had taken much of the credit. The failures and disputes of 1992 turned the commission into everybody's pet scapegoat, a cowed and feeble shadow of its former self. Morale among officials sunk to the low levels of the early 1980s. The commission lost the self-confidence to pursue measures which would incur the hostility of powerful governments. For instance in the autumn Leon Brittan mooted the use of 'article 90' – a rarely used but draconian power – to break up energy monopolies. His colleagues insisted that nothing so controversial could be considered while 'anti-Brussels' sentiment remained strong.

Delors worried that the political and economic uncertainty would worsen Europe's recession by discouraging investment and spending. For eight years he had made speeches about the need for EC governments to coordinate macroeconomic policy, but they had never listened. At the Birmingham summit Major had prevented Delors from making a presentation on an EC growth initiative. In the weeks before the Edinburgh summit, due on 11 and 12 December, Delors tried to revive the idea. He argued that even the announcement of a growth package, whatever its contents, would do something to restore confidence. This time, with the German economy starting to shrink, governments listened. Even the Eurosceptical Lamont thought an EC growth initiative a good idea – such a good idea that he sold it in Britain as his own.

In Edinburgh the governments agreed that, where possible, they would shift spending from the current to the capital account. They approved two of Delors's ideas: to give the European Investment Bank an extra facility of 5 billion ecus, for infrastructure projects; and to create a European Investment Fund, with 2 billion ecus of capital, to guarantee private sector project loans. The finance ministers speculated that the whole package might trigger 30 billion ecus of extra investment.

Delors helped the British to broker an impressive series of deals which saved the presidency's honour and did something to restore the Community's poise. After 30 years of argument over the seat of the European Parliament, Strasbourg was confirmed as the principal site for plenary meetings. Germany won 18 more Euro-MPs, so that the new German Länder would have representation. Membership talks with Austria, Sweden, Finland and Norway would begin in early 1993, but would not conclude until all 12 members had ratified the Maastricht treaty.

On subsidiarity, the commission promised to withdraw a plethora of draft measures – such as directives on zoo animals, the harmonisation of number plates and the regulation of gambling – and to simplify existing laws on pollution. A new procedure would allow any member of the Council of Ministers to suspend the discussion of a draft law, on the grounds that it breached subsidiarity, if a simple majority agreed. As for openness, the commission agreed to consult more widely before drafting proposals. A few meetings of the Council of Ministers would be televised, and some of its voting records would be published.

The summit agreed on a legally binding 'decision' and on several non-binding declarations that would allow Denmark to opt out of monetary union, defence policy, citizenship and judicial cooperation until 1996. However the original treaty had given the Danes an EMU opt-out and could not have forced them to do anything against their will in the other three areas. The point of the Edinburgh deal was to spell out and clarify this lack of obligation. Denmark's mainstream parties could then claim to have won concessions and support the treaty in a second referendum.

On the summit's second day Spain threatened to block an agreement on the Delors package. Everyone had agreed to Delors's idea of stretching the budgetary plans over seven years, rather than five, as a compromise that would give the 'poor four' more money, but later. However Britain and Germany would not concede a 1999 ceiling on EC spending of more than 1.27 per cent of Community GDP, while Spain demanded a higher ceiling so that regional aid to the poor four could double. Late in the evening, when Major suspended the session, Delors went into a huddle with British, German and Spanish officials. With the help of some creative accounting – which included shrinking the contingency reserve and even shifting 200 million ecus from the commission's administrative budget to the regional fund – Delors squared the doubling of regional aid with the 1.27 per cent ceiling.

The budgetary settlement delighted Delors. His plan for spending more on 'industrial competitiveness' had been squashed, but he had achieved his other objectives. The first Delors package, which ran from 1988 to 1992, had increased the structural funds from 8 billion ecus a year to an average of 13 billion ecus during those years, in 1992 prices. During the second package, which ran from 1993 to 1999, they would average 25 billion ecus a year.

After the summit Delors praised Major's chairing and welcomed the return of 'family spirit' to the EC. But for all its successes, the Edinburgh European Council failed to exorcise the demons. Nine members had ratified the Maastricht agreement, but it could not become law unless three others did so. Denmark's electorate, Britain's parliament and Germany's constitutional court (which had delayed German ratification) had yet to approve the treaty.

ANATOMY OF AN 'ANNUS HORRIBILIS'

The European Community's crisis in 1992 – and beyond – stemmed from three, intertwined historical episodes: an economic recession, the end of communism and a reaction to the EC's growing power and influence. Delors cannot be blamed for the first two but had a lot to do with the third.

The Community has always flourished in periods of economic growth and festered during downturns. Between January 1986 and January 1991, when the single-market programme was in full swing, the EC gained a net 9 million jobs. But the EC's unemployment rate, having fallen from 11.5 per cent in 1986 to 8.5 per cent in 1990, started to edge up in 1991. Lengthening dole queues increased the pressure for protection and harmed the cause of economic liberalism. In countries where the EC is seen as a liberal enterprise – such as France, Switzerland and Sweden – its image suffered accordingly.

The economic downturn sapped the strength of the German, Spanish, British, French and Italian governments, and made them meaner; hence France's tough talk in the Uruguay Round and Spain's brinkmanship on the negotiation of the Delors budgetary package. Several ERM members could not maintain their D-mark parities because of the contradiction between high German interest rates and recession-hit economies which needed cheap credit.

The Bundesbank insisted on high interest rates to counteract the German government's inflationary fiscal policy. Having won the November 1990 election on the promise of no tax increases, Kohl had to borrow heavily to support the new Länder. The error of a one-for-one rate of exchange for German monetary union, in July 1990, damaged the new Länder's competitiveness and increased their thirst for subsidies. By 1992 the German government's budget deficit had reached 5 per cent of GDP.

Yet the Bundesbank blamed a large part of the ERM's problems on the governments of weak economies, such as Britain, Italy and Spain. Bundesbankers criticised them for treating their currencies as symbols of national virility – and thus rejecting periodic German suggestions of a realignment. It was true that Italy's public debt and Britain's current account deficit had diverged from their partners', and that occasional realignments would have strengthened the ERM. But the continuing currency turmoil in 1993, culminating in the fall of the French franc – a currency backed by stronger economic fundamentals than the D-mark – showed the essence of the problem to be German interest rates. These required other ERM members to set interest rates of 2, 3 or 4 per cent higher than the optimal level for their economies.

The reunification of Germany had hurried along European integration in 1990 and 1991. Yet having helped to inspire the Maastricht treaty, German unity undermined it by slowing economic growth and by weakening the ERM.

The demise of communism harmed the Community by bringing the two Germanies together – and in other ways. During each of the four years 1989 to 1992, Germany admitted about 600,000 immigrants from former communist countries. Those figures exclude asylum-seekers, who numbered 400,000 in 1992. The influx of foreigners boosted support for Germany's extreme-right nationalists. Furthermore, the refusal of most EC members to share the burden of Yugoslav refugees (Germany took at least 300,000, while only a few thousand went to Britain and France) irked the Germans.

The EC's failure to bring about peace in Yugoslavia damaged its image, particularly among Germans, who followed the war more closely than most. By the spring of 1992 the United Nations had sent thousands of peacekeeping troops to Yugoslavia and joined the EC's efforts to find a diplomatic solution. That the 12 had kept to a common line, rather than back different republics, and had provided 75 per cent of both the humanitarian aid and the UN soldiers, did nothing to banish their shame. The world saw that the EC was not prepared to intervene militarily to end atrocities on its own doorstep.

Delors raged in his powerlessness. He said that international law should allow intervention in a country's affairs, in order to enforce peace.[19] In August, addressing an emergency meeting of the European Parliament, he fulminated against the 'destructive, anti-humanist ideology of the Belgrade regime'. Delors warned that if the epidemic of ethnic cleansing was not conquered, it would spread to the whole continent.

> *Do you have to hate to make a nation? We have shown in the EC the answer is no. Without the perspective of a credible military intervention, nothing will stop the subtle, expansionist and murderous strategy of the Serb leaders.*[20]

No EC government had called for military intervention, but Lady Thatcher did so in the same week as Delors. Both saw the Yugoslav problem as a moral issue.

The Community's critics attacked it – and by association the Maastricht treaty – for incoherence on foreign policy, inaction on immigration and instability in the ERM. Ironically, the treaty had been designed to deal with those very problems.

The wave of hostility to the Community appeared to be part of a wider-ranging phenomenon of 1992. Those who voted against Canada's draft constitution, for America's Ross Perot or for Italy's Lombard League all showed contempt for established politicians.

As the remotest elite of all, the Brussels Eurocrats had it coming. Until the mid-1980s the EC had touched groups such as farmers, steelworkers and scientific researchers, but had made little difference to the lives of most people. After Delors's arrival the EC encroached into more areas. Its laws opened markets and bankrupted firms, while commission edicts banned takeovers and outlawed state aid. The Maastricht treaty promised to change how Europeans would be defended, who would vote in their elections and which banknotes they would use.

Much of the hostility to the Maastricht treaty stemmed less from its contents than from the effects of the earlier single-market programme. Nevertheless the treaty, like Delors, became a symbol of everything that people disliked about the EC.

An apparent lack of democratic legitimacy did nothing to help the Community's image. Ministers debated and voted behind closed doors, far from the gaze of national parliaments, while the European Parliament had not yet won much credibility. Governments had contributed to the image problem by failing to explain what the EC was and how it worked. The three governments which held referendums informed their people of the Maastricht treaty's contents; the others did not bother.

National politicians found the EC a useful scapegoat for unpopular policies. They often referred, quite deliberately, to 'Brussels' making this or that mistake. That word implied the commission was to blame, when in fact – competition policy excepted – the Council of Ministers took most decisions.

Among the 12, the bug of Brusselsphobia was largely confined to Britain, France, Germany and Denmark. But it spread beyond the EC's frontiers after 2 June: public opinion in Sweden, Finland, Austria – and especially in Norway and Switzerland – shifted against membership of the EC. The inhabitants of the Benelux countries appeared to have been immunised by their faith in federalism. Many southern Europeans viewed the European Community as a source of money and of modernisation, and cared little about the sovereignty of their own (rather weak) parliaments. Some of the southerners' administrations are so inept that the one in Brussels may, by comparison, have appeared almost exemplary.

The events of 1992 humbled Delors. There were moments when he resembled a fish which insists on swimming in a certain direction, even when the tide is moving the other way; and then, when beached and gasping, wonders what has happened. Yet Delors's powers of analysis had not deserted him. In September he said:

> The EC has achieved its successes with only governments and institutions contributing. The successes of the next stage, such as EMU, will need the express support and participation of citizens.[21]

Delors showed some awareness of the EC's image problem. Shortly after the Danish referendum he commented: 'It's not in constructing the foundations that one makes the architecture of a house attractive; the drama is that one does not fall in love with a single market without frontiers.' The EC had been built on the double fear of Soviet imperialism and of another European war, he said; henceforth it should be built on reason, not fear. 'Reason is magnificent, but it's less mobilising.'[22]

Delors blamed part of the post-Maastricht crisis on the degenerate state of democratic life. 'If the nineteenth century was that of parliaments, and the twentieth that of the masses, we're entering the era of public opinion.' Delors did not welcome this change – which was hardly surprising, given how public opinion, made manifest through referendums, had damaged his plans.

> One has the impression that on one side there is the prime minister, and on the other public opinion; that's not democracy to my mind. You need mediators between the two. Thankfully there is the British tradition, which keeps a big role for parliament, which is very precious. If a government has to look at three or four opinion polls before taking a decision, it will achieve nothing. Democracy is about electing those who express people's aspirations but who are also competent to explain decisions to the people.[23]

In December 1992 Delors claimed that he welcomed the result of the 2 June referendum, for it had warned the politicians not to forget to take the people with them.[24] But whenever he was asked if the EC should not have concentrated on the single market, rather than take on so many ambitious projects all at once, he demurred. He said the EC had had to move fast because of German unity, the rapid changes in Eastern Europe and the unstable nature of the ERM. Otherwise, 'the forces of disintegration and national introversion are so strong that we would have risked losing everything we have gained over the past 40 years.'[25]

Some of Delors's fellow commissioners disagree. 'Delors tried to push the Community too fast. He could not take the citizens of Europe along with him because they did not understand what was happening,' says one of the most senior.

Many EC governments felt antipathy towards Delors and his institution, and were therefore reluctant to defend them against unjust attacks. Their hostility, which had been growing since about 1990, influenced as well as reflected public opinion. Some of the resentment was inevitable: Delors's plans for a federal Europe would, by definition, reduce the power of governments. But some of it was a reaction to Delors's personal style of running the commission.

Governments complained of the commission waging petty territorial wars against the Council of Ministers. Its main interest in foreign policy seemed to be to enlarge its own role. National capitals liked neither the commission's tendency to preach, nor the over-detailed character of some of its proposals, particularly on environmental and labour law. Delors's sidelining of several commissioners and his concentration of authority in the presidency did not endear him to governments.

'The commission should remember it's there to help the member-states and to arbitrate, for it has been too self-righteous,' said a senior Luxembourg official in October 1992. The following January a senior French official complained that the commission had gone 'beyond the threshold of legitimacy: Delors abused his position by pronouncing on subjects such as Yugoslavia and Russia. He took a risk in incarnating the commission and the Community in his own person, for now that they are attacked he is weakened.'

Delors's tactical errors in 1992 compounded his difficulties. His initial plan for the second Delors package was overambitious. His provocation of a debate on institutional reform, just before Denmark's referendum, proved ill-timed. During the French referendum campaign his fragile nerves sometimes frayed. He erred in imagining that subsidiarity could solve the EC's problems. His behaviour in the GATT trade talks was incomprehensible to everyone except the French.

Yet such mistakes should be seen in perspective. Delors soon realised he had overbid on the budget: the final compromise that he put together in Edinburgh won praise from the British presidency. After the French referendum campaign, an opinion poll found that he and Giscard d'Estaing had been the most convincing performers. By the year-end Delors had persuaded governments that subsidiarity was a serious idea and that the commission was moderating its activism. Even on GATT, the charitable could argue that, by forcing MacSharry to win better terms than those he nearly took in Chicago, Delors increased the chances of France signing an agreement. As for institutional reform, the commission's job is to think ahead and to alert governments to the consequences of enlargement.

Denmark's Ellemann-Jensen thinks it unfair to single out Delors for blame, when all the EC's leaders had become out of touch.

> *When the problems became apparent, Delors was one of the first to pick up the challenge, and was very helpful on subsidiarity. We foreign ministers should be blamed more because we had the contact with our constituencies. We should have started to realise that the EC looked like a centralised bureaucratic monster, and listened to complaints about square cucumbers and Ingrid Maria apples [which, to the chagrin of many Danes, the EC had outlawed because of their small size]. We were so busy trying to understand the new situation in Eastern Europe that we didn't listen to the signals.*[26]

CHAPTER ELEVEN

THE ENIGMA OF JACQUES DELORS

DELORS'S COMPATRIOTS have called him a *'grenouille de bénitier'*. That translates, literally, as a frog from the font, and idiomatically as a 'church hen' or simply as a prig. Delors attends mass every Sunday, knows the French archbishops and takes a close interest in the affairs of the Catholic Church. Yet he is a secular Catholic, who believes the church should steer clear of politics. He disagrees with the Vatican line on abortion and contraception and thinks that priests should not direct the consciences of individuals. He often says that being right-wing is just as compatible with Christianity as being left-wing.

Delors does not overtly exploit his Catholicism for political advantage. He never talks of religion in public and he seldom answers journalists' questions on the subject. Inadvertently, however, Delors has drawn political dividends from his faith. While the *grenouille de bénitier* image appeals to few socialist leaders, some Catholics on the centre and right of French politics are impressed. Opinion polls show Delors to be the only leader of the left who is held in esteem by substantial numbers of French electors who normally vote for centrist or right-wing parties.

On French radio Delors once spoke of 'a kind of invisible thread which never breaks, which sometimes is very thin, but which means that this faith always exists, and that when I'm inclined to forget it, it grabs me, happily, by the collar at the corner of a road.'[1] Delors believes in the resurrection of the body and the soul. He is not a determinist and believes that everyone has a margin of freedom to use for good or ill. Delors sees good and evil in every individual, including himself, but does not believe in a personalised devil. He describes the ideology of ethnic cleansing in former Yugoslavia as a manifestation of the force of evil. He says the gruesome murder in 1993 of 2-year-old James Bulger, by two 10-year-old boys, reveals the same force.[2] He also talks of the force of love.

Delors continues to believe, as his grandfather told him, that 'nothing is ever won and nothing is ever lost.' Unlike many on the French left, he has

never believed that science was going to allow man to dominate all his problems. I believe that man perpetually renews his alienations: you can make some progress, but then there's a little demon who comes and tears it up, and afterwards you start again.[3]

This stoical philosophy helped Delors to cope with the problems which beset the EC in 1992 and 1993. He had never thought the golden period of 1985 to 1990 would continue indefinitely. He says he believes in the pessimism of the reason but the optimism of the will. He means that man can, through sheer willpower, improve his lot and resist history's tendency to be tragic – even if the little demons tear up his work periodically.

Delors claims that his pessimism comes less from his religion or his parents than himself. 'I produce pessimism unceasingly and naturally. One does not succeed in improving oneself, the years pass and one always falls into the same sins.'[4] A strong sense of guilt feeds Delors's darker moods. He feels guilty that he loves people more than God. He admires and is slightly jealous of some of the Christian missionaries he has met, who are, he believes, filled with a divine grace that eludes him.

As a child he had a Christian conscience, but only as an adult did he develop 'this unpitying judgement on myself. When I realise in the evening that I've made the same mistakes as the week before, that I promised to myself that I would not make, I blame myself.' He says he feels guilty when he has treated his staff harshly without explaining why, when he has not paid enough attention to his family, and when he has talked to someone for only five minutes because he is busy.[5]

As Delors gets older, his sense of guilt gets stronger.

> *I feel more guilty today than I did 20 years ago, and still more guilty than 40 years ago. I need people around me like Lamy and Dethomas to tell me that everything which happens in Europe is not my fault, because I blame it on myself and I'm unhappy.[6]*

Delors sometimes appears almost to take a perverse pleasure in suffering. Jean-Pierre Cot, once a minister in the Mauroy government and now leader of the socialists in the European Parliament, says: 'Delors carries his cross, agonising and torturing himself. He suffers from the contradiction of being both a politician and a Christian moralist – yet he exploits his moral complexity to his advantage.'[7] He means that Delors's soul-baring does his popularity no harm.

Delors says that religion and politics should be kept apart, yet in his own personality they are inextricably linked. 'Jacques's faith plays a big role in his internal life,' says Antoine Lejay, his childhood friend. 'It also inspires his interest in the workers, the poor and the disadvantaged.'[8] Jacques

Moreau, a friend from the CFDT trade union, says Catholicism leads Delors to the principle that 'all men must be reconciled and brought to a compromise. Nothing is ever black and white and he never sees the "other side", such as businessmen, as the enemy.'[9]

Delors admits that his politics are more affected by his faith than he used to believe. 'The older I get, the more the social doctrine of the church appears to me to be good.' He defines that doctrine as follows: 'One must apply solidarity at all levels, to your neighbours and those you are close to, but also at the national and international levels.' He complains of a world increasingly dominated by money. 'I've never criticised money in moral terms, but I see everywhere the damage it does.' The welfare state is not enough, for the claiming of unemployment benefit is a bureaucratic and soulless procedure. 'The spiritual dimension is missing: the social doctrine of the church gives this dimension, and without it society dries up.'[10]

Delors's personalist Catholicism shapes his belief that a person's private life should reflect his or her political principles. 'I've always wanted to live soberly, because it's my personal ethic, but also because I find it good from the political point of view,' he says. 'In order that people believe the left wants to struggle against injustice, it should behave in that way.'[11] He avoids flashy cars, fast women, chic restaurants and any kind of *haute société* event. 'Do we really need to have three cars and four televisions in each family?' he asked French television viewers in October 1993.[12]

On one occasion at Brussels airport, when no photographers or journalists were present, Delors stopped to help a black woman who was unable to carry several large suitcases and her child. 'He's not a poseur,' says Alex Waelput, his Belgian bodyguard. Waelput notes that his previous employer – a Belgian prime minister – did not, like Delors, eat meals with his bodyguard and chauffeur.[13]

Mounier is never far from Delors's thoughts. Speaking to a conference on AIDS, in March 1992, he complained of

> *the weakening of traditional forms of solidarity and neighbourliness. Virtually nothing has replaced the steady disappearance of the traditional framework for life in the community. Families, schools and churches no longer play the same guiding role, giving useful information and support, or encouraging openness to others.*[14]

Delors's continual griping about the superficiality and dishonesty of French politics owes something to Mounier. 'Politicians always surprise me by their egocentrism and their belief in themselves,' he told *Paris Match* in November 1987.[15] He says the French are indifferent to their politicians because they dislike the way each camp denies the other's right to exist. Delors stresses that he is different: 'Many believe that everyone is made from the same model: ambition, satisfaction and sex. If you don't obey these criteria you disturb people but you can still have influence.'[16]

Père Henri Madelin, a Jesuit priest and the editor of *Projet*, a Catholic review, says Delors's faith explains his tendency to be censorious.

> *He gets angry about the gap between what people do and say : Christians tend to be more sensitive to that gap than most politicians, and French politicians are particularly inclined to exaggerate in their use of language.*[17]

Delors's faith prompts his sense of mission and his mania for work. He believes he has to serve God by proving his utility to man, and he feels guilty when he is not useful. 'What drives me is the worry – a sort of panic – that I might not do useful things. I am never satisfied. Evidently, those who are will be happier.'[18]

Delors counteracts his innate pessimism by acting. Early in his career, he worried about how he could help to modernise French society. Since the 1970s he has been obsessed with acting to reverse the decline of Europe, relative to Japan and America. Delors's desire to be useful justifies his taste for power, pushes him to perfectionism and drives him to work relentlessly.

THE TURKISH CARPET SALESMAN

Delors is no less dedicated to his work than Margaret Thatcher was to hers. On a typical weekday he enters the Breydel building, the commission's smart new headquarters, at 8 am. He leaves at 9 or 10 pm, taking work home. He works during most of the weekend, whether he spends it in the office or at one of his homes. 'It's his *raison de vivre* – he's never content with what's been done and he never says let's stop for a party,' says François Lamoureux, who spent six years in Delors's cabinet. 'He's a maniac for detail in his professional and private life.'[19]

Delors's appetite for reading reminds Pascal Lamy, his *chef de cabinet* for 10 years, of 'a whale who sucks in enormous quantities of water and keeps the plankton.'[20] While Delors reads he fills small, grey notebooks with summaries and comments. The best way to influence Delors, according to his officials, is to offer papers, statistics and graphs. In verbal discussions he is inclined to disregard arguments which contradict his own.

Delors's enthusiasm for work can be inspirational. In the spring of 1992 he sat on the same platform as Michel Rocard, Elysée officials and farmers' leaders, at a conference on the future of the rural world. When the conference began Delors started to take copious notes. Those beside him began to feel embarrassed and within half an hour all of them, including Rocard, were taking notes.

Having risen to prominence through hard work rather than birth or education, Delors is well aware that application is a source of power. He is effective at European Union summits because he knows the nitty-gritty better than anyone else. Senior British officials concede that Delors is often better prepared than Thatcher was or Major is (however Delors has the advantage of being able to focus exclusively on the Union, while prime ministers have to worry about the whole range of government business). Delors's ability to explain a complex issue succinctly – whether subsidiarity or Europe's failing competitiveness – gives him extra clout at such events. 'What's awful about me is that as soon as I learn something new, I think immediately, like a professor, about how I can teach it,' he says.[21]

In front of a large audience Delors may get carried away by his desire to please. It proved unwise to predict to the European Parliament, in July 1988, that in 10 years 80 per cent of economic legislation would come from the EC. He made a gaffe when he told a meeting of Rocardians, in August 1992, that those opposed to Maastricht should get out of politics. Some of Delors' advisers judge this tendency to go over the top as a serious weakness. Yet Delors is proud of the way he responds to a live audience.

> *I feel that I'm a crooner. I sniff the room. I say the same things but I shift the tone according to the public, so that they understand me. That's how I have a sense of compromise.*[22]

The Union's prime ministers and foreign ministers have often relied on Delors to unearth compromises where others could find none. Nils Ersboll, secretary-general of the Council of Ministers, says:

> *No task is too humble for Delors to perform: he's the mechanic who works out the lowly details which make an agreement possible. He is brilliant at satisfying a country by finding tiny changes in a text, or a sum of money, which others would not have thought of because they would not have known the details.*[23]

Both the Brussels summit of 1988 and the Edinburgh summit of 1992 depended on Delors to sew up the final agreements on budgetary packages.

Delors's performance at a foreign ministers' meeting in July 1993 showed that his deal-making derring-do has not diminished with advancing years. The Edinburgh summit had decided to spend 156.5 billion ecus (£125 billion) on the 'structural' funds and the cohesion fund, over the six years 1994 to 1999. Of that money, 96 billion ecus was set aside for the EC's most backward regions. The commission had the task of deciding how much money should go to each member-state. The governments had no say on this decision, but Bruce Millan, the commissioner for regions, had promised to consult them.

On 19 July in Brussels, the foreign ministers discussed some crucial regulations on the administration of regional aid. They had to pass them that day if the European Parliament was to approve them in time for the new regional funds to flow from January 1994. However several ministers said they would block the regulations unless Millan promised them precise amounts of money. Most governments wanted a bigger slice of the cake than Millan, a prudent Scot, would offer.

Willy Claes, the Belgian foreign minister in the chair, failed to break the deadlock. He telephoned Delors who, stricken with sciatica, was resting at his Burgundy home, and implored him to help. Delors's chauffeur drove him the 300 km to Brussels. At 9.30 pm, hobbled over a walking stick and high on painkillers, the commission president arrived at the Council of Ministers. Delors announced there was more money available than Millan had offered. Millan disagreed and the pair argued in front of the ministers. When Claes told them to speak with one voice, Millan went home.

One after the other, Delors invited each foreign minister and his EC ambassador to a 'confessional' in a small room. His offers were slightly more generous than those of Millan. 'Delors was like a second-hand car salesman,' recalls one of the ambassadors. 'He would lick his pencil and make new calculations on his little bit of paper.'

Another of the ambassadors thought Delors 'like a Turkish carpet salesman, applying rudeness, finesse, insight, and diplomatic skill all at the same time, while promising more than there really was.' When this ambassador demanded a larger portion of aid for his country, Delors told him he was crazy and that he had gone too far. Delors directed his curses at the ambassador, avoiding eye contact with the minister. 'If you think I'm not honest, say so!' he yelled, wincing with the pain from his back.

The most extraordinary aspect of Delors's performance, notes that ambassador, was that he guessed the government's bottom line. If Delors had offered one ecu less, the minister would have vetoed the agreement. 'It was as if he had bugged our delegation room,' says the ambassador. Officials from other countries report similar powers of divination on Delors's part.

By 6 o'clock in the morning everyone had accepted Delors's offers and approved the regulations. But no one knew exactly what Delors's promises added up to, for nothing had been written down – except on his little scrap of paper. Many countries had been offered *fourchettes*, bands between an upper and a lower limit, rather than a precise amount, which made it hard to calculate the total cost of the compromise.

Some of those present estimated that Delors had promised 1–2 billion ecus more than the 96 billion ecus which he had to offer. The complexity of the EC's structural funds allowed him some scope for creative accounting, yet he had taken risks.

In October 1993 the commission published precise figures on how much each country would get. Dick Spring, the Irish foreign minister, accused Delors of reneging on a pledge that Ireland would have 7.8 billion Irish pounds (£7.4 billion), the top end of its *fourchette*. 'I always have the custom of fulfilling my promises; this is a lie,' Delors told Irish television on 20 October. In the end everyone agreed on a form of words which allowed the Irish to back down quietly. Throughout his career – from the coal miners' strike of 1963 to the regional aid settlement of 1993 – Delors's flair for finding compromises has proved a winning card.

Another has been Delors's ability to generate ideas. 'Generally, those who have ideas do not like to, and do not know how to act, but I try and combine the two,' he says. 'So for some I am too intellectual or idealist, or too much a believer in will-power; but for others I am too pragmatic.'[24] That self-analysis is fair. No other modern European politician – except perhaps for Margaret Thatcher – has paid such attention to ideas and to implementation, to ideology and to detail, to principle and to power.

Those who visited Delors's flat in the 1960s recall the presence not only of trade unionists and economists, but also of business people, philosophers and natural scientists. Delors found such wide-ranging contacts stimulating. Jean Boissonat, who met Delors in the CFTC in the 1950s and now edits *L'Expansion*, a business weekly, observes: 'Unlike most French intellectuals, who think a problem is solved when it's brilliantly posed, Delors has a pragmatic spirit. He tries to be a realist which means he sometimes has to do things he does not like.'[25]

Delors cannot always reconcile the two poles of his personality. In 1975 he wrote: 'One of my faults, which I've always had to struggle against, is a tendency to idealism – which involves being over-prescriptive and underestimating obstacles.'[26] Delors had a bad bout of 'prescriptionitis' in 1991 and 1992, when he pushed for a more federal European Community than the member-states would accept.

As Delors approached the end of his stint as commission president, the ideals burned as brightly as ever. But the ideas came less readily. 'There is no more hay in the barn of ideas, we have to add some new stock,' he said several times in 1992. In the earlier part of Delors's career, periods of intellectual reflection had alternated with periods of political action: after Citoyen 60 came the Chaban–Delmas government; after Dauphine University and Echange et Projets came the Mauroy government. But since 1981, apart from four-and-a-half months at the end of 1984, Delors has held office continuously.

Delors has tried to keep his neurones sparking during his 10 years at the commission. Twice a year, the commission sponsors 'crossroads of intellectuals' in different cities of Western and Eastern Europe. Delors attends each of these conferences and fills a stack of grey notebooks. In 1992 and 1993, Delors promoted debates on subsidiarity and on Europe's failing competitiveness.

But he admits to being less prolific than in his past. 'Either, after a certain age, one is no longer imaginative and creative, or it's the lack of available time.' He believes that the time he has to spend on managing the commission is primarily responsible. He grumbles that Monnet had the freedom to go for two-hour walks every day, and to meet many interesting people. 'The one to one-and-a-half hours that I devote to intellectual work every day is not enough.'[27]

PRIDE AND POWER

Few politicians are capable of such humility and such pride as Delors. He is humble about his person but proud of his office. However, during the long years in Brussels Delors began to identify his person with his office, the commission and even the EC. The pride – sometimes verging towards arrogance and occasionally towards authoritarianism – became increasingly prominent. In July 1992 Delors castigated France's Parti Socialiste for failing to give him a head of state's welcome at its congress. 'I'm already in history thanks to Maastricht,' he told French journalists. 'What I've done, of course, no prime minister will ever do.'

During the inter-governmental conferences of 1991, Delors treated attempts to restrain the commission's power as personal attacks – which some of them were. By then governments and others were complaining that he had become less willing to listen, too sure of his own rectitude and too grasping of power for the commission. Simone Veil, who was president of the European Parliament when he was a Euro-MP, says:

Delors is a bulimic for the commission, he wants it to gobble up every kind of business. It was not realistic of him to think the commission could represent the EC to the world.

But she is fond of Delors, saying that 'he is the opposite of cynical and lacks the killer instinct.'[28]

Niels Ersboll notes that 'the private Delors is modest, but the public figure is surrounded by EC ambassadors, commission officials and journalists who hold him in awe. It would take a very strong personality to resist all that.' Delors made more mistakes in his last few years as president, Ersboll believes, because he had less objective advice and because the EC's agenda grew so large.[29]

When Delors attends an official dinner, accompanied by advisers, he likes to hold the spotlight. An adviser who talks too much is liable to earn a disapproving look. In 1987 Antoine Lejay turned up to a meeting of Clisthène, a club consisting of those who had worked for Delors in the ministry of finance. He remembers that when a group of commission officials arrived, they treated Delors differently from the others. 'They were very deferential. He no longer gets openness and confrontation from those around him, which is not healthy.'[30] Among past and present Brussels officials, Delors has called only Pascal Lamy *tu* rather than *vous*.

Despite the deference which often surrounds him, Delors does respect officials and politicians who argue back. Thus he has a high regard for Sir David Hannay and Sir John Kerr, two doughty negotiators who served as British ambassadors to the EC.

Many of these Delorist traits are reminiscent of Thatcher. Like Delors, she always believed her ideas were right. After several years as prime minister she began to identify herself with her government, and even with Britain. Thatcher had too many sycophants around her but, like Delors, respected someone who could drive a hard bargain. In her final years she sometimes appeared out of touch with reality, and her errors of judgement became more frequent.

The difference between Thatcher and Delors is that she took everything to a greater extreme. Delors has had less scope to centralise power in his own hands, for he has not controlled the apparatus of a modern state. Delors is capable of authoritarian behaviour but his instincts are less dictatorial and he lacks her ruthless streak. For instance, while Delors has managed the Brussels press corps astutely, he has not gone as far as Thatcher in using a spokesman to rubbish colleagues. The ethical side of Delors's personality moderates his desire for power and – from time to time – makes him humble.

Uffe Ellemann-Jensen, Denmark's foreign minister during most of Delors's presidency, observes:

> Unlike most French politicians, Delors is capable of self-irony and is uninterested in questions of protocol – such as where he sits or which car he takes. He annoys most Danes because he says clearly what he thinks, but that's why I like him. Sometimes he's a pain in the neck but he's deeply moral and I never felt cheated by him.[31]

Some of those who have crossed a tired or anxious Delors would use stronger language than 'pain in the neck'. Ministers, officials and members of his family have all suffered his ire. At his regular lunches with the EC ambassadors, says one of them, 'by the time you see the second glass of red wine go down, you know that he may pick a quarrel with someone, or just be indiscreet.' At one of these lunches he turned on the Dutch ambassador and accused him of working for a government controlled by multi-nationals.

None of Delors's subordinates in the commission finds him easy to work for. One of them told *Le Monde*, anonymously, in June 1992: 'He has the vocation of an apostle and takes himself for a martyr, but never plays the role of confessor and rarely gives you absolution.'[32] Delors can exploit his temper to get what he wants – and make his protagonist feel guilty. In July 1993 he became angry with a German junior minister and told him he was being obstructive. Instead of fighting back the minister replied: 'Please be calm, *monsieur le président*, we have not forgotten all the help you gave us during German reunification.'

One root of Delors's difficult behaviour is a deep sense of insecurity. He is proud to have pulled himself up by his bootstraps and still reveals, occasionally, the chip he bears on his shoulder. If he suspects that people do not respect him – such as when employers' leaders told him to tone down social legislation, in November 1988 – he may bristle with the defensive pride of a trade unionist. He says:

> I've certainly got an inferiority complex because I didn't attend the grandes écoles *or do real studies. That's why I'm ill at ease in public meetings where I'm the star, for I'm not a leader. But I know Rocard likes that role.*[33]

Delors's successes at the commission made him more self-assured. In his second and third presidential terms (1989 to 1994), talk of resignation and explosions of choler became less frequent. Nevertheless one senior com-

245

missioner estimates that in the early 1990s resignation threats – both direct and indirect, to the college of commissioners and to the Council of Ministers – numbered at least a dozen a year. 'He is like a little boy trying to apply emotional blackmail – who does he think he is?' asks a top official of the French foreign ministry. Rocard notes drily that he himself has threatened to resign only once in his career – when the Fabius government introduced proportional representation in 1985 – and that he did so.[34]

The puritan streak in Delors's personalist philosophy sharpens some of his edges. He will not tolerate imperfection, whether in his own or his colleagues' work and behaviour. 'He is a semi-mystic rather than a technocrat, so to do his job he has to suppress half his nature,' says a close friend. 'He lives on his nerves so if something goes wrong he explodes.'

Despite his difficult nature, most of those who know Delors like him and are only too ready to forgive his failings. They have discovered that the private man is warm and kind-hearted. Max Kohnstamm, Jean Monnet's aide, says:

> *Delors's weaknesses, such as his self-questioning, make you want to protect him. If he kicks someone, you don't ask if he's plotting against them, because you know he's doing it for the cause of Europe.*[35]

When Delors throws a tantrum in front of the EC's foreign ministers or prime ministers, they generally say something like 'there, there, it's not so bad.' They tolerate his moods because he is useful: they often depend on Delors to find the compromise which will allow them all to go home.

Although Delors gives his staff a hard time, most of them remain fiercely loyal, even when they have moved elsewhere. A stint with Delors does not bring evident benefits, for he is notoriously bad at arranging new jobs for members of his team. But these Delorists profess to be inspired by his ideals, intellectual rigour and honesty.

BOOKS, JAZZ AND WOMEN

When Jean-Paul Delors fell ill, in 1978, he wanted to enjoy some rural tranquillity. So his father bought a farmhouse in Fonteyne-la-Gaillard, a village which lies in gentle Burgundian hills, near the cathedral town of Sens. Jacques and Marie Delors now spend two weeks in August and occasional weekends at Fonteyne-la-Gaillard.

Built in the nineteenth century, the farmhouse has six small rooms on two floors. The furniture is cheap and simple, and bookcases cover the walls. Delors feels less stressed and more himself in Fonteyne than anywhere else. He invites close friends, many of whom share his Catholicism, humble origins and trade union links. Officials and politicians are not invited. Delors's mother, daughter and granddaughter pay visits. So does Jacqueline Housseaux, once Jean-Paul's partner and now a Parisian publisher, who has become another member of the family.

In 1990 Delors bought a small field adjoining the garden, fulfilling a wish of his son. He also built a new house close to the old one, in the same style, so that he could work undisturbed. The new house consists almost entirely of one huge room, with wooden beams leading up to an arched roof. Books on politics, economics, jazz and the cinema take up most of the wall space, with film posters filling the gaps. Large books on Federico Fellini, Woody Allen, François Truffaut and Pierre Mendès-France are prominently displayed.

A wooden spiral staircase leads to a gallery under the eves. Delors's archive – every speech, article and paper that he has written since the 1950s – is stored on shelves in the gallery. The new house has three machines: a high-definition television, a fax and a record player. Delors is inept with machines and spends much of his time struggling to make the fax and the record player work.

Delors seldom forgets about work for more than the shortest of periods. 'The nearest I get to relaxation now is to switch from one subject of pressing concern to another.'[36] Whether in Brussels, Paris or Fonteyne, Delors avoids cocktails and dinners and never entertains formally.

He claims that on holiday he has learned to stop thinking about work.[37] Cabinet members who spend their Augusts in Brussels, awaiting hourly faxes from Fonteyne, have their doubts. They reckon he is more irritable than usual on holiday because he feels guilty about not working.

Delors's life is not always austere. At Fonteyne he plays ping-pong and *belote* – a four-person card game – and walks in the woods. When he sits down to eat with close friends or family he becomes a raconteur – specialising in wicked little jibes at the expense of fellow politicians. Delors cooks nothing himself but enjoys the simple French country cooking that his wife and daughter prepare. He smokes both cigars – the best Cuban ones supplied by Felipe Gonzalez – and a pipe.

Delors reads a lot during his holiday. In 1989 he claimed to have read 10,000 pages on the history of Western Europe. In 1992 he found time to reread Stendhal's *Le Rouge et le Noir* and Flaubert's *L'Education Sentimentale*. The latter, Delors's favourite novel, is the story of a young man's amorous and political ambitions in the mid-nineteenth century. When Delors talks of the novel he seems more interested in the description of the 1848 revolution than in the love affairs.

When Delors works at home – whether in the farmhouse, the flat in Brussels or the flat in Paris – he listens to jazz as background music. In the late 1940s Delors discovered live jazz in Parisian cafés, where he saw, among others, the trumpeter and novelist Boris Vian. These days he frequents Ronnie Scott's jazz club when he is in London. Liking neither traditional jazz nor avant-garde free jazz, he remains faithful to the musicians who dominated his twenties and thirties. Starting with Coleman Hawkins (whose 'Body and Soul', he says, began modern jazz) he likes Bud Powell, Sarah Vaughan, Dina Washington, Miles Davis, Dizzy Gillespie and Charlie Parker, whom he once saw in Paris. Delors places the saxophonist Sonny Rollins above all others, because he devotes his 'virtuosity to imagination, sonority and lyricism, he has all three.'[38]

Delors's analysis of the origins of jazz reveals something of his own, contradictory nature. In 1975 he said:

> *The art which issues from this religious people corresponds to my conception of existence: we have our feet on the ground – in the sensual world, in the broad sense – and at the same time we aspire to have our head in heaven, to be transcendent. Our life is made from this gap, or dialectic. There's no music which better expresses this double desire – the attachment to the earth, to the men and women of this world, and the aspiration to something wondrous – than jazz.[39]*

Delors still follows sports with the enthusiasm of his youth, although he no longer plays them (in 1993 arthritis made him abandon his early-morning gymnastic routine). His expertise on cycling is second to none, and he has commentated for French television on the Tour de France. Delors sometimes interrupts a meeting to watch the conclusion of a cycling race on his high-definition television.

Delors's explanation of why he likes cycling – as with jazz – says a lot about himself. He told *L'Equipe*, France's sports newspaper:

> *Cycling is a lesson in life. That's because these sportsmen are authentic and they have to search in the depths of themselves. It is undoubtedly one of the sports where the suffering is greatest.*

Having proposed an EC team for the Olympics, Delors regaled *L'Equipe*'s readers with a piece of homely, personalist philosophy:

> *All human activity which allows people to surpass themselves, to meet others and to work in a team is creative and reinforces the good in humanity. That goes from cycling to the choir which sings Beethoven.[40]*

Thirty-five years after their marriage, Jacques and Marie Delors remain close. Delors is one of the few French politicians whose name has never been linked to an extra-marital liaison. Yet Delors is less of a prig than he may appear. With close male friends he enjoys a blue joke. He peppers public speeches with references to 'porn-shows' and 'strip-teases'. Just after his first summit as commission president – in Brussels in March 1985 – he confessed to a dinner of EEC ambassadors that he had felt as nervous as a 17-year-old boy on his first visit to a brothel. 'That kind of imagery shows he is repressed,' is the view of a close friend.

Delors flirts with women, in an innocent, 1950s sort of way. In September 1989, at an informal meeting of finance ministers in Antibes, Delors engaged in a long conversation with a female security guard – until his wife steered him away. Many women find Delors's sparkling blue eyes and warm, persuasive voice an appealing combination.

By 1993 the leading ladies of the Parti Socialiste had succumbed to Delors's charms, in the political sense. Most of the women who served in the governments of Edith Cresson and Pierre Bérégovoy (which ran from May 1991 to March 1993) – Elizabeth Guigou, minister for Europe, Ségolène Royal, minister for the environment, Frédérique Bredin, minister of sport and, of course, Martine Aubry, minister of labour – aligned themselves with Delors rather than Rocard.

So did Cresson herself. 'Some of his qualities are those I find in women,' she says. 'He's sincere and a man of convictions. He's not ambitious and he doesn't betray people.' She likes him because 'he doesn't treat us [women] as inferiors and unlike all the other men in French politics he's not sure of himself.'[41] Guigou, who like Cresson is close to both Mitterrand and Delors, says that 'what interests women in politics are concrete subjects. Delors tries to bring people with diverse positions together, so that things move forward in a concrete way.'[42]

The four women who matter most to Delors – his mother, wife, daughter and granddaughter – all have strong personalities. Jeanne Delors recently moved from Corrèze to sheltered accommodation in Paris. Her relationship with Delors is sometimes difficult, but she has turned out to public events such as the launching of his club Témoin, in October 1992. She never wanted her son to be a politician and has advised him not to run for the French presidency.

Marie Delors has always accepted and respected her husband's political life. He consulted her on whether he should take the job of commission president, and she encouraged him. However Martine notes that 'my mother doesn't like the milieu of politics, which she finds too individualist. She thinks politicians forget their ideas in attacking each other.'[43]

Marie would like her husband's political career to end before he becomes an old man. She has argued strongly against a campaign for the Elysée – and her views carry more weight than anyone else's. 'I've always had a debt to her,' says Delors, speaking of how, in the early years of their marriage, he was often absent because of political or trade union activity. 'She doesn't tell me to pay – but I haven't been a good husband and I have a bad conscience.'[44]

Such a highly-strung and complicated man could probably not have led such a successful career without an emotional anchor like Marie. She keeps his feet on the ground and talks about family, neighbours and shops. She tells Delors what ordinary French people think and does not let him forget his origins. Those who know Marie use adjectives such as delicate, generous and sensitive to describe her. They often speak of her '*simplicité*', in the sense of unpretentious rather than unintelligent. She reinforces Delors's religious and moral side.

Marie is a perceptive judge of human qualities and failings, and Delors listens to her views. She says what she thinks and is sometimes highly critical of people. 'She has her own hierarchy of what is important and what is not, which is different from that of Delors,' says one of his aides. 'Her priority is the family.' She and the officials sometimes struggle over how much time Delors should spend in Brussels and how much in Paris.

Marie was so *enraciné* in her *quartier* around the Boulevard de Bercy that the move to Belgium, in 1985, proved painful. She had no friends in Brussels and, because of her husband's travel schedule, found that she was often on her own. In time she busied herself with voluntary work and befriended the wives of commissioners and ambassadors. 'If I want to find out what Delors is thinking, I send my wife round to Marie,' says one European Community ambassador. 'She will tell my wife what is top of his agenda.'

Marie helps Delors at social events. 'She's good at small talk, smiling and asking people about their children,' says one of Delors's staff. 'With him, once you've done football and jazz there's not much left to say.' She often accompanies Delors on foreign trips and to European Union summits and 'informal' meetings. At an informal gathering of foreign ministers, at Brocket Hall in Hertfordshire in September 1992, Britain's Douglas Hurd challenged Marie to a game of croquet. He left the croquet field stunned, claiming that in all his life he had never met such an aggressive player.[45]

When the Delors moved to Brussels they kept their Paris flat and spent occasional weekends there. They could have afforded a larger flat in a more salubrious part of Paris (by 1993 Delors's presidential salary had reached 7.4 million Belgian Francs a year – £140,000 – after tax, plus a car and entertainment allowances). For many years Delors pondered moving but Marie resisted the idea. Finally, in 1992, Martine persuaded her parents to find an apartment closer to where she lived. So they bought a more spacious flat, in the Rue Saint Jacques, a plush area of the Rive Gauche near the Jardin du Luxembourg.

From then on the Delors spent more weekends in Paris, so that they could see their granddaughter, on whom they dote. Clementine, who celebrated her 16th birthday in 1994, has inherited her grandfather's passion for sport and her mother's determination. A keen horsewoman, she has participated in national show-jumping tournaments. Delors took her to the 1992 Olympics in Barcelona.

To Marie's great regret, Martine had only one child. Like her father, Martine is a sincere and persuasive conviction politician. She too is inclined to be self-righteous, although she lacks her father's religious faith and self-doubt. Close friends of the family say that, compared with her father, she is rather less interested in ideas and rather more interested in power. She can be stubborn and as hard as nails. 'She's a fighter!' Delors says proudly of his daughter.[46] Some of his friends admit to being slightly frightened of her.

Father and daughter feel mutual admiration and fierce rivalry. Martine says: 'We argue non-stop and never agree on anything, but our debates are not personal. He says I'm too hard, I say he's too tolerant of the behaviour of others.'[47] Those who have witnessed their scrapping say that she can be excessively aggressive to her father. She complains that the European Union overemphasises financial and monetary affairs at the expense of the real economy. While minister of labour she berated Delors for not doing enough to promote the EC's social dimension.

When Martine Aubry lost office, in March 1993, she set up the Fondation Agir Contre l'Exclusion (the Foundation for Action Against Poverty). Martine is among the toughest, most eloquent and most telegenic leaders of the Parti Socialiste. Her father believes she has a much better chance of becoming French president than he does, and he is probably right.

THE MYTH OF JACQUES DELORS

For as long as Jacques Delors has worked in Brussels, Parisian commentators have speculated on his ambitions in France. For just as long Delors has claimed that he is too lacking in self-confidence, too decent and too naïve for the Machiavellian world of French politics. Unlike other politicians, he says, he simply wants to serve humanity. 'I am never happier than when I work for the underclass. I feel comforted when I move closer to poor people and to those in difficulty.'[48]

The myth of other-worldliness that Delors has cultivated is partly true and partly false. In 1984 he said:

> *I conduct my life without thinking about image. If I am popular, it is for other reasons: I've invented a style of politics which is different from that of the communications professionals. I address myself to people, to their intelligence, to their heart. I don't hide. I make mistakes, I lose my temper, but people say, that guy, he's human. I shall never be a great politician because I cannot get concerned about my image.*[19]

That claim is disingenuous, for in analysing his popularity in France he has, unwittingly, described his highly successful image.

In 1990 Delors overtook Rocard in the opinion polls and became a serious *présidentiable*, as the French describe their potential presidents. Since then he has hesitated between a commitment to French politics and his European career. When asked if his sights are on the Elysée, Delors has offered ambiguous replies.

In May 1991 Mitterrand sacked Rocard and appointed the pugnacious Edith Cresson as France's first woman prime minister. Delors adopted a higher profile in French politics with Cresson, a personal friend, in the Matignon. Cresson's government soon became the most unpopular in the history of the Fifth Republic. Both her blunders and bitter faction-fighting among the socialists bore the blame. Delors's image remained untainted by the government's difficulties. Many Mitterrandists started to see him as the only credible alternative to Rocard as the Socialist candidate in the May 1995 presidential election.

In the shorter term the Socialists faced the prospect of defeat in the regional and local elections of March 1992 and in the general election a year later. Some of them argued that the best way to stave off electoral disaster would be to make Delors prime minister. Others said Mitterrand should keep Cresson until the general election, and then, if the left suffered a moderate defeat, ask Delors to head a socialist-centrist coalition.

Mitterrand stirred the speculation by telling friends that Delors and Raymond Barre were the only living French statesmen, other than himself. Pierre Joxe, a minister close to Mitterrand, said in August 1991 that 'Delors has a role to play ahead of him, in Europe and without doubt in France.' In September the French president told television viewers he had *the highest esteem and a great friendship for M Delors, with whom I have worked for so many years. He has become a political personality of the European world, for whom I have only praise ... Has he a future? Of course, but it's not for me to decide it.*[50]

Serge July, the editor of *Libération*, compared '*l'effet Delors*' to '*l'effet Rocard*' of the 1970s – when it had been Rocard's turn to be seen as the saviour of the left.[51] Delors's closest advisers believe that if he had been asked to go to the Matignon in the autumn of 1991, he would have accepted. If he had gone and then restored the Socialists' fortunes, he would have been well placed to stand for the presidency. But the call never came.

Early in 1992 the Cresson government's popularity sunk to new depths. 'The principal trump of Mitterrand remains Jacques Delors; to leave him in Brussels is becoming a luxury beyond the means of the left,' wrote Alain Duhamel, the doyen of France's political commentators, in January. When a moral crisis was wracking French politics, Delors represented 'the nostalgia of values ... isn't he tailor-made for missions of sacrifice?'[52]

Yet the man who had coveted the prime ministership for so long was starting to have second thoughts. Delors knew that if the job was offered and he turned it down, many Socialists would call him a coward for refusing to help in their hour of need. However he worried that Laurent Fabius, a longstanding enemy who had become party leader, would make life uncomfortable for a prime minister Delors. Furthermore, much important EC business, including the ratification of the Maastricht treaty, remained outstanding. Delors feared that quitting his post for the sake of domestic ambition would damage his image – and that of France – in Europe.

The proximity of the next general election, in March 1993, weighed heavily with Delors. The Socialists were so unpopular that they appeared to have little chance of recovering by then. Delors's potential strength as a prime minister would be his closeness to the Christian democratic CDS. But with an election so close he would have little chance of prising these centrists away from their electoral alliance with Chirac's RPR and Giscard's UDF; that task would be easier in a new parliament. Thus becoming prime minister could hinder rather than help Delors's chances of the presidency.

On 26 March Delors lunched with Mitterrand in the Elysée, without either of them discussing the prime ministership directly. Two days later the Socialists scored a surprisingly low 18 per cent in the cantonal elections. Mitterrand told Cresson she would have to go. Kohl visited Mitterrand in a bid to persuade him to leave Delors in Brussels. Pascal Lamy advised Delors to take the job if it was offered. Kohl and Gonzalez rang Delors and urged him to remain commission president.

Delors went to Paris and, after another convoluted and indirect conversation with Mitterrand, gathered that the job had been offered. Mitterrand understood that Delors did not want it. Mitterrand was furious that Delors had turned him down for the second time in nine years. No one else in the history of the Fifth Republic had declined the prime ministership even once. Pierre Bérégovoy, the pragmatic finance minister and a Mitterrand loyalist, replaced Cresson.

Throughout Delors's time as commission president, his relationship with Mitterrand proved as tortured as it had been when he was finance minister. By the late 1980s Delors's successes in Brussels had given him some independence from Mitterrand. The French president told Cresson he was more impressed by Delors's work at the commission than at the finance ministry.[53]

Delors welcomed every opportunity to see and to influence Mitterrand. Before each meeting he would compile a checklist of points which he wanted to discuss; afterwards, he would tick off those on which he had made progress. Delors became miserable if he had to wait months before seeing the president. Mitterrand complained that Delors would sometimes speak for too long, for instance when lecturing him on Yugoslavia. He also found it irritating that Delors constantly championed EC institutions.

Delors's agonising over his own ambition exasperated Mitterand. One of the French president's closest advisers says:

> *Mitterrand has a Darwinian view of the world: people must cope on their own and take their chances. He won't arrange Delors's political career for him. Delors has always been appointed to jobs, but the one job you're not appointed to is the presidency. Mitterrand is not going to send for him with four horses and a chariot.*

Despite Delors's decision to stay in Brussels, he continued to mark out his own, idiosyncratic profile in French politics. On television in May 1992 he said: 'The Fifth Republic has killed the faults of the Fourth Republic, but also its sense of coalition. The French need to rediscover a sense of compromise and coalition government.' Delors attacked the idea that

> *it's paradise for each individual to stay in his niche – it's the destruction of society, the weakening of democracy and the end of national ambition. For a nation which has no cohesion and participation of citizens is condemned to perish.*

On the same programme Delors was asked if he was a candidate for the French presidency.

To succeed in politics you must bouffer de la vache enragée [literally,
to eat mad cow, meaning to suffer humiliations]. You must plan for it a
long time in advance, be sure of yourself and sometimes consider yourself
stronger than the others, which makes many conditions.

He said that he had never been a candidate for any job. 'I've been offered
things and I said yes or no.' He said he was neither a virtual, potential or
declared candidate, 'and I live better for it. I do my job and the criticisms
slide off my back like water off a tile.'[54] In fact few politicians have thinner
skins.

In July 1992, at the Socialists' conference in Bordeaux, Delors paid the
price for refusing the Matignon. Fabius introduced Rocard as the party's
'natural' presidential candidate. Henri Emmanuelli, the president of the
National Assembly, captivated the chamber with a passionate rebuttal of
allegations of financial impropiety. Fabius asked Delors to speak straight
after Emmanuelli, which was the worst possible moment. Fabiusians and
Rocardians chattered and laughed throughout his speech. This humiliation made Delors fume. Three months later he complained that while
Rocard had telephoned to apologise, Fabius had never done so.

The referendum on Maastricht failed to dent Delors's popularity, which
continued to surpass that of Rocard, Chirac or Giscard. *Le Monde* wrote:

He incarnates the dream – or the myth – of the renaissance of a centre
which would break free from the right and ally with the Parti Socialiste.
[The result would represent] the blending of the two reformisms which
have competed in France since the nineteenth century, that which is born
of Catholicism and that which comes from the secular workers' move-
ment.[55]

In October 1992 Delors founded Témoin, a club dedicated to the renewal of social-democratic ideas. Many of the youngest, brightest and most
telegenic ministers took an active role in the club – including Ségolène
Royal, Elizabeth Guigou, Martine Aubry, Bernard Kouchner, Dominique
Strauss-Kahn and Michel Delebarre. Delors denied that Témoin was a
presidential stable. He told journalists:

Michel Rocard is a friend, don't stop him from sleeping at night with
your articles – for the time being there is only one présidentiable. We are
to a presidential stable what an artisanal enterprise is to a multinational
– it is true that artisans are sometimes more innovatory than multi-
nationals, who therefore buy them up.[56]

Speakers at Témoin's first conference, on European socialism, included not only Rocard but also Spain's Felipe Gonzalez, Britain's John Smith, Norway's Gro Harlem Brundtland, Sweden's Ingvar Carlsson and Portugal's Antonio Gueterres. Delors told the conference it was time to attack the stereotypes of neo-liberal ideology, such as the denigration of tax, a belief in the miracles of deregulation and a hostility to the state 'which is the expression of the responsibility of citizens.' Neo-liberal ideology 'no longer exercises the fascination of the boa.'[57]

In December 1992, during a television interview, Delors was asked what he would do for middle-class people whose standard of living had declined. He replied that 20 per cent of the French suffered from unemployment, poverty or marginalisation.

> To believe that we can help those 20 per cent through state action, without the middle classes making an effort through taxation and collective life, is a lie. The middle classes must snap out of their navel-gazing and, it has to be said, of a certain egoism.

Delors then eulogised public spending. 'So let's stop telling people they pay too much tax. In essence, taxation is the best mark of citizenship.'[58] Such unfashionable ideas revealed Delors's intellectual honesty – as well as the apparent archaism of his thinking.

As Delors's years in Brussels neared their end, he continued to tell the French how he differed from the rest of their political leaders. Yet for all the disclaimers, and all the myth making, Delors is a wily and effective, if unconventional politician. He has risen to fame at a time when traditional politics, in France and elsewhere, has fallen into disrepute. A skilful actor, Delors has milked his originality for all it is worth. 'He's not at all what he says he is, he's a *faux naïf*,' says a former member of his finance ministry cabinet. 'He is capable of making subtle political analyses.'

Delors portrays many of the characteristics of a successful political leader. He is a strategist who plots a course and sticks to it with tenacity. He can squeeze a compromise from a group of diverse individuals. He can master a brief and argue a convincing case on television. He knows how to win the attention of journalists and to flatter them. Having held office for so long, he has learned to wield authority and to make subordinates jump. He often has a general's tactical instinct for spotting an opening, timing an offensive and concentrating resources on a target. 'Delors has a sense of power and how to exercise it: he uses all possible means to pursue a goal,' says Carlos Westendorp, Spain's minister for Europe.[59]

In many other respects, however, Delors is a bizarre politician. He often shies away from personal confrontations with ministers or other commissioners. He shuns opportunities to woo party activists or glad-hand the populace. Adverse press comment stops him sleeping at night. 'He is permanently crucified by criticism, and he does not forget what people say,' notes his friend Cresson.[60] During the March 1993 election campaign, the Gaullist Alain Juppé accused Delors of betraying France over GATT; the wound festered for months.

Delors undoubtedly believes that his career at the commission has not been that of a conventional politician. In 1989 he said:

> *Some of the houses I build stand up, some crumble: I think of myself as an engineer, and less as a philosopher or political leader. Mitterrand has different responsibilities and is accountable to the French people. My job is to provide momentum, ideas, initiatives.*[61]

Delors is crafty but not devious. His theatrical ability allows him to exaggerate opinions and emotions, but he does not think one thing and say the reverse. 'Unusually for a politician he means what he says, and he's the least cynical person I know,' says Jean-Pierre Cot, who is no friend.[62]

Delors's lack of self-confidence is genuine, although it has diminished in recent years. A succession of mentors gave Delors valuable advice early in his career. Monsieur Fruit at the Banque de France; Albert Detraz and Paul Vignaux at *Reconstruction*; André Cruizat at Vie Nouvelle; Pierre Mendès-France; and Pierre Massé at the Plan were among those who helped Delors to appreciate his qualities.

Delors says he had mentors because he liked to learn and to listen. 'I was lucky to meet these people, because I was born with neither great talent nor a silver spoon in my mouth. They marked out a path for my life.' In the 1970s Jacques Chaban-Delmas and then François Mitterrand took Delors under their wing – though he claims that by then he no longer needed a mentor.[63]

With all these masters, Delors worked behind the scenes as an *eminence grise*. After Mitterrand's victory in 1981, Delors asked if he could be secretary-general of the Elysée rather than a minister. That gives credibility to Delors's claim that he cares more about implementing ideas than political glory. But by the time Delors reached Brussels, one was not possible without the other. 'Delors is not attracted to power for its own sake, but he always believes his ideas are right, which justifies his ambition,' says Thiérry de Beaucé, who worked with him under Chaban-Delmas.[64]

Conventionally ambitious politicians do not, like Delors, prefer to work with clubs rather than parties. After Vie Nouvelle in the 1950s came Citoyen 60 in the 1960s and Echange et Projets in the 1970s. He set up Clisthène, a club of longstanding friends and former finance ministry colleagues, in 1984. In the late-1980s the *transcourants* became an influential force in the Parti Socialiste. Also known as the '*quadras*' – because they included many forty-somethings – the *transcourants* wanted to transcend the factions which plagued their party. Their study group, Démocratie 2000, adopted Delors as its leader. In 1992 Démocratie 2000 transformed itself into Témoin, Delors's most recent club.

From Citoyen 60 onwards, Delors has been the *patron* of all these clubs, which may be one reason why he finds them congenial. Each time Delors created a club or changed his job, he spawned a new circle of supporters. The sum of these overlapping circles is a network of several thousand Delorists, many of whom hold prominent positions in French public life and in European institutions. In the event of a bid for the French presidency, the network would spring to his aid.

But does Delors want that job badly enough to challenge Rocard for the Socialist nomination in the 1995 election? Rocard says:

> *It's true that Delors's less ambitious than me, he has doubts about the ethics of taking my place [as socialist candidate]. It's rare to find someone who's been in politics so long, who is so popular and talented, who has these doubts – many less talented people see presidential wings growing.*[65]

One of Rocard's entourage compares the pair thus: 'One dreams of it, the other wants it. Delors would have a real presidential ambition on condition that 80 per cent of the French political class begged him to stand.'[66]

After the March 1993 general election, in which the Socialists won only 20 per cent, Edouard Balladur took office with a centre-right coalition. In April Rocard deposed Fabius as leader of the Parti Socialiste. Delors took pains to point out that he would do nothing to undermine Rocard's position. 'While my ideas are very close to his, I don't see why, for personal reasons, I should stand against him.' Such an ethical approach allowed Delors to suffer a little. 'Those who criticise me say, he just can't shoot. However I'm made that way. It's a strength for my conscience but a weakness in politics.'[66]

Delors said that for the past year or year and a half, he had understood that Mitterrand wanted him to declare his candidacy.

He's disappointed with my lack of ambition, he thinks I'm frightened of an electoral test but I've had others. I consider that I've taken on a task here and that for the moment it would be very difficult and ungrateful to abandon it.[68]

Rocard had the advantage of controlling the party which would nominate the candidate. Many of the party barons, including Fabius, made tactical alliances with Rocard. Delors knew that he was unlikely to win the nomination without engaging in the kind of no-holds-barred fight to which he was temperamentally unsuited.

Balladur's consensual style of government soon made him the most popular politician in France. Yet throughout 1993 and early 1994, Delors continued to outscore Rocard in the opinion polls, sometimes by as much as 20 points. By April 1994, social unrest had damaged Balladur's standing and allowed Delors to regain his lead in the popularity ratings. Some of Mitterrand's friends urged Delors to set his sights on the Elysée, as did Delorists who fancied their prospects if he became president. Delors continued to say that he would not be a candidate 'in the present circumstances'. When the Socialists come to choose, if the polls suggested that only Delors could beat the right's candidate – whether Balladur or Chirac – they would consider abandoning Rocard for Delors.

For a man who professes not to be ambitious, Delors has held high office for an extraordinarily long time. Since 1962 he has exercised bureaucratic or political power continuously, except for the years 1973 to 1981. He has never carried out any of his innumerable threats to resign. Others may judge him an opportunist, but Delors's conscience is clear: he had to hold positions of authority in order to fulfil his sense of mission and to enact his ideas.

Delors's belief that he is not a conventional political leader helps him to overcome a profound contradiction in his personality. The Mounierist thinks politics to be a dirty, nasty world, yet the pragmatist knows ideas cannot be implemented without power. Delors's answer is to hold office without considering himself a real politician.

CHAPTER TWELVE

FIN DE RÉGIME

NEITHER the successes of the Edinburgh summit, at the end of 1992, nor the official launch of the single market, at the start of 1993, revived the fortunes of the European Community. The *diablotins* – a favourite word of Delors's, meaning little demons – which had struck on 2 June 1992, when the Danes rejected the Maastricht treaty, continued their attack. The arguments over that treaty, the GATT trade talks and Europe's stricken currency system ensured that the 12 remained at loggerheads.

For much of 1993, however, Delors's judgement appeared sounder than in the previous two years. Taking heed of 'it's the economy, stupid', the slogan which had helped Bill Clinton to win America's presidential election in November 1992, he laid aside his grand institutional ambitions.

Delors thought the EC's difficulties had three roots:

> the Yugoslav war, which shows Europe's powerlessness; a lack of agreement over the Community's long-term objectives; and the return of Europe's economic decline, which has haunted me since the 1970s.[1]

Delors knew that neither he nor the commission could make an impact on the first or second problems. However, if the EC could be seen to do something for the economy, it might succeed in brightening its image. Dole queues were lengthening: by the end of the year nearly 18 million EC citizens, 10.5 per cent of the workforce, would be unemployed.

Delors thought something more than the Edinburgh 'growth initiative' was needed. He decided to provoke a debate on the theme with which he had begun his presidency: Europe's declining competitiveness. He asked the commission's staff to analyse the problem and to propose solutions. He discovered that while America and the EC had had the same growth rate between 1983 and 1990, employment had risen by 2.5 per cent a year in America, yet only 0.8 per cent in the EC. Between 1970 and 1990, America had created 29 million jobs, Japan 11 million and the EC 9 million.

Searching for useful ideas, Delors consulted entrepreneurs such as John Sculley, formerly of Apple, and surviving 'founding fathers' such as Max Kohnstamm, Jean Monnet's aide, and Emile Noël, the commission's first secretary-general. He reread Monnet's memoirs and the works of economists such as Keynes, Hicks and Schumpeter. He demanded briefing notes on technological innovations such as 'multimedia' information highways.

Delors knew his pronouncements on competitiveness would make little impact unless he trod a delicate path between right-wing and left-wing analyses. He understood the liberal argument that expensive welfare states and rigid labour markets discouraged job creation. Yet his deepest instincts told him that the 'European model of society' had to be preserved. He admitted that the European model had been applied harmfully, but insisted that the model itself was not redundant.

Delors claimed the model's strength had been to combine solidarity with competitiveness. Companies could not compete effectively unless they motivated their workers, for instance through allowing them to participate.[2] He praised Sweden's system of welfare, which combined generous benefits with an obligation on recipients to accept retraining or job offers. In Sweden, Delors noted with interest, 50 people worked on training or advice for each 1000 unemployed; in most EC countries, there were no more than 5 or 10 per 1000.

On 18 May the Danes ratified the Maastricht treaty at the second attempt, with a vote of 56.8 per cent in favour. The next day, however, Delors declined to visit the commission press room. In a written statement Delors said he could not express joy when Europe was impotent in the face of the Yugoslav tragedy. On the same day, during an interview with the author, he said he could not sleep at night because of Yugoslavia. The Serbian policy of ethnic cleansing was undermining his own idea of Europe. 'For a year and a half I've been absolutely sapped by this Yugoslav business. I have a bad conscience that I cannot do anything about these events, which stresses me.'[3]

A few days later a severe bout of sciatica, a painful inflammation of the spinal nerve, struck Delors. His doctors told him that stress accounted for 50 per cent of the illness. The only cures for sciatica are a long period of rest or an operation. Delors opted for the former but nevertheless attended the Copenhagen European Council of 21 and 22 June.

On the summit's first day, after four injections of morphine, Delors lectured the heads of government on the causes of Europe's economic malaise. To simplify the argument he talked around a set of brightly coloured graphs (even so, he confided to journalists that evening, with a touch of pride, 'it was too technical for some of them'). John Major complained that the Social Charter was a 'recipe for job destruction'. But all the heads of government welcomed Delors's presentation and asked the commission to prepare a white paper on jobs, competitiveness and growth for December's Brussels summit. As an interim measure they extended the Edinburgh facility for infrastructure projects from 5 billion to 8 billion ecus. They also set 1995 as the date by which Austria, Sweden, Finland and Norway should enter the Community.

Delors was delighted that the commission had a chance to prove its utility. But at his press conference he made the mistake of commenting on the apparently healthy state of the Exchange Rate Mechanism (ERM). He said the recent drop in interest rates in several member-states showed that the ERM 'was not dependent on one single dominant currency or country.' Although it was not yet time 'to start singing the Marseillaise, we should be comfortable with a situation in which France and the Benelux countries could become the anchor for a while.'[4]

At the time, Delors's analysis did not seem so far-fetched. The currency markets had suffered squalls in January 1993, but in February a cut in Bundesbank rates had saved the French franc from devaluation. In March Delors attacked competitive devaluations, as practised by Britain and Italy since September 1992, as 'the most deadly poison which exists inside the Community'; they made it harder for currencies such as the French franc to maintain their parities. He called for an acceleration of moves to EMU, even if some countries had to be left behind.[5]

The landslide election victory of the French right, on 28 March, raised doubts about the viability of the franc's parity with the D-mark (and contributed to the suicide of Pierre Bérégovoy, the outgoing prime minister, on 1 May). Edouard Balladur's new government of right-wing and centre parties contained many more Euroenthusiasts than Eurosceptics. However a powerful faction of the Gaullist RPR argued that the best way to tackle unemployment would be to follow Britain's example and quit the Exchange Rate Mechanism.

In May Denmark's vote for Maastricht calmed the currency markets. A convergence of French and German interest rates indicated market confidence in the franc. Both the EC's committee of central bank governors and its monetary committee (made up of top central bank and finance ministry officials) published reports on the ERM. They proposed more regular realignments, in line with economic fundamentals, to pre-empt speculative attacks. But they concluded that the mechanism was fundamentally sound.

How mistaken those committees were. As the summer wore on, France's recession deepened and its rate of unemployment touched 11.5 per cent. Investors began to doubt the Balladur government's willingness to sustain interest rates at the level required to support the D-mark parity of 3.43 francs. Continuing uncertainty over British ratification of the Maastricht treaty unsettled the markets still further.

On 23 July, in the House of Commons, Thatcherite Conservatives made a last-ditch attempt to stop the government ratifying the Maastricht treaty. They supported a Labour Party motion in favour of Britain adopting the treaty's social chapter. Major lost by eight votes but said he would try to reverse the defeat with another motion on the social chapter the following day. He said that motion would be tied to a vote of confidence, and that if he lost he would call an election. The Conservative rebels feared they would lose their seats, given the government's unpopularity, and so backed Major.

In late July several ERM currencies, including the French franc, came under renewed pressure. They rallied when the Bundesbank dropped hints of an imminent interest rate reduction. On Thursday 29 July, at a meeting of the Bundesbank council, Hans Tietmeyer, the deputy president and a believer in EMU, called for a cut in the discount rate. Helmut Schlesinger, the president and an EMU sceptic, warned that a cut would fuel German inflation. His implicit argument was that the Bundesbank could not behave like a *de facto* European central bank without compromising its constitutional commitment to maintain the value of the D-mark. The council cut the Lombard rate by 0.5 per cent but left the more important discount rate unchanged at 6.75 per cent.

The French, Belgian, Danish, Spanish and Portuguese currencies immediately hit the bottom of their ERM bands. On the Thursday and the Friday the French and German central banks spent the equivalent of $50-60 billion supporting the French franc, to no avail. On Saturday 31 July the EC's monetary committee met in Brussels. Gossip of a Franco-German currency union turned out to be just that. The Germans proposed widening the ERM's 'narrow band', which allowed the value of a currency to move up to 2.25 per cent on either side of its central rate, to 6 per cent. The French demurred, fearing that widening the bands to 6 per cent would seem like a way of disguising a franc devaluation, and that it would provoke a new onslaught from speculators. Germany rejected French pressure to promise lower interest rates.

Eventually the French and the Germans agreed that the D-mark would leave the ERM until Germany had digested the economic consequences of reunification. But the Dutch, unwilling to break the guilder's link to the D-mark, insisted on following the D-mark out of the system. The Belgians and Danes said that if the Dutch stuck to the D-mark, so would they.

On Sunday the 12 finance ministers flew to Brussels in an effort to break the deadlock. Delors's sciatica had kept him in bed at Fontaine-la-Gaillarde, but he sent the ministers a message. He called for the D-mark to leave the ERM and warned that a general float should be avoided at all costs. However by Sunday night no deal had been reached and a free float seemed likely.

Then France suggested a wide band of 15 per cent for all ERM currencies except the D-mark and the Dutch guilder. This would avoid the need to change parities and preserve the structure of the ERM. At 1.45 am, minutes before the opening of Tokyo's currency markets, the finance ministers agreed on this new, flexible ERM. Later that day, by coincidence, Britain ratified the Treaty of Maastricht.

The European Monetary System, an essential building-block for EMU, had been all but destroyed. Many of France's politicians blamed its humiliation on the Germans, for not cutting rates, and on 'les Anglo-Saxons', for undermining the ERM through speculation. French and German ministers declared that they would press ahead with plans for Economic and Monetary Union. British ministers, unable to conceal their Schadenfreude, responded with sniggers.

Delors kept quiet but a statement from the commission said that progress towards EMU would be impossible without closer coordination of economic policy. It pointed out that competing currencies would undermine both the single market and the Common Agricultural Policy. Delors became deeply pessimistic about the prospects for EMU. He confided to friends that Europe would end up with a Bundesbank-managed D-mark zone rather than a monetary union.

In 1986 Tommaso Padoa-Schioppa had warned Delors that fixed exchange rates were incompatible with both the free movement of capital and autonomous monetary policies (see Chapter 7). The transitional phase of EMU – between the abolition of exchange controls, in July 1990, and the abolition of national monetary policies – had always appeared a risky venture.

Delors's memory of that warning may explain his unscripted remarks when, free from sciatica, he addressed the European Parliament in September. He declared that it was time to study the means of limiting international monetary movements. 'Why shouldn't the Community take the initiative and agree on some rules? Cars are free to drive around but there are still speed limits.'[6] Delors's wistful longing for the days before his own proposals had outlawed exchange controls found no echo among governments.

A week later Major attacked Delors's vision of Europe in The Economist.

> I hope my fellow heads of government will resist the temptation to recite the mantra of full EMU as if nothing had changed. If they do recite it, it will have all the quaintness of a rain dance and about the same potency.[7]

This angered EC governments (and Delors) as much as it delighted Conservative party activists.

The German constitutional court approved the Maastricht treaty on 12
October, allowing Germany to become the 12th and last member-state to
ratify. To mark the treaty's coming into force, on 1 November, the EC's
Belgian presidency called a special summit. Meeting in Brussels on 29
October, the heads of government decided that henceforth they would call
themselves the European Union rather than the European Community.
They picked five areas where they would endeavour to apply the treaty's
provisions on common foreign policy: Eastern Europe, Russia, the Middle
East, South Africa and Yugoslavia. European Union observers would
monitor the forthcoming elections in Russia and South Africa. The
summit chose Frankfurt as the site of the European Monetary Institute,
and Alexandre Lamfalussy, the Belgian chairman of the Bank for International Settlements, as its first president.

In the weeks before the December Brussels summit, drafts of Delors's
white paper began to circulate. On 22 November, at a meeting of finance
ministers, Kenneth Clarke, Britain's rumbustious Chancellor of the
Exchequer, savaged parts of a draft. Afterwards he informed the press that
10 countries had squashed Delors's plans for work sharing. Delors thought
Clarke had grossly misrepresented his views, for the document had merely
described work sharing as an option for firms to consider. 'Next time I'll
install a cricket pitch since he always likes there to be winners and losers,'
Delors complained.

Four days later, during an interview with the author, Delors could not
contain his anger with Clarke. 'Even Mrs Thatcher' had not put such
words into his mouth, he said. 'My corpse is still twitching a little, we'll see
a serious incident, I shall explode, that will last just an instant but at least I
shall unbottle myself.'[8] He said he had warned the British government that
he would not tolerate the way its ministers were treating him.

Delors hit back. The finance ministers were supposed to debate the final
version of the white paper at their pre-summit meeting on 5 December.
Delors knew they would treat his ideas – and especially those costing
money – more roughly than the prime ministers. So he withheld publication until 6 December. Duly provoked, Clarke poured scorn on the
document when it did appear.

The college of 17 commissioners approved 'Growth, competitiveness,
employment: the challenges and ways forward into the 21st century', but
many of its 184 pages reflected the president's own views. Delors succeeded in steering the white paper towards the middle ground of politics: some
socialists found the radical ideas on labour market liberalisation heretical,

while many right-wingers dismissed proposals for infrastructure spending as outmoded Keynesian demand management. Delors's own views on economics have often swung between an acceptance of the need for markets and a visceral hostility to liberalism (see Chapter 8); the white paper showed that in 1993 Delors had veered to the former.

The document began with a disclaimer.

> *There is no miracle cure – neither protectionism, nor a dash for economic freedom [through boosting public spending], nor a generalised reduction in working hours and job-sharing at national level, nor a drastic cut in wages and a pruning of social protection to align our costs with those of our competitors in the developing countries.*

Europe needed an economy that was open and decentralised, yet tempered by solidarity, especially between those in and out of work. That meant productivity gains should go into investment and job creation rather than wage rises.

The paper carried blunt prescriptions for the creation of a more flexible labour market. In some southern member-states, employers should be able to sack workers more easily. Some northern countries needed to cut certain unemployment benefits and taxes on low incomes. Minimum wages needed to be 'adjusted' (meaning cut). Some companies would benefit from introducing more flexible working hours.

The relative cost of unskilled and semi-skilled labour should fall. It was wrong that in eight member-states, social security contributions bore more heavily on those with low incomes. The non-wage costs of employment should be lowered by 1–2 per cent of GDP by 2000. The commission's proposal for a CO_2 tax would help governments to offset lost revenue. Roughly two-thirds of government spending on the unemployed was 'passive', in the form of unemployment pay, rather than 'active', in the form of training and job placement; the proportions should be reversed. Workers should enjoy a lifelong right to education and training.

Improving the quality of life, through the increased provision of services such as childcare, help for the elderly, urban renewal and environmental protection, could generate 3 million jobs. The public sector could stimulate demand for such services by offering citizens vouchers or tax rebates.

Most of the white paper consisted of a menu of options for governments. But it also called for European Union action on 'trans-European networks' – cross-border transport, energy and telecommunications links – to reduce the fragmentation of the single market and to foster links with Eastern Europe. A series of taskforces would establish priorities and timetables for each type of network. The white paper claimed that 150 billion ecus needed to be spent on information networks by the end of the decade. A further 250 billion ecus should be spent on energy and transport links, such as gas pipelines and high-speed railways.

The private sector and governments would bear most of the cost. However the white paper suggested a Union contribution of 20 billion ecus a year: 5.3 billion ecus from the Union budget, 6.6 billion ecus from the European Investment Bank (EIB) and 8 billion ecus from 'Union bonds'. The commission would manage these bond issues, which the Union would guarantee.

The white paper went down well at the Brussels summit of 10 and 11 December. Even Major, whose officials had earlier described the white paper as 'rubbish', said it was intellectually impressive. The heads of government adopted its conclusions as an 'action plan' on competitiveness and agreed to carry out annual reviews of progress. They approved the schemes for trans-European networks, but were unenthusiastic about the commission becoming more involved in borrowing. They decided to consider 'Union bonds' only if the EIB ran out of money.

Delors's white paper on the 1992 programme, which contained legislative proposals, had transformed the nature of the Community. The white paper on jobs and competitiveness - subjects largely reserved for governments - consisted mainly of recommendations and so could not have such an impact.

However the focus on trans-European networks suggested a Big Idea for the future. In January 1989 Delors had called Karel Van Miert, who had just become transport commissioner, into his office. Delors pulled a map of Europe out of a cupboard. 'I want you to make plans for pan-European transport links,' he said. 'Strictly we're not allowed to but do it anyway.' Taking a pen, Delors drew his own priorities for high-speed rail links on to the map. He told Van Miert to take the map away and get cracking. In 1991 Delors had ensured that the Maastricht treaty gave the European Union the legal competence to make proposals on networks. The emphasis on them in the 1993 white paper proved canny: it would be hard for anyone to argue against projects which would, almost by definition, promote the single market; and hard to oppose a commission role in their management.

The white paper helped to stimulate a debate on the causes of unemployment. Its labour market prescriptions both reflected a shift in the thinking of governments, and gave them a useful cover for unpopular policies. Thus in January 1994 the Spanish government made it easier for employers to fire workers, while the German government cut wages on job-creation schemes.

The Brussels summit's welcome of his white paper left Delors as proud as a peacock. He said on French television:

> *I have the reaction of an artisan who, having been told he's done a good piece of work, feels content. I was looking for a way of putting back some élan. They've accepted this white paper as a kind of road map for the coming years.*[9]

By making Delors and his commission appear useful, the document had restored some of their battered credibility.

INTO THE UNKNOWN

Delors had never felt so uncertain over Europe's future as at the end of his presidency. 'Until 1989 I thought one day there would be a political Europe, with a federal structure and a common foreign and security policy in certain domains.' The collapse of communism forced him to change his ideas. The new challenge 'is to extend the values which have made the EC to [the East European] nations.'[10] As well as deepening their own ties, the Union's members had to organise the wider Europe to 'banish the viruses of nationalism, racism and ethnic or religious conflict.'[11] The vision of the founding fathers remained relevant but had to be adapted to respect facts. 'I cannot say where we'll get to in 2010 or 2020. I'm searching but it would be premature to make a design'.[12]

By 1991 Delors had realised that the EC's responsibility for the East European states meant they would have to be granted membership. He expects some of them to join between 1998 and 2000. Nevertheless Delors rejects the 'let'em in quick and don't worry about the consequences' attitude of many British politicians. He told the European Parliament in May 1993: 'We can't go on advancing in the fog, saying to ourselves, "let's enlarge, it's a sign of confidence in the Community, we'll see afterwards how it works out." '[13]

Delors wants governments to think about the Union's objectives and institutions before the 1996 inter-governmental conference.[14] In October 1993 he said his priorities at that event would be institutional efficiency, more democracy and the maintenance of the balance between the large and the small countries – code for more majority voting in the Council of Ministers and a more powerful parliament and commission. 'Only the federal model can achieve these objectives.'[15]

While Delors clung to Jean Monnet's supranational vision of European union, he feared that a rival, British conception was winning the argument.

I reject a Europe that would be just a market, a free-trade zone without a soul, without a conscience, without a political will and without a social dimension. That's where we're heading so I'm issuing a cry of alarm.[16]

He believes that Thatcher's ambition of a 'glorified free-trade zone', with a broader membership, would not be viable in the long term. It would be 'constantly menaced by the lack of common discipline and by the weakness of institutions.' Domestic political pressures would push governments to erect barriers against the single market.[17] Delors predicts that if the member-states continue to drift towards national egoism, the Union will burst asunder 15 years hence.[18]

Delors says:

The English don't have enough economic strength to propose things, but they are capable, thanks to the Foreign Office, of blocking, and they've no one against them. There's no longer a body of people with the same ideas as me on a united Europe. The construction of Europe defies nature and is difficult. It demands vision, force of character, courage vis-à-vis public opinion and institutions which work effectively.[19]

In the days before the Brussels summit of December 1993, Delors's vision of the future darkened.

I became the symbol of an idea of Europe which is in the process of vanishing. I am discouraged to the extent that I can no longer be useful. I can no longer stamp my mark on Europe, it's finished.

The combination of Europe's economic crisis, Yugoslav ethnic cleansing and the virtual collapse of the ERM meant that 'frankly I am no longer the man for the job.'[20]

However, Delors's moods are as changeable as the British weather. A few days later the success of his white paper and the conclusion of the GATT round raised his spirits. By early 1994, Delors's last year as commission president, he had other reasons to be moderately cheerful.

Europe's economic recession had passed its low point. On 1 January the second phase of economic and monetary union (EMU) began, the European Monetary Institute came into being and the Banque de France became independent of the French government. The French, Belgian, Danish, Spanish, Portuguese and Irish currencies had returned to their former narrow bands in the ERM. Inflation and interest rates were converging at low levels. Long-term yields on French franc and D-mark bonds were almost equivalent, reflecting market confidence in the durability of their exchange rate.

The European Economic Area had entered into force on 1 January. Spain and Belgium announced that they would join the Franco-German 'Eurocorps', which was expected to have 40,000 troops by 1995. The nine members of the 'Schengen agreement' prepared to scrap passport controls between their borders.

In March the membership talks with Austria, Norway, Finland and Sweden reached their climax. The foreign ministers of the 12 and the four negotiated continuously for three days and three nights without a breakthrough. The assertive Klaus Kinkel, Germany's foreign minister, dominated the final bargaining, but he needed help from the Turkish carpet salesman. Delors unearthed some extra money which allowed the Swedes a substantial rebate on their first five years' budgetary contributions. When Sweden agreed to terms, Austria and Finland followed suit. Norway, however, rejected Spanish demands that Union boats be allowed to fish for its cod. Another ministerial meeting was needed before Delors found the solution: the Union would buy extra fishing rights in Russian waters and pass them to Spain.

To the surprise of the applicants, Britain – which for so long had championed their membership – suddenly became an obstacle. The accession treaties could not be completed without an adjustment of the Union's system of qualified majority voting. The four new members would raise the number of votes in the Council of Ministers from 76 to 90. Ten of the 12 wanted a proportional increase in the votes required to block legislation, from 23 to 27. That would mean, they argued, that a Union of 16 would find it no more or less difficult to pass legislation than one of 12.

Britain and Spain, however, wanted the 'blocking minority' kept at 23 votes, to prevent the relative strength of large countries declining. That argument impressed neither Delors nor the other 10, who thought big institutional questions – such as the under-representation of large countries in the Council of Ministers – were better left for the 1996 conference. The foreign ministers held three meetings without reaching an agreement. The delay increased the risk of the European Parliament being unable to approve the new treaties in time for the applicants to join in January 1995.

John Major, seeking to curry favour with his party's Eurosceptics, made the tactical error of raising the stakes. He declared that Britain would continue to block 27 votes, and that it was too bad if that delayed enlargement. He accused John Smith – who had gingerly committed the Labour Party to 27 votes – of being 'Monseiur Oui, the poodle of Brussels'.

The European Union lurched towards another crisis, yet a week later, after a fourth meeting of foreign ministers, Major accepted a humiliating climbdown. The blocking minority would be 27 votes, although outvoted countries could delay decisions for a 'reasonable' period. In practice that meant a few months.

Clutching at straws, Major told the House of Commons that the commission had assured him there would be no social laws under the guise of 'health and safety' measures in 1994. In fact, as the commission's work programme revealed, no such laws had been planned. However the commission had drafted a directive on consultative workers' councils – the first law to be based on the Maastricht social chapter – in a way that would affect some British workers. Major said that Delors had promised to redraft the directive so that Britain's opt out would not be undermined. Despite pleas from Major and Leon Brittan, Delors refused to put any of these assurances on paper.

Major had upset his party's pro-Europeans by threatening enlargement and isolating Britain, and the anti-Europeans by raising and then dashing expectations. On 30 March the *Daily Mail* devoted its front page to a cartoon which brought together its two principal hate figures. Delors, dressed as a Parisian prostitute in high heels and fishnet stockings, led a fluffy poodle – with the head of Major – on a leash.

Another crisis has passed. In April Hungary and Poland applied for membership of the European Union. In May the European Parliament approved the treaties of accession for Austria, Finland, Norway and Sweden. The 'diablotins' appeared to have flown elsewhere, although they may have been merely pausing for breath.

THE BIRTH OF DELORISM

ONLY ONE portrait hangs in the Brussels office of Jacques Delors: a charcoal drawing of a balding, mustachioed and dapper Frenchman. Delors never met Jean Monnet, who died in 1979, but owes him the essence of his philosophy of European integration.

Unlike Delors, Monnet had travelled widely before he became interested in the unification of Europe. Born in the town of Cognac in 1888, Monnet joined the family export business at the age of 16 and never went to university. He sold brandy in the United States, Canada, England, Russia, Sweden and Egypt. During the First World War Monnet persuaded the British and French governments that they should, in the interests of efficiency, transfer control of their shipping to a joint 'transport executive' – a prototypical European Commission. In 1919 Monnet became deputy secretary-general of the League of Nations. He spent much of the 1920s and 1930s as a merchant banker in America, China, Poland and Romania.

In May 1940, with de Gaulle's support, Monnet convinced Winston Churchill to offer France a political union with Britain – involving a single parliament, currency and army. The collapse of the French government aborted that plan. Monnet moved to Washington, where he garnered supplies for the British war effort. In 1945 he persuaded de Gaulle to set up a planning commission and to make him its first *commissaire-général*. In 1951 he was involved in the creation of the European Coal and Steel Community (ECSC), and he became the first president of its High Authority.

In 1955 Monnet retired and established the Action Committee for a United States of Europe. For the next 20 years he exploited his huge network of political friendships to promote the European cause. Behind the scenes he wielded considerable influence. For instance, in 1975 he had a hand in the decision to turn the EEC's irregular meetings of heads of government into a formal institution, the European Council.

Monnet's experience of the League of Nations, and his observation, in the late 1940s, of the United Nations, of the European Organisation of Economic Cooperation and of the Council of Europe, convinced him that international bodies had to be supranational if they were to be effective.

> *Inter-governmental systems, already weakened at their birth by the compromises which their negotiators had to agree to, are soon paralysed by the rule of unanimity which governs their decisions.*[1]

Delors would not have fought so hard against the inter-governmental 'pillars' of the Maastricht treaty if he had not shared that belief.

Monnet told the first meeting of the ECSC assembly, the forerunner of the European Parliament, in October 1952:

> *The union of Europe cannot be based on goodwill alone: rules are needed. The tragic events we have lived through and are still witnessing may have made us wiser. But men pass away; others will take our place. We cannot bequeath them our personal experience. But we can leave them institutions. The life of institutions is longer than that of men; if they are well built, they can accumulate and hand on the wisdom of succeeding generations.[2]*

Monnet had an almost religious belief in the potential beneficence of institutions. 'Human nature cannot be changed, but common rules and institutions, which bind and protect at the same time, can change behaviour for the better,' he told Max Kohnstamm, the High Authority's first secretary.[3] He said that in the EEC's worst moments, the European spirit survived in the institutions, which 'once created have their own force, that supersedes the will of man.'[4]

Delors shares this faith in institutions, describing the commission as 'a sort of militant memory of European construction.'[5] He notes that Monnet's institutional model – the commission–council–parliament triangle – has 'during so many years, proved its worth: no one has put forward an alternative scheme which [would be so good] at taking decisions and acting.'[6] Delors says the lesson of the Community's failures is that 'no move to integration can succeed without genuine institutional dynamism.'[7]

Monnet believed that deadlines concentrated the minds of governments. Several dates appeared in the ECSC and EEC treaties, and Delors copied the technique with '1992'. A more fundamental part of the Monnet method, according to Kohnstamm, involved 'looking for the point which, when touched, would set off a series of consequences. What counts is having the capacity to find that strategic point.'[8] That would appear to be self-evident for any political leader, yet few of them have a broad enough vision to be able to apply such tactics.

'There are no premature ideas, only opportunities for which one must learn to wait,' Monnet wrote.[9] Delors shares his obsession with the importance of timing. Before taking any initiative, Delors agonises over whether the moment is right. In 1985 he judged, correctly, that promoting the 1992 programme would have a knock-on effect. In 1988 he sought to apply the

Monnet method' again, pushing the EC towards monetary union. In 1989 Delors decided – perhaps prematurely – that the 12 were ready for some kind of political union.

Walt Rostow, the American economist, compares his friend Monnet to a great battlefield commander who

> *drew to his side in each engagement a few first-rate lieutenants; he had both a large view of the field of engagement and took immense pains to generate a flow of accurate, detailed intelligence; he knew when to wait and when to strike swiftly. Above all, he understood the critical importance of concentrating effort and resources on a narrow front where a breakthrough would yield victory.*[10]

That description could apply to Delors at the height of his powers, for instance during the battles over the Single European Act.

Monnet and Delors were natural strategic thinkers. Knowing what they believed in gave them a head start over those who did not. In Delors's first presidential speech to the European Parliament, in January 1985 (see Chapter 5), he set out his plans for the next four years: a single market, a treaty revision, a social dimension and moves towards monetary union. Monnet's vision, if anything, ranged even wider than Delors's. Monnet told Rostow in June 1947:

> *First we must modernise France. Without a vital France there can be no Europe. Then we must unite Western Europe. When Western Europe unites and gathers strength, it will draw to it Eastern Europe. And this great East–West Europe will be of consequence and a force for peace in the world.*[11]

Monnet, like Delors, wanted America to treat Europe with respect and as an equal partner. But having sold the Americans brandy and mastered their language at the age of 18, Monnet felt more at ease with them than Delors ever did. In the very long term, Monnet believed, some kind of transatlantic Community was likely. Delors lacked Monnet's opportunities to travel and gained little practical knowledge of the wider world until he was in his fifties.

Delors's principles are slightly more realistic than those of Monnet. 'I didn't like his phrase where he says it's about uniting peoples, no, it's about uniting peoples and bringing together nations.'[12] Monnet once said he did not know what the word 'patriotism' meant: he did not see why he should treat someone differently because they lived on the other side of a border.[13] Delors, however, is both a European patriot and a French patriot.

The two men worked in contrasting ways. Delors, unlike Monnet, becomes easily engrossed in technical details. Delors likes to control strategy and the implementation of policy. Monnet was more ready to delegate administrative details to his staff. Monnet's calm style of management fostered a better team spirit than Delors's more nervous approach. Unlike Delors, however, Monnet never had to suffer the strains of running a bureaucracy of 17,000 people; the French Plan and the High Authority had no more than a few hundred staff.

The biggest difference between the two men is that Delors became a politician. Delors, unlike Monnet, sought to influence public opinion by dramatising the issues at stake. Monnet never had links with a political party and was primarily an initiator of organisations; he stayed no more than a few years at each of the bodies he helped to set up. In 1955 he decided that he could achieve more through informal contacts than through running a bureaucracy. An independent income, which Delors lacked, gave Monnet the freedom to be his own man. Quite apart from considerations of money, however, Delors had a greater penchant for office.

'At the end of 1992 I wondered if I should not leave [the commission] to carry out the kind of work which Monnet did,' says Delors. With the EC in mid-crisis, Delors decided that the captain should not abandon ship.[14] Nevertheless when he does leave the commission – unless French politics distracts him – he will probably adopt a Monnet-like role.

Some of Monnet's disciples criticise Delors for laying himself open to a conflict of interest: he remained commission president when, at the same time, he was a serious contender for the French presidency. They argue that, in those circumstances, Monnet would have renounced one or the other.

Monnet had a more rounded character than Delors. He behaved like a debonair English gentleman and won almost universal respect – even from those, like de Gaulle, who detested his ideas. Max Kohnstamm, who worked with Monnet for 25 years and who has known Delors since 1976, observes:

> *When Monnet entered a room he filled it, like a great actor upon a stage. Delors lacks Monnet's self-assurance. Only once or twice did I hear Monnet say he was perplexed; Delors is most of the time.*[15]

Delors is a more complicated and difficult human being but his lacunae make his successes all the more impressive. He lacked Monnet's suave manners, wealth and international experience. He had to pull himself up from the *école communale* of the Rue Saint-Maur, from six years of night school, from sorting securities in the Banque de France and from a trade union research department. Delors had to work in a more competitive and complex world than Monnet. Yet he still fathered the 1992 programme and two revisions of the European constitution – which Monnet, for all his achievements, could not match.

THERE IS NO SUCH THING AS AN INDIVIDUAL

Since Helmut Schmidt lost office, in 1982, how many European socialists can claim to have led successful careers? That Mitterrand remained president for 14 years was an achievement in itself, for the French right had held power almost continuously since the Second World War. Gonzalez won four elections and proved a competent manager of Spanish capitalism.

But it is Delors who stands out as the successful socialist of the 1980s and early 1990s. In an age of resurgent neo-liberal conservatism, when socialist ideas had become discredited, Delors exercised authority at the highest level from 1981 to 1994. Many political leaders say they want to change the world. But Delors – unlike Mitterrand, Gonzalez and most of their contemporaries – was not content to manage the system he inherited more efficiently. He succeeded, to a startling degree, in repainting Europe's political landscape.

Liberals and Christian Democrats have always felt more at ease with the idea of a united Europe than Conservatives and Gaullists. Socialists in most countries have been divided over the issue. Delors's long stint at the commission, and his campaign for European social legislation, persuaded many social democrats to accept a degree of supranational government. For instance, his 1988 visit to the Bournemouth TUC conference helped to banish the British labour movement's Euroscepticism. Conversely, some right-wing politicians turned against the EC because Delors gave the commission a socialist image.

Europe apart, Delors made an original contribution to social democratic politics. In the 1950s and 1960s Delors's ideas helped to shape France's 'Second Left', which opposed the Jacobin traditions of nationalisation, class struggle and a centralised state. In the early 1980s Delors convinced socialists in France – and elsewhere – that fiscal rectitude and fixed exchange rates were desirable.

Yet by the early 1990s Delors's idea of socialism appeared to look backwards as much as forwards. He praised the virtues of taxation, industrial policy and a role for trade unions. His laments for disappearing rural communities sounded almost conservative. He complained that people did not talk to their neighbours, and that families, schools and churches no longer gave moral guidance to the young. Such old-fashioned themes led to smiles among many of the younger generation of sharp-suited, cordless phone-using social democrats.

For Delors, socialism is not primarily about equality, efficiency, power or an ideological analysis of economic forces. It is about morality: the way individuals, groups and institutions treat people. Asked to define socialism, he responds:

> *A rejection of the idea that each individual stays in his niche. The individual should become a social being, participate in collective life and see his civic spirit raised.*

He stresses that each individual is morally responsible for his actions.

> *I never believed the state could make people happy. You have to allow everyone to fulfil themselves and that means giving them a margin of manoeuvre; each person should have his chances and take his responsibilities . . . Thus liberty, responsibility and solidarity go together.*

He says he wants equality of opportunity but not equality of outcome.[16]

Delors's belief, inspired by Christian personalism, that people are social beings or not their true selves, may help socialists to redefine their ideas. In the past few years British and American socialists have shown an increasing interest in the value of communities. Amitai Etzioni, a professor of sociology at George Washington University and the leader of a movement called 'communitarian', has become a best-selling author. Democrats such as Bill Clinton and Al Gore, Republicans such as Jack Kemp and Labour politicians such as Gordon Brown and Tony Blair have praised his books.

Etzioni argues that societies cannot cohere without shared notions of right and wrong that are clearly signalled through law and everyday practice. Modern Western societies have overemphasised the importance of rights and underestimated the significance of responsibilities. He says that many current forms of economic and social life have tended to foster selfishness and self-absorption rather than an awareness of the needs of others. The modern sense of social malaise stems, in part, from an unbalanced relationship between the individual and the community.

One of Etzioni's practical suggestions is that parents – men as well as women – should spend more time with their children, even at the expense of their careers. Employers should therefore provide better parental leave.

He also wants youths to perform a year of community service when they leave school. Delors has proposed the same ideas himself. Etzioni's philosophy is strikingly similar to that of Mounier and Delors.[17]

Europe's left-of-centre parties often admit to intellectual bankruptcy. Their leaders find it hard to define what social democracy stands for. Meanwhile ordinary people are increasingly worried about crime, the upbringing of children and the erosion of community feeling. 'Communitarian' ideas are no panacea for such problems, which are often better tackled at local, rather than national or European level. Furthermore, such ideas could be hijacked by conservatives who preach 'family values'. Nevertheless, Delors's emphasis on morality and community could offer socialists a basis for responding to deeply felt popular concerns.

THE IDEAL AND THE NECESSITY

For Jacques Delors, socialism means that individuals cannot fulfil themselves except in a community; federalism means that European nations can achieve more in a community than on their own. That Europe's nations should share a single market is already taken for granted: that there should be no customs barriers within the European Union, that each citizen has the right to work in any member-state, that a bank licensed in one country can operate in another, that a manufacturer of widgets can target 272 million consumers, and so on. That kind of market did not exist before Delors and Lord Cockfield, his British colleague, arrived at the commission in 1985.

Delors was fortunate to become president when he did. France, Germany and Britain, the EC's most influential members, had strong leaders who believed that economic deregulation and some kind of institutional reform were necessary. Yet by focusing attention on the 1992 programme, which led to the Single European Act, Delors exploited his luck skilfully.

There would not have been a treaty on EMU if Delors had not cajoled Kohl and the other leaders into appointing the Delors Committee in 1988. If and when Europe has a monetary union, the central bank will be based on the design – Delorist in parts – of the Maastricht treaty of 1991. Some of that treaty's provisions for political union disappointed Delors; yet it was he, in the autumn of 1989, who had propelled the EC towards that goal.

In 1989 and 1990, Delors welcomed German reunification warmly and ensured East Germany's smooth entry into the EC. He thought up the European Economic Area, which has extended the single market to five members of the European Free Trade Association. He helped to conclude 'Europe Agreements' with six East European states, thereby tightening their political and economic ties to the EC.

The commission president played a central role in the negotiation of the two 'Delors packages' which would, among other things, quadruple EC spending on poorer regions between 1987 and 1999. He oversaw two reforms of the Common Agricultural Policy (CAP), which cut its share of the EC budget from 65 to 45 per cent. Delors thought up the Social Charter, the 'social action programme' of employment laws and – at the Maastricht summit – the 'social chapter'. He provoked debates on subsidiarity and, of more consequence, on the causes of European unemployment.

Such a list of achievements is impressive, for a politician can more easily make a mark on a European government than on European institutions. The constitutions of nation states are hierarchical: a prime minister or president with a parliamentary majority has huge opportunities for bringing about change. The European Union, however, is a complex network of supranational bodies (the commission, the European Parliament and the Court of Justice), inter-governmental bodies (the Council of Ministers) and national governments. The three sorts of institution contribute to the legislative and to the executive process. For instance, both the Council of Ministers and the commission take decisions on aspects of the CAP, while national governments administer those decisions.

The links between the various bodies are horizontal. The Union has no leader with a strong executive authority. Ultimately, the Council of Ministers takes the most important legislative and executive decisions. But before any decision is taken, officials from several parts of the commission, from the Council of Ministers' secretariat, from the European Parliament and from national ministries are consulted. So are Euro-MPs, commissioners, junior ministers, EC ambassadors and hundreds of lobbyists.

Committees, 'working groups' and all-night meetings – rather than powerful individuals – are the cogs which drive this machinery forward. The Union never has been and never will be a right-wing or a left-wing entity; too many people of too many persuasions have to agree to the compromises. Decision making is so slow and consensual that decisive leadership from the centre is almost impossible – as Delors's predecessors discovered.

That Delors provided such leadership is a tribute to his energy, imagination, determination and cunning, and to the skills of his close advisers. Discreet support from friends in high places – such as Kohl, Mitterrand, Gonzalez, Lubbers, Andreotti and Howe – strengthened Delors's role. He gave the commission the intellectual lead and the sense of purpose which it needed in order to be effective. However, the concentration of its power in the presidency, which reinforced Delors's authority in the wider world, led to problems within the commission.

The huge influence of Pascal Lamy and the 'Delors network' – and their sometimes dubious methods – undermined traditional chains of command and the role of other commissioners. Delors and Lamy justified strong-arm tactics with the argument that, in such a creaking and ramshackle bureaucracy, there was no other way to get things done. However they never tried to reform the fundamentals of that bureaucracy. Had they done so, and succeeded, they would not have needed a management style which ended up causing some damage to the institution.

Another of Delors's mistakes was to appear too ambitious on behalf of the commission. The institution's growing power, and the perception that Delors wanted even more for it, had irked several governments by 1991; the commission duly suffered in that year's inter-governmental conferences. In 1992, when North European public opinion turned against the EC and the commission, most governments did not defend them. In common with many national politicians, Delors had not realised that few people understood the Community or what it was trying to do. He had become too wrapped up in the logic of the EC's institutional mechanisms.

Many Thatcherites and Gaullists accuse Delors of ignoring the revolutions in Eastern Europe. They argue that instead of constructing the tighter, more federal union of the Maastricht treaty, the 12 should have granted immediate membership to the East European states. Undoubtedly the EC should have given these countries' farmers and steelworkers better market access, and it could have made an unambiguous promise of membership earlier than June 1993. But to admit the 'Visegrad four' – Poland, Hungary, the Czech republic and Slovakia – in the early or mid-1990s, before their fragile economies were ready for the rigours of the single market or their democratic reforms had put down deep roots, would do neither them nor the European Union much good (Delors believes the EC was mistaken to let in Greece as soon as 1981).

Delors argues, justifiably, that the Union needs more strength and solidity before it can cope with integrating the East Europeans. The Treaty of Maastricht did not, as some claim, create obstacles to their joining the Union: most East European governments would gladly take part in European defence arrangements, if they were given a chance, while the provisions for monetary union concern only ready and willing members. The Maastricht treaty provides a framework and direction which will probably help rather than hinder the Union's mission to support Eastern Europe.

The Union's success, or not, in dealing with enlargement will determine whether it becomes a looser entity, responsible for little more than trade policy and the single market; or whether it continues to deepen its political and economic ties. A round of enlargement in 1995 will bring some or all of

Austria, Sweden, Finland and Norway into the Union. They will make the Union a little greener and richer but leave its fundamentals unchanged. A further round at the end of the 1990s, probably including Malta, Cyprus, Poland, Hungary and the Czech republic – and possibly Slovenia and the Baltic states – will almost certainly have a revolutionary effect on the Union.

The existing institutions could not cope with 20 members. Ministers would find it hard to reach unanimity about anything. Even when majority voting applied, bargains and compromises would be harder to find. The quality of decisions made could degenerate to that of the lowest common denominator. As Delors never tires of saying, an effective Union would require a different constitution.

A 20-member Union would have to rethink its budget from scratch. Under the second Delors package, which expires in 1999, the CAP and the structural funds account for 80 per cent of spending. The commission estimates that the application of the CAP and current regional policies to the Visegrad four, Slovenia and the Baltic states would swell the Union budget – 69 billion ecus in 1993 (£53 billion) – by 24 billion ecus. Neither the Germans nor anyone else will want to pick up the bill. The arrival of Poland's farmers will ensure the departure of the CAP in its current form.

The task of the 1996 conference will be to prepare the Union for this wider Europe. Will the large countries – whose relative weight dwindles with each round of enlargement – insist on changing the voting rules in their favour? Will governments deprive the commission of its right of initiative? How can the Union be made more democratic? In which areas should the national veto be preserved? And how will future treaties be ratified – could a Maltese referendum determine the fate of Europe?

More 'variable geometry' will offer a way of reconciling Britain's minimalist agenda with the Delorist perspective of many continental governments. But which activities should be compulsory? Would opt-outs from foreign policy damage the Union's coherence or facilitate more decisive joint actions? Delors has always accepted the principle of variable geometry – on his terms. He said in 1989:

> Any increase in the complexity of [the Community's] goals will inevitably mean a reinforcement of the centre [because it] must both manage the objectives of the most ambitious sub-group and coordinate the policies and tasks of the whole ensemble.[18]

In 1996 the scope for unbridgeable differences, ambiguous compromises and uninspiring language will be even larger than at Maastricht. If the governments cannot agree on a minimal number of common objectives, and on institutions which work effectively for 20 or 25 members, the Union may regress to a pre-Delorist phase of existence – when steel cartels, anti-dumping duties, milk quotas and their like provided the chief interest.

The Union still has to resolve the German question. Delors has long understood that the way Germany and its partners manage their relationship, particularly in monetary affairs, is crucial for the future of Europe. The arrival of Austrians, Nordics, Slavs and Magyars will place the 80 million Germans at the geographical heart of the Union. More than most members, Germany will fret about potential instability in Eastern Europe, the Balkans and Russia. Germany will not want to tackle those regions' problems on its own; for the sake of its own security, it will probably favour a tighter political union.

Since 1950 most members of Germany's political elite have believed that it can exercise more power, more effectively, in a European union than by acting alone. They think neighbouring countries are less likely to fear a Germany that is 'tied down'. Thus Germany will probably remain in the camp of those countries which desire a more federal Europe. But will the *communautaire* spirit move Germany as far as monetary union?

Come the late 1990s there will almost certainly be an ERM, or something like it, because an efficient single market requires currency stability. So does the fight against inflation. Continental governments have not forgotten a lesson which the British never learned: over the 10 years which began in 1983, when Delors kept the French franc in the ERM, that mechanism curbed the inflationary tendencies of most of its members.

As long as some kind of system links Europe's currencies, the Bundesbank will determine the interest rates of all those taking part. Most of those countries will find that politically intolerable. 'Better to be ruled by a European institution than by Germans,' they will say. So long as the Germans refuse monetary union, there will not be a European central bank. But until there is a monetary union, the argument will go on, and on, and on.

Germany's partners, and especially France, will use all their cunning to make it abandon the D-mark. 'Oh, so you want protection against those bellicose threats from Russia? So you need help when you mediate in the Slovakian civil war? *Bien sûr, chers amis – mais donnez-nous votre monnaie. Non?* You mean you are not good Europeans? You prefer to reawaken the nationalist demons of the past?' If Delors were to be in the Elysée in the late 1990s, he would certainly use such arguments. So, most probably, would any other French president.

Even without such pressure, most German business people, bankers and politicians would probably, like today, favour EMU. But if, at the end of the decade, German public opinion remained as hostile as it now is, the politicians would probably balk at currency union.

Popular sentiment in Germany did not swing against EMU until after reunification, when first inflation and then recession created a climate of economic insecurity. If Germany sorts out its economic problems and regains a sense of power and self-confidence; if the politicians make an effort to sell EMU to their citizens; if, following a prolonged period of European economic growth, the countries which aspire to monetary union have an inflationary record as good as Germany's; and if the people have come to regard the European Monetary Institute, the forerunner of the central bank, as Teutonic; then many Germans may be ready for permanently fixed exchange rates, if not for a single currency called the ecu. And that would be a major advance towards Delors's dream of a federal Europe.

Whether or not he has retired from public life, Delors's ideas will haunt the arguments on EMU, enlargement and institutional reform in the second half of the 1990s. Delorism and Thatcherism will define, as they do today, the extremes of the European debate.

The Community or Union always has been and always will be a compromise between federal and inter-governmental philosophies. The practical arguments, in 1996 and beyond, will be over the balance between those rival principles. To put it another way, how much, and for how long, can Europe's economies grow together before political integration catches up? The economic process appears inevitable, the political one less so.

The Delorists will argue for the efficiency of deciding more economic, foreign and defence policy at Union level. They already point to a little-noticed development of the early 1990s: in areas of foreign policy such as South Africa, Russia and Yugoslavia, the 12 have agreed on a common line and stuck to it. Their failure to stop the Yugoslav war has obscured this modest but significant success. Even the British and French governments, which have the strongest traditions of diplomatic independence, recognise that they can often achieve more through working with their partners than on their own. France, Britain and Germany may come to a tacit understanding: Germany will guide the Union's monetary affairs, while France and Britain will lead diplomatic and defence policy.

Progress towards common foreign and military policies is likely to be slow and organic, rather than dramatic – but a dangerous and unstable Russia would quicken the pace. By 1995 America will have no more than 100,000 troops in Europe, compared with 300,000 in 1990. Having for so long been hostile to the idea of common European defence, Britain now accepts that there will be occasions when it makes sense for the Europeans to act together, through the WEU, rather than through NATO. Having shunned NATO for so long, France has started to work closely with the organisation. The climate for European defence cooperation has never been more favourable.

On the other side of the debate, Thatcherites and Gaullists will argue that the Maastricht treaty gave too much power to the Union, and that electorates would reject any further slide to federalism. More distant decision making is harder for ordinary people to understand and is therefore less accountable. If European institutions became more powerful, they would be even more unpopular. Many national politicians and officials, fearing a loss of influence to the Union, will support this camp.

Thus Europe faces a contradiction between the need to transfer further powers to the Union, for the sake of a more effective market and greater international authority; and the readiness of public opinions and national elites to tolerate additional centralisation. The contradiction is already apparent: the Maastricht treaty went too far for large elements of public opinion, yet not far enough to allow the 12 to tackle a problem such as Yugoslavia in a unified and decisive manner.

Just after the Maastricht summit, Delors wrote:

> *The construction of Europe corresponds both to an ideal and to a necessity. The ideal often appeared to dim, after the post-war euphoria; the necessity has always been present, even insistent for those who did not accept the historical decline of Europe.*[19]

The legacy of Delors, an insistent man, is a series of simple ideas: a Europe that remains a collection of competing nations will become enfeebled, compared with other world powers; the countries of Europe have enough in common – in their history, culture and values – to make it worthwhile for them to manage joint policies in certain areas; and if the Europeans can pool their economic, diplomatic and military resources, they will hold their own among the superpowers and exert a benign influence on the world.

NOTES

Chapter 1

1. Interview with Martine Aubry, 20.11.92.
2. Interview with Delors, 5.6.93.
3. Interview with Antoine Lejay, 24.7.92.
4. Interview with Delors, 2.9.92.
5. *Changer*, Jacques Delors, Stock, 1975.
6. Interview with Delors, 5.6.93.
7. *Changer*, Jacques Delors, Stock, 1975.
8. Interview with Delors, 2.9.92.
9. *Changer*, Jacques Delors, Stock, 1975.
10. Interview with Delors, 2.9.92.
11. Ibid.
12. Interview with Delors, 5.6.93.
13. Interview with Delors, 2.9.92.
14. *Changer*, Jacques Delors, Stock, 1975.
15. Interview with Jean Leclere, 13.5.93.
16. Interview with Delors, 19.5.93.
17. *Qu'est-ce que c'est le personnalisme?*, Emmanuel Mounier, Seuil, 1947.
18. Ibid.
19. Ibid.
20. Ibid.
21. Ibid.
22. Interview with Delors, 19.5.93.
23. *Changer*, Jacques Delors, Stock, 1975.
24. Mounier, cited in *Delors*, Alain Rollat, Flammarion, 1993.
25. Interview with Delors, 2.9.92.
26. Interview with Delors, 2.9.92.
27. Interview with Jean Leclere, 13.5.93.
28. Interview with Edmond Maire, 18.11.92.
29. Interview with Delors, 2.9.92.
30. Interview with Martine Aubry, 20.11.92.
31. Interview with Delors, 5.6.93.
32. *Radioscopie*, French radio, 25.3.75.

Chapter 2

1. Interview with Delors, 2.9.92.
2. Ibid.
3. Ibid.
4. Interview with Delors, 19.5.93.
5. Interview with Jacques Moreau, 8.11.92.
6. *Changer*, Jacques Delors, Stock, 1975.
7. *Citoyen 60*, 1959.
8. Interview with Delors, 2.9.92.
9. *Citoyen 60*, 1963.

. *Citoyen 60*, 1961.
1. Ibid.
12. *Citoyen 60*, 1963.
13. Interview with Delors, 2.9.92.
14. Interview with Henri Madelin, 17.11.92.
15. Interview with Delors, 2.9.92.
16. *L'Expansion*, March 1982.
17. Interview with Delors, 2.9.92.
18. *Changer*, Jacques Delors, Stock, 1975.
19. Interview with Delors, 2.9.92.
20. Ibid.
21. Ibid.
22. Interview with Marie-Thérèse Join-Lambert, 10.12.93.
23. Interview with Delors, 2.9.92.
24. Ibid.
25. Ibid.

Chapter 3
1. *Radioscopie*, French radio, 25.3.75.
2. Interview with Delors, 19.5.93.
3. Interview with Edmond Maire, 18.11.92.
4. Interview with Delors, 19.5.93.
5. Ibid.
6. Interview with Simon Nora, 23.7.92.
7. Yves Cannac, quoted in *Jacques Delors*, Gabriel Milési, Belfond,1985.
8. Interview with Thiérry de Beaucé, 28.1.93.
9. Interview with Marie-France Garaud, 12.5.93.
10. Ibid.
11. Delors quoted in *Jacques Delors*, Gabriel Milési, Belfond, 1985.
12. Jacques Chaban-Delmas, quoted in *Jacques Delors*, Gabriel Milési, Belfond, 1985.
13. Delors quoted in *Delors*, Alain Rollat, Flammarion, 1993.
14. Interview with Antoine Lejay, 24.7.92.
15. Interview with Pierre Mialet, 19.3.92.
16. Preface to *La Révolution du Temps Choisi*, Echange et Projets, Albin Michel, 1980.
17. Ibid.
18. Chaban-Delmas, quoted in *Jacques Delors*, Gabriel Milési, Belfond, 1985.
19. Interview with Delors, 19.5.93.
20. Interview with Delors, 26.11.93.
21. Cited in *Delors*, Alain Rollat, Flammarion, 1993.
22. Interview with Michel Rocard, 5.11.92.
23. Interview with Delors, 19.5.93.
24. *Changer*, Jacques Delors, Stock, 1975.
25. Ibid.
26. Interview with Delors, 19.5.93.
27. Ibid.
28. Ibid.
29. Ibid.
30. Interview with Rocard, 5.11.92.
31. Interview with Delors, 19.5.93.

32. Ibid.
33. Delors quoted in *Jacques Delors*, Gabriel Milési, Belfond, 1985.
34. Interview with Simone Veil, 28.10.92.

Chapter 4

1. *L'Express*, March 1982.
2. Delors quoted in *La Décennie Mitterrand*, Vol I, Pierre Favier and Michel Martin-Roland, Seuil, 1990.
3. Interview with Delors, 5.6.93.
4. *La Décennie Mitterrand*, Vol I, Pierre Favier and Michel Martin-Roland, Seuil, 1990.
5. RTL, French radio, 29.11.81.
6. Interview with Edmond Maire, 18.11.92.
7. Interview with Elizabeth Guigou, 17.11.92.
8. Interview with Edith Cresson, 10.5.93.
9. Interview with Jean-Louis Bianco, 4.2.93.
10. Ibid.
11. Mitterrand quoted in *La Guerre des Deux Roses*, Philippe Bauchard, Grasset, 1986.
12. This episode is recounted in *Jacques Delors*, Gabriel Milési, Belfond, 1985; *La Décennie Mitterrand*, Vol I, Pierre Favier and Michel Martin-Roland, Seuil, 1990; and *Delors*, Alain Rollat, Flammarion, 1993. See also *Le Président*, Franz-Olivier Giesbert, Seuil, 1990; and *Verbatim*, Jacques Attali, Fayard, 1992.
13. Interview with Delors, 5.6.93.
14. Multiple sources already cited.
15. Interview with Delors, 5.6.93.
16. Reported in *Delors*, Alain Rollat, Flammarion, 1993.
17. Interview with Delors, 5.6.93.
18. *Euromoney*, October 1983.
19. Interview with Geoffrey Howe, 26.2.93.
20. Delors quoted in *Jacques Delors: artiste et martyr*, Bernard Maris, Albin Michel, 1993.
21. Interview with Philippe Lagayette, 19.3.92.
22. Interview with Edith Cresson, 10.5.93.
23. Interview with Delors, 5.6.93.
24. Ibid.
25. Delors quoted in *Jacques Delors*, Gabriel Milési, Belfond, 1985.
26. *La Décennie Mitterrand*, Vol I, Pierre Favier and Michel Martin-Roland, Seuil, 1990.
27. *Verbatim*, Jacques Attali, Fayard, 1992.
28. *The Downing Street Years*, Margaret Thatcher, HarperCollins, 1993.
29. Interview with Delors, 5.6.93.
30. Interview with Rocard, 5.11.92.
31. See 'Le Delorisme en économie', Jérôme Vignon, *Les Cahiers Français*, No 218, Oct–Dec 1984.

Chapter 5

1. *L'Europe Interdite*, Jean-François Déniau, quoted in *Le Monde*, 27.10.91.
2. *Mémoires*, Jean Monnet, Fayard, 1976.
3. Speech to European Parliament, 14.1.85.
4. Interview with Michel Petite, 13.11.92.
5. Interview with Arthur Cockfield, 26.11.92.
6. Interview with Charles Powell, 26.11.92.

7. Europe 1, French radio, 15.2.93.
8. Interview with Delors, 5.6.93.
9. Interview with Geoffrey Howe, 26.2.93.
10. Interview with Delors, 5.6.93.
11. Ibid.
12. Interview with Delors, 19.5.93.
13. Transcript of press conference, London, 6.12.86.
14. *Financial Times*, 6.10.86.
15. *Questions à domicile*, French television, 12.11.87.
16. Speech to Democracy 2000, 30.8.86.
17. *La Croix*, 23.9.86.
18. *Questions à domicile*, French television, 12.11.87.
19. Interview with Delors, 19.5.93.
20. Interview with Zygmunt Tyszkiewicz, 26.6.93.
21. Interview with Delors, 5.6.93.
22. Speech to Etuc in Stockholm, 15.5.88.
23. Interview with Tyszkiewicz, 26.6.93.
24. Interview with Delors, 19.5.93.
25. *Questions à domicile*, French television, 12.11.87.
26. Speech in Bordeaux, 1.3.91.
27. Interview with Delors, 19.5.93.
28. Speech to European Parliament, 6.7.88.
29. *Financial Times*, 28.7.88.
30. *Le Soir*, 29.9.88.
31. Speech in Bournemouth, 8.9.88.
32. Interview with Delors, 5.6.93.
33. Interview with Charles Powell, 26.11.92.
34. Interview with Geoffrey Howe, 26.2.93.
35. Interview with Delors, 19.5.93.

Chapter 6

1. *Reflections on the Delors Cabinet*, George Ross, Harvard Centre for European Studies, August 1991.
2. Interview with Pascal Lamy, 7.6.93.
3. Ibid.
4. Ibid.
5. Interview with Joly Dixon, 30.6.93.
6. Interview with Pascal Lamy, 10.9.93.
7. Interview with Delors, 5.6.93.
8. Ibid.
9. Cited in *Reflections on the Delors Cabinet*, George Ross, Harvard Centre for European Studies, August 1991.
10. Interview with Pascal Lamy, 7.6.93.
11. Interview with Peter Sutherland, 28.10.92.
12. Interview with Lamy, 7.6.93.
13. Interview with Delors, 2.9.92.
14. Interview with Lamy, 7.6.93.
15. The official minutes of Delors's speech to the European Parliament, 28.10.87
16. Interview with Delors 5.6.93.

NOTES

17. Interview with Carlo Ripa di Meana, 9.6.93.
18. Ibid.
19. Ibid.
20. Ibid.
21. Interview with Arthur Cockfield, 26.11.92.
22. Interview with Peter Sutherland, 28.10.92.
23. Interview with David Hannay, 20.3.93.
24. Cited in 'Jacques Delors and the Renewal of European Integration: The Cyclist', George Ross, unpublished manuscript, 1994.
25. For a detailed analysis of Phare and Tacis, see *The Economist*, 10.4.93.
26. Interview with Lamy, 7.6.93.
27. Interview with Leon Brittan, 2.4.93.
28. Interview with Delors, 5.6.93.
29. Ibid.

Chapter 7
1. *The Padoa-Schioppa Report*, OUP, 1987.
2. *Sud-Ouest*, 28.10.87.
3. Interview with Tommaso Padoa-Schioppa, 9.6.93.
4. Interview with Delors, 5.6.93.
5. Ibid.
6. Interview with Karl Otto Pöhl, 29.5.92.
7. Interview with Charles Powell, 26.11.92.
8. Interview with Pöhl, 29.5.92.
9. Ibid.
10. Interview with Delors, 5.6.93.
11. Interview with Jacques de Larosière, 13.5.93.
12. Interview with Pöhl, 25.9.92.
13. Interview with Delors, 5.6.93.
14. Interview with Padoa-Schioppa, 9.6.93.
15. Interview with Delors, 5.6.93.
16. Ibid.
17. *Le Figaro*, 25.5.89.
18. Speech to European Parliament, 17.1.89.
19. See Delors's speech to the Council of Europe, 26.9.89.
20. Speech in Bonn, 5.10.89.
21. Speech in Bruges, 17.10.89.
22. Delors on German television, 12.11.89.
23. Speech in European Parliament, 21.11.89.
24. Interview with Powell, 26.11.92.
25. Interview with Teltschik, 11.5.92.
26. Speech in European Parliament, 17.1.90.
27. *L'Heure de Vérité*, French television, 23.1.90.
28. *Financial Times*, 25.1.90.
29. Jean-Pierre Chevènement, cited in *Le Monde*, 25.1.90.
30. Interview with Elizabeth Guigou, 11.5.93.
31. Delors press conference, Brussels, 26.4.93.
32. Interview with Powell, 26.11.92.
33. Interview with Delors, 26.11.93.

34. Interview with Dietrich von Kyaw, 12.5.90.
35. Interview with Teltschik, 11.5.92.
36. Interview with Delors, 5.6.93.
37. Interview with Delors, 21.9.90.
38. *Le Monde*, 12.10.90.
39. Interview with Pöhl, 24.10.90.
40. Interview with Delors, 21.9.90.
41. *The Independent*, 13.12.90.
42. Delors press conference, Rome, 15.12.90.
43. *Financial Times*, 18.12.90.

Chapter 8
1. *Changer*, Jacques Delors, Stock, 1975.
2. Interview with Delors, 26.11.93.
3. Speech to a conference of French farmers, Bordeaux, 1.3.91.
4. *Financial Times*, 6.10.86.
5. Speech to European Parliament, 14.1.85.
6. *Financial Times*, 5.8.91.
7. Interview with Delors, 5.6.93.
8. Ibid.
9. Speech to European Parliament, 17.1.89.
10. 'De nouveaux enjeux pour la politique industrielle de la Communauté', Alexis Jac-quemin and Jean-François Marchipont, *Revue d'economie politique*, Jan–Feb 1992.
11. Speech in Brussels to meeting of socialists, 5.2.93.
12. Interview with Delors, 5.6.93.
13. Interview with Uffe Ellemann-Jensen, 26.4.93.
14. Speech to European Parliament, 28.10.87.
15. Interview with Peter Sutherland, 28.10.92.
16. Ibid.
17. Interview with Delors, 26.11.93.
18. Ibid.
19. *Marché du Siècle*, French television, 26.2.92.
20. Interview with Delors, 5.6.93.
21. *L'Heure de Vérité*, French television, 23.1.90.
22. *Financial Times*, 5.8.91.
23. Interview with Delors, 5.6.93.
24. Delors press conference, Brussels, 15.10.92.
25. Speech at Boston University by George Bush, 21.5.89.
26. Interview with Robert Zoellick, 16.3.93.
27. Interview with James Dobbins, 9.2.93.
28. Speech by James Baker in Berlin, 12.12.89.
29. Interview with Zoellick, 16.3.93.
30. Interview with Delors, 5.6.93.
31. *Marché du Siècle*, French television, 26.2.92.
32. Interview with Delors, 26.11.93.
33. Speech to 'Forum de l'Expansion', Brussels, 24.9.92.
34. Interview with Delors, 5.6.93.
35. Ibid.
36. Speech to Forum de l'Expansion, Paris, 4.3.93.

37. Delors, press conference, Rome, 15.12.90.
38. Speech in Bordeaux, 1.3.91.
39. Speech to Le Monde Rurale, December 1990.
40. France Inter, French radio, 4.9.92.
41. Interview with Ray MacSharry, 31.5.93.
42. Interview with Delors, 5.6.93.
43. Interview with MacSharry, 31.5.93.
44. Ibid.
45. Ibid.
46. Ibid.
47. Interview with Delors, 5.6.93.
48. Interview with MacSharry, 31.5.93.
49. Interview with Delors, 5.6.93.
50. Ibid.
51. *Grand Jury*, French television, 6.12.92.
52. Ibid.
53. *Grand Jury*, French television, 17.10.93.
54. Interview with Delors, 5.6.93.
55. Interview with Pascal Lamy, 7.6.93.
56. Interview with Zygmunt Tyszkiewicz, 26.6.93.

Chapter 9
1. Interview with Delors, 5.6.93.
2. Speech to European Parliament, 23.1.91.
3. *The Wall Street Journal*, 7.3.91.
4. Speech to the International Institute for Strategic Studies, 7.3.91.
5. Interview with Carlos Westendorp, 17.4.91.
6. Interview with François Lamoureux, 29.9.92.
7. Interview with Joseph Weyland, 15.6.92.
8. Interview with Delors, 5.6.93.
9. Interview with François Lamoureux, 13.9.93.
10. See 'A German view of Europe', *The Economist*, 27.7.91.
11. *Financial Times*, 5.8.91.
12. Interview with Delors, 5.6.93.
13. Ibid.
14. *The Economist* forecast that the Maastricht summit would break down over social policy unless Britain won an opt out. See 'Workers of the EC (except Britain) unite', 19.10.91 and 'Seven stops to Maastricht' 9.11.91.
15. *The Independent*, 6.11.91.
16. Ibid.
17. Speech to European Parliament, 21.11.91.
18. *Le Monde*, 7.12.91.
19. Delors press conference, Brussels, 5.12.91, quoted in *The Strange Superpower*, David Buchan, Dover, 1993 – the best book on European foreign policy.
20. Interview with Delors, 5.6.93.
21. Ibid.
22. Ibid.
23. Ibid.
24. Ibid.

25. Interview with François Lamoureux, 30.7.93.
26. Interview with John Kerr, 6.7.93.
27. Interview with François Scheer, 6.5.93.
28. Interview with Niels Ersboll, 1.3.93.
29. Interview with Delors, 5.6.93.

Chapter 10
1. *L'Heure de Vérité*, French television, 5.1.92.
2. Speech to European Parliament, 7.4.92.
3. See *The Economist*, 14.3.92 and 1.4.92.
4. *Sept sur Sept*, French television, 21.6.92.
5. Speech in European Parliament, 6.6.92.
6. *The Sunday Times*, 21.6.92.
7. For a detailed analysis of Delors's views, see Ken Endo, 'The Principle of Subsidiarity: From Johannes Althusius to Jacques Delors', *Hokkaido Law Review*, Vol. XLIV, No. 6, 1994.
8. Speech to European Parliament, 21.3.91.
9. Interview with Delors, 19.5.92.
10. *The Guardian*, 21.3.92.
11. *Le Figaro*, September 1992.
12. Delors, press conference, Brussels, 15.10.92.
13. Speech in Quimper, 28.8.92, cited in *Jacques Delors: artiste et martyr*, Bernard Maris, Albin Michel, 1993.
14. *Le Monde*, 2.9.92.
15. *Le Monde*, 30.8.93.
16. *La Croix*, 19.9.92.
17. *Le Nouveau Concert Européen*, Jacques Delors, Odile Jacob, 1992.
18. Speech to Forum de l'Expansion, Brussels, 24.9.92.
19. *Sept sur Sept*, French television, 21.6.92.
20. Speech to European Parliament, meeting in Brussels, 10.8.92.
21. Delors, press conference, 13.9.92, Brocket Hall, Herts.
22. *Le Figaro*, 18.6.92.
23. Interview with Delors, 19.5.93.
24. *L'Heure de Vérité*, French television, 13.12.92.
25. France Deux, French television, 1.1.93.
26. Interview with Uffe Ellemann-Jensen, 26.4.93.

Chapter 11
1. *Radioscopie*, French radio, 25.3.75.
2. Interview with Delors, 26.11.93.
3. Interview with Delors, 19.5.93.
4. Interview with Delors, 5.6.93.
5. Ibid.
6. Ibid.
7. Interview with Jean-Pierre Cot, 8.4.92.
8. Interview with Antoine Lejay, 19.11.92.
9. Interview with Jacques Moreau, 18.11.92.
10. Interview with Delors, 5.6.93.
11. Ibid.

12. RTL, French radio, 17.10.93.
13. Conversation with Alex Waelput, 5.6.93.
14. Speech to conference on AIDS, 25.9.92.
15. *Paris Match*, November 1987.
16. Quoted in *Jacques Delors*, Gabriel Milési, Belfond, 1985.
17. Interview with Henri Madelin, 17.11.92.
18. Quoted in *Jacques Delors*, Gabriel Milési, Belfond, 1985.
19. Interview with François Lamoureux, 29.9.92.
20. Interview with Pascal Lamy, 6.8.93.
21. Quoted in *Jacques Delors*, Alain Rollat, Flammarion, 1993.
22. Quoted in *Jacques Delors, artiste et martyr*, Bernard Maris, Albin Michel, 1993.
23. Interview with Niels Ersboll, 1.3.93.
24. Interview with Delors, 5.6.93.
25. Interview with Jean Boissonat, 19.11.92.
26. *Changer*, Jacques Delors, Stock, 1975.
27. Interview with Delors, 19.5.92.
28. Interview with Simone Veil, 28.10.92.
29. Interview with Niels Ersboll, 1.3.93.
30. Interview with Antoine Lejay, 24.7.92.
31. Interview with Uffe Ellemann-Jensen, 26.4.93.
32. *Le Monde*, 27.6.92.
33. Interview with Delors, 5.6.93.
34. Interview with Michel Rocard, 5.11.92.
35. Interview with Max Kohnstamm, 4.5.93.
36. *The Guardian*, 21.3.92.
37. Interview with Delors, 5.6.93.
38. Interview with Delors, 26.11.93.
39. *Radioscopie*, French radio, 25.3.75.
40. *L'Equipe*, September 1992.
41. Interview with Edith Cresson, 10.5.93.
42. Interview with Elizabeth Guigou, 11.5.93.
43. Interview with Martine Aubry, 20.11.92.
44. Interview with Delors, 26.11.93.
45. Interview with Douglas Hurd, 26.5.93.
46. Interview with Delors, 5.6.93.
47. Interview with Aubry, 20.11.92.
48. Interview with Delors, 5.6.93.
49. Quoted in *Jacques Delors*, Gabriel Milési, Belfond, 1985.
50. Mitterrand on French television, 13.9.91.
51. *Libération*, 9.9.91.
52. *Le Point*, 18.1.92.
53. Interview with Cresson, 10.5.93.
54. *L'Heure de Vérité*, French television, 17.5.92.
55. *Le Monde*, 6.10.92.
56. Ibid.
57. *Le Monde*, January 1993.
58. *L'Heure de Vérité*, French television, 13.12.92.
59. Interview with Carlos Westendorp, 8.6.93.
60. Interview with Cresson, 10.5.93.

61. Quoted in *Inside the New Europe*, Axel Krause, HarperCollins, 1991.
62. Interview with Jean-Pierre Cot, 8.4.92.
63. Interview with Delors, 26.11.93.
64. Interview with Thiérry de Beaucé, 28.1.93.
65. Interview with Michel Rocard, 5.11.92.
65. Interview with Delors, 19.5.93.
67. Ibid.

Chapter 12
 1. Interview with Delors, 19.5.93.
 2. Speech to European Parliament, 13.10.93.
 3. Interview with Delors, 19.5.93.
 4. Press conference, Copenhagen, 22.6.92.
 5. Speech in Paris to Forum de l'Expansion, 3.3.93.
 6. Speech to European Parliament, 15.9.93.
 7. *The Economist*, 26.9.93.
 8. Interview with Delors, 26.11.93.
 9. *Sept sur Sept*, French television, 12.12.93.
 0. Interview with Delors, 19.5.93.
11. Interview with Delors, 26.11.93.
12. Interview with Delors, 19.5.93.
13. Speech to European Parliament, 26.5.93.
14. Interview with Delors, 26.11.93.
15. Speech in Vienna, 1.10.93.
16. RTL, French radio, 17.10.93.
17. Interview with Delors, 26.11.93.
18. RTL, French radio, 17.10.93.
19. Interview with Delors, 26.11.93.
20. Ibid.

The Birth of Delorism
 1. *Mémoires*, Jean Monnet, Fayard, 1976.
 2. Speech by Monnet to ECSC assembly, 10.9.52.
 3. Interview with Max Kohnstamm, 4.5.93.
 4. *Mémoires*, Jean Monnet, Fayard, 1976.
 5. Speech in Bruges, 17.10.89.
 6. Interview with Delors, 19.5.93.
 7. Delors, 7.7.91, source uncertain.
 8. Interview with Kohnstamm, 4.5.93.
 9. *Mémoires*, Jean Monnet, Fayard, 1976.
10. Unpublished paper by Walt Rostow, 'Preparing the Future: Jean Monnet, master inventor-innovator', January 1992.
11. Ibid.
12. Interview with Delors, 19.5.93.
13. Interview with Kohnstamm, 4.5.93.
14. Interview with Delors, 19.5.93.
15. Interview with Kohnstamm, 4.5.93.
16. Interview with Delors, 19.5.93.
17. I am indebted to Geoff Mulgan, the director of Demos, the London think tank, for

pointing me to Etzioni's ideas. Demos has published some of Etzioni's works in Britain.
18. Speech to the Centre for European Policy Studies, Brussels, 30.11.89.
19. *Le Nouveau Concert Européen*, Jacques Delors, Odile Jacob, 1992.

BIBLIOGRAPHY

Jacques Attali, *Verbatim*, Fayard, Paris, 1993.

Philippe Bauchard, *La guerre des deux roses. Du rêve à la réalité*, Grasset, Paris, 1986.

David Buchan, *Europe. The Strange Superpower*, Dartmouth, London, 1993.

Michael Calingaert, *The 1992 challenge from Europe: Development of the European Community's Internal Market*, National Planning Association, Washington, 1988.

Patrick and Philippe Chastenet, *Chaban*, Seuil, Paris, 1991.

Nicholas Colchester and David Buchan, *Europe Relaunched. Truths and illusions on the way to 1992*, Hutchinson/Economist Books, London, 1990.

Jacques Delors, *Changer*, Stock, Paris, 1975.

Echange et Projets (preface by Jacques Delors), *La Révolution du Temps Choisi*, Albin Michel, Paris, 1980.

Jacques Delors, *Le Nouveau Concert Européen* (a collection of speeches), Odile Jacob, Paris, 1991.

Jean de Ruyt, *L'acte unique européen: Commentaire*, Editions de l'Université de Bruxelles, 1987.

Ken Endo, *What is 'Delorism'? The convictions of Jacques Delors*, unpublished thesis, Catholic University of Louvain, August 1992.

Ken Endo, 'The Principle of Subsidiarity: from Johannes Althusius to Jacques Delors', *Hokkaido Law Review*, Vol XLIV, No 6, 1994.

Pierre Favier and Michel Martin-Roland, *La Décennie Mitterrand*, Seuil, Paris. Volume 1: *Les Ruptures*, 1990. Volume 2: *Les Epreuves*, 1991.

Franz-Olivier Giesbert, *Le Président*, Seuil, Paris, 1990.

Lucien Guissard, *Mounier*, Editions Universitaires, Paris, 1962.

Robert O. Keohane and Stanley Hoffmann (eds), *The New European Community. Decision-making and institutional change*, Westview, Oxford, 1991.

Axel Krause, *Inside the New Europe*, HarperCollins, New York, 1991.

Nigel Lawson, *The View from No. 11*, Bantam, London, 1992.

Dick Leonard, *The Economist Guide to the European Union* (Fourth Edition), Hamish Hamilton/Economist Books, London, 1994.

Bernard Maris, *Jacques Delors, artiste et martyr*, Albin Michel, Paris, 1993.

David Marsh, *The Bundesbank: the bank that rules Europe*, Heinemann, London, 1992.

BIBLIOGRAPHY

David Martin, *Europe: an Ever Closer Union*, Spokesman, London, 1991.

Jean Monnet, *Mémoires*, Fayard, Paris, 1976.

Gabriel Milési, *Jacques Delors*, Belfond, Paris, 1985.

Emmanuel Mounier, *Oeuvres, 1944–50*, Seuil, Paris, 1962.

Tommaso Padoa-Schioppa, *Efficiency, Stability and Equity. A strategy for the Evolution of the Economic System of the European Community*, Oxford University Press, 1987.

Jean-Louis Quermonne, *Le système politique européen*, Montchrestien, Paris, 1993.

Alain Rollat, *Delors*, Flammarion, Paris, 1993.

George Ross, 'Jacques Delors and the Renewal of European Integration: The Cyclist', unpublished manuscript, 1994.

George Ross, *Reflections on the Delors Cabinet*, Harvard Centre for European Studies, 1991.

Margaret Thatcher, *The Downing Street Years*, HarperCollins, London, 1993.

Charles Zorgbibe, *Histoire de la construction européene*, Presses Universitaires de France, Paris, 1993.

INDEX

INDEX

INDEX